JOURNAL FOR THE STUDY OF THE OLD TESTAMENT SUPPLEMENT SERIES
275

Sheffield Academic Press

Chronicles and Exodus

An Analogy and its Application

William Johnstone

Journal for the Study of the Old Testament
Supplement Series 275

To my students in Aberdeen,
who made me try to explain it this way

Copyright © 1998 Sheffield Academic Press

Published by
Sheffield Academic Press Ltd
Mansion House
19 Kingfield Road
Sheffield S11 9AS
England

Typeset by Sheffield Academic Press
and
Printed on acid-free paper in Great Britain
by Bookcraft Ltd
Midsomer Norton, Bath

British Library Cataloguing in Publication Data

A catalogue record for this book is available
from the British Library

ISBN 1-85075-881-6

CONTENTS

Abbreviations   7

Chapter 1
INTRODUCTION   9

Part I
THE PROPOSAL:
CHRONICLES AS GATEWAY TO PENTATEUCHAL CRITICISM

Chapter 2
CHRONICLES, CANONS AND CONTEXTS   50

Chapter 3
THE EXODUS AS PROCESS   74

Part II
LOOKING AT THE GATEWAY:
CHRONICLES IN ITSELF AND IN ITS RELATION TO THE PENTATEUCH

Chapter 4
GUILT AND ATONEMENT: THE THEME OF 1 AND 2 CHRONICLES   90

Chapter 5
THE USE OF LEVITICUS IN CHRONICLES   115

Chapter 6
PROSPECTIVE ATONEMENT:
THE USE OF EXODUS 30.11-16 IN 1 CHRONICLES 21   128

Part III
LOOKING THROUGH THE GATEWAY:
APPLYING THE ANALOGY TO THE PENTATEUCH

Chapter 7
REACTIVATING THE CHRONICLES ANALOGY IN
PENTATEUCHAL STUDIES, WITH SPECIAL REFERENCE
TO THE SINAI PERICOPE IN EXODUS   142

Chapter 8
THE DECALOGUE AND THE REDACTION OF THE
SINAI PERICOPE IN EXODUS   168

Chapter 9
THE TWO THEOLOGICAL VERSIONS OF THE
PASSOVER PERICOPE IN EXODUS   198

Chapter 10
THE DEUTERONOMISTIC CYCLES OF 'SIGNS'
AND 'WONDERS' IN EXODUS 1–13   217

Chapter 11
FROM THE SEA TO THE MOUNTAIN. EXODUS 15.22–19.2:
A CASE STUDY IN EDITORIAL TECHNIQUES   242

Chapter 12
FROM THE MOUNTAIN TO KADESH,
WITH SPECIAL REFERENCE TO EXODUS 32.30–34.29   262

Part IV
THE VIEW BEYOND

Chapter 13
SOLOMON'S PRAYER (2 CHRONICLES 6):
IS INTENTIONALISM SUCH A FALLACY?   282

Chapter 14
JUSTIFICATION BY FAITH REVISITED   298

Index of References   307
Index of Authors   329

ABBREVIATIONS

AEL	E.W. Lane, *Arabic–English Lexicon* (8 vols.; London: Williams and Norgate, 1863–93)
AnBib	Analecta biblica
ANET	James B. Pritchard (ed.), *Ancient Near Eastern Texts Relating to the Old Testament* (Princeton, NJ: Princeton University Press, 1950)
AusBR	*Australian Biblical Review*
BBB	Bonner biblische Beiträge
BDB	Francis Brown, S.R. Driver and Charles A. Briggs, *A Hebrew and English Lexicon of the Old Testament* (Oxford: Clarendon Press, 1907)
BETL	Bibliotheca ephemeridum theologicarum lovaniensium
BHS	*Biblia hebraica stuttgartensia*
Bib	*Biblica*
BKAT	Biblischer Kommentar: Altes Testament
BZ	*Biblische Zeitschrift*
BZAW	Beihefte zur *ZAW*
CBQ	*Catholic Biblical Quarterly*
EA	J.A. Knudtzon, *Die El-Amarna-Tafeln* (Leipzig: J.C. Hinrichs, 1908–15)
EncJud	*Encyclopaedia Judaica*
EurHS	Europäische Hochschulschriften
EvT	*Evangelische Theologie*
ExpTim	*Expository Times*
GKC	*Gesenius' Hebrew Grammar* (ed. E. Kautzsch, revised and trans. A.E. Cowley; Oxford: Clarendon Press, 1910)
GNB	*Good News Bible*
JB	*Jerusalem Bible*
JBL	*Journal of Biblical Literature*
JJS	*Journal of Jewish Studies*
JPSV	*Jewish Publication Society Version*
JSOTSup	*Journal for the Study of the Old Testament*, Supplement Series
JTS	*Journal of Theological Studies*
LD	Lectio divina
NCB	New Century Bible
NEB	*New English Bible*
NRSV	New Revised Standard Version

OBO	Orbis biblicus et orientalis
OTG	Old Testament Guides
OTL	Old Testament Library
OTS	*Oudtestamentische Studiën*
RB	*Revue biblique*
RSV	Revised Standard Version
SBS	Stuttgarter Bibelstudien
SBT	Studies in Biblical Theology
SJT	*Scottish Journal of Theology*
SOTSMS	Society for Old Testament Study Monograph Series
ST	*Studia theologica*
SVTP	Studia in Veteris Testamenti pseudepigrapha
TDOT	G.J. Botterweck and H. Ringgren (eds.), *Theological Dictionary of the Old Testament*
TGUOS	*Transactions of the Glasgow University Oriental Society*
TLZ	*Theologische Literaturzeitung*
TQ	*Theologische Quartalschrift*
TRu	*Theologische Rundschau*
TynBul	*Tyndale Bulletin*
TOTC	Tyndale Old Testament Commentaries
UBS	United Bible Society
VF	*Verkündigung und Forschung*
VT	*Vetus Testamentum*
VTC	S. Mandelkern, *Veteris Testamenti Concordantiae* (Leipzig, 1925)
VTSup	*Vetus Testamentum*, Supplements
WBC	Word Biblical Commentary
WMANT	Wissenschaftliche Monographien zum Alten und Neuen Testament
ZAW	*Zeitschrift für die alttestamentliche Wissenschaft*

Chapter 1

INTRODUCTION

A Change of Direction

As is now well documented, since at least the 1970s profound and far-reaching changes have been taking place in Pentateuchal criticism.[1] It would be idle to claim that the train of thought represented in the essays in this collection has not been encouraged and influenced by that changing climate. Yet it has been stimulated also—perhaps, even, mainly—by specific local factors, the commonplace character of which, however, prompts the hope that the following account will spark some recognition among fellow-travellers through this controversial terrain.

The fundamental local factor stimulating change in my strategy in Pentateuchal study was the requirement in 1972–73 to teach a final honours course in the religion of ancient Israel to students who, as students of Religious Studies, had no formal training in Old Testament criticism. The challenge was to construct a course that would not only be accessible to the students concerned but also provide a reliable and intellectually defensible guide to the biblical material. It seemed to me that the only possible starting-point for such students was to begin at the end, with the Hebrew Bible as it is in the possession of all, rather than with the reconstruction of beginnings based on prevailing critical

1.   For the Pentateuch as a whole, see for example J. Blenkinsopp, *The Pentateuch: An Introduction to the First Five Books of the Bible* (London: SCM Press, 1992); C. Houtman, *Der Pentateuch: Die Geschichte seiner Erforschung neben einer Auswertung* (Contributions to Biblical Exegesis and Theology, 8; Kampen: Pharos, 1994); E.W. Nicholson, *The Pentateuch in the Twentieth Century: The Legacy of Julius Wellhausen* (Oxford: Clarendon Press, 1998). For Exodus, M. Vervenne (ed.), *Studies in the Book of Exodus: Redaction–Reception–Interpretation* (BETL, 126; Leuven: Leuven University Press/Peeters, 1996); T.B. Dozeman, *God at War: Power in the Exodus Tradition* (New York: Oxford University Press, 1996).

hypotheses. There simply was no time in the course to justify these hypotheses and to consider their relation to the reconstruction of the history of Israel's religious institutions, a discussion that would in any case, as like as not, merely have ended in indeterminacy. The likelihood is that what can be described from the Hebrew Bible in its completed form is the religion of Israel in the period of the Second Temple. It is only once the data on that final picture have been assembled—for example, the systems of sacrifice, the organization of the priesthood—that historical questions can be asked: whether these data are coherent; whether the religious institutions portrayed are uniform; whether they correspond to Second Temple practice, or represent at least in part fossilized elements of older custom, or are merely an ideal that bears only approximate relationship to the organization of Israel's religion at any time (the Pentateuchal material does, after all, concern the Tabernacle, not the Temple). It is not claimed that, by this approach, any problems are thereby solved at a stroke; merely that an agreed basis for raising questions has been established.

But a number of additional factors soon led to the conviction that the strategy of beginning from the end was appropriate not just for one set of students with particular interests but for all. The chief of these factors was growing disenchantment with the course on the history of Israel, then a staple element in most Old Testament curricula, which perforce sought to begin at the beginning with the recreation of Israel's origins. I had begun teaching such a course a couple of years after the first British publication of John Bright's famous *A History of Israel*.[2] My initial impression of this book was that it was the definitive account of the topic which afforded the inexperienced lecturer little scope for variation and invention. But inhibition soon gave way to the perception that on major issues affecting not least the latest and the best-documented periods of Israel's history (in particular, Bright's two major excursuses—to begin with the later—'The Date of Ezra's Mission to Jerusalem' and 'The Problem of Sennacherib's Campaigns in Palestine') there was not only much room for debate but also, in Bright's presentation, considerable special pleading, especially about matters of chronology. For a teacher in a faculty of divinity, a particularly pressing question was whether the portrayal of the faith of Israel could be left at the mercy of the reliability of historical reconstruction. Indeed, the suspicion was aroused that Bright's harmonizing approach was, with no

2.   London: SCM Press, 1960.

doubt the best of intentions, merely succeeding in obscuring the theological intention of the writers.[3] But, if such uncertainty prevails in the latest and the best-documented periods of Israel's history, what must the situation be like with regard to earlier? With the appearance of T.L. Thompson's *The Historicity of the Patriarchal Narratives: The Quest for the Historical Abraham,*[4] it seemed to me that the *coup de grâce* had been administered to Bright's reconstructions of the earliest periods of Israel's history. But, if that was the case with regard to the 'patriarchal age', how, then, did matters rest in connection with the reconstruction of the next earliest period, the exodus, the fundamentally crucial period, theologically speaking?

At about the same time, doubts began to surface about the recoverability of the traditional J and E documents of classical Pentateuchal criticism, and thus about the propriety of requiring students to master such topics as 'the theology of the Jahwist' or 'the kerygma of the Elohist'.[5] The catalyst for me here was the chance homiletical observation of the interconnection between Exod. 23.20-33 and Judg. 2.1-5: thereby a seed of doubt was sown in my mind about Martin Noth's then regnant hypothesis of the necessary separation of the Tetrateuch from the Deuteronomistic History embracing Joshua–2 Kings prefaced by Deuteronomy.[6] The unsatisfactory nature of Noth's general position on Pentateuchal criticism was compounded, in my view, by his no less unsatisfactory account of details in the text, in particular those passages that he acknowledged to be a 'deuteronomistic supplement' or

3.   Two of my early engagements with Bright's thought were the review article on his *The Authority of the Old Testament* (London: SCM Press, 1967) in *SJT* 22 (1969), pp. 197-209, and 'The Mythologising of History in the Old Testament', *SJT* 24 (1971), pp. 201-17.

4.   BZAW, 133; Berlin: W. de Gruyter, 1974.

5.   Not least in the wake of the translation into English of the first volume of G. von Rad's *Theologie des Alten Testaments* (*Old Testament Theology*. I. *The Theology of Israel's Historical Traditions* [trans. D.M.G. Stalker; Edinburgh: Oliver & Boyd, 1962]). Cf. the articles by H.W. Wolff, 'Das Kerygma des Jahwisten', *EvT* 24 (1964), pp. 73-93; 'Zur Thematik der elohistischen Fragmente im Pentateuch', *EvT* 29 (1969), pp. 59-72.

6.   As it happened, this observation occurred not long after Noth's views had gained wider currency through the translation into English of his *Überlieferungsgeschichte des Pentateuch* (*A History of Pentateuchal Traditions* [trans. B.W. Anderson; Englewood Cliffs, NJ: Prentice–Hall, 1972]).

'section', for example Exod. 12.24-27a; 13.1-16.[7] I found it difficult to
envisage the procedure by which a Deuteronomist, a canonizer of
scripture if ever there was one (cf. Deut. 4.2; 12.32), would be content
merely to insert sporadic adjustments to the text. If Deuteronomistic
elements are found in the text, it is much more likely that a representative of that school would be putting forth a complete edition of the
whole. In that case, 'supplement' is far too weak a term: the observation of Deuteronomistic elements within the Pentateuch prompts,
rather, the search for a Deuteronomistic editor of the Pentateuch. The
chief inhibiting factor in looking for such a 'late' date for an edition of
the Pentateuch is, of course, the 'early' subject matter which the Pentateuch contains. But the legitimacy of finding a Deuteronomistic, and
therefore 'late', edition of such a fundamental text of the Hebrew Bible
as Exodus gained its necessary sanction, it seemed to me, from the
work of Lothar Perlitt on covenant:[8] as he convincingly argued, covenant, the central concept in both Exodus and Deuteronomy, had not yet
become a major presupposition of prophecy even by the eighth century;
rather, as an overarching theological category, it was a relative late-
comer on the scene.

It has been under such influences that I have been developing
throughout the period represented by the following essays an argument
about the formation of the Pentateuch, in particular of the book of Exodus. Instead of making the search for origins with all the hazards connected with historical reconstruction the first step in the interpretation
of Exodus, one should, rather, begin with the text of the book as it now
stands. But, given the unquestionably composite nature of that text (the
diverging views in Exodus on Passover and on the itinerary of the
Israelites through the wilderness with its associated chronology are
cases in point, among others, that will bulk large in the following dis-
cussions), one cannot rest content merely with describing the final form
of the text. There are at least two dominant views represented therein.
A complete description of the text demands that those diverging views
be recognized and expounded; indeed, I have come to believe that it is

7.   *Exodus* (trans. J.S. Bowden; OTL; London: SCM Press, 1962), pp. 97, 101.
8.   *Bundestheologie im Alten Testament* (WMANT, 36; Neukirchen–Vluyn:
Neukirchener Verlag, 1969). In recognition of his liberating thesis, I had the privilege of inviting Professor Perlitt as distinguished foreign scholar to the summer
meeting of the Society for Old Testament Study in 1990.

precisely in the dialectic between these diverging views that the vitality of the whole to a significant extent consists.

In order to disentangle these contrasting presentations one must, I shall argue, begin with the known, the text as it now stands (not with the least known, the speculative origins of the text), and thence proceed to the less certain. The principal instrument in separating layers in the text is provided, I shall suggest, by the series of reminiscences in Deuteronomy of events contained in Exodus. This Deuteronomic version is significantly different in many respects from that of the final edition of Exodus. It is by the subtraction[9] of that material in Exodus that matches the reminiscence in Deuteronomy that enables the overlying layer in Exodus to be delimited and the distinctive features of both that final layer and the layer matching Deuteronomy to be appreciated. The objective existence of the reminiscence in Deuteronomy imparts a welcome degree of objectivity to the description.

The procedure is analogous, I suggest, to that involved in the interpretation of the books of Chronicles. Just as it is clear that Chronicles constitutes the final edition of the history of Israel, yet is based on, and incorporates in part, the earlier version contained in Samuel–Kings,[10] so, I argue, Exodus in the form in which it now stands represents the final edition based on an earlier version still embedded within it which is to be recovered with the help of the reminiscences of the exodus now to be found in Deuteronomy. The success of the recovery of that

---

9. The term 'subtraction' has been brought most vividly into my consciousness by the work of B. Renaud, *La théophanie du Sinaï. Ex 19-24: Exégèse et théologie* (Cahiers de la Revue Biblique, 30; Paris: J. Gabalda, 1991), though it is the P document that he seeks first to 'subtract'—which is part of the very question at issue. See my review in *JTS* NS 43 (1992), pp. 550-55.

As in elementary calculation it is always advisable to check the addition of digits by the subtraction of at least one from the total, so in Pentateuchal criticism: when I deduct 'D' from the total I am left with nothing that resembles traditional 'JE'.

10. The challenge to this view by A.G. Auld, *Kings without Privilege* (Edinburgh: T. & T. Clark, 1994), namely, that the evidence suggests not dependence by Chronicles on DtrH, but that both presuppose a common text, would simply change the focus to the question of the relationship between Chronicles and this common text. I have to state that at no point in the preparation of a commentary on Chronicles (see n. 12) did I find this a necessary hypothesis. Quite the reverse: Chronicles frequently presupposes a text to which Samuel–Kings is the sole witness. It is a short step to the affirmation that Samuel–Kings is that text. Cf. my review of Auld in *SJT* 50 (1997), pp. 256-58.

version embedded in Exodus by means of the Deuteronomic reminiscences justifies the application to that version of the term 'Deuteronomistic', in a way that is just as appropriate as the conventional application of that term to Samuel–Kings as part of the 'Deuteronomistic
History'.

One difference of this thesis about the growth of the text of Exodus
from most that are currently being offered[11] is that it presents the most
economical theory possible: two literary levels only are being identified. Further, in pursuit of this argument, it attempts to follow the
route that is critically most neutral and reliable—the comparison of
objectively available texts. As will be indicated in the discussion in
some of the essays below, much contemporary work, invaluable though
it undoubtedly is in the mass of detailed observations that it provides,
either approaches the subject from rather different angles from that
followed here (e.g. from the traditional critical four-documentary hypothesis, J, E, D and P, or a modification of it), or, where it attempts to
extend literary analysis into the reconstruction of pre- or post-Deuteronomistic levels of the text, becomes, in my opinion, too ambitious. It
is not claimed that my procedure provides an exhaustive account of the
development of the present form of the text of Exodus: in the legal
collections, especially, it is probable that there are still earlier literary
elements embedded. Yet it is unlikely that earlier levels can be
uncovered in the narratives to any degree approaching certainty by
further analysis of these two literary editions. An alternative model has
to be applied: the Pentateuch has not 'grown' from 'kernels'; it has
been composed from selected materials. The question is thus not so
much one of recreating origins as of appreciating function. Behind the
Deuteronomistic version, and freely tapped by it, lies the vast reservoir
of religious practices and institutions of the monarchic and, doubtless,
pre-monarchic periods. These have been the bearers and interpreters of
their own traditions (the law-code itself in Exod. 20.22–23.33 provided
with a later Deuteronomistic covenantal framework is a good example
of how independent earlier materials of an institutional nature have
been exploited by the D-writer; see Chapter 7). DtrExodus provides us
with the earliest recoverable literary version of these traditions and is to
be dated to the exilic period; this version was subsequently given its
final 'canonical' edition by Priestly writers in a far-reaching revision
probably late in the postexilic period. That much can be affirmed with a

11. See n. 1.

high degree of probability. The recovery of any earlier level is much more speculative. While 'speculative' is an honourable word in my vocabulary as critic, the lack of anything approaching comparable levels of probability in connection with the reconstruction of these putative earlier levels must be noted. I have been unable to burden my students with them.

Economical though the theory presented here is, it still produces radical enough conclusions. For example, a major contention in the essays below is that there has been a substantial amount of transposition of Deuteronomistic materials by the final P-editor: for instance, until the final edition there was no material *in this position* between Exod. 15.22a and 19.2b (see Chapter 11); the text of Exodus 32–33 as it now stands represents similar importations of adapted D-material into the present contexts (see Chapter 12). Further, even if the theory is not exhaustive, it nevertheless represents, in my view, at least the first necessary stages in any more elaborate programme of recovery of still earlier levels in the text.

This collection is complementary to fuller-length studies of both Chronicles and Exodus. A commentary has already been completed on Chronicles for its own sake;[12] an exploratory volume on interpretative issues has been published on Exodus,[13] which it is hoped eventually to develop into a full-scale commentary.[14] But this collection permits wider-ranging consideration of angle of approach, and greater scope for engagement with the work of other scholars and for the development of more systematic studies, than are possible within a commentary.

The essays are presented in four sections, each section, except the last, beginning with a programmatic essay. The collection as a whole opens with a statement of the programme as originally proposed and of the reasons for proposing it: the twin-track approach involving both Chronicles and Exodus (Chapter 2). This is followed by an essay, rather earlier in date, which marks the disenchantment with, and disengagement from, the search for origins so characteristic of scholarship

12. W. Johnstone, *1 and 2 Chronicles*. I. *1 Chronicles 1–2 Chronicles 9: Israel's Place among the Nations*; II. *2 Chronicles 10–36: Guilt and Atonement* (JSOTSup, 253, 254; Sheffield: Sheffield Academic Press, 1997).

13. W. Johnstone, *Exodus* (OTG; Sheffield: Sheffield Academic Press, 1990).

14. A sketch of what such a commentary might look like will be found in my 'Exodus', in J.W. Rogerson and J.D.G. Dunn (eds.), *Commentary 2000* (Grand Rapids: Eerdmans, in press).

up to the 1970s: it is essentially a critical review, so far as it concerns the exodus, of R. de Vaux's authoritative *Histoire ancienne d'Israël*[15] (Chapter 3). The intention is not simply to be destructive but to suggest a way ahead. The essay seeks to show that attempts to demonstrate the historicity of the exodus of Israel from Egypt as a single datable event, or sequence of events, merely succeed in reducing the exodus either to insignificance or to a commonplace. The historical approach has to be complemented by a study of Israel's religious institutions: it is only by understanding the material in Exodus as the casting into narrative form not only of historical but also of institutional—and still other—materials that the complexity of the account can have full justice done to it— and also its force: how to make the dead past live on as appropriated possibility in the life of the continuing faith communities.

While the motive for studying Chronicles is, in the first place, to acquire some kind of objectively available instrument for discriminating between Deuteronomistic and post-Deuteronomistic materials and to apply that model to Exodus, it has seemed important also to appreciate the work of the Chronicler in its own right. Accordingly, Part II is devoted to three studies of the Chronicler for his own sake. The programmatic essay at the beginning of this section (Chapter 4) argues that Chronicles is first and foremost a work of theology, which evaluates the Davidic monarchy in terms of the Levitical doctrine of guilt and atonement. The following chapter restates and defends that view in debate with the influential interpretation of Chronicles propounded by Sara Japhet. Chronicles, as the last word in the canonical arrangement of the Hebrew Bible, is, so to speak, a systematic theology of the Hebrew Bible in narrative form: Chapter 6 thus seeks to draw together in more systematic manner materials on one aspect of the Chronicler's thesis of guilt and atonement: atonement is not simply a matter of the retrospective repairing of the damaged relationship between God and his people; first and foremost, it involves rites for the prospective maintenance of an already existing, ideally undamaged, relationship.

Part III constitutes the heart of the collection. It applies to the book of Exodus the analogy of the use that the Chronicler makes of the underlying Deuteronomistic version in Samuel–Kings. The section begins with another programmatic essay (Chapter 7): it tests out the theory with a preliminary sweep of the text of Exodus 19–24 and

15. 2 vols.; Paris: J. Gabalda, 1971; ET London: Darton, Longman & Todd, 1978.

31.18–34.28. The five subsequent essays seek to pursue the question in greater detail and with greater precision in these and other parts of Exodus: the Decalogue in Exodus 20; the Passover narrative in Exodus 12–13; the 'plague' narrative in Exodus 1–13 (with, for the sake of completeness, a new appendix on Exod. 14.1–15.21, not otherwise dealt with in this collection); and the itineraries, and their associated chronologies, in the materials on 'From the Sea to the Mountain' in Exodus 15–19 and 'From the Mountain to Kadesh' in Exodus 31–34. In these essays, it is argued, the parallels between Exodus and Deuteronomy extend far beyond the merely verbal. The highly distinctive views in Deuteronomy of the 'signs and wonders' in Egypt, of the itinerary of Israel through the wilderness and the chronology associated with that itinerary, and of the Passover, and the integral connection in the laws of Deuteronomy between the freeing of slaves, the offering of the first-born and the celebration of the Passover, all have, I believe, a matching D-version in Exodus, now somewhat, but not completely, smothered by the overlying P-edition.

The final section is of a rather different nature. Here an attempt is made to indicate how the significance of these findings might be pursued beyond the confines of the Hebrew Bible. There is theological utility in distinguishing these two editions of Exodus: in their complementarity and dialectical integration they correspond to the doctrines traditionally termed in Christian theology 'justification' and 'sanctification'. First, the appropriateness of finding such a firmly enunciated theological intention embedded in the text is defended in the essay in Chapter 13 on the so-called 'intentional fallacy'; though the question has been raised in the context of Exodus, it is illustrated by material from Chronicles (2 Chron. 1–9), thus linking together once more the two biblical books. The observation that the theology of the D-version and that of the P-edition of Exodus appear to correspond respectively to two traditional Christian doctrines then prompts the final essay. Just as in the inaugural lecture (Chapter 2) it was argued that the study of the Hebrew Bible has to be conducted within a wider cultural context, so, in the concluding essay, it is not inappropriate to consider the possible impact of the findings of that study on one of the most significant of these contexts in Christian theology. The particular question I have in mind in that last essay is: if this is what the Old Testament teaches about justification and sanctification, what can Paul have meant by 'justification by faith'?

Response to Some Recent Pentateuchal Criticism

Of all the works that have appeared in the interim,[16] the closest to my approach is probably that of Erhard Blum, especially, as regards Exodus, his *Studien zur Komposition des Pentateuch*.[17] This, and the fact that it is rightly regarded as a landmark study,[18] justifies a consideration of it at some length. In identifying two main 'compositions' in the Pentateuch, Blum's work bears out to that extent my own findings. Blum's work is all the more welcome to me since both his studies and mine have been carried out in total independence.[19] But there are also

16. J. Van Seters's article, 'The Deuteronomistic Redaction of the Pentateuch: The Case against It', in M. Vervenne and J. Lust (eds.), *Deuteronomy and Deuteronomic Literature* (Festschrift C.H.W. Brekelmans; BETL, 133; Leuven: Leuven University Press/Peeters, 1997), pp. 301-19, does not, I think, despite its apparently threatening title, materially affect the discussion from my point of view. Much of the article is taken up with a rebuttal (with which I am in sympathy) of the argument of R. Smend (whose approach but not whose results I note with approval in Chapter 2) and H.-C. Schmitt for a Nomistic redaction of DtrH. The part of Van Seters's argument that does impinge on mine is his statement that his 'J', which he dates later than Deuteronomy, has broken up the 'very simple, staighforward [*sic*] theme... of conquest of the land after the departure from Horeb' in Deut. 1–3 and has 'interspersed it with a series of narratives mostly about the trials or murmurings in the wilderness that now completely obscure this theme' (p. 317). But other material in Deuteronomy on precisely Israel's murmurings is an embarrassment for this thesis, particularly Deut. 9.22-24, which is central to my argument (see Chapter 11). Van Seters (pp. 311-12) dismisses that passage as 'a late addition [which is based upon his late J] interrupting the original account'. But one would have to attribute the whole of Deut. 9.7–10.11 to such a 'late addition', for 9.22-24 is entirely integral to that section: these verses provide further items on the list of occasions of 'enraging the LORD' begun in 9.7-8. I continue to find no place for 'J' in my scheme of things, whether late (Van Seters; see also Chapter 11, n. 1 below) or early (see my engagement with representative views in, e.g., Chapter 8, §III; Chapter 9, n. 4; Chapter 10, n. 34).

17. BZAW, 189; Berlin: W. de Gruyter, 1990. The similarity of views is noted by Nicholson, *Pentateuch*, p. 171 n. 12.

18. Nicholson cites J.L. Ska's comment that Blum is a new Wellhausen (*Pentateuch*, p. 174; so G.I. Davies, 'The Composition of the Book of Exodus: Reflections on the Theses of Erhard Blum', in M.V. Fox *et al.* [eds.], *Texts, Temples and Traditions* [Festschrift Menahem Haran; Winona Lake, IN: Eisenbrauns, 1996], p. 77). To judge from the crude statistics of references in the index, Nicholson devotes most space, after Wellhausen himself, to the consideration of Blum's work.

19. Only my essay reproduced in Chapter 7 was available to Blum at the time of his writing (although in truth my programme was already well developed: Chapters

contrasts between our methods and our findings; a preliminary statement of agreements and contrasts may help to keep the line of argument clear.

As far as Exodus is concerned, I am at one with Blum that the book in its present state is the result of the combination of two accounts, one bearing the imprint of Deuteronomy and the Deuteronomistic History, and a later concerted edition of that account, P, which never existed independently but arose from the work of an editor engaging in a complementary and sometimes polemically corrective way with that underlying account (in my terms, what the Chronicler is to Samuel–Kings— certainly editor, even midrashist, but not merely independent editor of other sources or passive redactor—the final editor of Exodus, P, is to the underlying account, D).[20]

2–4 and 8 had also already been published, as had my *Exodus* [n. 13 above]; the paper published as Chapter 9 was already in the public domain as a lecture): Blum cites it (*Studien*, p. 70 n. 111) with approval of its argument about Exod. 34 but to affirm, on his part, that his conclusions were reached independently. Cf. also Blum's comment in Vervenne, *Studies in the Book of Exodus*, p. 358. I find it necessary to stress the independence of our work in view of the sometimes remarkable coincidence of expression, even down to detail: for example, Blum (*Studien*, p. 163 n. 271) cites the rabbinic dictum, אין מוקדם ומאוחר בתורה ('there is no earlier or later in the Torah'), which I have quoted in Chapter 13 and with which I have begun the *Commentary 2000* Exodus; he also uses, as I do in the same introduction, the term 'dialectic' for the relationship between the two main compositions (*Studien*, p. 345 n. 41); he even has a few words to say in defence of an 'intentionalist' approach to the understanding of the (many levels of the) text (*Studien*, pp. 380-82; cf. Chapter 13 below). But there are, in fact, many places where our interpretations diverge. Thus, even though he agrees with me that Exod. 34.17-27 represents the resumption of the end of the legislation of the Book of the Covenant, Exod. 23.12-19, I do not agree with his view that Exod. 34.11-16 corresponds to Exod. 23.20-33 (*Studien*, p. 370; the sequence itself would be odd); in my view, Exod. 34.11-16 is, rather, the elaboration of the second commandment of the Decalogue on the prohibition of the worship of other gods, already alluded to in 34.5-8 (cf. in particular the coincidence of vocabulary between 34.6, 7, 14 and 20.5-6; the centrality of the 'chief commandment' in v. 14 Blum in fact acknowledges, *Studien*, p. 373), here in terms of avoidance of marriage contracts with the indigenous population and the recognition of their gods which those would imply. By citing both the beginning of the Decalogue and the end of the Book of the Covenant, Exod. 34 makes it clear that the covenant is remade on precisely the same terms as before (see Chapter 7).

20. Blum terms Exod. 19.20-25 'a sort of midrashic definition of Exod. 19.11ff.[-13?]' (*Studien*, p. 382 n. 77).

Blum's method of argument, however, I find deficient.[21] He begins
with the Deuteronomic/Deuteronomistic composition, 'KD' in his
terms, and seeks to delimit it on 'text-immanent' grounds of narrative
coherence; by this means he endeavours to distinguish it both from the
underlying traditions that build up its 'profile' and from later superimposed literary editions. But this procedure surely begs a number of
questions of both external and internal delimitation. The distinction of
KD from 'KP', his term for the priestly composition, is not uncontroversial. As will be indicated below, there will be repeated occasions
when Blum's delimitation of the P-material must be disputed (e.g. in
Exod. 24).[22] Further, in the discussion of P, not only does its physical
extent have to be established; its editorial technique has also to be recognized, in particular, its reuse and transposition of D-materials
(acknowledged by Blum in Exod. 18, but not in Exod. 15–17; 32–34;
see Chapters 11 and 12). As for internal delimitation, Blum is much
more ambitious than I think the evidence warrants: KD, for instance, he
holds is not a 'flat landscape' but has a 'profile' or 'relief':[23] it incorporates earlier materials, which, though they cannot always be distinguished in themselves in literary form, nonetheless stand distinct 'diachronically' from KD as the 'main composition'.[24] I am sceptical at this
point. I have no doubt whatever that the two main compositions contain
much traditional material; but I do not know how one can successfully
distinguish between a main composition as a self-consistent written
literary layer and the traditions that it incorporates whose own literary
form cannot necessarily be recovered. Do these amorphous incorporated traditions not thereby simply become part of the composition?

---

21. As an anticipation of his argument, Blum's words (in this case about KP, for
which see below) may be cited: 'Für unsere relativ einfache Hypothese *eines* über-
greifenden "Gestaltungswillens" spricht zum einen die weitgehende *Vernetzung* der
sprachlichen/inhaltlichen Konnexionen, zum anderen, wohl nicht weniger ents-
cheidend, die konzeptionelle Dichte und Geschlossenheit des postulierten *Ganzen*'
('Our relatively simple hypothesis of a *single*, superimposed "creative intention" is
evidenced by the far-reaching *network* of interconnections of language/content, on
the one hand, and, on the other, indeed no less decisively, by the conceptual com-
pactness and consistency of the postulated *whole*'), *Studien*, p. 107 (Blum's italics).
22. Despite Blum's comments on *Studien*, p. 221 about the consensus, astonish-
ing for Old Testament studies, that the definition of the extent of Priestly texts in
the Pentateuch is virtually beyond dispute.
23. Cf. Blum, *Studien*, p. 382.
24. Blum, *Studien*, e.g. p. 215.

The Passover is a case in point: one may assume that it is an age-old rite, but to attempt to recreate the history of Passover observance on the basis of analysis of the biblical text alone leads only to enigmas and confusion (see Chapter 7). One may assume, indeed, that matters were far more complex than the short digests in the biblical materials indicate. I am thus content to affirm a D-version (but of a much larger extent than Blum's D-composition), without attempting to establish a 'profile' of his sources.[25] The period and place I should envisage for the composition of the D-version—the exile in Babylon (Blum places KD, as presupposing DtrH, in the early postexilic period)—suggest that creative synthesis dependent on a reservoir of shared memories and practices is likely to be the best model. This is not to say that there are no prior written sources: the Book of the Covenant, which, I have argued, has passed through editing by the D-writer (Chapter 7), is the main case in point. But on the whole the search for written or unwritten sources behind the D-version is as speculative—and futile—as the search for the Chronicler's extra-biblical sources:[26] they may or may not exist; what matters is the new creative synthesis produced.[27]

Further, in my view, the argument that he uses for the existence of the main D-composition is not the strongest that can be deployed. The 'reminiscences' in Deuteronomy 1–11 enable much more precisely the extent of the D-version to be established, which at once distinguishes it from the later P-edition and, at the same time, provides some controls over the question of the exploitation of traditions in that version,

25. I naturally agree with and welcome his strictures on the search for 'pre-, proto-, or early Deuteronomistic' literary levels in the text; *Studien*, p. 167 (see Chapters 11 and 12).

26. A preoccupation which accounts, I believe, for a certain inconclusiveness in sections of Japhet's commentary on Chronicles (see Chapter 5).

27. Equally dubious, it seems to me, is Blum's search for a 'composition history' of still later literary D-editions, his 'Joshua 24 edition' (*Studien*, p. 363) to which he assigns the burial of Joseph tradition (Gen. 33.19; 50.25-26; Exod. 13.19; Josh. 24.32), and, even more crucially, his intervening 'Mal'ak edition' (pp. 365-77), to which he assigns Exod. 14.19a; 23.20-33*; (32.34aβ;) 33.2,3b*, 4; 34.11-27 (28a); Judg. 2.1-5. His argument about the distinctiveness of vocabulary and viewpoint over against KD seems to me over-refined: the statement, for example, that צרעה in Josh. 24.12 sets this material apart does not seem to me to cohere with the only other occurrences of the word in the Hebrew Bible (Exod. 23.28; Deut. 7.20). I am quite unconvinced that such text elements can be held to evidence an independent edition or that the distinctions drawn can bear the weight placed upon them.

whether these be embedded as self-contained blocks or absorbed into the composition. I can only acknowledge that, in the following collection, the essay that has required most revision, in the light of the process of trying to write a short commentary,[28] has been that on the 'plague narrative' (Chapter 10): not the least of the reasons for reconsideration is that it is precisely in Exodus 1–13 that the parallels in Deuteronomy are at their vaguest and most ambiguous and that is it to less certain criteria, such as considerations of narrative coherence, that one is driven back. The establishment of a D-version in Exodus must begin where the parallels are closest, especially, 31.18–34.29 and, to a lesser extent chs. 19, 20 and 24. Only then can the findings be extrapolated into other areas where the less objective criteria of use of language, literary coherence, shared outlook and so on must be brought into play. Narrative coherence is to be brought in only as, so to speak, a 'third-level' argument when all else fails: first, the parallels between Exodus and the reminiscences in Deuteronomy must be thoroughly explored; then distinctive characteristics, primarily diverging views of *Realien*, 'hard facts', such as dates, itineraries and religious institutions, and, to a lesser degree, vocabulary; and only finally, in an auxiliary capacity or when these other indices are missing, narrative coherence, where passages necessary for the course of the narrative must be deemed to belong to the account in question. In my view, Blum, by beginning his argument from this third level, sets out from one of the weakest points. He is aware of the problem and, later in the book, even concedes that it might have been better if his argument had proceeded from the first criterion, the parallels in Deuteronomy.[29]

A number of points of detail may now be looked at.

Blum begins with chs. 1–14(15). Here he identifies a network of interconnected verses, built up in the first instance from the correspondence

---

28. See n. 14.

29. 'Als eine andere—in der Sache vielleicht erste—Möglichkeit, das Verhältnis der D-Komposition zur deuteronomistischen Traditionsschule zu prüfen und gegebenenfalls zu präzisieren, bietet sich der direkte Vergleich mit der Überlieferung im Deuteronomium selbst an' ('Direct comparison with the material as it is in Deuteronomy itself presents itself as another—perhaps in the nature of the case first—possibility of testing and on occasion defining the relationship of the D-composition to the Deuteronomistic school of tradition'), *Studien*, p. 172. On p. 137 n. 153 he speaks of the parallel in Deut. 10 as at least 'partially "external evidence [for a pre-P tradition of the construction of the ark]" '. Cf. his acknowledgment of the danger in his approach of arguing in a circle (*Studien*, p. 107 n. 30).

of 14.31 to 4.31, which he terms the 'loadbearing pillars' of the composition, to which he explicitly ascribes 3.1–4.18, 29-31; 5.22–6.1; 10.2; 11.1-3; 12.21(25)-27, [33-34, p. 38] 35-36, 39b; 13.3-16; 14.13-14, 30-31.[30] These passages, self-contained within a framework with matching beginning and end, and bound together by narrative coherence and dramatic tension, constitute, says Blum, the final 'compositional layer' of the pre-P composition of Exodus 1–14, which can at the same time be distinguished from the pre-existing tradition(s) (even though not written sources)[31] that it incorporates.

Scarcely surprisingly, there is much that is debatable in his discussion of this part of Exodus and in his excerpting of these passages. Fine distinctions are drawn. The elusive character of these incorporated traditions is acknowledged, for example, 'the contours of an "incorporated" "Vorlage" cannot be traced'.[32] From pericope to pericope, the traditions that make up the 'profile' of the composition may lie at any point on the spectrum represented by the poles of *Traditionsgeschichte*—that is, the mere knowledge of an ancient tradition without fixed literary form (which, presumably then, KD incorporated in his own words!)—and *Überlieferungsgeschichte*—that is, the incorporation of such tradition in recoverable earlier literary form. But, once free composition is granted, the attempt diachronically to differentiate KD from a textually undefinable 'substratum'[33] becomes nugatory. The point may be illustrated in connection with Blum's discussion of the revelation of the divine name, 'YHWH'. Beyond reasonable doubt the tradition of the revelation of the name existed in ancient Israel long before KD (Blum cites Hos. 1.9; 12.10; 13.4; Ezek. 20.5). In the present account in 3.14-15, KD is thus dependent on earlier versions 'of whatever kind'. But, once that concession has been made, there is no possibility of differentiating KD as a compositional level from the earlier material embedded within it. Blum's concluding statement, 'We content ourselves here with the fact of a reception of older tradition in Exod. 3 (KD)',[34] becomes so non-explicit and uncontroversial as hardly to be worth making.

In his identification of KD in Exodus 1–14 there are, further, striking

30. Blum, *Studien*, pp. 18-19.
31. Blum, *Studien*, p. 19.
32. Blum, *Studien*, p. 41 n. 155.
33. Blum, *Studien*, p. 41.
34. Blum, *Studien*, p. 42.

omissions and controversial attributions. For example, he endorses
W.H. Schmidt's view that 4.21-23 is an editorial element presupposing
the P-composition.[35] But, on the contrary, if it is viewed in the light of
D's legislation on the release of Hebrew slaves and the offering of the
first-born in Deut. 15.12-23 (not to mention Passover in 16.1-8), which
in my view it must be (see Chapter 10, below), this passage integrates
thematically the whole of Exodus 1–14 (1–24, indeed) at the D-level in
a much more apposite and powerful way than Blum's proposals do.

Strikingly, Blum denies the plague cycle to KD: 'the great complex
of the plagues narrative and along with it the substance of the episode
in Exodus 5 (which provides its narrative preparation) evinces no
Deuteronomistic formulation'.[36] But he has immediately to modify the
point.[37] There are 'at least' two places where KD has supplemented the
plague cycle: the introduction of Moses' staff in 7.15b in 'explicit
cross-reference to 4.2ff.' (he runs into this problem later in connection
with 17.5);[38] and the element of instruction of children in 10.2a. Indeed,
10.1-2 Blum takes to be original to KD: 10.2b=7.17aβ and so marks an
inclusio in the first six of the original seven plagues subsumed by
KD[39]). While I agree with Blum on the extent of the pre-P seven-plague
cycle (plagues III, VI and IX are added by P; the cycle begins in 7.14
and includes 12.29-36), I argue in Chapter 10, in the light particularly
of the use of 'signs' and 'wonders' in Deuteronomy, that these plagues
are integral to the D-version and that Exod. 10.1b-3aαi is in fact to be
attributed to P. Further, can he both cite with approval Buber's insight
about the connection of the verb פלה in 33.16 and in the plague
narrative of 8.18; 9.4; 11.7, and its foreshadowing in פלא in 3.20,[40] and
deny the formulation of the plague cycle to KD?[41] Is it not more natural
to attribute all to the same D-version?

A critical point is the discussion of the Passover legislation in 12.21-
27.[42] Blum agrees that the legislation in vv. 25-27 agrees with
Deut. 16.1-8 (Passover not as domestic rite but as sanctuary-based

35. Blum, *Studien*, p. 28 n. 100.
36. Blum, *Studien*, p. 36.
37. Blum, *Studien*, p. 37 n. 141.
38. Blum, *Studien*, p. 151 n. 210.
39. Blum, *Studien*, p. 15 n. 28.
40. Blum, *Studien*, pp. 63-64 n. 80.
41. Blum, *Studien*, p. 36.
42. Blum, *Studien*, pp. 38-39.

זבח-sacrifice). This he takes as evidence that KD 'has in 12, 21*-23(24) integrated an already firmly formulated section and further developed it in vv. 25-27'. KD could not alter that underlying material, or else it would have destroyed the connection with the sparing of the first-born. This view is, it seems to me, quite the opposite of the state of affairs: it is D that provides the older account in vv. 25-27 which P has overlaid by insertion into a new context! I should argue at the outset that v. 28 has to be added to the context under discussion: quite apart from the paragraph marker in MT at the end of v. 28, it is with v. 29 that the narrative of the tenth plague is resumed from 11.8. The importance of the observation lies in the fact that v. 28, resuming, with the mention of Aaron, v. 1 which belongs, as Blum agrees, to P, places a P-framework round the paragraph. Verses 21-24 equally belong to that P-context: the point is almost conceded by Blum when he attempts to defend his view of the D-provenance of this material by critique of J. Van Seters's arguments (with which in this context I agree) that the terminology is P.[43] After remarking that technical terms for rites such as those observed at Passover must have been current long before P, and are, thus, non-specific as regards attribution to sources, he acknowledges that the P-writer elsewhere shows a tendency to correct inherited traditions and might well have introduced this material to reaffirm, against KD, traditional practice. Belatedly he adds: 'v. 28 might support the contention that the P-level "integrated" this section', though only 'at the level of *composition*'. Against Blum it must be observed that only the recognition that D-material has been placed in vv. 21-28 in a new P-context explains the illogicalities that have thereby been introduced into the narrative: in the immediate context, the command to stay indoors all night, v. 22, is at variance with the (D) denouement in vv. 29-36 (Moses' audience with Pharaoh at midnight and Israel's expulsion forthwith that night); in the wider context, it makes the Passover the focus of the plague cycle, when, as the tenth plague indicates, it should be the offering of the first-born. The logical sequence indicated in the legislation in Deut. 15.12–16.8 and its originally matching narrative in the D-version of Exodus 1–24, is here, as elsewhere with other D-materials, transposed by P (in this case from the original D-version in ch. 13) in order to be polemically corrected in its new context in ch. 12 (see Chapter 9 below).

Though Blum thereafter turns to a consideration of the Sinai pericope

43. Blum, *Studien*, p. 39 n. 149.

(chs. 19–34),[44] for the sake of continuity of presentation I include at
this point comments on his discussion of the itinerary materials in
15.22–19.2. He attributes to KD matching pairs of 'murmuring' episodes tied aetiologically to place-names both before and after Horeb—
the substratum of 15.22-26 (Marah) and 17.1-7 (Massah), with their
legitimate complaint about lack of water, corresponding to the two
incidents in Numbers 11 (Taberah; Kibroth-hattaavah), with their nag-
ging complaints about lack of food.[45] At first sight, this is a compelling
set of observations. In my view, however, it is erroneous. It runs
counter to Blum's own (correct, in my opinion) observation of Israel's
ready responsiveness in chs. 19 and 24.[46] That contradiction is avoided
if the reminiscence in Deut. 9.22 is taken as prescriptive for the
restoration of the D-version of Exodus (as I think it should): the
matching Massah narrative should fall between the Taberah and
Kibroth-hattaavah narratives, that is, between Num. 11.3 and 4, as I
argue in Chapter 11, where I also argue that the Marah narrative in
15.22-26 represents reuse of D-material by P. By contrast, in Blum's
opinion it is Deut. 9.22 that is anomalous: Massah there *may* (Blum's
italics) be attributed to a 'marginal gloss'.[47] In 17.8-16 there is doubtless D-material, as Blum argues (the role of Joshua, for instance, corresponds to that portrayed in ch. 32; the oracle against Amalek in v. 14
coincides almost word for word with the legislation in Deut. 25.19).
But it must be doubted whether Hur, for example, as part of the
'quartet' in 17.8-16 is evidence for the pre-P composition, as Blum
claims: Hur recurs in 24.14, which I, though not Blum,[48] regard as P
(he may be identified in 2 Chron. 1.5 as the grandfather of Bezalel, who
occurs in Exodus [31.2, etc.] only in contexts universally regarded as
P). As regards Exodus 18, Blum follows the lead of Ibn Ezra, substantiated by the evidence of Deut. 1.9-18 (my very argument!) and Num.
10.29-36, that the material has been displaced from the end of the
Horeb narrative in Numbers 10.[49] But if displacement can be allowed in
this context, on the evidence of Deuteronomy, why not more widely?

As for the opening section of the Sinai pericope in Exodus 19–24,

44. Blum, *Studien*, pp. 45-72.
45. Blum, *Studien*, p. 151.
46. Blum, *Studien*, p. 193.
47. Blum, *Studien*, p. 149 n. 202.
48. Blum, *Studien*, p. 89.
49. Blum, *Studien*, pp. 153-58.

Blum argues that KD embraces 19.3b-8, 20.22 and 24.3-8. But here he finds that KD bears more strongly the character of an 'edition': it has incorporated an older narrative which includes 20.18-21, B, and 24.1-2*, 9-11*. The distinction between these two pre-P layers is based on two main observations: the difference in concept of the nature and content of the revelation at Horeb in 20.22 (Decalogue as well as B, though Blum leaves open the question whether KD actually incorporated the Decalogue at this point); and the deliberate contrasting by KD of the 'young men' in 24.5 with the 'elders' in what he regards as the earlier narrative in 24.9-11. Thus 24.3-8 constitutes the 'point of intersection' of two lines of pre-P composition.[50]

The latter observation may be disposed of briefly first. Blum himself acknowledges[51]—correctly in my view—that the insertion in Exod. 24.1, 9 of Nadab and Abihu, who occur elsewhere only in P contexts,[52] is evidence of 'priestly tradents'. But there are still further features in these verses that are typical of P: the cultic vocabulary (which Blum notes), and the preoccupation with hierarchy. In my view, therefore, these verses are part of P's rearrangement already witnessed in 18.13-27. The counterpoising of 'elders' to 'young men' is simply further evidence of P's preoccupation with hierarchy, as I argue in Chapter 7.

The main point—the attempt by Blum to distinguish between a D-version and a 'pre-Deuteronomic' version—rests on a comparison between the presentation in Exodus and the reminiscences in Deuteronomy, especially Deuteronomy 4–5, and the assumed differences between them. In this argument, Blum bases himself to a significant extent on E.W. Nicholson's article, 'The Decalogue as the Direct Address by God'.[53] Some consideration of Nicholson's argument is, therefore, appropriate at this point.

Nicholson argues that the Decalogue in its present position in Exod. 20.1-17 is clearly intrusive: as direct address by God to the people,[54] it interrupts the description of the theophany which is broken off at 19.19, only to be resumed at 20.18. The Decalogue as direct address by God to Israel at Horeb is, however, a characteristic conception of Deuteronomy, for whom, indeed, it constitutes the sole basis of the covenant

50. Blum, *Studien*, p. 99.
51. Blum, *Studien*, p. 89 n. 196.
52. Blum, *Studien*, pp. 230-31.
53. *VT* 27 (1977), pp. 422-33.
54. So Blum, *Studien*, p. 93.

(Deut. 4.13).[55] The presence of the Decalogue in its present position in Exodus is thus attributable to a Deuteronomic redactor.[56]

I should wish to question, however, both of these points (that for Deuteronomy the Decalogue was 'the direct address of God' to the people; and that it alone constituted the basis of the covenant). At first sight it does indeed appear that in Deuteronomy what the people hear for themselves is the very words of the Decalogue. This would be the obvious interpretation of such phrases as, 'so that I may make them hear my words, which they will learn...and teach their children' (4.10, explained in v. 13 as the Decalogue; cf. v. 15, etc.). Even more pointed seems to be 5.4: 'face to face the LORD spoke with you at the Mountain' (though the continuation, 'from the midst of the fire' shows the strongly figurative sense of the verse). Deuteronomy 5.5, however, which suggests that Moses mediated also the content of the Decalogue to the people, is a problem for Nicholson's interpretation and he is obliged to consider it 'a later gloss inserted by an editor'.[57] But, I should respond, perhaps Deut. 5.5 is not to be regarded as a gloss but is to be taken as integral to its context, explaining precisely what occurred. It was not the *content* of the Decalogue that the people heard at the foot of the mountain, but the *sound* of the revelation to Moses at the top of the mountain (an interpretation that would be fully compatible with Deut. 4.12, 'קוֹל דברים'; cf. 4.33). As we shall see below in connection with the discussion on Deuteronomy's view of the basis of the covenant (sometimes Decalogue alone, sometimes Decalogue plus 'statutes and ordinances'), Deuteronomy may on occasion use an abbreviated version, in this case 'words' alone, as well as 'sound of words'.

On that basis, I should argue that the two accounts in Exod. 19.16–20.22, including the Decalogue, and Deut. 4.9–5.33 are fully compatible with one another. The pre-P text of Exodus reflected in both suggests that, so far from hearing intelligible utterance, the central experience at the mountain was overwhelming terror induced by exposure to the shattering sound of natural and cosmic phenomena, accompanied by the blaring ram's horn, all proclaiming the theophany of

55. So Blum, *Studien*, p. 198.
56. Nicholson, 'Decalogue', p. 431. Cf. p. 429: Exod. 20.22-23, interpreted as referring to Decalogue—correctly, in my view—is also attributed to a Deuteronomic redactor (= Blum's KD, at least for v. 22).
57. Nicholson, 'Decalogue', p. 431 n. 13.

God. The basis of the relationship between God and people is the indelible impression left by this immediate encounter with God. Amid that clamour no intelligible word could be made out; the rational element of the definition of the terms of the relationship is then spelt out in detail in the Decalogue and B, both of these involving communication by God to Moses alone (Exod. 19.19; 20.21). (The curious fact that only the first two 'words' of the Decalogue are the direct speech of God, while in the remainder God is referred to in the third person, is compatible with this scenario that even the Decalogue itself is mediated by Moses.) It is essential, therefore, that this awesome visual and auditory experience, which is only subsequently 'decoded' in rational discourse, is prepared for in 19.3-9 by an assurance of election and a preview of the terms of the covenant. The compositions in Exodus and Deuteronomy are thus complementary but linked by verses that are anomalous in each: Deut. 5.5 links with the awesome presentation of Exodus and the necessary mediatorial function of Moses even for the Decalogue; Exod. 19.19b links with the intelligible discourse of Deuteronomy. Each, it may be said, fully presupposes the other, the difference being explained by the fact that D is reminiscence (cf. the way in which it passes rapidly over the detail in 4.13), hortatory and didactic (and is thus at the same time expansive and repetitive, as in 4.14-15), whereas Exodus is narrative. The link between the two is aided by the ambiguity of the word קוֹל ('sound' as well as 'content of speech'; cf. the variety in the senses of קוֹל in Exod. 19.19; 20.18. In 20.18 the participial construction implies that the reaction of the people, including their withdrawal to some distance from the mountain, is simultaneous with the foregoing opening utterance of the Decalogue). דברים is hardly less ambiguous; cf. Deut. 4.9, where it refers to things seen, not words heard. The mediatorial role that Moses has to play also in connection with the Decalogue accounts, then, for the reading in Exod. 24.3 (cf. Deut. 5.5), where דברים are included as well as משפטים as the basis of the covenant. 19.9 confirms the point: the people are witnesses to the fact that God speaks with Moses; their knowledge of what is actually said depends on his subsequent communication with the people.

The freedom of the agreement between Exodus and Deuteronomy is very striking. The sequence of events is identical in the two presentations: Moses brings the people to the mountain; they experience an overwhelming theophanic display; they hear for themselves the sound but not the words of the revelation of the Decalogue;

in terrified response, they recoil in terror for their lives; they request that Moses alone should hear and communicate any further revelation by God to them; further revelation directly from God to Moses duly follows.

There is also agreement in the depiction of the essentials: the mountain (הר), wreathed in cloud (ענן) and fog (ערפל, Deut. 4.11, etc.; Exod. 19.16), the people seeing (ראה) and hearing (שמע) the speaking (דבר; אמר, Deut. 4.9-10, etc.; Exod. 19.9, etc.) of God to Moses; the speaking of God from heaven (Deut. 4.36; Exod. 20.22); the reaction of fear (ירא) and mortal (מות, Deut. 5.25; Exod. 20.19) terror on the part of the people.

There are, however, many varieties in the depiction of the details. Moses assembles (Deut. 4.10, הקהיל; Exod. 19.17, הוציא) the people; Exodus alone mentions the camp (19.16, 17), though D alone has Israel return 'to your tents' (5.30) pending Moses' return; D has them 'approach' (קרב, 4.11; 5.23, cf. 27) the 'foot' (4.11, תחת; Exod. 19.17, בתחתית) of the mountain; in D the people simply 'stand' at the mountain (4.10), whereas in Exod. 19.17 they 'present themselves' (in Exod. 20.18, and its resumptive phrase in 20.21, they 'stand back'); the theophany D describes also in terms of 'fire burning into the heart of the heavens' (4.11) and of 'darkness' (4.11, though that may be a construct form referring to the darkness of the enveloping cloud and fog) and of God speaking 'from the midst of fire' (מתוך האש, 4.12, 15, etc.; cf. 5.23, 'the mountain burning with fire'). Exodus adds thunder and lightning (19.16; 20.18); and the sounding of the שפר (19.16). In Deuteronomy the approach to Moses is through the hierarchy of 'heads of tribes and elders' (5.23) and their speech is greatly elaborated (5.24-27), as is the response of God (5.28-33). The subsequent revelation to Moses alone is termed חקים ומשפטים (4.14; 5.31 adds כל־המצוה; the correspondence of these descriptors to the content of the Book of the Covenant, Exod. 20.22–23.33, is striking [cf. table of the varieties of law in Chapter 7]). The purpose of the theophany in terms of impact on the people is described in different terms: ליסרך in Deut. 4.36; in Exod. 20.20 it is לבעבור נסות אתכם (but for the interchangeability of יסר and נסה in Deuteronomy compare 4.34 and 11.2) and לבלתי תחטאו ובעבור תהיה יראתו על־פניכם.

Particular concerns bulk out the presentation in Deuteronomy 4: for example, the insistence on instruction (למד, 4.10); the emphasis that no תבנית was seen, only a קול was heard (4.12), which is part of the setting of D's reminiscence as preparation for the impending settlement in the land in year forty in which warnings about idolatry feature prominently; the expected emphasis on covenant (4.13).

As has been anticipated above, Nicholson's other observation that in Deuteronomy the covenant is concluded on the basis of the Decalogue alone[58] does not seem to me to cover all the data, in particular the reference to 'statutes and ordinances' 'revealed at that time' in Deut. 4.14; cf. 5.31. Neither of these verses is cited by Nicholson, but they are

---

58. Nicholson, 'Decalogue', pp. 422, 425, 432.

discussed by Blum in a sense similar to Nicholson's overall argument:[59] the reference to 'statutes and ordinances' in these verses, claims Blum, is to the parenesis and laws that are to follow in Deuteronomy, now revealed to Moses at Horeb in order to be later handed on to the people in Moab. But, on the contrary, the reference in these verses to 'statutes and ordinances' (see again the table of varieties of laws in Chapter 7) is most naturally to be taken as to the Book of the Covenant, revealed there and then. The reference to 'observing them in the land whither you are crossing' does not imply that these statutes and ordinances were only subsequently communicated in the guise of the Deuteronomic code in Moab on the eve of the settlement, any more than the prospective legislation on Passover, unleavened bread and firstlings, in which a similar phrase occurs (Exod. 12.25; 13.3, 5, all belonging to the D-version in my view), is to be communicated in Moab. 'The LORD commanded me at that time' (Deut. 4.14) relates the material specifically to Horeb; Deut. 5.31 belongs to the retrospect on Horeb.

The upshot of these observations is that the reminiscences in Deuteronomy 4–5 of the events at Horeb are compatible in every detail with the presentation of Exod. 19.17, 19; 20.1–23.33; 24.3-8. Nicholson's note 13 has to be emended:[60] Deut. 5.5 is contributed by *the* editor, the Deuteronomistic editor, who is responsible for both narrative in Exodus and reminiscence in Deuteronomy. Nicholson speaks of one text being 'dependent upon' or 'presupposing' the other;[61] on the contrary, identity of conception is evidence of identity of authorship, just as in the case of other parallels, not least Jeremiah 52//2 Kgs 24.18–25.30. It seems to me, therefore, that Blum's confining of his compositional layer KD only to Exod. 19.3b-8; 20.22; 24.3-8 is equally unwarranted. His leaving as an 'open question' whether his KD was responsible for the incorporation of such a fundamental text as the Decalogue is the unnecessary consequence of his over-elaboration of the process of the production of the text (cf. his subsidiary argumentation that, for example, נסה in Exod. 20.20 means 'to allow to experience', while it is interpreted in Deut. 5 in the sense 'to test' [the verb נסה does not actually occur in Deut. 5!]). On the contrary, in my view, the Decalogue and the Book of the Covenant are both integral to the D-version of Exodus, as the parallel in Deuteronomy 4–5 makes clear.

59. Blum, *Studien*, pp. 93, 199.
60. Nicholson, 'Decalogue', p. 431.
61. Nicholson, 'Decalogue', p. 431.

Because of his highlighting of apparent differences between Exodus
and Deuteronomy, Blum has to propose a complex history of transmission for these traditions.[62] In view of the unmistakable agreement in
basic structure and in individual details, it is impossible not to see here,
he agrees, reciprocal relations between the two (*Wechselbezüge*)[63] in
terms of a history of transmission. He maintains (as has Perlitt, whom
he cites) that Deuteronomy 4–5 is to be regarded as a set of interpretations of Exod. 20.18-21: in particular, the interpretation of the Decalogue as the direct address of God in Deut. 4.10ff.[-13?], 36 and the
instruction about the appropriate reaction of the people in Deut. 5.28-
29. Yet, on the other hand, he argues that Exod. 20.22 (covenant on the
basis of Decalogue plus B) represents a development beyond
Deuteronomy 4 (covenant on the basis of Decalogue alone). That is,
Blum proposes the following *Überlieferungsgeschichte*: the pre-
Deuteronomic tradition reflected in Exod. 20.18-21 → Deuteronomy 4–
5 → KD in Exod. 20.22. Furthermore, he claims to find a compositional
difference between the two latter stages: whereas Deuteronomy represents free reformulation, KD's formulation is restricted by the now
authoritative D. Deut. 5.5, also a problem verse for Blum, he is consequently constrained to consider as a correction (by whom?) of Deut. 5.4
in the light of KD's picture of Moses as sole mediator in Exod. 33.11,
Num. 12.8 and Deut. 34.10.[64] This, it seems to me, is unnecessarily
complicated. This complementarity between Exodus and Deuteronomy
is simply another example of the 'conundrum' of which I speak in
Chapter 12 below: both the D-version in Exodus and Deuteronomy
show knowledge of each other; the explanation of this knowledge is not
that there is a complex history of interchanging dependence of one
upon the other but that both emanate from the same school. The *Wechselbezüge* are synchronic, not diachronic.

It seems to me that it is, thus, possible to argue for a basic shared D-
text which has undergone its own elaboration in Deuteronomy and a
Dtr elaboration in Exodus, where it has been thoroughly reused and
revised by the P-edition. This is perhaps the most economical theory
possible to account for the processes involved, but it is sufficient to
account for the differences between Deuteronomy and pre-P Exodus.

P builds in Exod. 19.20-25 on the fact that the following Decalogue

62. Blum, *Studien*, pp. 176-77.
63. Blum, *Studien*, p. 181.
64. Blum, *Studien*, p. 177 n. 346.

is part of the material mediated by Moses (cf. the rough transition between 19.25 and 20.1). It is equally concerned to remove through its hierarchy all possibility of misunderstanding of Deuteronomy's 'face to face' of the people's encounter with God (Deut. 5.4), as it is, I have argued, in the case of Moses' own encounter with God in Exodus 33 (Chapter 12).

Reuse by P would be the fire (19.18), and the fact that the people had not gone up the mountain (19.12-13 [in v.13 the ram's horn is now יבל], 20-25). P's distinctive concerns with purity and hierarchy are also found in 24.1-2. D does not fully clarify how God relates himself to the mountain—Exod. 19.11b, 18, 20 has him descend (contrast 'come' in 19.9; 20.20); he also 'speaks from heaven' (20.22; Deut. 4.36), another example of D's lack of consistency and precision.

Brief comments of a similar nature may be made on the remaining passages. For example, Blum delimits P in 24.12-18 as vv. 15b[I assume from context, though '15a' is read]-18a.[65] But surely v. 14 is also P (cf. Aaron and Hur, quite apart from the 'elders', who reflect the P-displaced position of 18.13-27). Blum's main—correct—argument, that ויעל at the beginning of v. 18 is resumptive, can apply as well to v. 13 as to v. 15.

In the discussion of Exodus 32–34 he begins with 32.7-14, which, he says, has the advantage that there is 'an unusually broad consensus' among scholars that that passage is an 'expansion' in Dtr style.[66] He thus with some confidence assigns it to his KD. Its importance is confirmed by the fact that in it so many of the lines developed in chs. 33–34 intersect (he notes the complex network of cross-references between Exod. 33–34, Num. 11–12, Deut. 31.14-15, 23; 34.10[-12] concerning the אהל מועד, YHWH's descent [ירד] in the עמוד הענן, Moses' face-to-face encounter with God, Moses and prophecy, and Joshua as משרת and successor of Moses).[67]

But, once more, Blum's discussion of the parallels between Exodus and Deuteronomy is controversial.[68] Blum notes the obvious discrepancy that in Deuteronomy Moses' intercession occurs but once—on the occasion of Moses' second period of 40 days and nights on the

65. Blum, *Studien*, p. 89 n. 194.
66. Blum, *Studien*, p. 73.
67. Blum, *Studien*, p. 76.
68. Blum, *Studien*, pp. 181-88. Oddly he defines Exod. 32–34 as the limits of comparison to Deut. 9.7–10.11. Surely 24.12, 18; 31.18 must be brought into consideration as well.

mountain (i.e. that Deuteronomy fails to provide a parallel to vv. 11-14 of his key text, Exod. 32.7-14). Blum's conclusion is that Deuteronomy is 'extremely idiosyncratic' (*höchst eigenwillig*).[69] On the basis of the model that he has worked out in connection with Exod. 20.18-22// Deuteronomy 4–5 (which I have criticized above), he assumes that similar processes are at work here: the underlying tradition of Exod. 32.30-35 is assumed to have undergone free expansion in Deuteronomy, whence it has been received and redeveloped by KD in 32.11-14. Once again I should argue very differently. If Exodus is admitted on all hands to have passed through a process of editing probably more far-reaching and complex than that of Deuteronomy, are the reasons for the divergences between Exodus and Deuteronomy not to be sought on the side of Exodus? As I argue in Chapter 12, it is the P-editor who has transposed the sole intercession of Moses which should figure in the parallel position in Exod. 32.30-35 into 32.11-14, where he has developed it, and then replaced it with his own composition (which also includes D-material) in 32.30-35. Blum's observation that Deuteronomy presupposes the narrative in Exodus, without which it is unintelligible, is welcome to me: the mutual interaction of the texts is, however, to be explained by the origin of both in the one school, before the work of the final editor, P.

The above remarks have criticized Blum's angle of approach (his beginning with narrative coherence rather than with the parallels between Exodus and Deuteronomy), his over-elaboration of his KD (a literary compositional layer, which has both incorporated earlier, mostly non-literary, traditions and undergone further literary editions), and details of his delimitation of his KP. But these criticisms have not affected his basic thesis about the two main 'compositions', a Deuteronomic/Deuteronomistic and a P, which is highly congenial to my own thesis of a D-version, re-edited by a P-edition. It is that fundamental agreement that makes me wish to side with him against some recent criticism of his position.

Chief among that criticism is, perhaps, a couple of articles by G.I. Davies, in particular, ' "K^D" in Exodus: An Assessment of E. Blum's Proposal'.[70]

---

69. Deut. 10.6-7 he—rightly, in my view (see Chapter 11)—takes to be an 'Aaronic corrective gloss' (p. 181 n. 359).

70. In Vervenne and Lust (eds.), *Deuteronomy and Deuteronomic Literature*, pp. 407-20. Davies has also provided an extended review of Blum's work in his

A preliminary point about Davies's angle of approach may be made. Davies is sympathetic to the idea that there is an underlying pre-P composition to be found in Exodus, but he is hesitant about assenting to the proposition that such a redactional layer does in fact exist and, certainly, about describing it as 'Deuteronomic'. As a commentator on Hosea, it is natural for Davies to emphasize the Exodus tradition assumed by that prophet. He refers more than once to Blum's list of these allusions in Hosea:[71] 'the exodus from Egypt (2.7; 11.1; 12.14 [Moses as נביא!]; 13.4 [cf. also Amos 9.7]), and also the wilderness wandering and conquest as stages in the "Heilsgeschichte" (2.16f.; 9.10 [Baal Peor!]; 13.5)'.[72] One detects the hope behind Davies's cautious words that it may be possible to discover some such older 'Hoseanic' layer in Exodus. While not averse to finding Hoseanic influence (see Chapter 8, §IV), there seem to me to be two preliminary problems with that search. (1) The extremely speculative and hazardous nature of an attempt to reconstruct the layer of tradition presupposed by Hosea must be noted by contrast to the 'Deuteronomic canon', evidenced at least in D, DtrH and DtrJeremiah, if not also, indeed, in some of the 'minor prophets', Hosea and Amos included. The materials available for the reconstruction of a pre-P layer on the basis of references in Hosea, for instance, are far more fragmentary than the reminiscences in Deuteronomy, on which, I believe, the case for the recovery of the D-version of Exodus is substantially based. The

essay, 'The Composition of the Book of Exodus: Reflections on the Theses of Erhard Blum' (see n. 18 above). I am grateful to Dr Davies for supplying me with an offprint of that article. In it he helpfully points out that recent debate on the composition of the Pentateuch centres largely on two theses: (1) that the 'earliest major composition extending from the patriarchs to the beginning of the settlement in Canaan...was produced in a Deuteronomistic environment'; (2) that P 'comprises a supplement...to this composition, not an independent account...that once existed separately...and was secondarily combined with it by a redactor' (p. 71). Since it is, in the main, concerned with the critique of the second of these theses and with the defence of the existence of P as originally a separate 'source-document' (p. 74), that article is of less significance for my present purpose. Davies's articles have been influential in Nicholson's review (cf. Nicholson, *Pentateuch*, p. 203 n. 8). Presumably for typographical reasons, the first of these articles uses the form 'K[D]' rather than Blum's own 'KD'. I am grateful to Dr Davies for reading a draft of this chapter and saving me from a number of misrepresentations of his views.

71. Davies, 'Composition', p. 74; 'K[D]', p. 419 n. 43.

72. Blum, *Studien*, p. 218 n. 44.

recreation of such a layer, in preference to the D-canon, would involve the opening up by at least 200 years of a still longer gap in time between the two main editions of the Pentateuch. (2) Davies does not deny the presence of Deuteronomistic 'additions' in Exodus (he lists three:[73] itinerary notes derived from Numbers 33; the Decalogue; and the cross-reference to the Decalogue in Exod. 34.28b. That list, in my view, is at once too long and too short. On the one hand, the first item[74] I regard as most improbable,[75] as I shall argue below; on the other, the presence of Deuteronomistic elements is much greater than the other 'additions' allowed by Davies). My problem with the concept 'additions' has already been noted at the beginning of this Introduction: how to envisage the procedure. Why and under what conditions would a Deuteronomist wish to make merely sporadic additions— though of materials of major significance, in the case of the first two listed by Davies—particularly when that is not his method elsewhere? In the postulate of an exilic D-version one can at least see that a coherent response to the unparalleled catastrophe of 587 is being produced. Shattering though the sack of Samaria in 722 was (and would no doubt be an influential factor in promoting the gathering of Northern traditions, a 'Hoseanic canon'—but the speculative character of such a collection is obvious), it marked the downfall of a schismatic and apostate regime. Matters are quite different in 587: with the sack of Jerusalem and its Temple, the entire Zionist, messianic, Immanuel, Melchizedek tradition of theology, with all that it meant for the status of the House of David and the doctrine of the inviolability of Jerusalem, lay in ruins. The composition of a theological response, the production of a work of fundamental theological reconstruction, is what is required in that context. It is credible to believe that the D-version of the Pentateuch is that response.

A third general problem may be added: the conception of the processes involved at the redactional level. Davies makes considerable use of the concept of 'derivation' or 'dependence':[76] the itinerary notes in Exodus are 'derived' from the list in Numbers 33. But may it not be that both arise from the one conception of the one writer? In that case,

---

73. Davies, 'K^D', p. 407.

74. Repeated in 'Composition', p. 79 against Blum.

75. As does Blum, *Studien*, p. 125 n. 96.

76. E.g. in his earlier article, 'The Wilderness Itinerary and the Composition of the Pentateuch', *VT* 33 (1983), pp. 1-13 (7); 'K^D', pp. 414-15.

the itinerary notes are but another example of the kind of conundrum I propound at the end of Chapter 12 (though in the case of the itinerary notes of Num. 33 affecting, as I shall argue below, P not D): it is impossible to establish the priority of 'quotation' from Deuteronomy in Exodus or from Exodus in Deuteronomy, for the texts are in fact inter-related and both belong to the one conception of the Dtr editor (cf. again Jer. 52//2 Kgs 24.18–25.30), where the parallel betokens not 'dependence' but shared origin in the Deuteronomic movement.

Before looking at Davies's critique of Blum it is necessary, then, first to question his contention that it is largely a redactor influenced by D/Dtr who has added the extracts from the wilderness itinerary from Numbers 33 (as will be seen in Chapters 7–12, I fully endorse Davies's view that an older version of the Decalogue and Exod. 34.28b—but much else besides in Exodus—are Deuteronomistic). The question of the wilderness itineraries and their associated chronologies is a funda-mental element of my argument. As already indicated above, in order to identify redactional layers in the Pentateuch, it is not sufficient, in my view, to rely on differences, or consistently distinctive uses, of vocabulary or of theological outlook, indispensable though these are when other evidence is lacking. Rather, it is a matter of determining the existence of integrated versions which are characterized by con-sistent views of *Realien* and by coherent frameworks. The chain of references to the itineraries obviously provides one such overarching framework. I believe that the two latest editorial layers in the Penta-teuch, D and P, each has such an overarching view of Israel's itinerary and of the chronology associated with it, but that these two views are radically different from one another, and that it is P, as the later of these, that is responsible for the dominating itinerary and chronology in the extant Pentateuch.

For his discussion of the itinerary notes Davies refers back to his article, 'Wilderness Itinerary'. On the basis of a still earlier argument of his that the summary itinerary in Numbers 33 represents a later edi-tion of an earlier version,[77] he seeks to establish the affiliation of the

---

77. 'The Wilderness Itineraries: A Comparative Study', *TynBul* 25 (1974), pp. 46-81, especially pp. 50-51: an original list of 'points of departure', מוצאים, relics of whose title are 'possibly' contained in v. 2a, has now been recast as a series of 'stages', מסעים: 'whereas the list in its present form is said to consist of מסעים what Moses is supposed to have written is a list of the מוצאים of the Israelites. It is probably correct to see in the reference to a Mosaic composition...

itinerary notices in the narratives in Exodus and the earlier chapters of Numbers. He begins with Exod. 19.1-2. There are 'doublets' in the text: Exod. 19.2a repeats material on the arrival at Sinai already given in Exod. 19.1, which, he agrees, is P, and in its account of setting out from Rephidim for Sinai it is indeed logically prior to v. 1. Davies therefore argues that v. 2a belongs to 'a different source or stage of composition'.[78] Equally, the repetitions between v. 2a and v. 2b about encamping in the wilderness suggest that v. 2 is in turn to be assigned to two different sources. Since v. 2a matches the summary itinerary of Numbers 33 (v. 15), it must be derived from Numbers 33. Similar 'doublets' about the setting out for the wilderness of Paran in Numbers 10–13 point in the same direction: Num. 10.12 is a doublet of 11.35 and 12.16; the itinerary notes must then belong to two sources, P and non-P. The identification of the non-P itinerary source as Deuteronomistic[79] is based on the argument that the itineraries of Num. 21.10-13 are glossed with expressions derived from DtrH at Judg. 11.18.

I find a number of difficulties with this account. There are so many features characteristic of P in Numbers 33 that it perfectly satisfactory, in my view, to attribute the list in its entirety to P,[80] without D elements: Israel is referred to as 'hosts' (v. 1);[81] the chronology of 'the fifteenth day of the first month' as 'the day after the Passover' (Num. 33.3), which does not correspond with the Deuteronomic concept of the Passover as lasting for one night plus seven days (Deut. 16.1-8); the expression 'judgments on the gods [of Egypt]' (v. 4; a P-expression as in Exod. 6.6); 'Sinai' as the name of the mountain of God (vv. 15-16).

The discussion of Num. 21.10-13, which lies at the heart of Davies's argument, is unconvincing. The parallel text in Judg. 11.18 cites none

---

evidence of a document which was utilized by the editor who put Numbers 33:1-49 into its present form.' (In that article the discussion of Deut. 1.6–3.29 is deliberately excluded [p. 49].) It is thus 'a real possibility', argues Davies, that Num. 33 represents 'a late reworking of a perhaps much earlier text' ('Wilderness Itinerary', p. 6).

78. Davies, 'Wilderness Itinerary', p. 3.

79. So in Davies's earlier work, *The Way of the Wilderness: A Geographical Study of the Wilderness Itineraries in the Old Testament* (SOTSMS, 5, Cambridge: Cambridge University Press, 1979), p. 59, and again in 'Composition', p. 79.

80. So Blum, *Studien*, pp. 121 n. 81; 125 n. 96.

81. Cf. Num. 10.25; in 'Wilderness Itinerary', p. 12 n. 21, Davies recognizes this as a P locution—but does not cite Num. 33.1.

of the place-names in Num. 21.10-13 that recur in the Numbers 33
itinerary: stations 37 and 38 of Num. 33.43-44 which figure in
Num. 21.10-11bα are conspicuous by their absence in Judg. 11.18.
Judges 11.18 can then hardly be used as evidence for the Dtr origin of
Numbers 33. I find particularly puzzling Davies's statement that the
Deuteronomistic character of Numbers 33 is confirmed by the absence
in Deuteronomy of the place-names in that list. The words are so sin-
gular that they deserve verbatim quotation:

> The view that a redactor in the Deuteronomistic tradition was responsi-
> ble for inserting the main series of itinerary-notes...would explain why
> Deuteronomy itself shows no knowledge of any of the place-names
> which occur solely in these itinerary-notes, which it could be expected to
> do if they appeared already in one of the older sources.[82]

But how can absence in Deuteronomy be evidence of creation by Dtr
outside Deuteronomy? It is much more probable that, if place-names
are to be found neither in Deuteronomy nor in DtrH nor in the postulated 'older sources', they were in fact known to none of these but only
to a later source, namely, P.

Major difficulties in the text of Numbers, which, in my view actually
preclude the identification of the itinerary notes with D/Dtr, Davies
does not allude to. A fundamental divergence between D and Numbers
33 concerns the location of Kadesh: reached in year 1 at the beginning
of the wilderness wandering according to Deut. 1.19; 2.14; station 33
only reached in year 40 according to Num. 33.36-38. A further incom-
patibility, to be noted below, concerns the location of the crossing of
the Sea: an eastern arm of the Nile Delta in Num. 33.7-8 at station 4; at
the Red Sea in Deut. 11.4 (= station 7 in Num. 33.10). Reflections of
both of these itineraries are to be found in Exodus (along with the suppression of Red Sea as station 7 in Exod. 16.1; see further below), and
these divergences in itinerary are merely 'the tip of the iceberg': they
reflect differences in ideology of a most far-reaching kind, as I attempt
to delineate in Chapters 11 and 12.

Particular details of Davies's argument may be solved in simpler
ways. The repetitions (Davies's 'doublets') in Exod. 19.1-2 can be
accounted for by redactional arguments. In the light of a parallel formation in Num. 33.9 (which I should hold for the reasons stated above
is P),

---

82. Davies, 'Wilderness Itinerary', p. 12.

ויסעו ממרה ויבאו אילמה ויחנו שם

the text of Exod. 19.2a (which is not in fact exactly parallel to Num. 33.15) should read, not as it stands

ויסעו מרפידים ויבאו מדבר סיני ויחנו במדבר

but

ויסעו מרפידים ויבאו מדבר סיני ויחנו שם.

The reason for the change from שם to במדבר at the end of v. 2a is clear: the incorporation of the separate source in v. 2b (ויחן־שם ישראל נגד ההר)—and I agree that is a separate 'source', though I should identify it as D—would otherwise have brought together the awkward repetition of the two phrases ויחנו שם and ויחן־שם. The changed formulation in v. 2a thus shows P's redactional activity as he prepares to incorporate the D-material. The supposed repetition between vv. 1 and 2a is to be explained by the fact that v. 1 gives the chronology (an important point of polemical correction which P wishes to make of D [see Chapter 11 below], which thus accounts for the illogical order of vv. 1 and 2a), while v. 2a links that chronology with P's schematic itinerary. It must be observed in the bygoing that with its 'Sinai' it is already unconvincing to attribute v. 2a to D.

I find Davies's discussion of the 'other end of the Sinai-pericope' also unsatisfactory.[83] While allowing that Num. 10.11-28 is P, rightly in my view, he denies that 11.35 and 12.16 can be P because P has already provided a 'doublet' at 10.12. I should rather regard the similarity of language—and radical difference of conception of the itinerary from D's view—as evidence that these three passages all belong to the same 'source'. The evidence is as follows:

ויסעו בני־ישראל למסעיהם ממדבר סיני וישכן הענן במדבר פארן:	Num. 10.12
מקברות התאוה נסעו העם חצרות ויהיו בחצרות:	Num. 11.35
ואחר נסעו העם מחצרות ויחנו במדבר פארן:	Num. 12.16
ויסעו ממדבר סיני ויחנו בקברת התאוה:	Num. 33.16
ויסעו מקברת התאוה ויחנו בחצרת:	Num. 33.17

In my view all of these materials are to be regarded as coming from the same source. The variations among them are not to be accounted for at the rather superficial level that they are 'doublets'; much wider editorial dynamics must again be taken into account, in particular the

83. Davies, 'Wilderness Itinerary', p. 3.

radically different conceptions of itinerary in his own and in the inherited material with which the final editor is juggling. The narrative in Numbers 10–13 records no arrival at Taberah and Kibroth-hattaavah (only the latter occurs in the summary itinerary in Num. 33 where it is station 13 [vv. 16-17]) in the manner of Numbers 33. In Numbers 11 there is only a narrative of the events that took place at Taberah and Kibroth-hattaavah. But in Deut. 9.22-23 this narrative is related to Kadesh. In the narrative of Numbers 10–13 as it now stands, however, Kadesh has been almost totally suppressed and replaced by the vague 'wilderness of Paran'. The only stray reference to Kadesh is in Num. 13.26 and this reference has been facilitated by the identification of the location from which the spies start their reconnaissance of the land as 'the wilderness of Zin' in Num. 13.21, which is identified in Num. 33.36 with Kadesh. In other words, in Numbers 11–13 the older D-narrative referring to year 1 has now been edited to refer to year 40 by the introduction of the 'wilderness of Paran'. Thus Davies is correct in identifying two accounts combined in these chapters: but the 'doublets' in Num. 10.12, 11.35 and 12.16 are themselves evidence not for these two accounts but rather for the final editor's polemical correction of the itinerary in the older narrative. The essential similarity of the for-mulation of the verses cited bears this out: the differences between them and Num. 33.16-17 are explained by the fact that, while Numbers 33 is a formalized list, in Numbers 10–13 they fall within narrative sections that also have to meet editorial purposes.

By these means Davies drastically reduces the number of itinerary notices to be assigned to P to Exod. 19.1; Num. 10.12; 20.1aα; and 22.1.[84] But, for a start, one may note that the last of these essentially coincides with the notice on station 42, the final stage of the wander-ing, in Num. 33.48: if, then, Davies attributes to P the final itinerary note, why does he not attribute the remainder of the itinerary notes in the narratives and in the summary in Numbers 33 to P as well?[85]

---

84. So also in *The Way of the Wilderness*, p. 114 n. 1.

85. Davies makes an important concession in 'Composition', p. 82 n. 50, in connection with arguing for the original independence of P as a separate source: 'by a surprising coincidence, a trace of the original Priestly account of the final plague can be seen in Num. 33.3-4, which is (with vv. 38-39) one of the few places where the itinerary has been amplified with extracts from the complete Priestly narrative'. The coincidence is, in my view, not in the least 'surprising'; it is, rather, valuable evidence for the inherently P-character of the whole of Num. 33, as these key

Further, Davies is then constrained to suppose that Exod. 14.2 must be a 'special case':[86] though he admits Exod. 14.1-4 is a P-section, he claims that v. 2 has been derived from a hypothetical 'older account'. Again wider consideration of the divergent accounts of the itinerary makes this impossible. As already noted, Exod. 14.1-4 envisages the crossing of the sea at an eastern branch of the Nile Delta, as in Num. 33.7-8; this contrasts with the 'older account', as reflected in Deuteronomy, which locates it at the Red Sea (Deut. 11.4). There is no hint in Exod. 14.1-4 that the crossing of the sea takes place at the Red Sea.

It is important to establish these weaknesses in Davies's own argument and general approach, for a consistent element in his, in the end quite cautious, criticism of Blum is just that the evidence is 'not sufficient': yet within a wider and more satisfactory framework, not least consideration of how texts functioned rather than how they originated, Blum's arguments can appear to be more convincing. Given relative views of levels of consistency that can be expected of an ancient literary text, Davies at times demands an unattainable standard of verification (e.g. 'Even if the conclusion is justified in these cases [where formulae such as "land flowing with milk and honey" or lists of pre-Israelite population are given] that deuteronomistic editors have been at work...it does not mean that, when the same formulae occur in passages without such "clearly" deuteronomistic language, a deuteronomistic reworking of these passages need be inferred'[87]). On the other hand, Davies's confidence in the recoverability and, consequently, reliability of ancient traditions is high: for example, Moses would not have been called a prophet in the early period, therefore Num. 12.7-8 could be early.[88]

To return, then, to Davies's evaluation of Blum. His critique is essentially twofold: (1) the pre-P 'composition' is not necessarily Deuteronomistic—it is, rather, older (cf. Hosea) and such Deuteronomistic elements that are present do not cohere as a version; (2) there are, he claims, elements that positively militate against identifying the pre-P composition as Deuteronomistic.

I have not myself made use of some of Blum's arguments about the network of narrative interconnections in favour of a D-composition

narrative sections amid the otherwise stereotyped list of stations make clear.
    86. Davies, 'Wilderness Itinerary', p. 4.
    87. Davies, 'K^D', p. 412.
    88. Davies, 'K^D', pp. 410, 413.

that Davies cites and criticizes (to that extent these points would be simply ancillary to my position): parallels in Exodus to linkages in other parts of DtrH (Exod. 1.6, 8//Judg. 2.8a, 10; Exod. 3.16-17//Gen. 50.24; Exod. 14.13, 31//1 Sam. 12.6a, 16, 18); the portrayal of Moses as prophet in Exod. 3.18-22 in the respect that he is given a detailed preview of events to come as in the Dtr addition in Amos 3.7. I should agree with Davies's hesitations about the strength of Blum's argument here but not with Davies's proposal that Exod. 3.18-22 should be regarded as secondary. Motifs are introduced here which dominate the entire presentation down to 15.21 (and beyond): for example, the 'three days' journey', which I believe is integral to the D-version's chronology (see, e.g., Chapters 9 and 10), 'the wonders' that herald the following plague narrative. The passage in question is about the signs that are confirmatory of Moses' role as leader of Israel in the exodus (a much wider role than 'prophet'). The connection between fore-knowledge and events is most likely to be understood at the literary level, as indeed Davies's feeling about the 'insertion' of 3.18-22 pre-cisely makes clear (cf. how Exod. 4.22-23 equally anticipates the entire sequel down to 15.21).

This section of Davies's argument seems to me to illustrate well the exaggerated demands for consistency that he makes and his words deserve to the quoted in full. Davies is quite impressed by Blum's argument about the preview in Exod. 3.18-22. But he refuses to be convinced:

> there is evidence in the context that 3,18-22 was a late addition…as 4,1 connects much more closely with 3,16-17…This argument, therefore, probably does indicate a late, post-deuteronomic date [presumably in the light of Amos 3.7] for 3,18-22 but not for the surrounding context and not for the verses later in Exodus which 3,18-22 anticipate.[89]

One can only ask, 'Why?' There is evidence of hypercriticism in the related footnote:

> There remains some difficulty in the fact that the previews in 3,18-22 do not coincide exactly with what is said later on: e.g. the reference to the women alone in 3,22 (contrast 11,2; 12,35-36). This may mean that the intrusive matter [i.e. 3.18-22] was drawn from a late account of the Exo-dus which was slightly divergent at this point from the one which became canonical.

89. Davies, 'K^D', p. 413.

This seems to me to be an unnecessarily complex conclusion. It demands a consistency of literary usage that amounts to an inappropriate mechanical fixity (Blum has anticipated the point; he terms such a demand 'schoolmasterish pedantry'[90]). On that one can only comment that if one sets up such high criteria of verbal consistency one will be driven to such expedients. Once again, the argument has to be conducted on a much broader basis. There are vital wider points of interconnection of the narrative at this point with this block of legislation in Deuteronomy: the link between Exod. 3.21 and the law on the release of Hebrew slaves in Deut. 15.12-17 is only one of a series; the law on the release of Hebrew slaves in Deuteronomy 15 is followed by the legislation on the offering of firstlings (Deut. 15.19-23) and, most significantly of all, on the Passover understood as including unleavened bread (Deut. 16.1-8), all of which, as I argue in Chapter 9, have had a fundamental influence on the formation of the D-version of Exod. 1.1–24.8. These I should regard as confirmation of coherence which has to be established on other grounds (above all recoverable narratives in Exodus that match the reminiscences, and even the legislation, of Deuteronomy, with their matching concepts of *Realien*).

This demand for consistency is seen in evidence elsewhere in the overdrawing of fine distinctions: for example, Davies claims there is a distinction to be drawn between the portrayal of Moses as 'paradigm prophet' in Deuteronomy and Num. 12.7-8 where he is merely superior to all prophets, that is, not yet classified as a prophet (Hos. 12.14 may be the origin of that classification, Davies suggests[91]).

Davies does engage with Blum on passages that I regard as central to the argument for the recovery of the D-version—parallels in Exodus to reminiscence in Deuteronomy. An important instance is Exod. 32.7-14, the account of the end of Moses' first period of 40 days and 40 nights on the mountain. Davies has some incisive comments to make on Blum's view that this is a D-composition.[92] He rightly points out that the direct parallels in fact hold only as far as Exod. 32.10. But in alleging that 'Deut. 9 contains no parallel to Moses' prayer in Exod. 32,11-13',[93] he has overlooked the fact that there are indeed such parallels in Deut. 9.26-29, which, however, Deuteronomy places in the

90. Blum, *Studien*, p. 19 n. 38.
91. Davies, 'K^D', p. 410.
92. Davies, 'K^D', pp. 415-16.
93. Davies, 'K^D', p. 416.

context of Moses' second period of 40 days and nights on the mountain. The conclusion to be drawn from this is not that Exod. 32.11-14 is non-D (how can it be non-D if the language is parallel to Deut. 9?), but (as I argue in Chapter 12) that serious disturbance has been introduced by reuse and transposition of this D-material by the P-editor. Once again a much wider contextual view has to be taken of this particular case: this reuse and transposition is only one example of many such reuses and transpositions in Exod. 15.22–19.2 and 31.18–34.29 (see also Chapter 11). Part of the reason for Davies's counter-argument is his conviction that underlying the passage there is 'the original story'. To that I can only respond that, once all the Deuteronomic vocabulary has been noted and accounted for, there is no residuum left: for all we know, an earlier tradition may underlie D's narrative but it cannot be recovered; its existence is purely speculative. The important—and only sure—point is the use to which both D and P put the narrative. As before, function, not origin, is the key issue.

The 'Sinai pericope' in Exodus 19–24 is a further passage where Davies engages closely with Blum's argument. Davies reviews Blum's view, noted and extensively commented on above, that Exod. 19.3b-8; 20.22 and 24.3-8 express the 'organizing intention' of KD. On the contrary, Davies argues, Exod. 19.3b-8 is 'a late addition':[94] it is not presupposed by 20.22 and 24.3-8, and indeed (a favourite argument of Davies) 'anticipates and duplicates' the latter. Exodus 20.22 is a secondary insertion 'connected with the introduction of the Decalogue into the Sinai pericope' and does not 'belong' with 24.3-8; Exod. 21.1 'is a perfectly satisfactory beginning' for B. But, in the light of the above discussion (the integral character of the Decalogue to the D-version; the necessity for rational explanation to envelop the uncanny experience of the theophany; the conjoint basis for the covenant in both Decalogue and B, both of which are mediated by Moses), I cannot accept any of these points. The view that the Decalogue is 'an insertion' is *ex hypothesi*—that because the Decalogue 'first' appears in Deuteronomy, and given that there is already an 'older' source in Exodus, it must then be an insertion in Exodus. A further consideration may be added. It cannot be said that 21.1 'is a perfectly satisfactory beginning' for B without the structure of B as a whole being considered. The structure of B as covenant code requires that it begin with the second-person address of 20.22-26, just as it concludes with

94. Davies, 'K^D', p. 417.

second-person address in 22.20–23.33; this second-person address in fact contaminates 21.1, the opening of the law-code of חק ומשפט which is largely couched in the third person as far as 22.19. A similar failure by Davies to take the wider context into consideration is evident in 'K[D]',[95] where it is denied that 24.12-15a is Deuteronomistic simply because it connects with '32–34': the comparison with Deut. 9.9–10.11, however, suggests that D-material is to be found in 24.12abα, 13, 18b; 31.18* before continuing in chs. 32–34.

Davies's second main line of criticism of Blum is that there are elements in the Exodus and Deuteronomy presentations that are so contradictory that they positively militate against identifying the pre-P composition in Exodus as Deuteronomistic.[96] Davies cites the view that the 'blood ritual' in Exod. 24.3-8 is 'an element which is quite foreign to Deuteronomy and the deuteronomistic literature'. But, given that the blood-rite is unique in the Hebrew Bible, that cannot of itself prove or disprove affiliation to any of the Pentateuchal sources. As a unique text it is to be regarded as belonging to the imaginative presentation of how a covenant—which is surely the central concept of the D-literature—between God and people might have been instituted. There is, indeed, a strong argument for associating the passage with a D-version. As I have argued (Chapter 9), again on the basis of taking a much wider view of context, the chronology within which the passage is presented matches that of the presentation of Passover in Deut. 16.1-8. The use of precisely the ritual terminology of the communion sacrifice, זבח, in both Exod. 24.3-8 and Deut. 16.1-8 supports the connection.

Davies further holds (like Blum), on the basis of his understanding of Deut. 5.31 (and 6.1) as referring to the promulgation of the laws of the later chapters of Deuteronomy at Mt Pisgah, that Deuteronomy differs from Exodus in regard to the basis of the covenant: in D it is based on the Decalogue alone, while in Exod. 24.3-8 it is based on the Decalogue plus B. As I have argued above, this seems to me to be an unlikely reading of Deut. 5.31: there is not a hint in the narrative or in the paragraphing of MT that Deut. 5.31 is anything other than the continuation of the reminiscence of the preceding verses of events at Horeb (cf. Deut. 4.14). This is a crucial point, in my view. If Deut. 5.31 refers to events at Horeb (as it seems to me it clearly does), then

95. Davies, 'K[D]', p. 417 n. 38.
96. Davies, 'K[D]', p. 417.

Deuteronomy is of the view that the covenant at Horeb was indeed based, as Exodus 20–24 says it was, on both the Decalogue and Book of the Covenant, thus flatly contradicting Davies's view.

Davies further cites Deut. 5.22, 'The LORD spoke these words [i.e. the Decalogue]…at the Mountain…and added no more', contending that the last phrase supports his interpretation. That is a weak point: Deut. 5.22 precisely states, in agreement with Exod. 20.18-21, that the revelation of the Decalogue was all that was heard directly by the קהל, the lay assembly. The continuation of Deuteronomy 5 goes on to describe the conditions under which the further revelation (i.e. B) was made.

Yet again, Davies argues that the account of the remaking of the covenant on the basis of the second set of tablets in Deut. 9.7–10.11 cites only the Decalogue. That is correct: but it is no different from Deuteronomy's identification of the original covenant with the Decalogue in 4.13, only in 4.14 to add that 'at that time the LORD commanded me to teach you statutes and ordinances [i.e. B]'. In any case, the reminiscence of Deut. 9.7–10.11 represents a highly condensed summary as, for example, the bald references to Taberah, Massah, and Kibroth-hattaavah in 9.22, which are incomprehensible without the narratives in Exod. 17.1-7 and Numbers 11, make clear. In fact, as I have argued, the parallel between Deut. 10.1-4, which is cited with the necessary adjustments from reminiscence to narrative in the pre-P version of Exod. 34.1-4, 28, is absolutely crucial in showing the mutual development of both texts (see the opening of Chapter 9, conclusion of Chapter 12).

Further 'conflict' between Deuteronomy and Exodus, Davies finds in the legislation of the Passover: even the alleged '"older" material' in Exod. 12.21-27, Davies argues, implies that the Passover is a domestic rite as opposed to Deut. 16.5-7's central sanctuary rite. The existence of such 'older material' embedded in *this* text is, of course, part of the very question at issue. It seems to me to be, once again, an unnecessary hypothesis. Exodus 12, I have argued (Chapter 9), is in part a polemical correction of Deut. 16.1-8: P reuses much of the D-material to set it in a new context; the much-modified remnant of the D-material is to be found in Exodus 13; Exod. 12.21-28 is precisely a reworking of some D-material in preparation for the resumption of D-material on the tenth plague in Exod. 12.29-36, as has already been noted above.

Davies cites with approval Van Seters's argument that the view of

Moses' mediatorial role diverges between Exodus and Deuteronomy: according to Exodus 3, Moses is mediator since his call; according to Deut. 5.24-27, Moses only becomes mediator after the terror of hearing the Decalogue. There seem to me here to be unnecessary fine distinctions: Exod. 3.12 is after all about what is going to happen at the mountain; in Deut. 5.5 Moses is already mediator at the moment of the revelation of the Decalogue, as discussed above.

These 'differences' I thus find to be either non-existent or explicable more economically by other means. Davies's last point is on omissions in Deuteronomy of material in Exodus (Moses' call, Midianite marriage, and advice from Jethro):[97] on these matters lack of evidence hampers discussion and simply leads to speculation. The non-incorporation by D of one incident of praise and a balancing one of blame does not seem to me to be of enormous significance given that D does justice to both in other terms: for example, Deut. 1.37. The third of these incidents I have discussed at the end of Chapter 11: since, in my view, Exod. 18.13-26 is part of the P-edition's reuse of D-material, it is impossible that D could have made use of it.

It would be an unwarranted reduction of the scale of recent discussion to restrict the debate to the interpretation of a handful of verses. Yet the upshot of the above comments is that there are a few key texts in Deuteronomy the interpretation of which, it emerges, is a crucial issue for the case being made below. These verses include Deut. 4.12-14; 5.5, 31; 9.22-24, 25-29. In every case, I have argued that they should taken at full face value and as integral to their contexts, and that to do so not only does justice to them in themselves but is also fully compatible with the thesis presented in the following chapters, that the reminiscences in Deuteronomy provide the primary means for the recovery of a D-version in Exodus.

97. Davies, 'K^D', p. 419.

Part I

THE PROPOSAL:
CHRONICLES AS GATEWAY TO PENTATEUCHAL CRITICISM

Chapter 2

CHRONICLES, CANONS AND CONTEXTS*

You may remember the story in the press last autumn[1] of the debate in the Oriental Faculty in the University of Cambridge about retaining the Iranian Studies Tripos. No doubt the fact that impressed most readers was the statistic that over the past 33 years the course had attracted only 16 undergraduates. It may be that some regard the Aberdeen Department of Hebrew and Semitic Languages, considering its exotic range of languages—Arabic, Aramaic, Phoenician, Syriac and Ugaritic besides Hebrew—and the half-dozen students in the Arts Faculty who annually take its courses, as the local equivalent. Let me quickly clear up any possible misunderstanding. On the matter of student numbers it must be stated that the Department's fundamental function is to teach the interpretation of the Hebrew Bible to students in Divinity, all of whom are required to study Hebrew Bible for at least one-and-a-half courses, most of whom in fact opt for two, and a few of whom aspire to Honours. The number of students studying in the Department this session is thus nearer 50.

What attracted my attention to the press report of the debate in the Cambridge Oriental Faculty was, rather, the opening couple of sentences:

> Ilya Gershevitch, Reader in Iranian Studies... and author of *A Grammar of Manichaean Sogdian* (now in its second edition), is dazzled by limelight. For the past 33 years, his notion of excitement has been the discovery of a new Central Asian language, his idea of celebrity the acknowledgement of half a dozen equally distinguished peers.

* Inaugural Lecture delivered on 25 January 1982, originally published in *Aberdeen University Review* 50 (1983), pp. 1-18; marginally adjusted to be uniform with this collection (new material is enclosed in square brackets).
1. *The Sunday Times*, 25 October 1981, p. 2.

In coming to the inaugural lecture of a new professor it may be something of the excitement of such new discovery that you desire to hear about. If the restrictedness of the number who can truly appreciate the significance of what one says is a criterion of pureness of scholarship, then I can indeed assure you that I have shared that kind of excitement. When I was engaged in the excavation of a Carthaginian warship, the results of which were finally published four months ago,[2] my preliminary researches, which had led off into the field of ancient ship-building, were communicated by a colleague to an international conference in Italy from which I received the following message on a picture post-card: 'Your discoveries re construction [of the ancient warship] had a great effect on the 5 people in the world interested in ship architecture.' Last summer I got the number down still further. An Emeritus Professor of Harvard argued on the basis of the alleged similarity of a rim sherd from New Mexico to bowls in a museum in Spain, which are inscribed in what he identified as the Iberian language written in Chalcidian script, that the magnetic compass, using a needle floating on mercury, had been invented at least as early as somewhere between the third century BCE and the first century CE and implied that it had been used in an actual crossing of the Atlantic Ocean in that period.[3] It sounds a fairly tall story but how can one refute such a claim? The chink in his armour is that he has used a *Dictionary of Modern Written Arabic* to decipher his Iberian on the assumption that Iberian was 'a dialect of early Arabic, closely allied to Ancient Maghrib of Morocco'. As a result, the Iberians had not only anticipated by a millennium the date usually assigned to the invention of the magnetic compass; they had also by uncanny prescience foreseen that Arabic was going, for example, to adopt a Persian loan-word meaning 'copper basin' and in modern times to invent a technical term for the rim of a wheel.

Tonight, however, I do not propose to lead you to such areas at the frontiers of research, or, if you prefer, the margins of knowledge; should you wish to know about such or similar matters, I invite you to

2.   In H. Frost *et al.*, *Lilybaeum (Marsala)—The Punic Ship: Final Excavation Report* (Notizie degli Scavi, 1976, 30, Supplement; Rome: Accademia dei Lincei, 1981), pp. 191-240.

3.   B. Fell, 'Ancient Iberian Magnetic Compass Dials from Liria, Spain', *The Epigraphic Society Occasional Publications* 3.57 (September 1976); 'Additional Lirian Compass Dial Inscriptions from Spain and New Mexico', *The Epigraphic Society Occasional Publications* 7.142 (April 1979).

attend a series of four lectures beginning next Wednesday evening at
Marischal College under the aegis of the Extra-Mural Department in
which I shall cover such things as the borrowing of the Phoenician
alphabet by the Greeks, the origins of *phi, chi* and *psi*, not to say
digamma, in the Greek alphabet,[4] Late Bronze Age Cyprus,[5] Canaan[6]
and the coming of the Philistines, Early Bronze Age Syria and the
Amorites, and other matters. Rather, I should like to consider with you
questions relating to the more central responsibilities and interests of
the Hebrew Department, for, it may be, the inaugural lecture has also
the function of assessing the point that study in the subject area has
reached and of offering proposals for the continued development of the
subject. The unarticulated question, which your troubling to come at all
this evening may put, may perhaps be that which was explicitly posed
to me last 22 May when new appointees and retiring long-service
employees were presented to the Moderator in the General Assembly of
the Church of Scotland. At the complimentary meal beforehand, I, with
all the lofty condescension of the new professor, enquired of the depart-
ing Baird Fellow, 'What do you propose to do with your retirement?'
With the swift thrust of an Ulsterman's rapier wit he replied, 'And what
do you propose to do with your professorship?' The best answer I could
muster on the spur of the moment was, 'Rebuild from the foundations'.
Tonight let me try to repeat that answer in rather more fully developed
form.

By an odd coincidence I was in receipt last month of letters from the
editors of two proposed new monograph series—the one a series of
commentaries on books of the Hebrew Bible, the other a series of intro-
ductions to books or sections of the Hebrew Bible—confirming that,
after a period of negotiations, protracted in the case of the first, my proposals for contributions to each had been accepted. In each case I have
had a relatively unrestricted choice of books, or areas, of the Hebrew
Bible on which to write. If one is seeking to rebuild the interpretation
of the Hebrew Bible from the foundations, which books should one
choose, and why? It is my reasons for the choice of the book of the

4.   W. Johnstone, 'Cursive Phoenician and the Archaic Greek Alphabet', *Kad-
mos* 7 (1978), pp. 151-66.

5.   W. Johnstone, 'A Late Bronze Age Tholos Tomb at Enkomi', in C.F.A.
Schaeffer *et al.*, *Alasia*, I (Leiden: E.J. Brill; Paris: Klincksieck, 1971), pp. 51-122.

6.   W. Johnstone, 'The Sun and the Serpent: The Interpretation of the Ugaritic
Text RS 24.244', *TGUOS* 26 (1979), pp. 44-62.

Hebrew Bible for the commentary series that I should like to consider with you tonight.

But is there really much of a problem here? If one wishes to rebuild Hebrew Bible studies from the foundations, should one then not start at the beginning? Let me illustrate some of the problems from one of the staple elements in any course on the Hebrew Bible: the history of ancient Israel. The problems here concern the availability of truly primary sources and the specialized character of the biblical material. If one is reconstructing the history of ancient Israel from scratch, where does one begin? With Abraham, would appear to be a not unreasonable answer. But to write the history of a period one must have access to appropriate primary sources, not merely contemporary chronicles or the more public documents, but, better still, the diaries, letters, account books and other private papers of the principal personages involved. For the writing of the history of Abraham and the other patriarchs of Israel we possess none of such records. Even on the most traditional view of the authorship of the book of Genesis, the final writer Moses lived, if we take the biblical chronology at face value, at least 400 years after Abraham and the resultant record is at best his selection and arrangement of traditions handed down over many centuries. The book of Genesis as it now stands cannot be called a primary historical source but is already a work of interpretation stemming from a period long after the events of which it gives an account. If, as I would, one does not even accept that Genesis was written by Moses, then the possibilities of remoteness of the book of Genesis as we now have it from the events of Abraham's time become all the more extended.

Since truly primary sources for the historical reconstruction of the life of Abraham are lacking in the Bible, scholars have turned to archaeology. But Abraham was a nomad wandering on the fringes of the civilizations of the ancient Near East. It is unlikely that he would have left any tangible artefacts, such as a house and its contents, for the archaeologist's spade, or that his name would appear in any of the contemporary records of the settled societies. The most the archaeologist can hope to achieve is to recover in general terms the social, economic and political circumstances of the age. But what *is* the age of the patriarchs? Perfectly competent and reputable scholars have argued for periods as far apart as towards either end of the second millennium BCE.[7] I should argue myself that the biblical account is a generalized

7. E.g. R. de Vaux, *The Early History of Israel* (2 vols.; London: Darton,

and highly over-simplified presentation, though not misleading in its general drift, of a lengthy and, in its detail, highly complex process. The exodus, which must in some sense have marked the birth of ancient Israel as a political entity, I should regard as a biblical short-hand for a series of events that were extremely complicated in themselves.[8] Even the figure of Moses is highly elusive to the historian: he has been likened to a lump of sugar in a cup of tea—you can tell by the sweetness that the sugar is there, but it has lost all recognizable shape.[9]

Where, then, does the history of Israel begin, in the sense that there are available to the historian contemporary primary sources? There is no history of Israel before David, in the opinion of one writer,[10] but even the existence of David, as Magnus Magnusson was not slow to point out in his television series, *BC: The Archaeology of Bible Lands*, receives no corroboration in any text outside the Bible.[11] The first Israelite king attested in extra-biblical texts is Omri, who figures in the Assyrian records of the early ninth century BCE.

Even when primary historical records become thereafter relatively plentiful, the problems for the historian of ancient Israel scarcely diminish in their acuteness: it now becomes clear that all along the problem has been not only the scarcity of sources but also the character of the biblical sources. The writers of the Hebrew Bible are not primarily interested in the reconstruction of the actual course of historical events as such or for their own sake. Rather, their concern lies in the use of historical data and circumstance as the means of communicating the inner significance of Israel's experience: their purpose is to make theological statements by means of narratives cast in historical form. An example of this is the incident of the Assyrian king Sennacherib's invasion of Judah during the reign of King Hezekiah, an event that is apparently one of the best dated and on which there are perhaps more

Longman & Todd, 1978), I, pp. 263ff.; S. Herrmann, *A History of Israel in Old Testament Times* (London: SCM Press, 1975), pp. 45ff.

8.   See Chapter 3.

9.   Cited by C.F. Evans, *Explorations in Theology* (London: SCM Press, 1977), p. 97.

10.   J.L. McKenzie, *The World of the Judges* (London: Geoffrey Chapman, 1967), p. 5.

11.   M. Magnusson, *BC: The Archaeology of Bible Lands* (London: Bodley Head; BBC, 1977), pp. 155-56. [This was in the days before the discovery of the 'House of David' inscription at Tel Dan—and the controversy it has unleashed.]

copious sources than any other in the entire Hebrew Bible. Yet any attempt to combine the biblical and the ancient Near Eastern data leads to anomalies. From the Assyrian annals, Sennarcherib's sole known campaign took place in the year 701 BCE. This date, however, conflicts with the biblical chronology, according to which the invasion took place in Hezekiah's fourteenth year, which, given that he succeeded his father on the throne about 727 BCE, must have fallen in the year 713. Various expedients have been urged to harmonize the data: for example, Hezekiah's dates have been moved from 727–698 to 715–686,[12] or the biblical texts, which give the date of the invasion as Hezekiah's fourteenth year, have been amended to the twenty-fourth.[13] The key, however, probably lies in an appreciation of the theological purpose of the biblical writer. Hezekiah reigns 29 years; in his fourteenth he falls grievously sick; in his extremity he prays to the Lord who graciously hears him, restores him to health and promises him a further 15 years of reign and deliverance from the Assyrians. The writer has then moulded a complex mass of disparate materials around the theme of Hezekiah's fourteenth year to bring into sharp focus the conjunction of submission to the divine will and the fulfilment of the divine promises.[14] To insist on the year 701, or to add the data together mathematically as if they were digits of the same order, is to misconstrue the theological purpose of the writer.

Nor do matters improve much in the postexilic period from the sixth century BCE onwards. The writers of Ezra and Nehemiah do not bat an eyelid at associating the events under Darius and Artaxerxes, though these Persian rulers reigned a good 60 or so years apart, or at intertwining the missions of Ezra and Nehemiah, though these were from half to one-and-a-half generations apart.

Faced with the twin difficulties of lack of primary sources and the specialized character of the biblical sources where they do exist, where can the biblical critic begin in order to reconstruct the history of Israel? Within the context of a lecture such as this, it is appropriate to try to relate one's own efforts to the ongoing stream of scholarly endeavour and to acknowledge, however briefly, one's debt to the past. It perhaps sounds like special pleading that one should propose to offer a review

---

12. E.g. Bright, *History of Israel*, p. 259 n. 22.
13. H.H. Rowley, *Men of God* (London: Nelson, 1963), p. 113.
14. Cf. A.K. Jenkins, 'Hezekiah's Fourteenth Year', *VT* 26 (1976), pp. 284-98.

of the course of research in a discipline in terms of the figures who happen to have been associated with it in Aberdeen and the North-East of Scotland. Yet it is not regional chauvinism, nor even Burns' Night intemperance, which leads one to affirm that this part of the world has had an illustrious association with Hebrew Bible and Semitic studies and has mirrored accurately in its local exponents the wider trends of research. It is invidious to single some out for mention and pass over others in silence. Within the present circle of the University there are many living links with the past. To my knowledge the North-East has produced two Regius Professors of Hebrew in the University of Oxford;[15] the daughter of one is presently on the staff of our University. The Principal of the University himself from 1909 to 1935 was a noted scholar of the Hebrew Bible,[16] one of whose daughters is happily still resident in Aberdeen. The present Professor of Logic is the great-grandson of the Professor of Old Testament at the turn of the century in what is now Christ's College.[17] I am personally delighted that tonight there is present here in our midst one who was not only the wife of the Professor who held this Chair from 1932–62, but was also the daughter-in-law of the only Scottish Divine to have been a Professor for 50 years, first in the Hebrew Chair here in Aberdeen from 1887–94, thereafter in Edinburgh.[18] Much as all of these and more deserve mention, there are perhaps a couple whose work is particularly relevant to our theme this evening.

It would, I think, be universally admitted that pride of place must be accorded to William Robertson Smith. Smith was born in 1846, son of the Free Church minister at Keig, near Alford. The range of his learning was truly remarkable as an outline of his career shows: assistant to the Professor of Natural Philosophy in the University of Edinburgh, appointed Professor of Old Testament in the Free Church College in Aberdeen at the age of 23; still under 30, he began contributing articles to the ninth edition of *Encyclopaedia Britannica*; these articles on Hebrew Bible topics immediately aroused a storm of controversy which eventually led to his being deposed from his Aberdeen Chair in 1881;

---

15. A. Nicoll, 1822–28 (*Dictionary of National Biography*, XIV [Oxford, 1917], p. 489); W.D. McHardy, 1960–78.
16. George Adam Smith.
17. G.G. Cameron, 1882–1913.
18. A.C. Kennedy and A.R.S. Kennedy.

meantime he had been offered and had turned down the Chair of Hebrew at Harvard and the Chair of Church History at Harvard and had applied unsuccessfully for the Chair of Mathematics at Glasgow. On being deposed from his Chair he first became editor of *Encyclopaedia Britannica* ninth edition, before at length he was appointed Professor of Arabic in Cambridge, where he died at the age of only 47.[19]

Smith's approach to the twin problems posed by the biblical sources that we have noted—their frequent remoteness in time from the period portrayed and their theological rather than historical interest in that period—was twofold, and matches rather neatly the two broad phases of his academic career. In the first phase he is the Old Testament teacher in the Aberdeen Free Church College; his thinking in this period is reflected in his two books *The Old Testament in the Jewish Church* (1881) and *The Prophets of Israel* (1882). In these books it is essentially with Israel's origins as seen through the Scriptures that he is concerned, the first treating mainly of the Pentateuch, the second of Israel's prophets down only to 700 BCE. His basic contention is the need for traditional affirmations about the Bible to be appraised by the internal evidence of the Bible itself: this internal evidence is to be elicited by the standard means of literary and historical inquiry that one would employ in the study of any other work of ancient literature. What is the resulting picture of the history of Old Testament religion? Smith, using very much the arguments of his older Continental contemporaries Kuenen and Wellhausen, argues that most of the Pentateuch is more recent than Moses. If, for example, Deuteronomy had been revealed to Moses, why are the next long centuries of Israel's life lived in flagrant *and uncondemned* contravention of its fundamental principle enunciated in Deuteronomy 12 that there is but one legitimate sanctuary and altar? Incidentally, it was Smith's views on the non-Mosaic authorship of Deuteronomy expressed in his article on 'Bible' in *Encyclopaedia Britannica* ninth edition that provoked the initial proceedings against him in the Free Church General Assembly of 1876. The ritual law was codified still later. In consequence, the eighth-

19. For the biographical details, see J.S. Black and G. Chrystal, *The Life of William Robertson Smith* (London: A. & C. Black, 1912). [A congress to mark the centenary of Smith's death was held in Aberdeen in April 1994. Cf. W. Johnstone (ed.), *William Robertson Smith: Essays in Reassessment* (JSOTSup, 189; Sheffield: Sheffield Academic Press, 1995).]

century prophets of Israel do not presuppose the Law except for the
Book of the Covenant in Exodus 20–23; the Law is, rather, the
formalization of the work of the prophets.

In the second phase of his work, Smith appears as Arabist, social
anthropologist and historian of religion as well as scholar of the
Hebrew Bible. Again two books mark the progression: the preliminary
sketch is in *Kinship and Marriage in Early Arabia* (1885); the summation was delivered as the Burnett Lectures at Marischal College from
1888, the first series of which was published as *The Religion of the
Semites* in 1889. In this phase Smith is still very much concerned with
Hebrew origins, only now inquired into using the methods of comparative religion. The assumption is that there are principles of general
applicability that govern the evolution of any religion. Thus on sacrifice
he writes:

> Sacrifice is equally important among all early peoples in all parts of the
> world where religious ritual has reached any considerable develop-
> ment...an institution shaped by the action of general causes...To con-
> struct a theory of sacrifice exclusively on the Semitic evidence would be
> unscientific...It is right to put the facts attested for the Semitic peoples
> in the foreground and to call in the sacrifices of other nations to confirm
> or modify the conclusions to which we are led. For some of the main
> aspects of the subject the Semitic evidence is...clear, for others it is
> fragmentary and unintelligible without help from what is known about
> other rituals.[20]

It is only right at this point that I should say that Smith's work in the
elucidation of Hebrew origins from the side of comparative Semitic
religion, language and culture has been brilliantly carried on by my
immediate predecessor and former colleague John Gray. In his case the
point of departure has been the discovery between the two world wars
and since of new Canaanite texts which have opened up the religious
situation in Palestine on the eve of Israel's settlement in quite revolutionary ways. I should like to record publicly my gratitude at having
had the opportunity to be associated with one whose work is exemplary
in both method and industry.

The other scholar associated with the North-East whom I should like
to mention in connection with this review of past quests for Hebrew

---

20. *The Religion of the Semites* (London: A. & C. Black, 2nd edn, 1907),
pp. 214ff.

origins is Alexander Geddes, who, like Smith, was concerned with a critically established understanding of the sequence of materials in the Pentateuch yet who with a sure insight pointed forward to a probably sounder appreciation of tradition than Smith, an insight that, however, like so much else in Geddes's work, lacked thorough development, only receiving sufficient attention in the first half of the twentieth century.

Alexander Geddes was born a couple of miles from Buckie in 1737 and died in London in 1802. As a Roman Catholic destined for the priesthood (his cousin John, Bishop of Morocco, is buried in the Snow Kirkyard in Old Aberdeen a hundred paces from where I usually teach), Geddes was never a student at Marischal or King's College (indeed, he studied for seven years at Scalan, the seminary in the Braes of Glenlivet), but was honoured by the degree of LLD of the University of Aberdeen (as Smith was) in 1780 for his 'Translation and Imitation of Horace'.[21] In the textbooks Geddes is chiefly remembered as the originator of the so-called 'Fragment Hypothesis' of the origin of the Pentateuch: but this term does scant justice to his account of the dynamism of tradition lying behind the materials now collected in the Pentateuch or to his view of the work of the final editors who drew the materials together. Here are his own words:

> From the intrinsic evidence, three things seem indubitable to me. 1st, The Pentateuch, in its present form, was not written by Moses. 2dly, it was written in the land of Chanaan, and most probably at Jerusalem. 3dly, it could not be written before the reign of David, nor after that of Hezekiah. The long pacific reign of Solomon (the Augustan age of Judaea) is the period to which I would refer it: yet, I confess, there are some marks of a posterior date, or at least of posterior interpolation... It is my opinion that the Hebrews had no written documents before the days of Moses; and that all their history, prior to that period, is derived from monumental indexes, or traditional tales. Some remarkable tree, under which a patriarch had resided; some pillar, which he had erected; some heap which he had raised; some ford which he had crossed; some spot, where he had encamped; some field, which he had purchased; the tomb in which he had been laid—all these served as so many links to

21. Biographical details are taken from R.C. Fuller, *Dr Alexander Geddes: A Forerunner of Biblical Criticism* (unpublished PhD thesis 6583; Cambridge, 1968) [now published in Historic Texts and Interpreters in Biblical Scholarship, 3; Sheffield: Almond Press, 1984].

hand his story down to posterity; and corroborated the oral testimony transmitted, from general to generation, in simple narratives or rustic songs.[22]

It was only when the twentieth-century German scholars—a Gunkel or a Noth—came along with their technical terms of *Überlieferungs-geschichte*, *Haftpunkt* and *Sitz im Leben* that these ideas received the currency that they deserve.

It is a melancholy but perhaps not so surprising fact—one hopes not a precedent—that these two distinguished sons of the North-East, Geddes and Smith, should both have completed their biblical interpretation under the censure of their respective churches. Neither gave nor expected quarter. 'I have throughout acted the critic, and occasionally the commentator', wrote Geddes defiantly.

> ...In both these characters I have freely used mine own judgement (such as it is) without the smallest deference to inveterate prejudice or domineering authority. The Hebrew Scriptures I have examined and appretiated, as I would any other writings of antiquity...I am well aware, that...the cry *heresy*! *infidelity*! *irreligion*! will resound from shore to shore. But my peaceful mind has long been prepared for...such harsh Cerberean barkings: and experience has made me (not naturally insensible) callous to every injury, that ignorance or malice may have in store for me...Reason, reason only, is the ultimate or only sure motive of credibility; the only solid pillar of faith.[23]

'Protestant shall contend with Papist, which shall throw the first stone at me.'[24] Already in 1792 the Vicar Apostolic had issued a Pastoral warning Catholics against Geddes's Bible translation, and when he died in 1802 he was buried without requiem. When I was presented to the Moderator in the General Assembly last 22 May, it was to within two days of the centenary of the deposition of Robertson Smith from his Hebrew Chair in Aberdeen and within the selfsame hall. I recently overheard a highly respected retired member of staff of this University say to one of my colleagues that perhaps the way to revival of interest in Hebrew Bible studies would be a trial of William Johnstone for

22. Preface to *The Bible*... (2 vols.; London: J. Davis, 1792–97), I, pp. xviii-xix.

23. Preface to *Critical Remarks on the Hebrew Scriptures* (London: Davis, Wilks and Taylor, 1800), I, pp. ivff.

24. Preface to *The Bible*..., II, p. iv.

heresy. *Absit omen*! But if it comes to that, I await the contest with relish.

After this review of a number of attempts associated with Aberdeen and the North-East of Scotland to approach the Hebrew Bible from the angle of origins, we return to our question: given the nature of the Hebrew Bible—that it is often written long after the event, and that even when nearer to the event it is moulded according to distinctive theological purposes—where is the surest ground on which to begin? The answer, of course, is that one must begin at the end. To begin at the beginning where the problems of distance of the material from the period and the depth of interpretation are at their greatest is to deal in vagueness and to proffer hypothetical reconstructions, which, however valid and necessary the attempt, can often only leave a feeling of great uncertainty. One is on firmer ground if one starts with the Hebrew Bible as it now is, the literature in its fully developed form, which must be regarded as an expression of the Jewish community's self-understanding towards the time of the completion of the Hebrew Bible, that is, sometime in the postexilic period, say third or second century BCE. This greater certainty does not altogether prevail on the historical side: history continues to be used with free plasticity as before (as in Ezra, Nehemiah or Daniel, for example). But the theological outlook and the religious institutions may be taken as reflecting more immediately the thought and forms of life of the postexilic community. There is presumably a greater convergence than heretofore of period and expression, though fossilized elements may have been preserved, archaic survivals (such as the ark of the covenant which had physically disappeared after 587), which had ceased to be functional in the community's life.

Given a relatively wide choice across the whole Hebrew Bible, which book have I therefore offered to write a commentary upon? The answer brings me at last to the title of this lecture—or at least the first element in it—Chronicles. Now why should one offer to write on a work of which there have been more one-line dismissals than of almost any other book in the Hebrew Bible? A Jewish commentator on the Mishnah, Obadiah of Bertinoro (d. 1501), classified Chronicles among 'the books that divert the mind and drive away sleep'.[25] Morton

---

25. Cited in H. Danby, *The Mishnah* (Oxford: Oxford University Press, 1933), p. 163 n. 2.

Smith's opinion may more accurately reflect the popular view: 'The Old Testament contains some of the world's most remarkable works of literary creativity. When one comes down from these heights to the Death Valley of the Chronicler, one finds an author whose brazen, clearly motivated contention is obvious on almost every page.'[26]

Why, then, Chronicles? There are three main areas of interest.

I

The first I have already indicated, namely, greater certainty about the relationship of writer to period. On any account, Chronicles stands at or near the end of the canon of the Hebrew Bible. In the standard Hebrew Bible it is printed as the last book. Its date cannot be precisely determined, but indications would point to at least as late as the fourth century BCE: 1 Chron. 3.19-24 offers a genealogy of the Davidic house stretching seven generations from and including Zerubbabel, one of the leaders of the return from exile, who was operative in attempts to restore the Temple around the year 520 BCE. Such data would suggest a date in the mid-fourth century. Chronicles thus stands at the gateway to a reading of the Hebrew Bible which begins from the more certainly datable sections and works back through the accumulated layers of Scripture to materials of less certain period. In this respect at least, the interpreter who begins with Chronicles resembles the excavator of a Middle-Eastern—or any other—archaeological site: he begins at the latest level of the tell, perhaps takes a deeper sounding in one area, before peeling off the layers of accumulated material, period by period. Alexander Geddes and Robertson Smith tried to begin the account from the beginning and immediately fell foul of ecclesiastical authorities who could not distinguish between theological truth and historical truth, between the theological significance of the Bible and its historical dress. To begin at the end enables one to do justice to the canonical status of the body of Scripture and all that that implies, and thereafter in calmer fashion to explore the historical roots.

My proposals for thus beginning at the latest level (though I must admit that I do not submit my students to the full rigour of this approach: Chronicles barely figures on the curriculum)[27] are by no

26. M. Smith, 'The Present State of Old Testament Studies', *JBL* 88 (1969), p. 29.

[27. For the record, we normally begin with Jeremiah, which introduces the evidence for multiple authorship (ch. 36) and, by its appendix (ch. 52), is clearly

means unique: it provided the starting-point for many of the literary critics of last century, for example, De Wette and Graf;[28] Wellhausen wrote a thesis on material from the early chapters in 1870.[29] Further, this approach brings me into contact with some strong, perhaps even dominant, trends in contemporary approaches to the Hebrew Bible, about which, however, the Chronicler poses probing critical questions. Three of these may be mentioned.

1. The approach nearest to that which I am advocating, which I have noted, is that of Rudolph Smend of Göttingen in his recent book on the origin and formation of the Old Testament, *Die Entstehung des Alten Testaments*. He writes,

> The usual presentation of the analysis of the books of the Bible and the history of its literature begins with the pre-literary and literary categories and then proceeds to the biblical books themselves. Thus as a rule there is progression from the older to the more recent, e.g., from a literary source or the authentic words of a prophet to the later additions and redactions. The present work proceeds in the opposite direction. The point of departure is the complete literary units, the Old Testament itself and its constituent parts. From these it works backwards to the redactions and the written sources used by them and from there back to the materials and units which underlie them.

He then alludes to 'the advantage of such a starting point: one works back step by step from the relatively more certain to what is usually less certain'.[30] My criticism of Smend would be that he does not carry through his programme with sufficient radicality: despite this statement, he still begins his book with the Pentateuch and deals with the succeeding parts of the Hebrew Bible in their conventional sequence. But this approach may overlook the possibility that the final stages of editing the Hebrew Bible may not have been confined to the individual

linked with DtrH. The comparison between DtrH and ChrH makes clear the differing theological intentions of the biblical writers. The unambiguous evidence of two editions of Israel's history—and the welcome 'hard' date of post-561 for the earlier of these (2 Kgs 25.37)—prompts the hypothesis of two corresponding editions of the Pentateuch.]

28. J.E. Carpenter and G. Harford-Battersby, *The Hexateuch* (2 vols.; London: Longmans, 1900), I, p. 46.

29. D. Mathias, 'Die Geschichte der Chronikforschung im 19. Jahrhundert' (unpublished dissertation; Leipzig, 1977), p. 83.

30. R. Smend, *Die Entstehung des Alten Testaments* (Stuttgart: W. Kohlhammer, 1978), p. 11.

books in their isolation from one another but that much broader shaping
of very much larger blocs may have taken place in order to produce a
unitary collection of Scriptures and that this process may have continued as late as the Chronicler. Thus, for example, it has been pointed out
that there is perhaps a deliberate coincidence in the choice of vocabulary in the last verses in the book of Genesis and in the last verses of
Chronicles, that is, the first and last books of the Hebrew canon end on
the same note: in the one, the dying Joseph in the land of the alien
Pharaoh of Egypt says to his kinsmen, 'God *will visit* you'; in the other,
the same verbal root (*pqd*) is used by the alien emperor Cyrus of Persia
when he says, 'The Lord...*has charged* me to build him a house at
Jerusalem'; in the one, the dying Joseph says, '*Take up* my bones' from
the alien Egypt to the Promised Land; in the other, the same verbal root
(*'lh*) is put on the lips of Cyrus, 'Whoever is among you from God's
people...*let him go up*' from alien Babylon to Judah restored.[31] The
observation has all the more force if Chronicles is written about the
time of the destruction of the Persian Empire at the hands of Alexander
the Great towards the end of the fourth century BCE.

2. The approach to Hebrew Bible studies through the latest levels
brings one into critical contact with that advocated in particular by our
latest honorary graduate in Divinity, Professor Brevard Childs of Yale.
He stresses the final form of the Scriptures, the biblical text as canonized, as the appropriate context within which interpretation takes place.
The following passage may be taken as representative of his writing:

> Recent continental scholarship has often radicalised [the] form-critical
> approach in an endless search for earlier forms and alleged traditions. As
> a result, the present biblical text has been atomised and hopelessly
> blurred by hypothetical projections of the traditions' growth. On the
> other hand, American scholarship has tended to impose Ancient Near
> Eastern patterns upon the biblical traditions with a heavy hand which
> has only succeeded in smothering the text [notice the similarities in
> the approaches stigmatised to those of Geddes and Smith]...Both
> approaches have failed to deal seriously with the present form of the
> biblical text and have focused their major interest, on some phase of the
> prehistory...The history of research has often demonstrated how effec-
> tively the study of the prehistory has functioned in obscuring the biblical
> text through false parallels and mistaken ideas of historical develop-
> ment.[32]

31. N.M. Sarna, 'Bible', *EncJud*, IV, col. 831.
32. B.S. Childs, *Exodus* (OTL; London: SCM Press, 1974), pp. 338-39; cf. his

There is much sound sense here: the approach has the merit of stressing what Israel in the end of the day intended to stress rather than creating an irrelevant historical account. The Hebrew Bible is summated literature: it does not present a historical reconstruction of events for its own sake; far less is each part a running transcript of the period with which it deals. Rather, it is the definitive presentation of what the believing community has affirmed as significant, the normative account of the accumulated tradition of the people as meaningful. It is the expression in terms of its classical past of the present it experiences and the future it awaits. It was the canon of Scripture which, as Robertson Smith pointed out exactly 100 years ago in *The Prophets of Israel*,[33] enabled the Jewish community, clustered round the written word of God in place of the shattered Temple cultus, to survive the Babylonian exile, whereas their northern brethren of Samaria had succumbed in the Assyrian exile of a century and a half earlier. It is this written canon of Scripture that, furthermore, has given access to the nations of the world to the treasured faith of Israel.[34]

Yet, though there is so much to be said in favour of Childs's approach, the books of Chronicles help to make a point in so obvious a way that it is inclined to be overlooked: the canonical form of Scripture is not necessarily the final form of Scripture; earlier canons are embedded in the final form of Scripture. Chronicles uses for much of its sources material derived from the books of Samuel and Kings. Chronicles represents a presumably later edition of Samuel and Kings; it is the final form of the history of Israel. Yet though it is the final form of the history of Israel, it does not rob the earlier presentation of its canonical status—quite the contrary; most would probably regard the earlier account in Samuel and Kings as the more valuable both historically and theologically. These facts about the relationship between Chronicles and Samuel–Kings illustrate an important truth about the canon of Scripture. The canon is not merely the end-product of a long process of accumulating, refining and summating. Rather, the final canon of Scripture stems from a long series of earlier canons of Scripture, which are taken up in the later without abrogation, as Samuel–Kings is taken up

Introduction to the Old Testament as Scripture (London: SCM Press, 1979), *passim*.

33. *The Prophets of Israel* (Edinburgh: A. & C. Black, 1882), p. 262.

34. D. Patrick, *The Rendering of God in the Old Testament* (Overtures to Biblical Theology; Philadephia: Fortress Press, 1981), p. 140.

into Chronicles, yet with continuing validity in its own right. What is visibly the case with Samuel, Kings and Chronicles is implicit in vast areas of the rest of the Hebrew Bible. To take the familiar example, most of Isaiah is not written by the prophet whose name the book bears but is, in the words of the subtitle of a recent book on Isaiah 1–35, 'mirror of half a millennium of Israel's religion'.[35] The point is this: the Bible does not represent a final result which in the end was canonized; rather, it grew from an original canonical nucleus, a decisive primary experience (an exodus, a Sinai, a conquest), which, constantly revived and reactualized in liturgy and experience, controlled the shape of things to come. In the Hebrew Bible we have a rolling, snowballing canon, on the one hand creative, on the other receptive, growing by means of its own liberating power. And so it remains in the believing communities of Synagogue and Church that have inherited it today: closed but not foreclosing, defined but not inert, final but not absolute, not the sum total of all that can be said, it remains the standard of what is in fact said. One cannot, after all, by affirming canon escape the history of tradition, for tradition is all part of canonical Scripture.

3. Chronicles poses searching questions to a further modish approach to the interpretation of the Hebrew Bible which can be only briefly alluded to here. This approach again affirms the final form of the text as it now stands and seeks to appreciate that form aesthetically as literature. A recent writer begins his book as follows: 'It is my belief that much Old Testament narrative belongs naturally to the life-sphere of art and entertainment and that to approach this material as a literary critic might an epic poem, a novel or a play, can be helpful to the modern reader.'[36] The same approach has been tried out on a section of the Chronicler.[37] The only trouble is that the Chronicler has not always digested his sources and, like a creative artist, re-expressed them in his own thought-forms. He is not freely composing his material from scratch but by a scissors-and-paste method is arranging blocs of material, sometimes of substantial length, derived from the Pentateuch,

---

35. J. Vermeylen, *Du prophète Isaïe à l'apocalyptique. Isaïe, I–XXXV: Miroir d'un demi-millénaire d'expérience religieuse en Israël* (Paris: J. Gabalda, 1977).

36. D.M. Gunn, *The Fate of King Saul* (JSOTSup, 14; Sheffield: JSOT Press, 1980), p. 11.

37. H.G.M. Williamson, 'We are yours, O David', paper to the Society for Old Testament Study, 18 July 1979 (on 1 Chron. 12.1-33), now in A.S. Van der Woude (ed.), *Remembering All the Way* (OTS, 21; Leiden: E.J. Brill, 1981).

Samuel–Kings and Psalms with blocs of material that have no parallel elsewhere in Scripture and which may plausibly be attributed to himself. While the arrangement of the blocs and the independent material can give us some clue about the author's immediate intentions, the aesthetic approach can hardly by itself do justice to the constraints under which the inherited material placed him or to the inner dynamics of the inherited materials themselves or to all questions of their relationship to Chronicles' own materials. The biblical interpreter has as part of his task to establish whether the final form of the text does in fact possess literary and aesthetic integrity. It may be that these last two approaches noted manifest and are motivated by a justified but misapplied reverence for Scripture.

II

While such motives and the appraisal of such issues are my initial reason for choosing Chronicles, one cannot in dealing with Chronicles confine attention to the issues of Hebrew Bible interpretation to which it happens to provide a gateway. Chronicles is important not only for the way in which it frames the vista beyond: the design, construction and decoration of the gateway itself deserve consideration. Chronicles merits study in and for itself. Of these interpretative issues, which Chronicles itself poses, I choose only the central one: what was the purpose for which Chronicles was written? Despite Morton Smith's assertion that the author's 'clearly motivated contention is obvious on almost every page', a number of rather different interpretations of the purpose of the work have in fact been given down the years. A recent review of interpretation of the books of Chronicles, emanating, it is not uninteresting to note, from the Karl-Marx University of Leipzig, spends 793 pages, including a bibliography of 185 pages, considering the suggestions that have been offered, confining itself in so doing only to the nineteenth century.[38] The traditional understanding of Chronicles is that it provides amplification of, or supplementation to, the material in Samuel–Kings (compare the title of the work in the Greek Version *Paraleipomena*, 'the things left out [sc. of the earlier version]'), but this cannot account for the extensive repetitions, overlaps and duplications between Chronicles and Samuel–Kings, nor, therefore, for its creative

38. Mathias, 'Geschichte'.

new handling of the matter. As representative of a typical nineteenth-
century attitude we may take Heinrich Ewald's view that Chronicles
was written about the time of the death of Alexander the Great by a
member of the guild of Temple musicians; it is a priestly history, as
opposed to the prophetic history of Samuel–Kings, aimed partly against
the Samaritans and partly at the new Greek overlords, ending as it does
with the benefactions of Cyrus to the Jews in 538 BCE with the purpose
of stimulating Alexander's heirs to similar deeds of generosity. Ewald
comments unfavourably on the Chronicler's literalistic faith and pious
timidity.[39]

What, then, is the purpose of the Chronicler likely to have been? It is,
I think, possible to read the work of the Chronicler as an essay in the
preservation of Israel's identity by the unification of her streams of
tradition in a time of political powerlessness and cultural pluralism. The
streams are the Levitical, the priestly and the royal; the uniting focus of
restored national life is the Temple in Jerusalem rebuilt on the ruins of
the First Temple destroyed at the time of the Babylonian exile. The
status of the Temple is enhanced by the attribution to King David of the
very plan of its structure revealed in a heavenly blueprint, the organization of its cultic personnel, its liturgy and cult. David functions as
standard and hope in the presentation of the past history: himself the
recipient of a unilateral covenant from God, his successors on the
throne enjoy success or are chastized by failure according as they are
loyal or disloyal to the central institution and maintain or neglect its
ordinances. The Davidized final edition of the Psalter[40] is here actual-
ized in terms of a presentation of Israel's history. The stress throughout
is on the reunification of the people: the phrase 'all Israel' occurs no
less than 48 times in Chronicles.[41] The reconciliation of the claims of
competing factions is attempted. A number of recent writers have
drawn attention to the divergent streams of theological outlook in the
postexilic community. The division of opinion lay perhaps between the
visionary idealists on the one side, who regarded themselves as the
heirs of the prophetic tradition now interpreted in more apocalyptic
terms (cf. Dan. 9.2 for such reinterpretation of the prophetic scriptures),

39. Mathias, 'Geschichte', pp. 47-48.

40. J. Becker's phrase in *Wege der Psalmenexegese* (SBS, 78; Stuttgart: KBW,
1975), p. 99.

41. F.L. Moriarty, 'The Chronicler's Account of Hezekiah's Reform', *CBQ* 27
(1965), p. 403.

and those, on the other hand, the practical realists, who saw in the maintenance of the Temple and its round of worship the true form of patient waiting upon God until the political tide turned in Israel's favour. It may be that Hanson is right in describing the Chronicler as marking the moment when 'the victorious hierocratic party returns to a more conciliatory position'.[42] The master-hand in the composition of Chronicles is most likely to have been a Levite or a group of Levites, whose function, as the book of Deuteronomy makes clear, was to act as Israel's teachers of the Law (cf. Deut. 33.8, 10). The book of Deuteronomy itself probably represents a substantial earlier Levitical exercise in creating a canon of Scripture (cf. the 'canonical formulae' at Deut. 4.2; 12.32), just as Samuel–Kings is part of a substantial Levitical history interpreting Israel's experience in the light of its obedience or disobedience to the word of canonical Scripture. Chronicles thus represents the next significant phase of Levitical activity. Here the Levitical author, who is bearer of the tradition of canonical Scripture, offers a new interpretation of Israel's past experience up to his time around 300 BCE to meet the needs of his contemporary community. For his purpose he has blended together his own dominant tradition of law, as canonized in earlier codifications of Scripture, with priestly traditions and with the messianic traditions of the Davidic monarchy; this combining of traditions is presented to the reader accessibly in the form of a running story. In other words, Chronicles presents us with a prime example of the reapplication of canonical Scripture in terms of an immediate social and political context. So saying, we have now reached the title of this lecture, which, in turn, leads me to the final reason for an interest in the Chronicler.

III

We have looked backwards through the gateway of Chronicles, for it is an appropriate point of departure for the study of the Hebrew Bible. We have also looked at some features of its own design and structure. But, if Chronicles is an example of the exposition and application of a canon of Scripture within the context of a contemporary society, then we can also look forward through this gateway, for, dropping the figure, in that case Chronicles provides an example of the central task of theology and

42. P.D. Hanson, *The Dawn of Apocalyptic* (Philadelphia: Fortress Press, 1975), pp. 269-79.

be no different. If Christ came not to destroy but to fulfil, then his message represents the *a fortiori*, the how much more, written across the pages of the Hebrew Bible. If that is true in local, national terms of the case study of ancient Israel, how much more is it true in the universal terms of the gospel of Jesus Christ? The Chronicler's summons to the theologian today is that in patient and faithful waiting upon God he offers in continuity with the past tradition of belief a new synthesis of the perceptions of the whole life of humankind.

There are here profound implications for the organization of the teaching of Divinity. Divinity enjoys the privilege of constituting a separate faculty in this University. Yet this is an honour which, if rigidly adhered to, dishonours her, for by cutting her off from active academic association with non-Divinity departments within the University she is disabled in her proper task of relating the heritage of Christian thought to the full range of contemporary concerns, and, at the same time, she is obstructed in any reconstructive role she may have. If theology is to attempt a synthesis of traditions and modern perception, of canon and context, she requires the input that only the other disciplines can provide; the membranes that separate her from her sister faculties must be permeable in both directions. Now this is hardly the time or the place for a political speech; but it is gratifying that students in Divinity can take courses in Arts or Science as part of their degree and that students in Science and Law can take graduating courses in Divinity. The route from Arts to Divinity is meantime somewhat restricted; I personally hope that in the future the traffic will flow still more easily.[45]

There remains some truth in theology's ancient title 'queen of the sciences' even if it is only in an attenuated and vestigial sense. Theology is a queen in that without her handmaids she is powerless and can scarcely fend for herself. It is not with imperialistic claims, but in grateful acceptance, that she lays under tribute the contributions of knowledge and learning from the rest of the University; in principle there is no subject area in the results of which she does not have an interest. It is for this reason that the endowments of the theologian and the biblical critic as theologians are never adequate. Already in 1786 Alexander Geddes reflected gloomily on the necessity for even the

[45. A hope in fact realized by the constitution of the joint Faculty of Arts and Divinity in 1989.]

translator of Holy Writ to be 'a universal scholar'.[46] I suppose that Robertson Smith, encyclopaedist of *Britannica*, ninth edition, natural philosopher, mathematician, social anthropologist, comparative religionist, semitist and theologian as he was, comes as near as any. But in an age when polymaths are few and far between, all we are left with is interdepartmental cooperation on the widest scale.

What the theologian makes of the canon reinterpreted in the light of the contemporary context he can offer to no one as prescriptive; like her master, theology though monarch is servant of all; or like the figure of Wisdom in the book of Proverbs, who has given herself to the University as its motto, 'The fear of the Lord is the beginning of wisdom' (Prov. 1.7), she stands by the wayside, at the crossroads, appealing to the passers-by for a hearing. Yet what she is attempting is no less than her traditional role as queen of the sciences. Hastings Rashdall put it thus in *The Universities of Europe in the Middle Ages*:

> Theology remained Queen of the Sciences, but a grander and nobler conception of theology arose—a conception which the modern world, alas! has all but lost. Theology became…the architectonic science whose office it was to receive the results of all other sciences and combine them into an organic whole…the ideal was one which cast a halo of sanctity over the whole cycle of knowledge.[47]

In our pluralist times it is hardly likely that any one synthesis can or should command assent, or that the task of creating syntheses be reserved to any one agency. With that view oddly enough Queen Wisdom of the Hebrew Scriptures would herself unhesitatingly agree. Yet theology must claim a hearing and from time to time even the apparently arcane disciplines of biblical criticism can break through creatively into wider fields. Alexander Geddes can serve yet once more as our example. In the opinion of a recent writer, who attempts to chart the dynamic impact on English literature from Samuel Taylor Coleridge to George Eliot of the new higher biblical criticism inaugurated especially in Germany in the last quarter of the eighteenth century, Geddes played a key role. Through his *Prospectus of a New Translation of the Holy Bible* of 1786, his *Proposals* of 1788, his *Answer to Queries* of 1790 and by the publication of the first volume of the *Translation* in 1792, the writer suggests that

46. Alexander Geddes, *Prospectus of a New Translation* (Glasgow, 1786), p. 140.

47. Cited by Evans, *Explorations*, p. 85.

[t]he fullest and most widely publicized accounts of recent German Biblical Criticism were those of the Roman Catholic Biblical critic Alexander Geddes... [I]t is certain that he [Coleridge] met Geddes before
leaving for Germany [in 1798] for he carried a letter of introduction
from Geddes to Dr Paulus, the head of the German rationalist theologians at Heidelberg...If Coleridge had read nothing but the reviews of
Geddes's Bible, he would have had a tolerable idea of the main heads of
the new criticism; if he read Geddes, as it is hard to conceive he did not,
he had an excellent conspectus of the higher criticism as it had developed in the hands of Herder and Eichhorn.[48]

All this may seem a long way from the biblical books of Chronicles;
yet I should argue that the creative way in which biblical criticism
acted upon the high seriousness of a Coleridge or a George Eliot in
their searches for an integrated vision (cf., e.g., the function of the
Jewish heritage in Eliot's *Daniel Deronda*) is entirely in the spirit of
the Chronicler's *midrash*, wherein he sought no less creatively to bring
inherited Scripture to bear on his quest for integration and wholeness
amid the factions of his time.

Nevertheless, Principal, in case I am entirely wrong in all I have said
tonight about the appropriate place to start in the interpretation of the
Hebrew Scriptures and the consequences of starting at that place, I have
also undertaken to write a book on Exodus.

48. E.S. Shaffer, *'Kubla Khan' and* The Fall of Jerusalem: *The Mythological
School in Biblical Criticism and Secular Literature 1770–1880* (Cambridge: Cambridge University Press, 1975), pp. 26ff.

Chapter 3

THE EXODUS AS PROCESS*

The biblical narrative of the descent of Israel's forebears into Egypt, their sojourn there, and ultimate exodus therefrom represents at least from the Egyptian point of view a gross over-simplification. Whereas the historical Egypt of the probable period was at the zenith of imperial might, the biblical record does not even trouble to name the three Pharaohs whom it recognizes as being involved; beginning with Joseph's rise to dominance over Egypt and ending with the humiliating destruction of the entire Egyptian host in the waters of the Red Sea, it allows to the Egyptians no brilliance of achievement in any field but only cruelty and intransigence and the fate such deserve. May it be that the presentation of the Israelite side is no less stylized? If the exodus narrative is an over-simplification of the course of events even from the Israelite point of view, then to attempt to defend its historicity point by point, to take it at face value as a running transcript of a series of immediately interconnected events, may be to mistake its character and thus run the danger of misrepresenting its purpose.

In what follows, the suggestion will be made that the exodus should not be regarded, as it usually is, as a *punctual* event, that is, one that took place at one point in time or in one specific locality or involved one particular group of Israel's forebears; rather, the exodus narrative as it now stands represents a theological interpretation of a historical *process* typical over an extended period of time for large numbers of people. In a manner characteristic of one way in which the Bible makes theological statements, the complexity of the actual historical process has been scaled down and contained within the form of a connected narrative.

* Originally published in *ExpTim* 91 (1979–80), pp. 358-63, now made uniform with this collection.

I

That a new line of approach to the problem of the exodus may not be unjustified is suggested by the difficulties that beset the conventional interpretation that seeks to understand it as a single, punctual event. Three notorious problems in particular—date, location and participants—may be instanced.

The inner-biblical relative chronology of the pre-monarchic period is uncertain, perhaps inevitably so: the apparently firm chronological date of 1 Kgs 6.1, for example, which relates the exodus to later history (it took place 480 years before the Temple in Jerusalem was founded), or Exod. 12.40-41, which relates it to earlier events (it took place 430 years after the descent), appear to be in conflict with the span of years implied by genealogies such as that of David in Ruth 4.18-22, in which David's forebear Nahshon, who according to Exod. 6.23, etc., was contemporary with the exodus, belongs to only the fourth generation after the descent into Egypt and the sixth before the founding of the temple. Both sets of data are embedded deep in the biblical tradition (contrast already Gen. 15.13 with Gen. 15.16), so that it is rather arbitrary to choose one in preference to the other; both, indeed, may be conditioned by the views of the biblical writers concerned (e.g. Exod. 12.40-41 places the exodus in the year 2666 after creation, or ⅔ through a period of 4000 years).[1]

In view of the ambiguity of the biblical data, the establishment of an absolute chronology relating biblical material to extra-biblical historical sources can hardly be other than tentative. The issue is further complicated by the fact that there is no cross-reference between the Israelite and Egyptian sources, though the notice in Exod. 1.11 about the building of the store-cities Pithom and Raamses, unless it is dismissed as an anachronism, would point to the Ramesside period, in other words, sometime from the late fourteenth century on, though even it can define no more precise a date. Historians are left to suggest the period of Egyptian history that seems to them to provide the most congenial background for the events recorded in the biblical narrative. Even within the past decade studies have appeared supporting a long

---

1.   A.H.J. Gunneweg, *Geschichte Israels* (Stuttgart: W. Kohlhammer, 1972), p. 21.

chronology (early descent, early exodus),[2] a short chronology (late descent, late exodus associated with the movements of the Aramaeans),[3] and a mixture of the two: the Patriarchs associated with Amorites; the exodus dated in the thirteenth century.[4] The arguments adduced are not all equally convincing. Bimson's involves such elements as a later dating for the appearance of bichrome ware than archaeologists are usually disposed to allow, and the playing-down of the significance of the Egyptian imperial presence in Palestine during the New Kingdom. Herrmann's interpretation that the Israelites were among the last spent forces of a wave of land-seeking Aramaeans who were unsuccessful in finding territory in Egypt to settle does not ring particularly true to the biblical record. It furthermore involves an excessive whittling-down of the biblical tradition: only elements of later Israel spend time in Egypt and that time has a 'basically temporary—indeed positively fleeting character';[5] as for the pursuing Egyptian army, 'we may assume that it was only a small contingent'.[6] It is difficult to see how an event so obscure and banal as Herrmann reconstructs it could have left so profound and lasting an impression on subsequent Israelite faith; if the *Geschichte* was so trivial, the *Wirkungsgeschichte* is incredible. In any case, the conception of the 'arrival' of semi-nomadic peoples, whether they be termed Amorites or Aramaeans, may turn out to be a dubious one in view of the researches of such scholars as M.B. Rowton or M. Liverani.

Equally problematical is the discussion of locality and personnel on the punctual theory of the exodus. The words quoted from Herrmann above represent a typical approach: the statistics in Exod. 12.37 of 600,000 men, not to mention women and children, that is, a total of two million and more, suggest a company that is impossibly large to pass through any stretch of water in a single night, let alone be supported on manna 'these forty years' in the wilderness. Interpreters therefore contend that the numbers must have been considerably fewer: even Bimson accepts the suggestion of 'about 72,000 for the whole migration';[7]

2. J.J. Bimson, *Redating the Exodus and Conquest* (JSOTSup, 5; Sheffield: JSOT Press, 1978).

3. S. Herrmann, *Israel in Egypt* (London: SCM Press, 1973).

4. De Vaux, *Early History*.

5. *Israel in Egypt*, p. 28.

6. *Idem, History of Israel*, p. 64.

7. *Redating*, p. 33.

much more radical are P. Weimar and E. Zenger who suggest a number of the order of 50 to 150.[8] This is surely the *reductio ad absurdum* of the punctual view.

A similar embarrassment, one suspects, lies, in part at least, behind the prevalent identification of the *yam suph*, the location of the exodus, as 'the reed sea', an identification that has been adopted into the text of JB and intermittently into the margin of NEB. It is impossible for the vast numbers of the biblical tradition to have crossed any stretch of water in the time available, let alone the Red Sea. Further, how could a stretch of water of any depth have 'dried up'? Therefore, upholders of the punctual theory appeal to an undoubted meaning of the word *suph*, namely, 'reeds', such as the infant Moses was concealed among. Suitable reed-swamps are then canvassed from Lake Manzaleh or Lake Sirbonis at the northern end of the modern Suez Canal to the Bitter Lakes towards the south. But it must be observed that elsewhere in the Hebrew Bible the *yam suph* always refers to the Red Sea, sometimes not even to the Gulf of Suez but even to the Gulf of Akaba (1 Kgs 9.26). The possibility that also in the exodus story it refers to the Red Sea is thus strong (cf. Exod. 10.19).

II

The difficulties and uncertainties confronting and raised by the punctual approach are apparent; its results are by no means so assured and agreed as to preclude any attempt at an alternative. What, then, are the arguments by which one might attempt to support the thesis that, historically, the exodus should be regarded as a process rather than as a punctual event?

The Egyptian records conventionally cited to support the historicity of the biblical tradition permit the process interpretation. Because of the vagueness of the biblical chronology, the history of Egypt has been combed for evidence of the arrival of Semites, like Jacob and his sons, in Egypt; their rise, like Joseph, to positions of prominence; even of their escape from Egypt. The very success of these endeavours, especially with regard to the first two elements, suggests that in fact descent, sojourn and exodus were, historically, recurrent possibilities.

A few examples illustrate the point:

8. *Exodus: Geschichten und Geschichte* (SBS, 75; Stuttgart: KBW, 1975), p. 114 n. 35.

- for the descent into Egypt, one often compares the Beni Hasan mural (about 1890 BCE),[9] or captive lists of Amenophis II (third quarter, fifteenth century BCE);[10]
- for the employment of Semites, cf. a text naming Asiatics in a Theban household (mid-eighteenth century BCE; the Asiatics receive Egyptian names as did Joseph [Gen. 41.45]),[11] or a text of Ramesses II mentioning the *'apiru* (probably related in some way to the biblical Hebrews) in building operations or of Ramesses IV in the army;[12]
- for the attainment of high office by Asiatics such as Joseph, cf. the position of Dod as chamberlain at the court of Amenophis IV,[13] or the rule by a Syrian between the XIXth and XXth Dynasties (end of the thirteenth century);[14]
- for escape/expulsion from Egypt and all the hazards attendant thereto, cf. the *Tale of Sinuhe* (twentieth century BCE),[15] the expulsion of the Hyksos (sixteenth century BCE),[16] or the pursuit of two runaway slaves (copy of text from end thirteenth century BCE).[17]

The conclusion to be drawn from a comparison of the biblical account and such material from so many disparate periods and sources can hardly be simply that the biblical material fits plausibly into the background of the time; rather it could be that the biblical material represents a drastically over-simplified and partial account—perhaps, even, a distant reminiscence—of an extended process with a very complex history.

The point concerning the periodicity of descent and exodus can be developed by reference to the practice of the semi-nomadic Semites of Transjordan, the Negev, and north Sinai, known in Egyptian texts as

9.   *ANET*, p. 229.
10. *ANET*, pp. 245ff.
11. *ANET*, pp. 553-54.
12. K. Galling, *Textbuch zur Geschichte Israels* (Tübingen: J.C.B. Mohr, 2nd edn, 1968), pp. 35-36.
13. *EA*, pp. 158, 164.
14. *ANET*, p. 260.
15. *ANET*, pp. 18ff.
16. *ANET*, pp. 233-34.
17. *ANET*, p. 259.

Shosu. A frequently cited text concerning the Shosu is 'The Report of the Frontier Official':[18]

> (We) have finished letting the Shosu of Edom pass the fortress...which is (in) Tjeku [a locality in the region called Goshen by the Bible]...to the pools of Per-Atum [? = biblical Pithom]...to keep them alive and to keep their cattle alive.

Some identify in this text, probably correctly, the phenomenon of transhumance whereby the shepherd with his flocks and black tents is annually forced by the onset of the drought of summer to abandon the withered pastures of the wilderness and enter the agricultural zone to graze his flocks on the stubble fields.[19] This is a practice that has been followed of necessity since time immemorial, and which can, indeed, still be observed today. It is a practice attested for the Shosu and Egypt not only by the above-cited text but from much earlier texts, such as 'The Prophecy of Nefer-rohu'.[20] A point strangely not often noticed, however, is that if such texts refer to transhumance then they attest not simply periodic descent of semi-nomadic Semites but also periodic exodus. W. Helck has drawn attention to this inference;[21] and in consequence W.H. Schmidt disputes the appositeness of such Egyptian material![22] For my part, I should affirm the relevance of the evidence as portraying something of the social context within which Israel's exodus as process took place. De Vaux's magisterial treatment of the period cited above suffers in my view precisely at this point simply because he does not follow to its conclusion the logic of the evidence he adduces. At one point he is forced by such evidence to concede that 'just as there were several entries into Egypt, so too it is possible that there were several exoduses'.[23] On the basis of an analysis of the material in Exodus he himself concludes that there were in fact two exoduses: in the first, elements of the Leah tribes were expelled by border police operations during the XVIIIth Dynasty; they followed a northern route out of

---

18. After *ANET*, p. 259, copy of text from end thirteenth century BCE.

19. E.g. de Vaux, *Early History*, I, pp. 316-17, and Herrmann, *Israel in Egypt*, pp. 25-26.

20. *ANET*, p. 446.

21. Review of Siegfried Herrmann, *Israels Aufenthalt in Ägypten* in *TLZ* 97 (1972), cols. 178ff.

22. *Exodus* (BKAT, 2; Neukirchen–Vluyn: Neukirchener Verlag, 1974–), p. 37.

23. *Early History*, I, p. 375.

Egypt to Kadesh Barnea and entered Palestine from the south. However, it is the second exodus that tradition has preserved 'as the real
exodus':[24] this concerns the flight of elements of the Rachel tribes
under Moses, who enter Palestine from the east after traversing Sinai
and Transjordan. De Vaux, it seems to me, is inhibited by his regard for
the biblical tradition as it now stands from drawing the conclusions his
evidence demands. Transhumance is not, of course, the sole means of
the periodic arrival of Shosu in Egypt: they regularly feature as captives
in conquest lists from Tuthmosis II onwards.[25] It may be speculated
that the presence of Shosu shepherds in Goshen provided Shosu prison-
ers-of-war in the same vicinity opportunity to rejoin their people and
escape from their bondage. While all this was a recurrent possibility of
experience, it may well be that under the Ramessides of the XIXth
Dynasty the treatment of Shosu—shepherd or prisoner—reached a new
peak of severity in the Eastern Delta.

The view of the exodus as process is, further, I believe, highly congenial to the character of the biblical records. In this regard, it is hardly
sufficient to confine oneself to literary criticism; for example, Weimar
and Zenger (*Exodus*) identify the earliest narrative in Exodus as a critical commentary derived from the early monarchy directed against the
royal use of Israelite forced labour. The literary sources identified, N,
L, J, E, P, or whatever, are merely as the belts of trees of different
varieties cladding a hillside which tell of the general configuration of
the ground that lies underneath but little of its geology. The biblical
narrative in Exodus is concerned not simply to describe the event of the
exodus (whether punctual or process) but to explain and justify continuing religious practice. This is clear from the very layout of the material,
for example, in chs. 12 and 13, where narrative and legislation are
intertwined. In these chapters some three religious institutions are
interrelated—Passover, the festival of unleavened bread, and the
offering of firstlings. A reasonable case can be made out for the view
that all of these institutions are immemorial observances of pastoralist
or peasant long antedating the exodus of Israel from Egypt, which are,
therefore, only secondarily associated with one another and with the

24. De Vaux, *Early History*, I, p. 388.

25. R. Giveon, *Les bédouins Shosou des documents égyptiens* (Leiden: E.J.
Brill, 1971).

exodus.[26] The matter is perhaps clearest with regard to the offering of firstlings: it is nowhere stated in Exodus that the passover lamb is a firstling; yet the offering to the LORD of firstlings is justified by reference to the slaying of the Egyptian first-born both of man and of beast on the eve of the exodus, though in fact, as the legislation of the Book of the Covenant (Exod. 22.30, English versions) makes clear, firstlings were offered on the eighth day after birth. It is hard to escape the conclusion that the continuing practice of later Israel has been justified by secondary historicization of these rites by means of reference to the exodus from Egypt, with its all-embracing significance. A similar process can be observed in Num. 3.12-13; 8.14-22, where the setting-apart of the Levites is similarly explained and justified (cf. the justification for *booths* at the feast of tabernacles by reference to Israel's *tents* in the wilderness [Lev. 23.42-43]!). It is likely therefore that the exodus has not given rise to any of these religious observances, though it has imparted additional significance to each. This is in no way to deny that the present association of these rites with the exodus and with each other is now more important than their original separation just as for the Christian Holy Communion is now more important than antecedent Passover. Such religious observances of Israel have come into being not because of some particularly significant event in the past; rather, they belong to the immemorial rhythm of life of the ancient Orient of which, for the semi-nomad, descent into and exodus from Egypt were an integral part. There is no pressure from these institutions to find a single event that could have given rise to them. To view the exodus as process is to relate it to the rites that came to be associated with it in a way that is congenial both to its character and to theirs.

It might even be possible to argue that the Passover *could* not have belonged historically to an exodus from Egypt in the spring. If the Passover is connected with the age-long semi-nomadic spring festival, then there are difficulties in relating it to a departure from Egypt. The semi-nomadic spring festival is a rite of *entry* into the agricultural area, not of departure from it; the purpose of the rite is to protect the pastoral group as they set out into the unknown and possibly hostile farming zone (it may be, as L. Rost has suggested, that the scapegoat ceremony of Lev. 16 with the offering of the goat for Azazel reflects the Israelite counterpart to a semi-nomadic autumn festival marking the return from

26. See, e.g., J. Henninger, *Les fêtes de printemps chez les Sémites et la pâque israélite* (Paris: J. Gabalda, 1975).

the sown to the desert).[27] Where and when, therefore, was the association of Passover (the semi-nomadic spring rite of entry) and unleavened
bread (the agricultural spring harvest festival) likely to be made? There
is a ready-made context for this in the worship of the sanctuary at Gilgal as recounted in Joshua 3–6: it is at Gilgal that Passover and unleavened bread can be conjointly celebrated by incomer and resident in the
context of ceremonial celebration of entry into the land across the river
whose waters are divided and of conquest of the land by the circum-
ambulation of the site of Jericho.[28] It may be for this precise reason that
there are these striking parallels between the Exodus narrative and that
in the early chapters in Joshua; the Exodus narrative, in particular the
miraculous crossing of the sea in ch. 14, may indeed have been written
up in the light of the Gilgal celebrations, as de Vaux holds,[29] again
without drawing, it seems to me, the full conclusions. That is, once
more the exodus has provided justification for a particular religious rite,
in this case the entry and conquest festival at Gilgal. As Benjaminite
historical traditions in all probability provide the basis for the conquest
narratives in Joshua 6–9, so Benjaminite liturgical traditions at Gilgal
provide basic materials for the celebration of freedom from Egyptian
domination and entry into YHWH's land.

What is true of the association of Passover, unleavened bread and
firstlings in the book of Exodus may be true also of the association of
the exodus and the revelation of Sinai. In the biblical narrative, these
are represented as consecutive punctual events; in fact they may have
been continuing concurrent or overlapping processes. The revelation of
the name YHWH is associated with 'this mountain' in Exodus 3. But the
possibility that YHWH was known by name long before Moses is
strong. Gen. 4.26, for example, preserves a tradition that the name
YHWH was known in the same generation as Cain, a piece of evidence
that, among others, has given rise to the Kenite hypothesis of the origin
of Yahwism. Irrespective of the soundness or otherwise of that hypothesis, there now appears to be evidence from Egypt from the time of
Amenophis III and Ramesses III for the association of the name YHWH
with the semi-nomads of Seir as in the biblical tradition of Deut. 33.2

27. His essay 'Weidewechsel und altisraelitische Festkalendar', now repub-
lished in his collection *Das kleine Credo* (Heidelberg: Quelle & Meyer, 1965).

28. H.-J. Kraus, 'Gilgal', *VT* 1 (1951), pp. 181ff.

29. *Early History*, I, pp. 384ff.

and Judg. 5.4.[30] There are thus reasonable grounds for regarding exodus and Sinai not as successive punctual events but as processes, each interpreted in the light of the other by those involved in both.

Literary arguments are thus complementary to historical: the record of historical process has been shaped by directions for periodic celebration and actualization. Recurrent celebration is the eminently congenial vehicle for the tradition of a historical process that was itself a recurrent possibility of experience.

An advantage of regarding the exodus as process is that it enables the biblical information concerning the locality of the exodus and the numbers of those involved to be accepted more or less as it stands without the unacceptable reduction of it to the point of banality. It is possible now to argue that *yam suph* possesses the meaning that it has elsewhere in the Hebrew Bible, namely, the Red Sea, though not in a precisely localized sense any more than the crossing of it is to be understood in a precisely punctual sense. What is being stated in narrative form might be something like this: after bitter subjection, Israel's forebears finally escaped from Egyptian sovereignty which for centuries had represented the greatest physical and metaphysical force in the ancient world to which Israel belonged; this new situation—the decline of the Egyptian Empire and the *'apiru*'s consequent gaining of freedom—constituted such an unexpected reversal of previous conditions that Israel could only attribute it to the agency of its God. The waters of the Red Sea were now finally established as an impenetrable barrier for the Egyptians keeping them firmly within their eastern frontier. Its waters had at last rolled back and cut Egypt off. Such a symbolic interpretation may at first sight seem fanciful, yet it is in line with the mythological features that undoubtedly become attached to the sea of the exodus elsewhere in the biblical traditions, for example, Isa. 51.9-10.

As for the participants, obviously an experience extended over a period of time could well become shared by a considerable number of people. A common approach to the problem of the numbers involved is to assume that the experience of the few considered to have been in Egypt is recognized by the many to have been so significant that it has been adopted as the normative tradition of all. However, a further point is worthy of consideration here. To the Hittites, the Egyptians' arch-rivals in the closing centuries of the Late Bronze Age, the 'land of Egypt' meant not simply metropolitan Egypt of the Nile Valley and

30. E.g. Document 16a in Giveon, *Les bédouins.*

Delta but in large part the land of Syria and Palestine; this is clear from such a text as 'The Plague Prayer of Mursilis'.[31] It is doubtful whether the expression 'the land of Egypt' is used in this sense anywhere in the Hebrew Bible (though cf. Judg. 6.9). The point is, however, this: for the peoples of the ancient Near East for much of the Late Bronze Age, and especially in the fifteenth and thirteenth centuries, Palestine and south Syria lay within the Egyptian orbit; the region was divided into three provinces; the chief cities in these provinces were organized as if they were part of metropolitan Egypt; their governors were installed as if they were mayors of metropolitan Egyptian cities. It must have been apparent that the power behind the myriad city-states, whose existence the Egyptians were happy to perpetuate in pursuance of a policy of divide-and-rule, was the Egyptian; for example, sons and heirs of the princelings of these city-states were held in Egypt as hostages and for training pending their taking over the reins of government in their areas in the Egyptian interest on the death of their fathers.[32] That is, until the decline of Egyptian power by the twelfth century BCE all the people of Palestine were Egyptian *ᵃbādîm*, that perplexingly vague term which can mean not only 'slaves' but 'vassals'. The *bêt ᵃbādîm*, traditionally 'house of bondage', could cover a very much wider area than the land of Goshen in Egypt. There is thus added force given to the contention that the experience of those physically in the land of Egypt in the narrower metropolitan sense simply reflected, though no doubt in harsher terms, the general experience of all, not least the *'apiru* in the Egyptian provinces of Asia. From the Amarna letters[33] corvée labour is known to have been exacted, for example, in the territory assigned by the Hebrew Bible to Issachar, 'the man of hire', who in Gen. 49.15 is described as 'subjected to slave-labour'. In the process of history, the forebears of all the elements that went to make up Israel suffered in some sense bondage in the land of Egypt; this is why at the exodus Israel is represented as numbering 600,000, not counting women and children. A further pointer in the same direction is the fact, often noted, that two foreign nations in the Hebrew Bible refer to the Israelites as 'Hebrews', namely the Egyptians and the Philistines. The explanation for this may

31. *ANET*, pp. 394ff.

32. Details may be found in W. Helck, *Die Beziehungen Ägyptens zu Vorderasien im 3. und 2. Jahrtausend v. Chr.* (Wiesbaden: Otto Harrassowitz, 2nd edn, 1971).

33. *ANET*, p. 485 and esp. n. 7.

lie not in mere coincidence of practice but in the probability that the Philistines simply took over the practice long established by the Egyptians in that area of Palestine.

Perhaps the main problem confronting the theory of the exodus as process is the role of Moses. It is difficult to see how a single dominating figure can fit into a lengthy historical process (though there is no difficulty in conceiving that the process could have culminated in a series of events in which Moses played the leading part). But then the historical role of Moses is difficult to define on almost any account of the period. What historical evaluation can be made of the many miraculous details of the narrative and the prodigious quality of the many roles the biblical tradition ascribes to him? The place Moses now occupies in the exodus narrative as it stands may be explained on literary grounds. By means of a linear narrative of ostensibly punctual events, Passover–exodus–Sinai, the Bible constructs the epic of national origins. It is in response to the requirements of this method of making theological statement and providing historical explanation by means of a consecutive narrative that the figure of Moses is developed in order that thematic unity may be imparted to the whole. A similar procedure is, in all probability, discernible in the treatment of the figure of Samuel: out of the obscure local seer of Ramah there is developed a national prophetic exponent of Deuteronomic orthodoxy, a procedure required by the nature of the narrative in 1 Samuel as a theological statement on the inception of the monarchy. So out of Moses the Levite of Kadesh Barnea, son of Jochebed and husband of Zipporah (if one may hazard a guess at the historical core), there is developed the national leader steadfast through every vicissitude, the archetypal prophet, bearer of the definitive revelation of God, in whose person the diverse experiences of groups and epochs are united into a single narrative statement.

In conclusion, it may be appropriate to consider some of the theological implications of understanding the exodus as process. A conventional interpretation of the exodus as a unique signal historical event leads easily to a theology of 'the mighty acts of God', the affirmation that the God of the Hebrew Bible is pre-eminently a God who acts in history, who demonstrates his nature in interventions on the plane of human experience. A consequence of this understanding may be that any interpretation that seems to undermine the historicity of the events as portrayed in the biblical account is viewed as threatening the structure of biblical theology itself. It may be, however, that in such an understanding of 'the mighty acts of God' the emphasis is wrongly placed. There is a danger here of the crass historicism, the attachment to the accidents of history, which vitiated Israelite belief from Amos's contemporaries who appealed to the historical fact of their election to the Jews of Jesus' day who claimed Abraham as their father. The interpretation of the exodus as process lays the emphasis on tradition, the age-long experience of the semi-nomads, endorsed through the successive generations, of their God as ever-present guide and protector (the divine title 'shepherd' may well come from this milieu). YHWH is not believed from now on to be redeemer because he brought his people out of Egypt; rather, because he has been long known as redeemer, and much else besides, he is believed to have brought his people out of Egypt. This deliverance is accepted as but the latest manifestation, no doubt in climactic and summating form, of the already-known God. This, it would seem, is precisely the affirmation of the biblical story: the new of the exodus is carefully bonded onto the old and already known of the patriarchal age. There is a fine paradox in the early part of the Moses story that he, Moses, who is the bearer of the revelation of YHWH, the new name of God, has himself a mother whose name Jochebed is in all probability compounded with the divine name YHWH. The point is more certainly made in Moses' experience at the burning bush: he who is YHWH, who will be what he will be, identifies himself as the already known God of Abraham, Isaac and Jacob. The new cannot be perceived unless it is related to tradition; only thus can it be received and endorsed by the experiencing community as the legitimate extension of the faith of the fathers. The linking of the new to tradition seems to me to be a constant element in biblical theology, present in the record of the ministry of Jesus himself as in the parable of Dives and Lazarus: 'If they hear not Moses and the prophets, neither will they be persuaded, though one rose from the dead' (Lk. 16.31). Herein lies the truly prophetic function of a Moses: the age-old faith is now projected beyond the limited horizons of the semi-nomadic wandering herdsman onto the military and political realities of the contemporary international scene. It is not the exodus as such which is important, but rather the truth about God of which it is an expression: a specification of the already-known character of God on an ever wider scale. The exodus is not so much proof as proving ground. A similar thought is put rather well by Weimar and Zenger:[34] linguistically the

34. *Exodus*, p. 97.

name YHWH is a short sentence with open predicate, 'He shows him-self as...'; it therefore demands concretizing through experience and is open to new experience in which the basic experience is renewed and vitalized; or again on p. 126: the earliest account of the exodus is a definition in narrative form of the divine name YHWH. One would only quibble about the limitation imposed by the word 'earliest'.

Part II

LOOKING AT THE GATEWAY:
CHRONICLES IN ITSELF AND IN ITS RELATION TO THE PENTATEUCH

Chapter 4

GUILT AND ATONEMENT:
THE THEME OF 1 AND 2 CHRONICLES*

I

It is clear that the books of 1–2 Chronicles[1] represent a highly ideological work. That that is so is apparent from a number of considerations.

1. Even if it were 'only' a work of historiography, it is obvious that any treatment of the entire history of Israel against the background of mankind as a whole, from Adam (1 Chron. 1.1) to the edict of Cyrus (2 Chron. 36.22-23) in 538 BCE, within the compass of two books of the Bible must be using ruthless principles of selection of the material available and must be arranging these materials according to some preconceived pattern.

2. The relationship of Chronicles to other works in the Hebrew Bible which deal with Israel's history, Samuel–Kings on the one side, especially, and Ezra–Nehemiah on the other, raises the question of the Chronicler's ideology still more sharply.[2]

*   Originally published in J.D. Martin and P.R. Davies (eds.), *A Word in Season* (Festschrift W. McKane; JSOTSup, 42; Sheffield: JSOT Press, 1986), pp. 113-38; lightly edited, and brought into uniformity with this collection.

1.   Chronicles is here sometimes construed in the singular as a single work. 'The Chronicler' refers to the author(s) of the work, without prejudice to critical decisions that might be reached concerning his (or their) identity, or the process of the composition or compilation of the books.

2.   I should be prepared to subscribe to the view that already both Samuel–Kings and Ezra–Nehemiah are highly ideological. In broad terms, 'covenant' is the 'hermeneutical key' (to use the term of P. Buis, *La notion d'alliance dans l'Ancien Testament* [LD, 88; Paris: Cerf, 1976]) in the former, whereby the history of Israel from Sinai to exile is interpreted by the criteria of the blessing and curse of the covenant: e.g. the 'blessing' narrative of the conquest in Josh. 1–12 and the 'curse' narrative in Judg. 1.1–2.5; or the way in which the histories of David, Solomon and Hezekiah are hinged round pivotal points (the Bathsheba incident in 2 Sam. 11–12,

(a) The relationship between Chronicles and Samuel–Kings is exceedingly complex: the Chronicler adds much, omits more and incessantly modifies material even where he reuses it.[3] It is obvious that principles of selection have been operated with added stringency and that, to a limited extent, materials have been rearranged.[4] It is unlikely,

the trafficking with Egypt in 1 Kgs 10.28-29 [cf. Deut. 17.16], and the 'fourteenth year' in 2 Kgs 18.13–20.11 respectively). Ezra and Nehemiah are constructed in such a way as to present the 'Return from Exile' as a single concerted event, as the layout of the books makes clear:

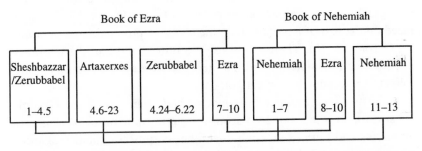

Book of Ezra   Book of Nehemiah

Sheshbazzar /Zerubbabel	Artaxerxes	Zerubbabel	Ezra	Nehemiah	Ezra	Nehemiah
1–4.5	4.6-23	4.24–6.22	7–10	1–7	8–10	11–13

The fact that the time-scale from Sheshbazzar to Nehemiah spans at least 100 years (whatever conclusion one may reach about the historical relationship between the activities of Ezra and Nehemiah) is apparently of little concern to the writer/editor of Ezra–Nehemiah.

3.   It is surprisingly difficult to compile accurate statistics of the relationship between the two corpora. Apart from the quite external factor of the occasional variation in verse numbering, the Chronicler intervenes so constantly in his Samuel–Kings source that at times it is almost arbitrary whether one regards the texts as parallel or whether the Chronicler's modification of a phrase should be counted as a plus to the Chronicler and a minus to Samuel–Kings. My assessment would be somewhat as follows: 1 Chron. 11.1–2 Chron. 36.21 contains 1341 verses; the parallel 2 Sam. 1.1–2 Kgs 25.30 contains 2229 verses; Chronicles in this part contains some 530 verses with parallels to Samuel–Kings; i.e. some $2/5$ of Chronicles (from 1 Chron. 11 on) has parallel material in Samuel–Kings, while some $3/5$ is independent of Samuel–Kings. Contrariwise, Chronicles uses only about $1/4$ of the material available in Samuel–Kings (again from 1 Chron. 11–2 Chron. 36).

4.   E.g. the sequence of materials derived from 2 Samuel in 1 Chron. 11–21, where the order begins:

1 Chron. 11.1-9	cf. 2 Sam. 5.1-3, 6-10
1 Chron. 11.11-41a	cf. 2 Sam. 23.8-39
1 Chron. 13.6b-14	cf. 2 Sam. 6.2b-11
1 Chron. 14.1-16	cf. 2 Sam. 5.11-25
1 Chron. 15.25–16.3	cf. 2 Sam. 6.12b-19a

however, that the Chronicler has made these modifications of his
underlying source for purely, or even mainly, historiographical reasons.
In comparison with Samuel–Kings, circumstantial detail revealing
human motive and intrigue has been still further reduced; for example,
the rivalries for the succession to David recorded in 2 Samuel 13–21
have been entirely suppressed by the Chronicler. Where his work can
be checked against an underlying source, it can be seen that the Chronicler has consistently simplified the presentation of historical events
(cf., e.g., the accounts of the raising of the siege of Jerusalem in 2 Kgs
19.35-37 and 2 Chron. 32.21-23). Elsewhere, his material includes
theological comment either on his own part (e.g. 1 Chron. 10.13-14) or
placed on the lips of a prophet (e.g. the series of prophetic interventions
in 2 Chron. 12–36). There can surely be little doubt that the Chronicler's selection of material and his incorporation of such comment are
motivated by some ideological purpose.

(b) Further indications of the motive and character of the Chronicler's work may be gathered from a couple of parallel passages in
Chronicles and Ezra–Nehemiah, that other corpus commonly regarded
as historiography. It has been widely held that Chronicles–Ezra–Nehemiah is, in fact, a single work by a single author, 'The Chronicler'.
Those familiar with the sequence Chronicles–Ezra–Nehemiah in the
Christian Bible may already be predisposed to this view. It is seemingly
confirmed by the overlap between the two works in the edict of Cyrus
(2 Chron. 36.22-23/Ezra 1.1-4), which links the earlier historical episodes of Chronicles with the later ones of Ezra–Nehemiah. There
seems, however, to be a growing number of interpreters[5] who would
subscribe to a view perhaps already implied by the sequence in the
Hebrew Bible, Ezra–Nehemiah–Chronicles: Chronicles is not primarily

---

5.   See, e.g., H.G.M. Williamson, *1 and 2 Chronicles* (NCB; Grand Rapids:
Eerdmans, 1982). It should perhaps be explained that the present chapter has been
written entirely independently of the substantial secondary literature on Chronicles
(though, as one tries to do one's own map-making, it is hard to avoid altogether
coming across tales that earlier travellers have had to tell of their pioneering explorations in this rugged terrain). It represents part of the preliminary thinking for a
larger-scale work (see Chapter 1, n. 12) and the development of an earlier contention that the work of the Chronicler is 'an essay in the preservation of Israel's
identity by the unification of her streams of tradition...the uniting focus...is the
Temple in Jerusalem' (Chapter 2, p. 68). I am concerned here to try to identify the
basic centripetal force, by which Israel's disparate traditions are brought into relationship with one another.

conceived as the historical account that provides the necessary pre-
amble to Ezra–Nehemiah; it is a later and independent work, which,
strangely enough, despite its being later, ends back at the point at which
Ezra–Nehemiah begins. I should argue that, while Ezra–Nehemiah
depicts the 'Return from the Exile' (see n. 2), Chronicles grapples with
the mystery that, despite the 'Return', Israel is still 'in exile', still
poised on the eve of the definitive 'Return'. It may be that already the
true lineaments of Chronicles as religious and theological writing,
using historical materials in symbolic fashion and not composed primarily for historiographical purposes, are beginning to appear.

In my view, one of the clearest indications of the priority of Ezra–
Nehemiah is provided again by parallel passages, in this case 1 Chron.
9.2-17 and Neh. 11.3-19. That dependence is on the side of Chronicles
is particularly clear from the lameness of 1 Chron. 9.2: 'The original
settlers, who were *in their [Neh.: 'his'] holding in their cities, were the
Israelites, the priests, the levites and the n^{e}tînîm.*' The harshness and
apparent redundancy of the statement (but see below at the end of the
chapter), which pull the translator up sharp, can be explained by the
fact that the Chronicler by his usual scissors-and-paste method has conjoined his own material, 'The original settlers, who were', which continues from his own previous verse summarizing the list of tribal
genealogies and territories itemized in the preceding chapters (1 Chron.
2–8), with material borrowed from Neh. 11.3, which makes fluent sense
in the Nehemiah context: 'These are the chief men of the province, who
resided in Jerusalem, while in the cities of Judah there resides, each one
*in his holding in their cities, the Israelites, the priests, and the levites
and the n^{e}tînîm…*' (parallel phrases italicized). The Chronicler, with
scant attention to the particularities of the Nehemiah passage (the dis-
approving comparison between the nine-tenths of the population, who
with heedless hedonism settled into their landed possessions, and the
pioneering one-tenth, who altruistically gave up such pleasures in order
to repopulate the capital), blandly turns the material to his own
purposes.

It is not perhaps so clearly demonstrable that the edict of Cyrus
material in 2 Chron. 36.22-23 is similarly derived from the parallel in
Ezra 1.1-4. Nonetheless, in a couple of features it would be entirely
characteristic of the Chronicler as dependent. Chronicles as the shorter
text could well be another example of the Chronicler's regular practice
of abbreviation and the excision of material redundant for his purpose.

By a subtle change in reading (unless it is merely an instance of textual corruption), the Chronicler alters the tentative greeting of the pagan emperor in Ezra, 'Let his God be with each among you, who is one of all his people', to the triumphant affirmation, 'YHWH his God is with each among you'.

3. The reference just made to 1 Chron. 9.2 introduces another indication of the Chronicler's intention of providing not a merely historical but a suprahistorical interpretation of his people's existence. Already in the genealogies in 1 Chronicles 2–8 he has used eclectically lists from a great variety of historical periods, as if they were all on the same time-plane, in order to complete his muster of the people of Israel.[6] Now in 1 Chron. 9.2-17 he borrows as his source for the inhabitants of Jerusalem a postexilic list from the time of Nehemiah (Neh. 11.3-19). The effect is that individuals of widely differing historical periods are brought into association with one another: these men of Nehemiah's time in vv. 3-17 rub shoulders with David and Samuel's appointees (the inversion of the historical Samuel and David is further evidence of the Chronicler's suprahistorical thinking!) in vv. 18-22. The Chronicler is not now interested in the historian's discriminations of time and epoch; rather, his purpose is to gather together in a global manner the fullness of Israel past and present in timeless contemporaneity. He is concerned to portray an ideal Israel in all-inclusive terms, not to reconstruct the actual population at some point in time.[7]

---

6.   E.g. the descent of the House of David is traced for some 38 generations in 1 Chron. 2.10-16; 3.1-24, whereas the obscurer branches of the Calebites are fobbed off with a couple of generations and are then indicated by the names of the places that they populated (e.g. 1 Chron. 2.19-20, 50-55; 4.1-8). Lineal descent and lateral spread are thus placed side by side in order to achieve the most ample presentation of the descendants of Israel. Statistics obtained under David in the tenth century (1 Chron. 7.2) stand alongside data from Jotham in the eighth century (1 Chron. 5.17).

7.   The RSV translation of 1 Chron. 9.2 (cf. also GNB), 'Now the first to dwell *again* [my italics] in their possessions', is conditioned by the knowledge of the parallel with Neh. 11.3, the reasoning being, presumably, that, since Neh. 11 is about the fifth century, 1 Chron. 9 must be about the postexilic repopulation of Jerusalem. This conclusion is simply symptomatic of the captivity of the modern mind to historicism. There is no word in the Hebrew corresponding to the RSV's 'again'; the RSV translation also ignores the fact that 1 Chron. 9.2 resumes 1 Chron. 8.28 and that the sequel to 1 Chron. 9 is the early monarchy. Even more serious is its misconstruing, in my view, of the Chronicler's intention.

Perhaps such indications are sufficient to make the necessary preliminary point that Chronicles is better understood as primarily a theological essay than as a work of historiography. Without accepting any of
the negative implications sometimes attaching to the term, I should be
happy to call it *midrash*.[8] This definition of genre is of the utmost
importance in shielding the reader from false expectations, and the
Chronicler himself from misguided reproaches that he is not fulfilling a
function that he never intended to fulfil.

II

If the Chronicler's work is primarily a theological essay, with what
purpose has it been written? A not unreasonable place at which to start
one's inquiry into the Chronicler's distinctive purpose is surely provided by those materials without parallel in Samuel–Kings, especially
those where he offers an evaluation of a historical incident, borrowed
or adapted from Samuel–Kings, to which he has just referred. Within
the narrative section of Chronicles, which begins with 1 Chronicles 10,
the first such comment is to be found in 1 Chron. 10.13-14. In the preceding verses he recounts, with significant changes in detail, the narrative of the last, fatal, campaign of Saul against the Philistines at Gilboa,
which is to be found in 1 Sam. 31.1-13. On this debacle he offers the
following independent evaluative comment:

> Thus Saul died for the *ma'al* (מעל), which he *ma'al*ed against the LORD:
> for the word of the LORD which he did not keep even to the extent of
> resorting to necromancy. He did not resort to the LORD; therefore, he put
> him to death and passed the monarchy over to David, son of Jesse
> (1 Chron. 10.13-14).

8.   In applying the term *midrash*, I am thinking of some such understanding of
it as that of J. Neusner: '*Midrash* represents…creative philology and creative historiography. As creative philology, the *Midrash* discovers meaning in apparently
meaningless detail. It…uses the elements of language not as fixed, unchanging categories, but as relative, living, tentative nuances of thought. As creative historiography, the *Midrash* rewrites the past to make manifest the eternal rightness of
Scriptural paradigms. What would it be like if all people lived at one moment?…
Midrash thus exchanges stability of language and the continuity of history for
stability of values and the eternity of truth' (*Between Time and Eternity* [Encino:
Dickenson, 1975], p. 52). The only two occurrences of the word מדרש in the
Hebrew Bible are in Chronicles (2 Chron. 13.22; 24.27).

The use of root מעל in such an evaluative context becomes all the more
striking when it is realized that this same root is used at key points in
similar evaluative comments throughout the Chronicler's work.
Already in the genealogies it occurs three times (1 Chron. 2.7; 5.25;
9.1). After 1 Chron. 10.13 there is a long gap, but there are a further 12
occurrences in 2 Chronicles (12.2; 26.16, 18; 28.19 [twice], 22; 29.6,
19; 30.7; 33.19; 36.14 [twice]).[9]

An examination of these passages shows that this distribution of the
root מעל can hardly be accidental. By means of it the Chronicler punc-
tuates the decisive periods of Israel's history; from first to last, on West
Bank and on East, in North and in South, Israel in its occupation of the
land has been characterized by מעל. 1 Chronicles 2.3 begins the
genealogies of the tribes of Israel with Judah. Almost immediately, the
incident recorded in Joshua 7 is alluded to: at Jericho, in the very first
campaign of the conquest of the West Bank, Achar, the 'troubler' of
Israel (the form of his name here is derived from Josh. 6.18; 7.24-26),
committed an act of מעל (1 Chron. 2.7). The first phase of Israel's settlement of the land is already vitiated. What is true of the West Bank is
equally true of the East (1 Chron. 5.25): the Chronicler, in free reminiscence of Joshua 22, where the root occurs seven times, records how the
two-and-a-half tribes of Reuben, Gad and Half-Manasseh committed
מעל against their ancestral God.[10]

In the summary on the genealogies in 1 Chron. 9.1, מעל is singled
out as the significant factor leading to the exile. After the occurrence,
which has already been noted, in 1 Chron. 10.13 in the evaluation of
the reign of Saul, the first episode in the history of Israel recounted in
any detail by the Chronicler, the root does not reappear until 2 Chron.
12.2. The reason for this gap is clear. The reigns of David and Solomon
(apart from the highly significant episode of 1 Chron. 21, to be noted

___

9.   The distribution of the remaining 47 occurrences of מעל throughout the rest
of the Hebrew Bible may be noted: Lev. 5.15 (2×), 21 (2×); 26.40 (2×); Num. 5.6
(2×), 12 (2×), 27 (2×); 31.16; Deut. 32.51; Josh. 7.1 (2×); 22.16 (2×), 20 (2×), 22,
31 (2×); Ezek. 14.13 (2×); 15.8 (2×); 17.20 (2×); 18.24 (2×); 20.27 (2×); 39.23, 26
(2×); Job 21.34; Prov. 16.10; Dan. 9.7 (2×); Ezra 9.2, 4; 10.2, 6, 10; Neh. 1.8;
13.27.

10.   Incidentally, one notes again the Chronicler's lack of interest in historiographical accuracy: while there may be other factors in his elevation of Judah to
pre-eminence among the tribes (e.g. the emergence of David from Judah) besides
the notoriety of their early history, his dealing with the West Bank before the East
reverses the sequence familiar from the Hexateuch.

below, where, however, not מעל but the associated root אשם is used) do not add to the fateful entail already announced in the genealogies. It is only with the Judaean king Rehoboam, son of Solomon and instrument of the break-up of the united monarchy, that the deadly course of מעל is resumed and continues down through the reigns of Uzziah (2 Chron. 26.16, 18), Ahaz (2 Chron. 28.19, 22; 29.19) and Manasseh (2 Chron. 33.19), until it issues in the shared מעל of the whole community under their last king, Zedekiah (2 Chron. 36.14). The pleas of the pious Hezekiah, urged precisely on the basis of this past history of מעל, are unavailing (2 Chron. 29.6; 30.7). The Chronicler's message is clear: his explanation for why Israel is 'in exile' is that from beginning to end of its occupation of the land, whether on West Bank or on East, whether in Northern Kingdom or in Southern, Israel has been guilty of מעל and has paid the penalty for it. Confirmation that the concept is indeed of distinctive significance for the Chronicler's thinking may be found in the fact that, in all its occurrences from and including 1 Chron. 9.1, the root is not to be found in the Chronicler's underlying sources but belongs exclusively to his own material.[11]

What, then, is מעל? The meaning of the term the Chronicler has already begun to make clear contextually. In Achar's case, it consisted in violation of the חרם, that is, of the spoils of battle, the fruits of victory, which ought to have been devoted wholly and exclusively to God in virtue of the fact that the victory had been won by him alone and that he is the sole giver of the land and of every gift that Israel possesses. The reminiscence of Joshua 6–7 is so clear that it is surely legitimate to assume that the concepts associated in Joshua 6–7 are also presupposed by the Chronicler. The חרם infringed by Achar is there defined as that which is holy (קדש) to the LORD and which ought to be deposited in 'the LORD's storehouse' (אוצר יהוה) (Josh. 6.9, 24). Terms synonymous with violating the חרם are 'to sin' (חטא), 'to transgress the covenant' (עבר את הברית, Josh. 7.11), 'to commit folly in Israel' (עשה נבלה בישראל, Josh. 7.15). The double-sided nature of the offence is also recognized: מעל is not only to deprive God of that which is rightfully his; it is also to misapply what has thus been wrongfully gained to one's own profit (Josh. 7.11, 'They have stolen, dissembled and put among their own goods'). The penalty for the individual guilty

11. Contrast, e.g., 2 Chron. 12.2 with 1 Kgs 14.25; 2 Chron. 26.16-21 with 2 Kgs 15.5; 2 Chron. 28.16-20 with 2 Kgs 16.7-9; 2 Chron. 33.18-20 with 2 Kgs 21.17-18; 2 Chron. 36.11-14 with 2 Kgs 24.18-20.

of מעל is stoning to death by the whole community of the culprit, his family and all living creatures within his household and the burning of the corpses. The whole community thus has a hand in extirpating wrongdoers from their midst and in purging the effect of their wrong-doing.

The model case of the individual guilty of מעל is then writ large in the life of the nation as a whole. Here again, מעל is failure to accord God what is his due (חטאת is used in 2 Chron. 33.19 in conjunction with it as in Josh. 7.11). The duty owed to God is, in particular, exclusive obedience and utter reliance (1 Chron. 10.13), the ancestral faith of Israel being sometimes stated as the ground for such trust (1 Chron. 5.25). מעל is evidenced in turning to other gods (2 Chron. 33.19), a particular irony since Israel's God had exposed their powerlessness at the conquest (1 Chron. 5.25). Thus Israel reduces itself to the level of the nations in a way that is as inexplicable as it is inexcusable, even to the extent of polluting and profaning its own sanctuary or of abandoning it altogether (2 Chron. 28.22; 36.14). The double fault of מעל, of defrauding God and misapplying that which is holy, is seen in the activities of Ahaz (2 Chron. 28.24). Uzziah is roundly informed that he is trespassing in the sphere of the holy (קדש), to which only those duly consecrated (המקדשים) have access, and that he had better depart from the sanctuary (המקדש) forthwith (2 Chron. 26.16-18). The penalties of מעל are recognized to be incapacitating illness (Uzziah, 2 Chron. 26.19), death (Saul, 1 Chron. 10.13-14), or exile (the people, 1 Chron. 9.1; 2 Chron. 30.6, 9), and the devastation of the land (2 Chron. 30.7); in a word, forfeiture of status, life or land.

The account in 2 Chronicles 29 of Hezekiah's rededication of the Temple after Ahaz's מעל provides a covenient summary of the Chronicler's view of the significance of מעל and the range of concepts associated with it, and of the institutions ordained to deal with the situation caused by it. מעל is expounded in vv. 6-7:

> Our forebears have committed מעל, have done what is evil in the estimation of the LORD our God and have forsaken him: they have disregarded the dwelling-place of the LORD and have abandoned it; they have locked the doors of the porch; they have extinguished the lamps; they have not burned incense; they have not sacrificed holocaust in the sanctuary to the God of Israel.

The penalties are grimly recorded: the men have been slain in battle, and their widows and orphans have been carried off as captives (v. 9).

God has made of them an awesome object lesson for all to see (v. 8). What is the remedy? Hezekiah proposes a covenant (v. 10). The prerequisite is the rededication of the sanctuary by the removal of defilement (הנדה, v. 5; הטמאה, v. 16) and the performing of the appropriate rites of atonement. Holocausts of bulls, rams and lambs are offered by the priests and goats for a sin-offering (חטאת, v. 21), with which the king and the whole community identify themselves by the imposition of their hands (v. 23). All is done to the accompaniment of the liturgy intoned by the Levites and as approved by the prophets (v. 25). When the focus of community life has thus been reinaugurated, the round of ideal normal life can recommence. Thus in one incident the Chronicler lays bare profound forces underlying and unifying the disparate elements of Israel's life: king, priests, Levites, prophets and people are harmoniously integrated with one another in a national act of atonement.[12]

III

It is hardly surprising, then, that beyond the confines of the books of Chronicles this circle of ideas and institutions related to מעל is primarily associated with priestly theology and practice. For a full appreciation of the term it is, therefore, necessary to consider its place in priestly theories of atonement, so far as these can be determined, especially in the book of Leviticus. In principle, it would be relevant to consider the significance of all rites connected with the sin-offering (חטאת, Lev. 4.1–5.13; cf. 2 Chron. 29.21 referred to above) and the Day of Atonement (יום הכפרים, Lev. 16; 23.26-32; cf. לכפר in 2 Chron. 29.24). In practice, the regulations concerning מעל itself in Lev. 5.14-26 serve to impose some limitation on the discussion: the sacrifice to be offered on the occasion of מעל is the אשם ('guilt-offering'). The rites of the אשם are similar to those of the חטאת (so Lev. 7.1-7). Indeed, that the אשם is regarded as the sacrifice for the graver offence is indicated by the offering required: whereas for the חטאת a female goat or female lamb was the most required in the case of the individual (Lev. 4.27-35), for the אשם only a ram sufficed (Lev. 5.18).

A number of the elements in Lev. 5.14-26 appear to be of particular significance for the Chronicler's argument.

---

12. With what degree of acceptability to the parties involved is, of course, quite another matter.

1. מעל may be defined as the act of defrauding (cf. the examples listed in Lev. 5.21-24 of the ways in which one may wrongfully gain possession of another's property). It is always in principle committed against God. Even where it is an act of defrauding of one fellow-Israelite by another, for example, by embezzlement, extortion or theft (Num. 5.2, 27 adds adultery), it is regarded as an offence against God (Lev. 5.21), because it involves violation of an oath taken in the name of God,[13] who is, in any case, the framer of Israel's entire social order. But the primary act of מעל specified is when an individual is guilty of defrauding God of some of the sacred dues (הקדשים, Lev. 5.15); a convenient list of such sacred dues is to be found in Num. 18.8-24, which includes tithes, firstlings and first-fruits, as well as prescribed portions of sacrifice (the Mishnah tractate on the subject, *M^e'îlâ*, provides a much fuller list). The double guilt of מעל is again clearly in evidence: it is not merely the denying of others their rights; it is also the misappropriation of goods belonging to another for one's own use and benefit. Where God is the party wronged, as he always is in principle, the wrongdoer must be guilty of sacrilege.

2. It should not be thought that the קדשים belong merely to the externals of religion. Inasmuch as they are offered from the produce of the land, they are tokens of Israel's acknowledgment that God is the giver of the land, indeed of the life that that produce sustains. Deuteronomy 26.1-15 gives classic expression to these concepts. מעל is, consequently, greatly extended in meaning: it is not simply failure to offer הקדשים, the symbols of Israel's submissive obedience to the one on whom they totally depend for all they have and are; it is an expression of defiant disobedience and failure to acknowledge the source of their being and possessions. מעל extends beyond the symbol to the whole of life represented by the symbol. The point is made explicitly in the continuation of the discussion in Leviticus 5: 'If anyone sins and does any one of the things which ought not to be done in all the commandments of the LORD' (v. 17).[14]

---

13. Cf. B.M. Bokser, 'מעל and Blessings over Food', *JBL* 100 (1981), p. 561.

14. Cf. the comment by J. Milgrom, *Cult and Conscience* (Leiden: E.J. Brill, 1976), p. 80: 'The increased importance of the asham at the end of the second Temple bespeaks a development whose significance cannot be overestimated. Heretofore, man tended to dichotomize the world into the sacred and the profane, the discrete realms of the gods and man...With the promulgation of Lev. 5.17-19...whereby the unwitting violation of any of the Lord's commandments required

It is thus that מעל, as failure in rendering הקדשים and sacrilegious use of them, provides the Chronicler with a powerful category by which to explain Israel's predicament. Not surprisingly in the light of their Pentateuchal background, as מעל is a key root in the Chronicler's vocabulary, so also is קדש.[15] The two are brought together in the same contrast as in Lev. 5.15 in the Chronicler's summary on the climactic occurrence of מעל under Zedekiah:

> Indeed all the leaders [of Judah],[16] the priests and the people committed as much מעל as the nations abominably practised: they polluted (ויטמאו) the house of the LORD, which he had consecrated (הקדיש) in Jerusalem (2 Chron. 36.14).

The holiness, which Israel has profaned, is typically understood by the Chronicler in terms of the Temple, its personnel, rites and furnishings, and also of the sacred dues and, significantly in view of Achar's מעל בחרם, the spoils of war (e.g. 1 Chron. 18.10-11). Yet the wider implications of the term are included. The account of Hezekiah's reformation can again suffice for illustration (not least since more than half of the occurrences of the root in קדש in Chronicles [44 out of 80] are to be found in that section [2 Chron. 29–31]). Behind the idyllic picture of the sanctuary restored, the cult reinaugurated in accordance with the most punctilious observance of the law, the land purged, and the people

expiation for sancta desecration, the boundaries of the sacred and profane are obliterated for ever. Henceforth the sacred is unbounded; it is coextensive with the will of God. It embraces ethics as well as ritual, the relations between men and not just those between man and God. In short, the violation of any of the Torah's prohibitions constitutes sacrilege, *ma'al*, the expiation of which is essential for Israel to remain in divine grace.'

15. The distribution of the root קדש in the Hebrew Bible is instructive. Not counting the 11 occurrences of קָדֵשׁ (m. and f., sg. and pl.), or proper names derived from the root, it occurs some 775 times in the Hebrew Bible. The major concentrations are in Exod. 25–31, 35–40 (77×), Lev. (except H) (76×), H (63×), Num. (72×), Isa. 1–39 (32×), Isa. 40–66 (40×), Ezek. (93×), Pss. (65×), and Chronicles itself (80×). The 16× in Dan. and 14× in Neh. are also proportionally significant. At the intermediate level are the rest of Exod. (17×), Deut. (15×), Josh.–Kgs (41×), Jer. (19×). The statistics for the remainder are Gen. (1×), Hos. (2×), Joel (7×), Amos (4×), Obad. (2×), Jon. (2×), Mic. (2×), Nah. (2×), Hab. (3×), Zeph. (3×), Hagg. (2×), Zech. (6×), Mal. (1×), Job (6×), Prov. (2×), Eccl. (1×), Lam. (4×), Ezra (5×) (statistics on the basis of *VTC*).

16. Reading with *BHS*.

fulfilling all their obligations in the payment of the sacred dues, stands the larger reality of the restoration of an ideal and wholly sanctified common life, on which blessing showers down in abundance (2 Chron. 31.10). It is equally recognized that beyond the Temple and its cult lies the heavenly dwelling-place of God, of which the earthly is but the local physical counterpart (2 Chron. 30.27; cf. 1 Chron. 28.29). The roots מעל and קדש are understood in their widest sense: the 'holy things' are not merely sacred dues, which are but the externals of religion, ends in themselves; rather, their dedication symbolizes and expresses the consecration of Israel's entire life to God the giver of all. Israel is guilty of מעל, because it has failed both in the symbol and in the reality behind the symbol. Where God required consecration and sanctity, Israel responded with desecration and sacrilege.

3. Leviticus 5.15-26 specifies the necessary remedial action for מעל. Where the fraud involves goods, the guilty person has, naturally enough, to restore in full the amount due. In addition, he has to pay 20 per cent. The Hebrew Bible does not make clear the reason for this 'added fifth', whether it is conceived in terms of compensation to the wronged party, or the surrender of value illegitimately enjoyed by the guilty, or punishment aimed at deterring further similar acts by himself or others within the community or, indeed, all of these.

But the fact that the מעל is, in principle, committed against God raises the matter to an altogether more problematical level. How can God, the giver of all, be compensated? On what terms can the relationship with him, disturbed by the individual's unilateral act of faithlessness, be restored? Can atonement for the sacrilegious act be made? The legislation in Lev. 5.15-26 required the sacrifice of a ram as a guilt-offering (אשם) along with the restitution and the 'added fifth'. The rite of the אשם is described in Lev. 7.1-7. Again the significance of the details of the rite is never explained in the Hebrew Bible. As in all other Israelite sacrifices, the victim was selected from among the domesticated animals. It was an integral part of the householder's own possessions; indeed, as presumably a breeding ram, and in any case fit for human consumption, upon it in part at least the support of the household might be said to depend. By its very nature, the victim was also a representative part of the household and its life. It is not clear whether the imposition of hands by the offerer on the head of the victim was a further symbol of its representative function; whether, indeed, there was implied an identification of the offerer with the victim, a substitution by the victim for the offerer, or an imparting to the victim of the guilt of the offerer or, again, whether there are elements of all included. What is clear is the emphasis on the grace of God. The guilty is aware that restoration of the relationship with God is not worked mechanically but depends upon God's gracious choice; humans cannot coerce God into forgiveness, nor can they wrest favour from him. Despite sacrifice, forgiveness may be withheld (cf. Hos. 8.11-14). All that the individual can hope for is the gracious acceptance of God, symbolized by the smoke of the burnt portion of the sacrifice ascending into the heavens, consumed by the fire, which is, in principle, God's own gift (Lev. 9.24; the point is made by the Chronicler in 2 Chron. 7.1, 3; cf. 1 Kgs 18.24, 38).

It is against this background of the guilt of מעל and its expiation that the fundamental purpose of the great central section of the Chronicler's work on the reigns of David and Solomon (1 Chron. 11–2 Chron. 9) can be appreciated. If Israel's life from start to finish is riddled with מעל, then the rearing of the altar of sacrifice, where atonement is effected, is cardinal for the continued life of Israel.

The Chronicler's design is heightened by the function of 1 Chronicles 21 in the overall structure of his work. The chapter concerns the reason for the ultimate choice of location for the altar of sacrifice, where the guilt of the Israelites may be expiated. It is the guilt of David himself, the king and cult-founder, which determines the selection. As David's adultery with Bathsheba is the hinge of the presentation of the reign of David in 2 Samuel (2 Sam. 11–12), so David's census of the people in 1 Chronicles 21, the presumptuous act of numbering the people of God, is the pivot of the presentation of the reign of David in 1 Chronicles. Before the census, David with immediacy of access to God functions as high-priest, clad in ephod and linen garments, before the ark (1 Chron. 15–16). But with the census all is changed: David himself incurs guilt, as is explicitly stated in 1 Chron. 21.3, in the words of Joab, again not in the Chronicler's underlying source in 2 Samuel 24, 'Why should my lord the king bring guilt (אשמה) upon Israel?' The aftermath was the terrible plague. But the angel of the Lord stayed his hand at the threshing floor of Ornan, and there David reared the altar of burnt-offering, which thenceforward was to be the place of sacrifice, where atonement between God and people was to be effected. But the result of David's guilt was loss of immediacy of access to God. As the Chronicler notes in 1 Chron. 21.29–22.1, in sentences that

inaugurate the Chronicler's independent account of David's measures
to found the cult in Jerusalem in 1 Chron. 21.27–29.30:

> The altar of holocaust was at that time at the high place at Gibeon. But
> David could not come before it to consult God because he was afraid of
> the sword of the angel of the LORD. So he said, '*This* is the house of the
> LORD God; *this* is the altar of holocausts for Israel.'

The Chronicler could have scarcely more eloquently stated his theme:
at the centre of Israel's guilt-laden life, as supremely indicated in the
very life of David the ideal king himself, there is raised the altar where
that guilt itself may be expiated. Where guilt occurs, there God himself
graciously provides the means of atonement. The Chronicler does not
neglect, therefore, to note, in words that are again his own, that, when
David had built the altar, the LORD 'answered him with fire from
heaven' (1 Chron. 21.26), the symbol of the LORD's gracious acceptance. It is hardly surprising that in 2 Chron. 3.1, with reference back to
1 Chronicles 21, the Chronicler alone in the Hebrew Bible picks up
from the story of Abraham's sacrifice of Isaac in Genesis 22 the name
of Moriah for the Temple Mount, the place where the LORD provides.

The Chronicler is, however, aware that the problem of the guilt of
Israel is altogether more serious than the situation envisaged in Lev.
5.15-26. There are two features in the legislation on מעל and its expiation, which make it not directly applicable to Israel's case: first, Lev.
5.15-26 concerns only the individual, not the nation; secondly, and
even more seriously, it concerns inadvertent מעל. By contrast, Israel on
the Chronicler's argument is guilty of corporate and deliberate מעל.
The inexcusability of Israel's national, wilful guilt is emphasized by the
Chronicler's theory of the centrality of the Levites, to be noted below,
and of the role of the prophets (in summary in 2 Chron. 36.15-16). If
the condition of the individual inadvertently guilty of מעל is precari-
ous, entirely dependent on the gracious decision of God, how much
more must Israel's be? If the fate of the individual, who, like Achar,
was guilty of defrauding God deliberately ('with a high hand', Num.
5.30), was summary extirpation from the community, what then was to
become of Israel?

The Chronicler is not the first in the Hebrew Bible to grapple with
this problem of the punishment, survival and restoration of Israel, corporately and wilfully guilty of מעל. He stands in the tradition pioneered
by the priestly writer of Leviticus 26 (where מעל explicitly occurs in
v. 40) and by the priest-prophet Ezekiel (see n. 9). The penalty for such

deliberate מעל in the case of the individual is summary extirpation to expiate the sacrilege in the holy things, and to restore and preserve the sanctity of the community symbolized by the precise rendering of the duty owed to the giver of the land. Where the whole community is guilty of such מעל, the total profanation of the community leaves no margin of sanctity for the rendering of the holy things, which are the tokens of Israel's dutiful response, let alone fit material for the payment of the 'added fifth'. The consequence must be the forfeiture by the entire community of the land for which they have so totally failed to show gratitude. In Leviticus 26 this forfeiture is interpreted in terms of the sabbatical years of which the land has been deprived, while in Ezekiel 20 Israel is represented as reverting to its condition before the conquest of the land of wandering in the wilderness, now understood typologically as the 'wilderness of the nations'.

It may be doubted whether the Chronicler advances much the thinking already found in Leviticus and Ezekiel on Israel's predicament as guilty of national, premeditated מעל. What the Chronicler is doing is to apply these ready-made categories as 'hermeneutical key' to the interpretation of Israel's past history and understanding of her present state: the Chronicler matches Ezekiel's typological 'wilderness of the nations' with his own typological 'exile', in which he perceives Israel still to languish. Using the materials of Israel's past history in a suprahistorical way, the Chronicler expounds in narrative form the teaching of both law and prophets on the guilt of Israel and its destructive consequences. If one were to be bold, one would say that, as the 'Deuteronomistic History' from Deuteronomy to 2 Kings constitutes an aggadic *midrash* on the Levitical doctrine of the blessing and curse of the covenant, so Chronicles constitutes an aggadic *midrash* on the complementary Levitical (including priestly) doctrine of guilt and atonement.[17] In the contemporary phase of scholarship, when much attention is being directed to Deuteronomy, the 'Deuteronomistic History' and the 'Deuteronomistic School', it is not inappropriate to redress the balance by drawing attention to this complementary presentation of Israel's history in the work of the Chronicler.

There is a further analogy between the work of the 'Deuteronomistic School' and that of the Chronicler. As in the end of the day the 'Deuteronomistic School' found itself constrained to transcend its

17. Cf. J. Milgrom's identification of an 'aggadic Midrash' on the law of sancta desecration in Jer. 2.3 (*Cult and Conscience*, pp. 70-71).

doctrine of covenant and await a final act of God himself, when God would 'both will and do of his good pleasure' by circumcising the heart of his people and writing the covenant code on that heart renewed (Deut. 30.6; Jer. 31.31-34),[18] so the Chronicler, the latest representative of the Levitical-priestly school, is forced to look beyond the limits of his theological category, not to the destruction of Israel, fully required though that would be for its colossal fraud, inherited and compounded generation by generation, but to its restoration through an act of the free grace of God already implied in the אשם for individual, inadvertent guilt, now prevailing immeasurably more for Israel's corporate, wilful guilt. He does not see that this restoration has yet taken place, any more than the Deuteronomist sees the fulfilment of his expectation of the new covenant. Meantime, though the return from the exile is, historically speaking, long past, theologically speaking, Israel is still 'in exile', still poised on the verge of 'the Return' proper (just as Deuteronomy leaves Israel poised on the verge of the settlement in the Promised Land). As Israel awaits the dawning of that day, it must seek to realize that total sanctity of life, untainted by any מעל sacrilege, which is its divinely willed destiny.

IV

The argument up until now has largely concerned the narrative section of Chronicles from 1 Chronicles 10. In conclusion, it may be appropriate to consider something of the function in the Chronicler's purpose of the genealogical section, 1 Chronicles 1–9, which presents such a formidable obstacle to the reader.[19] As has been noted above, the thematic term מעל has already been enunciated in the genealogical section; indeed, it binds the whole together. From start to finish, on West Bank and on East, Israel's history has been blighted by מעל (1 Chron. 2.7; 5.25; 9.1).

18. My indebtedness to W. Thiel, *Die deuteronomistische Redaktion von Jeremiah 26–45* (WMANT, 52; Neukirchen–Vluyn: Neukirchener Verlag, 1981) is obvious.

19. Thus *The Reader's Bible* (gen. ed. B.M. Metzger; London, 1983) retains only fragments of some 20 of the 407 verses of 1 Chron. 1–9. Lord Coggan writes in the Foreword (p. xi) that the book, 'shorn of...such things as long genealogies...just because of this, is more likely to convey the essence of what the Bible is really about'. If my interpretation is right, it is precisely this 'shearing' that will condemn Chronicles to continued misunderstanding.

Four major themes are handled in 1 Chronicles 1–9: the universal context of Israel's life; the divinely ordained ordering of Israel's life so that its destiny as God's people can be realized; the ideal vitiated by Israel; the necessary remedial action.

1. The work opens by setting the descendants of Abraham within the context of the whole family of humankind. The genealogical material, which the Chronicler freely quarries from Genesis, is wholly congenial to the Chronicler's developing theme (it is safe to assume that, throughout, he presupposes the narrative material in Genesis as well; e.g. 1 Chron. 1.27 clearly alludes to the narrative of Gen. 17.4-5). The history of humankind as a whole is characterized from the beginning by a pattern of false starts and abortive restarts, as God's original plan is vitiated by rebellious man and his new arrangement, by which his intention may yet be fulfilled, is again thwarted. Already in the first two names of the work in 1 Chron. 1.1 there is a premonition: Adam, the primal man, is succeeded by his third son Seth, whose very name means 'the substitute one' (cf. Gen. 4.25). In the tenth generation, Noah, the second father of humankind, is reached (1 Chron. 1.4). In 1 Chronicles 1, the Chronicler allows himself four evaluative comments on the character of this emerging world of the nations: in their pursuit of war (v. 10) and nationalism (v. 19), they are the origin of the powers which threatened Israel both physically (v. 11) and ideologically (v. 43). After a further ten generations there springs, from one of the three branches of Noah's descendants, Abraham, and, in turn, from one of the three branches of his descendants, Israel. Out of the broad mass of humanity, a single family has now been chosen; Israel is to realize on behalf of humankind what humankind as a whole cannot. But lurking in the background stands the world of the nations, from which Israel springs and to which it is kin. Israel's pursuit of the ideal is constantly threatened by reversion to that 'wilderness of the nations', from which it took its origins, or by invasion from these destructive nations. It is notable how often in Chronicles Israel's מעל is visited by the incursion of a foreign force (already in 1 Chron. 5.26). The ideal relationship between Israel and the world of the nations is portrayed in 1 Chronicles 14, where the gathering of all Israel to David (1 Chron. 11–13) is crowned by the recognition and pacification of the nations of the world (1 Chron. 14.17, yet another of the Chronicler's original statements).

2. The Chronicler then proceeds in 1 Chronicles 2–8 to portray Israel in its ideal tribal structure. He begins, conventionally enough in 1 Chron. 2.1-2, with a list of the 12 tribes in the order familiar from Gen. 35.23-25; Exod. 1.2-4 (except that Dan is now placed between the 'Leah' and 'Rachel' tribes, instead of following the latter). But thereafter (1 Chron. 2.3–8.40) he follows an entirely different sequence. Again its uniqueness may be taken to confirm that it reflects his specific purpose. The intention behind it becomes relatively clear, when it is tabulated as follows:

Judah Simeon	Reuben Gad Half-Manasseh	Levi	Issachar Benjamin Naphtali Half-Manasseh Ephraim Asher	Benjamin

The reason for this singular disposition of the tribes of Israel[20] is presumably that Judah (with Simeon incorporated) and Benjamin, the two tribes of the Southern Kingdom of Judah, were the elements of the whole nation, which endured the longest in their territories, surviving until the exile of 587 (but see also below under point 4). They form the enclosing bracket whereby the more vulnerable elements, Reuben, Gad and Half-Manasseh on the East Bank, and the remaining tribes in the North, are enclosed and thus have their status as permanent members of the Israelite tribal system, though 'in exile', preserved, at least ideologically, if not practically.

The major point of interest is, however, the centrality of Levi. The role of the Levites is, in the Chronicler's view, quite literally, central to Israel's life.[21] In what way they are central is indicated by his treatment of them in 1 Chron. 5.27–6.66. After noting the descent of the priests through Aaron from Kohath son of Levi (5.27-41) and the descent of the remaining Levites in the conventional order of the sons of Levi,

---

20. The absence of Dan and the repetition of Benjamin will be discussed below.

21. This device of central location to indicate prominence and leadership is used quite widely by the Chronicler, e.g. the House of David (1 Chron. 3.1-24) within Judah (1 Chron. 2.6–4.23), Solomon within David's sons, even to the extent of the Chronicler's making up the number of 19 to get the pattern 9–1–9 (1 Chron. 3.1-8). So also, as in the Pentateuch, in the case of the sons of Levi (see text below).

Gershom, Kohath and Merari (6.1-15), the section culminates in the specification of the chief duties of the Levites in the sanctuary (the music of the liturgy and the service at the altar, 6.16-38) and the settlements assigned to the Levites throughout the other tribes. Clearly for the Chronicler the means whereby Israel is to maintain its identity and sanctity as the people of God is the central ministry of the Levites, both as priests and officiants at the central altar and as teachers of the law in the 48 Levitical cities dispersed throughout the entire body of Israel. It is through the ministrations of the Levites, living in the midst, that all the duty that Israel owes to God will be performed.

Again the Chronicler points up his meaning by a characteristic addition to his underlying source. He begins his list of Levitical settlements in 1 Chron. 6.39 with a phrase not present in the parent list in Josh. 21.10-42: 'The following are their settlements according to their טירות throughout their territory.' By the comparatively rare word, טירות 'dwellings', used only seven times in the Hebrew Bible, typically in connection with nomadic populations (e.g. Ishmael, Gen. 25.16; Midian, Num. 31.10; 'sons of the east', Ezek. 25.4), the Chronicler stresses that the Levites remain as pastors of flocks with grazing grounds (מגרשים) in the midst of the tribes settled in their agricultural lands and are, therefore, dependent like the other landless ones on the tithes (part of the קדשים!) rendered by the community. As such, the Levites would become immediately aware of מעל, any shortfall in the payment of the sacred dues, on the part of Israel.

The ideal constitution of Israel has thus been stated: the community lives clustered round the Levites living in the midst, both centrally and in dispersion throughout the length and breadth of the land. It is to be remarked how comparable this system of the Chronicler is to other equally ideological systems of the Levites in the midst in the priestly materials in Numbers 2, 7 and 10 and in the priest-prophet Ezekiel (ch. 48). In 1 Chron. 5.20b, 22a, the Chronicler gives an example of the ideal trusting obedience of Israel to God, which he has in mind.

3. But Israel, chosen to realize on their behalf what the rest of humankind cannot, immediately vitiates the divinely ordained ideal order. Even within Israel, the same vicious pattern of false start and abortive restart is amply in evidence. Beyond the familiar examples of over-reaching and supplanting of Esau by Jacob, or of Manasseh by Ephraim, the Chronicler has others to cite. He begins his muster of the tribes with Judah (1 Chron. 2.3–4.23). But he is well aware that Reuben

should come first by right of primogeniture, but had forfeited that right by a deplorable act of incest. He knows, too, the tradition that, subsequently, the birthright was allotted to the House of Joseph. Nonetheless, he elevates Judah to first place in virtue of its military strength, as evidenced above all in the leadership of the House of David (1 Chron. 5.1-2). But, even after all these adjustments, the same pattern of the failure of the favoured first choice and his replacement by a secondary repeats itself. Judah's first three sons spring from a disastrous liaison with a Canaanite woman (one may recall that in Ezra–Nehemiah מעל is used above all of intermarriage between Israelite and non-Israelite, which is condemned as the contamination of the 'holy seed' [Ezra 9.2, 4; 10.2, 6, 10; Neh. 13.27]). The two oldest ones mark the false start and are eliminated; the third is relegated to the end of the Chronicler's account of Judah's progeny (1 Chron. 4.21-23). Even then, the replacement main line springs from the most dubious of circumstances. The Chronicler presupposes the narrative of Genesis 38 (1 Chron. 2.3a is freely composed from Gen. 38.1-5; v. 3b is virtually identical with Gen. 38.7), which records the irregular birth of Judah's two later sons by his daughter-in-law, twins who, like Jacob and Esau, are to be contentious from the womb, with the younger, Perez, from whom David is descended, ousting the originally intended elder, Zerah. It is from Achar, a scion of the latter branch of the House of Judah, which is itself the replacement leader of Israel at several removes, that immediately the first, trend-setting act of מעל arises (1 Chron. 2.7).

There are a number of details in 1 Chronicles 2–8 that stress Israel's מעל and its deadly effects. As has just been noted, 1 Chron. 5.20b, 22a provides an example of the ideal trusting obedience that Israel ought to have accorded God. The same passage continues to show how such reliance on God was soon abandoned in the perfidious turning to other gods, whose powerlessness before the LORD had first been exposed and acknowledged. The consequences of such treachery are that the East Bank tribes languish in exile from their forfeited land 'until this day' (v. 26). This act of מעל is then brought into immediate juxtaposition with the role of the Levites as officiants at the altar and as teachers throughout the land in 1 Chron. 5.27–6.66. But, by recording the names of Nadab and Abihu, the two eldest sons of Aaron, the archetypal chief priest descended from the central son of Levi, who were extirpated from the priesthood because of their irregular practice (Lev. 10.1-3), the Chronicler does not flinch from acknowledging that even among the

Levites, the fulfillers of the central role for the hallowing, and, therefore, for the well-being, of their people, the same pattern of false start is
reproduced. It is perhaps, then, not accidental that the line of the priesthood is traced in 1 Chron. 5.26-41 only as far as Jehozadak, the high-
priest carried off into exile by Nebuchadnezzar. Nothing could emphasize more clearly that the mere rites of the altar as such can neither
suffice nor avail to expunge the guilt even of its own officiants.

Another detail that may expose the fatal power of מעל is the omission of any mention of the tribe of Dan in the Chronicler's tribal system
in 1 Chron. 2.3–8.40. While Dan is mentioned in 1 Chron. 2.2, in
material derived from Genesis 35 and Exodus 1, as noted above, it fails
to recur in the subsequent detailed genealogical lists.[22] The omission is
not likely to be accidental: in 1 Chron. 6.46, there is a barely comprehensible text, 'And to the remaining Kohathites there were assigned by
lot ten cities from the clan of the tribe, from the half of the tribe of the
half of Manasseh', while Josh. 21.5, the parent text from which this
verse is derived, records with total intelligibility, 'And to the remaining
Kohathites there were assigned by lot ten cities from the clans of the
tribe of Ephraim and from the tribe of Dan and from the half of the
tribe of Manasseh.' The reason for the elimination of Dan is surely not
far to seek: unlike the East Bank tribes, whose מעל according to Joshua
22 consisted in their erecting an altar not for sacrifice but only as a
reminder of their devotion to the LORD, the Danites were the origina-
tors of a sanctuary of their own self-conceiving, in which a full-scale
and idolatrous cult was practised (Judg. 17–18) and which was eventually to become the focus of the schismatic and apostate kingdom of the
North.[23] The one who is guilty of מעל must suffer forfeiture and elimination, so that the community can be protected from the contagion of
uncleanness.

4. But the ideal vitiated is not the end of the matter. By his layout of
the genealogical material, the Chronicler indicates the divinely intended
remedy. It is thus that the oddity of the repetition of the genealogy of

22. There may be a vestigial trace in 1 Chron. 7.12: Hushim appears as a Danite
in Gen. 46.23. Aher may then not be a proper name but the adjective 'another', an
oblique reference to Dan, avoiding mention of the accursed name (so already
Bertheau, according to BDB).

23. N.H. Snaith, *Leviticus and Numbers* (NCB; London: Nelson, 1967), on Lev.
24.11, points out that Dan is omitted from the list of the 12 tribes of Israel in Rev.
7.5-8.

Benjamin can be fully explained. The repetition of Benjamin is only part of a series of interweavings of material in 1 Chronicles 7–10, which may be most conveniently presented diagrammatically (see below).

7.6-12	genealogy of Benjamin
7.13-40	genealogy of the northern tribes
8.1-27a	genealogy of Benjamin
8.28b	opening list of inhabitants of Jerusalem
8.29-40	the Benjaminites of Gibeon (family of Saul)
9.1a	conclusion of the ideal tribal muster
9.1b	the ideal marred
9.2	the primal ideal
9.3-9	the inter-tribal population of Jerusalem (Judah, Benjamin, Ephraim, Manasseh)
9.10-13	the priests resident in Jerusalem
9.14-34a	the Levites resident in Jerusalem
9.34b	= 8.28b
9.35-44	= 8.29-38 [*sic*]
10.1-14	the reign of Saul
11.1-9	the accession of David; Jerusalem the capital

An immediate, unambiguous point that can be made about this table is that there is repetition of material: 8.28b = 9.34b; 8.29-38 = 9.35-44. The reason for this repetition is, surely, not difficult to infer. The repeated material concerns, on the one hand, the population of Jerusalem, and, on the other, the family of Saul. Both are in origin Benjaminite (for Jerusalem as a Benjaminite city, cf. the definition of tribal boundaries in Josh. 18.11-28; apart from the Chronicler's genealogies, the Benjaminite origin of Saul is recognized in 1 Sam. 9.1-2); both are, therefore, appropriately included in connection with the genealogies of

Benjamin in 1 Chronicles 8. But both receive a supra-Benjaminite significance. In the immediately ensuing chapter (1 Chron. 10), in which the Chronicler begins his historical narrative proper, tracing the theme of guilt and atonement, it is Saul, the Benjaminite, who provides the Chronicler with his first example of מעל. But by this interweaving of materials the Chronicler associates with that, namely the first breakdown of the ideal order intended by God for his people, the new supratribal significance of the old Benjaminite city of Jerusalem, the place where the new centralized atonement cult will be introduced. The intention is expressed with great clarity: where Israel falls into guilt, there God provides the means of atonement. The reason that Benjamin appears last in the tribal genealogies is, therefore, not merely that Benjamin, as one of the last survivors, constitutes an enclosing bracket around the more vulnerable northern tribes; rather, it is that Benjamin provides the Chronicler with the double link of both guilt and atonement forward into this account of Israel's history.

Had the old model of the constitution of Israel (decentralized tribal life, hallowed by the presence of the Levites indwelling in the midst) remained intact, the tribal muster could well have ended at 1 Chron. 7.40, before the second appearance of Benjamin. The tribal muster would then have been sufficiently complete to justify the statement in 1 Chron. 9.1a, 'So all Israel was enrolled by genealogical descent' and the ideal portrayed in 1 Chron. 9.2, 'The original settlers, who were in their holdings in their cities, were the Israelites, the priests, the levites and the *nᵉtînîm*.' But the ideal has been destroyed by מעל; Judah is in exile (1 Chron. 9.1b).

Within the new context of the ideal marred, the climax to the genealogical section is now the new population of Jerusalem. The citizens are now drawn from several tribes, not merely from Benjamin (1 Chron. 9.3-9). The list passes swiftly to the chief inhabitants of the city, the priests, who officiate at the altar in the new House of God, at which atonement can be effected (1 Chron. 9.10-13). At first sight, it then seems a crass anticlimax that the portrayal of the new centralized order, through which the crisis provoked by Israel's מעל is to be handled, should culminate in the families and duties of the non-priestly Levites, in particular in their role as custodians of the Temple storehouses (1 Chron. 9.26-32). In fact, however, this conclusion exactly fits the Chronicler's theme. מעל, in the legislation of Lev. 5.15-26, concerns precisely the violation of the holy things, the supreme, tangible

token of Israel's rendering of its duty towards God as the giver of the
land and the possibilities of life within it. It is to the storehouses of the
Temple that such holy things were brought to the Levites to confirm
that Israel's duty towards God had been completely fulfilled.[24] Atonement for sacrilege is not an end in itself: it is the necessary means
whereby Israel, made for sanctity, can regain its status as holy. Atonement was made for Israel, not Israel for atonement.[25]

As a postscript, it may be commented that the Chronicler's thesis is
hardly unexpected. After the excitement and disappointments of the
'Zionist' phase of Israel's history from Second Isaiah to Ezra–Nehemiah, it is hardly surprising that, faced with the apparently meagre
achievements of the restoration period, the Chronicler, in a way no
doubt representative of many within the community, looks for a more
ultimate 'Return', not only for the thousands still in the Diaspora but
even for those physically present in the land. But this 'Return' and the
ending of the present 'exile' depend on atonement, an act in which the
initiative lies always and only in God himself. Meantime, in waiting for
that day, at the dawning of which Israel stands poised, it is levitical
instruction on Israel's duty toward God and the levitical custodianship
of the rendering of that duty that must stand at the heart of the community's life. Beyond the scrupulous rendering to God of every obliga-
tion due to him, the community waits in quiet expectation for the
restoration, which God alone can accomplish.[26]

---

24. The אצרות, 'storehouses', are specified in 1 Chron. 9.26. The occurrence of
the אוצר יהוה in Josh. 6.19 in the context of the חרם, in connection with which
Achan/r was guilty of מעל, is striking.

25. There may be added relevance, then, in the fact that Chronicles was one of
the works read out to the high-priest on the eve of the Day of Atonement (*m. Yôm.*
1.6; see Danby, *The Mishnah*, p. 163).

26. For an analysis of the rhythms of Zionism and the study of Torah in contemporary Judaism, see Neusner, *Between Time and Eternity*, pp. 171ff.

Chapter 5

THE USE OF LEVITICUS IN CHRONICLES*

Some years ago, I suggested that Leviticus supplies the Chronicler with his central theme: guilt and atonement.[1] Israel's guilt, according to the Chronicler, consists in מעל (conventionally, 'unfaithfulness' [NRSV]); for an exposition of מעל we have to turn to Lev. 5.14-26. But there מעל is not only defined; it is placed within the context of the אשם (conventionally 'guilt-offering' [NRSV]), and it is the אשם that opens the possibility of atonement for מעל.

In the interim, the massive commentary on Chronicles by Sara Japhet has appeared, which is surely destined to be a major point of reference in Chronicles study for years to come.[2] In her commentary, Japhet maintains that the connection between Chronicles and Leviticus on this point is merely verbal; the usage is entirely different in the two works. She writes: 'The root [מעל], which is used mainly in a limited technical meaning in the Priestly literature...takes on a very general meaning in Chronicles, covering the whole range of man's sins against God.'[3] It is

---

*   Originally published in J.F.A. Sawyer (ed.), *Reading Leviticus: A Conversation with Mary Douglas* (JSOTSup, 227; Sheffield: Sheffield Academic Press, 1996), pp. 243-55, adapted for this collection.

1.   See Chapter 4.

2.   S. Japhet, *I & II Chronicles* (OTL; London: SCM Press, 1993). This work has to be read in tandem (as Japhet herself explicitly states on p. 43) with her earlier work, *The Ideology of the Book of Chronicles and its Place in Biblical Thought* (Beiträge zur Erforschung des Alten Testaments und des antiken Judentums, 9; Bern: Peter Lang, 1989 [original Hebrew 1977]). These works provide a compendium of discussion of all manner of issues that is as impressive as it is invaluable, and I have gone on record in praise of the latter ('Which Is the Best Commentary? 11: The Chronicler's Work', *ExpTim* 102 [1990–91], pp. 6-11). They are, nonetheless, seriously flawed, I believe, in overall conception.

3.   Japhet, *I & II Chronicles*, pp. 229-30 in connection with 1 Chron. 10.13. She does not discuss Lev. 5 in *Ideology*, though the point is referred to on p. 202 n. 10: 'Regarding Priestly language, it must be noted that the meaning of a phrase

perhaps, then, apposite to reconsider the question whether there is or is
not a connection between Leviticus and Chronicles on this point and, if
possible, to defend and to develop my view in conversation with
Japhet's work.

Now, whether or not the connection between Chronicles and Leviticus through מעל can be maintained, I must insist on the centrality of the
concept for Chronicles.[4] The distribution and use of מעל in Chronicles
is striking:

1. It binds together the genealogies of Israel in 1 Chron. 2.1–9.1,
where it occurs three times in the relatively rare narrative sections or
evaluative comments, and each of these times is at an absolutely critical
moment in Israel's history:

   (a)   1 Chronicles 2.7, at the moment when Israel first sets foot in
         the land, Achar of Judah is guilty of מעל, by stealing some of
         the spoils of Jericho dedicated as חרם to the LORD;
   (b)   1 Chronicles 5.25, to account for the loss of the settlements of
         Reuben, Gad and Half-Manasseh on the East Bank;
   (c)   1 Chronicles 9.1, to account for the final loss of the land by
         Judah in the exile.

On West Bank and on East, from first to last, Israel has been guilty of
מעל, and it is מעל that accounts for Israel's forfeiture of the land and
exile.

2. This theme, having been enunciated in the genealogies, is
expounded at length in the narrative section of the work, where the root
occurs a further 14 times.[5] The use and distribution in the narrative
section is equally significant, in my view, to that in the genealogies:

   (a)   Despite the extensive parallels in the narrative section to
         Samuel–Kings, מעל only occurs in material peculiar to Chron-
         icles and may, thus, be legitimately regarded as diagnostic of
         his view.
   (b)   The distribution in the narrative section is particularly interest-
         ing: it accounts for the death of Saul (1 Chron. 10.13-14); it

when used in Chronicles may not correspond to its original technical definition.
The correspondence is one of literary form rather than content.'
   4.   The point is not pursued by Japhet; she does not annotate the word, for
example, on its first occurrence in 1 Chron. 2.7 (*I & II Chronicles*, pp. 75-76).
   5.   1 Chron. 10.13 (2×); 2 Chron. 12.2; 26.16, 18; 28.19 (2×), 22; 29.6, 19;
30.7; 33.19; 36.14 (2×).

then leaps over the reigns of David and Solomon (1 Chron. 11–2 Chron. 9) without mention but reappears in Rehoboam (2 Chron. 12.2), whence it continues its deadly path until it culminates in the Fall of Jerusalem in 2 Chron. 36.14.

3. The omission of מעל in the account of David and Solomon is to be explained by the fact that they approximate to the Chronicler's ideal of monarchy—but only 'approximate' in the case of David. The hinge event in the Chronicler's presentation of David's reign is David's census of the people in 1 Chronicles 21, where David incurs guilt (אשמה, v. 3). The explanation for the heinousness of the crime of counting the people the Chronicler gives in 1 Chron. 27.23: it is to count the people of God who, he had promised, would be as many as the stars in the heavens.

Incidentally, the topic of David's census in 1 Chronicles 21 gives me an opportunity to state the obvious, that Chronicles is presupposing much more material in the Pentateuch than Leviticus, as the use of genealogies in 1 Chronicles 1–9 from Genesis and Exodus (and Joshua and Nehemiah) already shows. 1 Chronicles 21 itself provides two examples of the use of Exodus. (a) I suspect that behind the outrage at David's census lies, in part, the legislation on the muster of the people (root פקד), in Exod. 30.11-16: there *is* a way to muster the people which already involves atonement (cf. the variations on the root פקד, 1 Chron. 21.5-6, plus 18 further times in Chronicles). (b) Another very striking feature of 1 Chronicles 21 is the use of the Passover motif of the משחית, the 'destroyer', of Exod. 12.13, 23, only this time turned in a 'negative Passover' against Israel itself (v. 12). This motif is then quite widely used in Chronicles (e.g. in the Egyptian invasion in the time of Rehoboam, 2 Chron. 12.2-12). But all that is another story.[6]

To resume: the term מעל does not occur in Chronicles under David and Solomon. But David's census provides opportunity for the use of the term 'guilt' (אשמה, 1 Chron. 21.3), which, of course, immediately relates the discussion again to מעל in Lev. 5.14-26. For it is precisely the so-called guilt-offering, אשם (better, I think, 'reparation-offering'), which provides the mechanism for dealing with מעל. Thus the immediate outcome of David's אשמה is the building of the altar of sacrifice on the threshing floor of Ornan (1 Chron. 22.1). At the place where guilt is incurred, there, up to a point at any rate—for David's status is

---

6. Developed in Chapter 6 below.

catastrophically changed from now on—the means of atonement is provided.

Admittedly, there are differences in the use of מעל in Chronicles from that in the immediate legislation in Leviticus, as I earlier acknowledged.[7] There are at least three such differences:

1. In the Leviticus legislation on the 'guilt-offering', the מעל is inadvertent; in Chronicles it is deliberate. Chronicles is, indeed, at pains to develop the theme of the consciousness of Israel of their guilt because of the ministry of the prophets.[8] The prophetic ministry is twofold:

(a)   the prophets have recorded in writing an unbroken *midrash* on the reigns of the kings of Judah in every generation down to the reign of Jehoiakim[9] (by *midrash* is meant here a critical account of events from a theological perspective);

(b)   the prophetic word (not always spoken through those officially designated prophets but through those who are prophetic in function)[10] has been communicated to every generation virtually without fail.

7.   Chapter 4, p. 104.

8.   It is this continuous and cumulative raising of consciousness through the generations to bring to repentance and in order to display the long-suffering patience of God that has been the function of the prophets, rather than merely 'warning' delivered *seriatim* to each generation, as on Japhet's argument (*Ideology*, pp. 176-91; the gaps in the series provide her, therefore, with some problems, p. 190 n. 561).

9.   I am assuming that, though there are some eight varieties in the terms used for the record of the reigns of the kings of Judah, they all refer to essentially the same enterprise. This is twice termed *midrash*—'the commentary of the prophet Iddo' on Abijah (2 Chron. 13.22) and 'the commentary on the book of the kings' for Joash (2 Chron. 24.27).

10.   Sometimes it is very generally stated (Ahaziah in 2 Chron. 22.7; Manasseh in 2 Chron. 33.10, 18). Most typically it is the prophets themselves (Shemaiah to Rehoboam; Oded to Asa; Micaiah ben Imlah and Jehu ben Hanani to Jehoshaphat; Elijah to Jehoram; Zechariah ben Jehoiada, among others unnamed, to Joash; an anonymous prophet to Amaziah; Isaiah to Hezekiah; Huldah to Josiah; Jeremiah to Zedekiah). But sometimes it is the priests (to Uzziah), occasionally the kings themselves (Abijah, Hezekiah). Sometimes it has been a non-Judaean prophet (Oded to Ahaz), sometimes even a foreign king, who has been not only God's instrument of punishment but even his spokesman (Neco to Josiah). Only very occasionally is no such intervention recorded (Jotham, and, naturally, in the light of the Chronicler's view of when the exile begins [see below], Jehoahaz, Jehoiakim and Jehoiachin).

2. Leviticus legislates for the מעל of the individual; in Chronicles the unfaithfulness is corporate and compounded generation by generation.

3. In Leviticus the unfaithfulness consists, in the main, in the defrauding of God in 'holy things', offerings in kind (such as are listed in Num. 18).[11] These are the tokens of the consecration of the whole of life. In Chronicles the defrauding of God consists not merely in the tokens but in that very totality of life.

At first sight at least, these differences between the uses of מעל in Leviticus and in Chronicles may, indeed, support the contention of Sara Japhet, quoted above: 'The root...used mainly in a limited technical meaning in the Priestly literature...takes on a very general meaning in Chron.'. I should like to maintain that, nonetheless, the use of מעל in Leviticus remains fundamental to the Chronicler's work. The reason for so arguing comes from two passages in Leviticus itself:

1. Leviticus itself broadens the applicability of מעל in 5.14-26, beyond the 'limited technical meaning' (the immediate reference to fraud in 'holy things'): specifically in v. 17, where it is extended to failure in 'any one of all the commandments of the LORD' (though there the trespass remains inadvertent).

2. More tellingly, Leviticus itself broadens the applicability of its own category of מעל in precisely the same way, it seems to me, as that in which Chronicles uses it. This broadening is to be found in Lev. 26.40,[12] precisely at the end of the Holiness Code, which encompasses all life, in the promise of blessing and the threat of curse which constitute the inducements to lead the holy life. It is not a matter of isolated verbal coincidence. The conceptual framework is the same: for example, the necessity for 'humbling oneself', acknowledging that one is in the wrong, before there is any possibility of atonement (כנע, Lev. 26.41; cf. 2 Chron. 7.14; 12.6-7).

The point being made in Leviticus 26 is that there *is* no possibility of atonement for Israel because of its מעל, at least not immediately. The

---

11. The importance of 'holy things' is well recognized in Leviticus: e.g. Lev. 22.1-16. The stress there on appropriate handling is matched in 2 Chron. 31. But—again—there is no need to tie up every connection between Chronicles and the Pentateuch with Leviticus alone.

12. A passage not noted by Japhet in *Ideology*, and skirted on pp. 1075-76 of *I & II Chronicles*.

legislation for the individual guilty of inadvertent defrauding of God in
the tokens of sanctity cannot possibly apply in the case of Israel guilty
of national, deliberate fraud in every aspect of life, compounded over
the generations. Nor can the penalty exacted on the individual guilty of
deliberate fraud, such as Achar, apply—the death of the defrauder and
the destruction of his whole family and possessions (Josh. 7.25): the
death penalty would simply wipe out Israel (cf. 2 Chron. 12.7). What,
then, is the alternative to the death penalty? The only alternative is forfeiture of the land. And for what purpose? So that the land can recover
from the rapacity of Israel, in *not* repaying its tithes and other holy
offerings in kind, and thus be regenerated.

That there is a deliberate exploitation by Chronicles of this sense of
מעל developed by Leviticus itself is, I think, evident. The wording of
part of the peroration of Chronicles, 2 Chron. 36.21, picks up the words
of the peroration of the Holiness Code in Lev. 26.34 (cf. v. 43): 'until
the land gets satisfaction for its sabbaths'; the hophal infinitive in the
phrase 'during all the days of its being devastated' occurs in the Hebrew Bible only in 2 Chron. 36.21 and Lev. 26.34-35, 43, even down to
its anomalous form with suffix, הָשַׁמָּה.[13]

Why should Japhet be resistant to such observations? Her resistance
derives, I believe, from her interpretation of the Chronicler's view of
Israel's relation to the land. In her view, Israel's relation to the land is a
matter of continuity from beginning to end.[14] Much of her interpretation of Chronicles hangs on this point:

1.   In the genealogies, the Chronicler traces Israel's origins back
     to Adam. Bypassing any doctrine of election or covenant, the
     Chronicler presents Israel's relation with God as *a priori*,
     simply a given that requires no justification.[15]

2.   Similarly, because the narrative section begins with the
     monarchy, omitting exodus and conquest, the Chronicler
     regards Israel's settlement in the land as continuous since
     Jacob.[16]

---

13. The reference to 'the word of the LORD through the mouth of Jeremiah',
with which 2 Chron. 36.21 begins, has a different function (see below).

14. Japhet, *Ideology*, p. 363.

15. It is 'an integral part of Creation'; Japhet, *Ideology*, p. 199.

16. 'The tie with the land is an undisturbed continuity'; Japhet, *I & II Chronicles*, p. 47.

3. Equally, at the other end of Israel's history, the exile is consistently played down by the Chronicler. This is so in terms of the sheer space he devotes to it: in place of the 57 verses of 2 Kgs 23.31–25.30, Chronicles offers only 23 (2 Chron. 36.1-23). The exile of 587 affects in truth only Jerusalem, not Judah.[17]

4. If there is no significant exile, then there can be no significant return; therefore, Chronicles can have no eschatology.[18]

5. The picture is static and continuous, not cumulative. The Chronicler's work is a series of vignettes of ancient Israel, presented generation by generation, each treated in its own right. There is no inherited, compounded sin; retribution takes place in the generation that has merited it.[19]

Let me give a couple of brief quotations from Japhet, in summary:

> Chronicles presents a different view of history [from the standard presentation in other postexilic writings]: the dimensions of the Babylonian conquest and exile are reduced considerably, the people's settlement in the land is portrayed as an uninterrupted continuum...The bond between the people and the land, like the bond between the people and its god, is described as something continuous and abiding. This bond cannot be associated with a particular moment in history, for it has existed since the beginning of time.[20]

> There is only one complete captivity in the book of Chronicles [namely, the East Bank]...Chronicles takes the account of Israel's exile and destruction and associates these disastrous events with the tribes who lived east of the Jordan...With respect to the land west of the Jordan, in both the northern and southern kingdoms, the effects of enemy invasions are minimized. Foreign armies come and go, but the people's presence in the land continues uninterrupted.[21]

Now this is not the place for a full-scale review of Japhet's work.[22] I have space only for a comment or two on her interpretation of the Chronicler's work on the exile:

17. Japhet, *Ideology*, pp. 364-73.
18. Japhet, *Ideology*, pp. 493-504.
19. Japhet, *Ideology*, pp. 162-63.
20. Japhet, *Ideology*, p. 386; 'axiomatic', p. 393.
21. Japhet, *Ideology*, pp. 372-73.
22. On the alleged absence of conquest narrative, one might reply that the conquest is indeed cited (2 Chron. 20.7, 11; cf. 1 Chron. 5.25; 16.18; 2 Chron. 33.9).

1. The space the Chronicler allots to the exile (23 verses as opposed to 57) may be given an entirely different interpretation, again related to material from Leviticus, this time Leviticus 25, as I shall hope to show in a moment.

2. 2 Chronicles 36.20 makes the explicit statement: 'He [Nebuchadnezzar] carried off into captivity in Babylon those who survived the sword.' Japhet seeks to tone down the statement by saying that it is modelled on material on Jehoiachin borrowed from 2 Kgs 24.15-16[23] and is, therefore, limited to Jerusalem. But the Chronicler has already made his selection of the 2 Kings 24 material on Jehoiachin in 2 Chron. 36.9-10; he has abandoned any close following of the Kings text at 2 Chron. 36.13aβ, and is hardly going to revert to an earlier section of it at v. 20. One cannot be expected to elevate the Chronicler's alleged editorial techniques above the plain sense of the text. The Chronicler is fully capable of making himself clear.

3. Her contention that 'there is only one complete captivity in the book of Chronicles'—that of the East Bank tribes—is based on a similarly complex redactional argument. The material on the exile of the East Bank tribes in 1 Chron. 5.25-26 absorbs the material in 2 Kings 17 on the exile of the North, so as to apply now only to the East Bank and no longer to the North, thus producing but one exile.[24]

4. I find Japhet's interpretation of 2 Chron. 36.15-16 equally unacceptable. The text runs:

> Now the LORD, the God of their fathers had sent by the hand
> of his messengers, at earliest opportunity and persistently...
> But they were ridiculing the messengers of God, rejecting his

One might as well argue that since the 'event' of Moses at Sinai is made little of (Moses is mentioned 21 times, Horeb occurs but once [2 Chron. 5.10] and Sinai never), Chronicles has a radically different view of revelation and of the tradition of Torah; a position that Japhet—rightly—does not adopt (e.g. *Ideology*, p. 497). In Chronicles, David figures as new Moses and Solomon as new Joshua (cf. the encouragement of David to Solomon as of Moses to Joshua, 'Be strong and of a good courage', 1 Chron. 22.13). The upshot is that the whole of Israel's past is presupposed, whether overtly mentioned or tacitly implied.

23. So, rather than 2 Kgs 25.15-16 as stated by Japhet, as the reference to the verb ויגל makes clear (*I & II Chronicles*, p. 1074; cf. *Ideology*, p. 368).

24. Japhet, *I & II Chronicles*, pp. 141-42.

> words and mocking his prophets, until the anger of the LORD
> was provoked to the point that there was no more healing.

In line with her view that there is no inherited guilt in Chronicles,[25] Japhet relates these verses exclusively to the reign of Zedekiah.[26] But surely the verses are most naturally understood in terms of a long process of events: Zedekiah is not alone in his culpability, but marks the climax of an age-long process.[27]

If such counter-arguments hold, then the Chronicler's argument is entirely different from Japhet's interpretation. There is only one unconditional element in the whole of Chronicles and that is enunciated in the first word in 1 Chron. 1.1: the existence of a relationship between God and humanity expressed in exemplary and instrumental terms in Israel. Israel's relation to the land is conditional (as Leviticus holds; cf. Solomon's prayer, 2 Chron. 6, e.g. vv. 36-39), just as the monarchy is conditional (cf. the exposition of the apparently unconditional promise to David, 1 Chron. 17.14, in totally conditional terms in 1 Chron. 22.11-13; 28.7).

Let me give, finally, an example of the consequences of following the view I am advocating, that concepts derived from Leviticus are functional in the Chronicler's argument. This is the question of the overall chronology with which Chronicles is operating—which takes us back again to Japhet's argument about the alleged insignificance of the exile.

It is clear that the Chronicler is working with a chronology of ten generations from Adam, the first father of humanity, to Noah, the second (1 Chron. 1.1-4). There are a further ten generations from Shem to Abraham, the father of a host of nations (1 Chron. 1.24-27). But what

---

25. Japhet, *Ideology*, p. 197: 'each king's account is settled with his death. A new unblemished and neutral chapter, freed from the influence of the past, opens with the accession of the succeeding king.'

26. Japhet, *Ideology*, p. 163: 'Only Zedekiah and his generation are responsible for the disaster that occurred in his time'; cf. pp. 188-89.

27. See 2 Chron. 29.6; 30.7 for the point made again specifically in terms of the history of מעל precisely as the Chronicler does here (v. 14). Other examples of continuity can be given: for example, the pernicious influence of the house of Ahab through four generations, from Jehoshaphat to the death of Athaliah (2 Chron. 18–23).

of the ensuing generations? Here I acknowledge the stimulus of a citation that Japhet makes from *Exod. R.* 15.26:

> The moon begins to shine on the first of Nisan and goes on shining till
> the fifteenth day, when her disc becomes full; from the fifteenth till the
> thirtieth day, her light wanes, till on the thirtieth it is not seen at all. With
> Israel, too, there were fifteen generations from Abraham to Solomon.
> When Solomon appeared, the moon's disc was full.[28]

Japhet is happy to endorse that statement so far: the 15 generations
from Abraham to Solomon. That the Chronicler has indeed 15 generations from Abraham to Solomon through the descent of David is
clear.[29] But, naturally, given that she does not believe in an exile when
Israel was completely on the wane, Japhet does not follow up the
implications of the second part of the quotation, the demise of the
monarchy. The text in *Exodus Rabbah* actually begins, 'Even before
God brought Israel out of Egypt, He intimated to them that royalty
would last for them only until the end of thirty generations'.[30]

At first sight it does not seem that 15 generations after Solomon to
the exile fits the Chronicler's presentation. In 2 Chronicles 10–36 nine-
teen kings are listed (from Rehoboam to Zedekiah). But suppose we
follow the lead of *midrash Exodus Rabbah* and look at the fifteenth
king in the sequence from Rehoboam to Zedekiah, what do we find?
We have reached the end of the reign of Josiah. Is it possible that
the *midrash* is correctly reflecting the chronology intended by the
Chronicler?

There are a number of indications that suggest that the Chronicler
does indeed regard the exile as beginning with the death of Josiah:[31]

1. The paragraph marker, *pᵉtûḥâ*, marking the end of the presen-
    tation of the reign of Josiah and the opening of the next
    section, is placed at the end of 2 Chron. 35.24 (I believe the

28. Japhet, *Ideology*, p. 75 n. 203.

29. The 15 are Abraham, Isaac, Jacob, Judah, Perez, Hezron, Ram, Ammi-
nadab, Nahshon, Salma, Boaz, Obed, Jesse, David, Solomon (1 Chron. 1.34; 2.1, 4-
5, 9-15; 3.5).

30. H. Freedman and M. Simon (eds.), *The Midrash Rabbah*, II (with introduction by I. Epstein; London: Soncino Press, 1977). The footnote at 'Josiah' reads
'Joash' by error.

31. That is, far from Chronicles underplaying the exile because of the Chronicler's drastic reduction of the coverage of it, as Japhet argues (*I & II Chronicles*,
pp. 106-107), Chronicles actually extends the exile to begin in 609!

paragraph markers of MT to be the absolute baseline in the interpretation of the Hebrew Bible).[32] This results in the rearrangement of the last three elements of the standard framework of seven elements within which the reigns of the kings are normally set (5, the record of the rest of the deeds; 6, the burial in Jerusalem; 7, the succession of the son). Element 6, the burial of Josiah in Jerusalem, is moved out of position and marks the end of the presentation on Josiah. Josiah is the last of the Davidic line to die in Jerusalem (the Chronicler has deliberately changed the text of 2 Kgs 23.29-30 so that Josiah is not killed at Megiddo, but dies in Jerusalem).

2.   All the succeeding kings are puppets of foreign powers; foreign dominion has begun.

3.   Not only so; all these kings are removed from Jerusalem and disappear in exile. For this purpose the Chronicler invents an exile for Jehoiakim (2 Chron. 36.6).

4.   The positioning of the paragraph marker throws into prominence the work of the prophet Jeremiah. The whole of these final paragraphs in 2 Chron. 35.25–36.23 is now held together by the words of Jeremiah—his lament over the death of Josiah with which they begin (2 Chron. 35.25), his unavailing presence under the last king Zedekiah (2 Chron. 36.12), and the edict of Cyrus as fulfilment of Jeremiah's prophecy of 70 years for the duration of the exile (2 Chron. 36.22).

5.   All this argument would hold, even if crude arithmetic did not support it. But it should be acknowledged that 70 years from the edict of Cyrus, conventionally dated 538, takes us close enough to the death of Josiah, conventionally dated to 609.

And so to return to the question of the Chronicler's chronology. If, in his view, the exile takes place in the sixteenth generation after Solomon, the exilic generation, held together by the prophecy of Jeremiah (2 Chron. 36.21) is the fiftieth generation from Adam (10 + 10 + 15 + 16 = 51, less one because Abraham is double-counted).

If that is so, then there is another interconnection between Chronicles and Leviticus, this time the legislation, again in the Holiness Code, on the Jubilee (Lev. 25.8-24). This passage is enormously suggestive for

---

32. Contrast Japhet, who takes the section on Josiah as extending from 2 Chron. 35.1–36.1 (*I & II Chronicles*, pp. 1038-59).

the eschatological character of Chronicles. The exilic generation is the time of Jubilee, of the proclamation of eschatological return to the land.

Let me give but two examples of the use of the vocabulary of Jubilee in Chronicles:

1. Lev. 25.13: בשנת היובל הזאת תשבו איש אל־אחזתו. In 1 Chron. 9.2, the ideal of all Israel's possession of the land is stated in terms of 'dwelling in their holding' (היושבים...באחזתם). 1 Chron. 9.2 is strategically positioned: it comes immediately after the explanation for the forfeiture of the land in 1 Chron. 9.1 (and before the account of the ideal population of Jerusalem in 1 Chron. 9.3-34). This becomes the point of reference for the restoration of the ideal under Hezekiah—or the nearest approximation to the ideal Israel is to be capable of achieving under the later monarchy—in 2 Chron. 31.1: וישובו כל־בני ישראל איש לאחזתו.

2. The fundamental principle of tenure of the land is enunciated in Lev. 25.23: הארץ לא תמכר לצמתת כי־לי הארץ כי־גרים ותושבים אתם עמדי. That last phrase in echoed in David's farewell prayer in 1 Chron. 29.15: כי־גרים אנחנו לפניך ותושבים ככל־אבתינו.[33]

I should further point out that there is, it seems to me, verbal interconnection between the proclamation of Cyrus's edict at the end of 2 Chronicles and the proclamation of the Jubilee in Leviticus 25. The formulation of 2 Chron. 36.22, 'He [Cyrus] *sent* proclamation *throughout all* his dominion' (העביר...בכל)—which are 'all the kingdoms of the world' (v. 23)—echoes the formulation of Lev. 25.9: 'You will *send* proclamation by trumpet blast *throughout all* your land (העביר...בכל)'.[34]

---

33. The connection is not noted by Japhet, *Ideology*, p. 340 n. 262; p. 416 n. 58, where it is related to Ps. 39.13.

34. It is taking the discussion too far afield to open the issue of the role of the foreign nations in Chronicles, raised by the edict of Cyrus to all the kingdoms of the world. Once again I find myself completely at odds with Japhet (e.g. 'Chronicles contains no reference to the nations in their own right, nor does it show any interest in reforming the world' [*Ideology*, p. 53]). The point of the Chronicler's beginning his history with Adam is not connected with any *a priori* relationship of Israel with God, independent of election (another aspect of the alleged 'autochthonous' character of Israel), as shown by tracing Israel's origins back to primaeval beginnings (cf. *Ideology*, pp. 117, 123). It is, rather, in my view, to

What kind of literature, then, is Chronicles? Not for the purpose of historiography (again I am at odds with Japhet),[35] but for the purpose of theology it weaves a tale of Israel's past on a highly eclectic use of already 'canonical' texts, using the Levitical concept of מעל as dominant theme. What else can one call it but a *midrash* on a theme of Leviticus?[36]

prepare a setting for Israel amid the nations of humanity, within three 'coaxial pyramids' at the apex of which stand Adam, Noah and Abraham, respectively (cf. the very significant alteration Chronicles makes to his underlying text with the addition of Adam in 2 Chron. 6.18). What happens in Israel then has an immediate bearing on the nations of the world, whether in ideal achieved under David as YHWH's vicegerent on earth (1 Chron. 29.30), or in exile and hope of return, as here.

35. For example, Japhet, *I & II Chronicles*, pp. 31-34.

36. Here I happily adopt Japhet's definition of *midrash* (writing on 1 Chron. 5.1-2): 'Its midrashic features are, first of all, the fact that the passage is formed as an interpretation of a given text. A citation is followed by an interpretation...Secondly, this interpretation introduces a new theological concept' (*I & II Chronicles*, p. 131).

Chapter 6

PROSPECTIVE ATONEMENT: THE USE OF EXODUS 30.11-16
IN 1 CHRONICLES 21

In this paper[1] I am seeking to justify a point I made in passing in
another connection: 'behind the outrage at David's census [in 1 Chronicles 21] lies...the legislation on the muster of the people (root פקד) in
Exod. 30.11-16'.[2]

B.E. Kelly gives a convenient recent review of a range of possible
interpretations of what David did wrong, in the Chronicler's view, in
the matter of the census:

> The Chronicler does not specify why this census was so sinful...but
> probably he saw David's act as a usurpation of Yahweh's prerogatives...
> the Chronicler affirms that the people are Yahweh's and so David's
> actions in numbering them must appear presumptuous and self-seeking.
> This census (in contrast...to those in Exod. 30.12 and Num. 1.2, 26.2,
> which are sacral and commanded by Yahweh) lacked authorization and
> legitimacy. Moreover, it was apparently for a military purpose (cf. vv. 2,
> 5) and betrayed lack of trust in Yahweh who had so far acted as Israel's
> commander in war.[3]

---

1. Unpublished paper, read at the Society for Old Testament Study, January
1997, under the title: '1 Chronicles 21: What did David Do Wrong?'
2. See Chapter 5, p. 117.
3. Brian E. Kelly, *Retribution and Eschatology in Chronicles* (JSOTSup, 211;
Sheffield: Sheffield Academic Press, 1996), p. 81. This, it seems to me, gets to
within a hair's breadth of the correct view: it misses the connection between Exod.
30 and 1 Chron. 21 in the use of the root פקד. The point to be argued below is that,
while it *is* legitimate for David to conduct a census, he has failed to apply the legislation on it in the Torah. Cf. M.J. Selman, *1 Chronicles* (2 vols.; TOTC; Leicester:
InterVarsity Press, 1994), I, pp. 205-206, who, correctly in my view, notes—but
does not fully expound—the connection with Exod. 30, but includes other grounds
which are not confirmed by the argument below.

Since the Chronicler indeed 'does not specify' the reason, the reader is left to infer from Joab's response to David what was wrong with David's census:[4]

> 1 Chron. 21.1 [Satan]...incited David to count (מנה) Israel. [2] So David said to Joab [and to all the captains (שׂרים) of the people, 'Go, count (ספר)] Israel...so that I may know their number (מספר)'. [3] Joab said, 'May the LORD increase his people a hundred times more than they are! O my lord the King, [does not my lord possess them all as slaves?]. Why does my lord [want to do this? Why should Israel incur guilt (אשׁמה) thereby?']... [5] Joab gave the number (מספר) of the muster (מפקד) of the people to David...[[6] But Levi and Benjamin he did not muster (פקד) among them because the word of the king was repugnant (תעב) to Joab.]

From this reply one might infer three objections to the census: it *can* not, it *need* not, and it *ought* not to be held. Joab's words in v. 3, couched in courtly rhetoric, begin with an exclamation, 'May the LORD increase his people...!' In the light of a similar invocation of blessing by Moses in Deut. 1.11, this exclamation amounts to a polite refusal (a close English equivalent would be, 'LORD preserve us!'). Teased out, Joab's reply would amount to something like: 'I *cannot* count the people, for they are far too many for me. Don't get me wrong; I wish that the LORD would increase his people a hundredfold, but even as they are they are uncountable.'

In the continuation, Joab suggests that the census *need* not be held. The immediate context is military: it is Joab the commander of the citizen army and the captains who are dispatched to do the counting, and the number that Joab brings back is that of the swordsmen. David's motive in taking the census is thus, presumably, to know Israel's military capability. Joab suggests that David does not *need* to know the number because he already has all the men he needs at his disposal, as the successful campaigns recently completed in 1 Chronicles 18–20 have amply demonstrated.

But Joab's refusal by invocation of blessing involves more than just a conventionalized expression of formal piety; the Chronicler's addition of the last phrase of v. 3, 'Why should Israel incur guilt thereby?', suggests theological factors: the census *ought* not to be taken because to do so would involve the violation of some theological principle. Three

---

4. In texts cited from Chronicles below, [...] =, approximately, material in Chronicles not in the parallel in Samuel–Kings. The English translation is by myself.

such principles might occur to one: the battle is the LORD's and he can
save by few or by many (as David had already learned in his first campaign, that against the Philistines in 1 Chron. 14);[5] to know the number
is to replace trust by knowledge, to rely on the 'arm of flesh' rather than
on the LORD (cf. 2 Chron. 32.7-8, where the allusion to the Immanuel
prophecy underpinning rule of the Davidic House in Jerusalem in Isa.
7.14 is unmistakable); in any case, the divine promise is that Israel will
be as many as the stars in the sky (Gen. 15.5). To attempt to count
Israel would be a faithless attempt to verify the LORD's promise. For
whatever reason, Joab seeks to invalidate the census: he omits two key
tribes, Levi and Benjamin, who provide the clergy and the artillery,
respectively.[6]

All this seems so far so reasonable. The problem is that such interpretations are undercut by the Chronicler himself in 1 Chronicles 27.
1 Chron. 27.1 makes it plain that it is perfectly legitimate to conduct a
census (מספר) of the population, by the same agency, the שׂרים, and
under the aegis of the king (indeed 1 Chron. 23.3 makes it clear that it
is legitimate to count the Levites, also on royal initiative). Further,
1 Chron. 27.23-24, referring back specifically to 1 Chronicles 21,
shows that David himself, by restricting the count to those over 20
years of age, did not violate the divine promise that Israel would be
uncountable.[7]

Can the paradox presented by these two passages, 1 Chronicles 21
and 1 Chronicles 27, then, be resolved? An easy way out would be to
go along with the view that 1 Chronicles 23–27 have been added.[8] This
seems to me to be excluded by the cross-reference to Joab in 1 Chron.
27.24 and by the fact that vocabulary, some added in 1 Chronicles 21
by the Chronicler himself, is picked up and developed in these chapters
(especially שׂרים, מספר [v. 2], and the all-important פקד [v .6]).

---

5.   Cf. 2 Chron. 14.10 [MT] and the motif of the Lord fighting for Israel in
2 Chron. 13.15; 17.10; 20.15, 17, 29; 25.8; 32.8.

6.   For the Benjaminites as habitually providing archers and slingers, cf.
1. Chron. 8.40; 12.2; 2 Chron. 14.8; 17.17.

7.   [1 Chron. 27.22 '...These are the captains (שׂרים) of the tribes of Israel.
[23] David did not record (ונשא) their (Israel's) number (מספר) from the age of twenty
and under, for the LORD had promised to make Israel as many as the stars in the
sky. [24] Joab...had begun to count (מנה) but had not finished. Thereby anger came
upon Israel. But the statistics (מספר) were not entered among the statistics (מספר;
BHK, BHS urge one to read ספר, 'book') of *The Chronicles of King David.*']

8.   Cf. the review of interpretation in Japhet, *I & II Chronicles*, pp. 406-11.

It may be helpful, first, to observe that a similar paradox is to be found in connection with other passages in Chronicles, especially the building of the Temple (which, be it noted, overlaps in context with the census). In 1 Chron. 17.5 it is stated that a Temple *need* not be built—the LORD has managed perfectly well hitherto without one; indeed that the Temple *can* not be built because the House of the LORD is already in being in the form of the House of David (1 Chron. 17.14); and, certainly, that David as a man of blood *ought* not to build it.[9] Yet, in 1 Chron. 17.12 and as the sequel in 1 Chronicles 21–2 Chronicles 7 makes clear, a Temple shall be built. The ultimate significance of the Temple is that it is to be the resting-place of the ark as the symbol of the pacification of the world by the LORD of hosts through his sacramental host, Israel, led by his vicegerent on earth, David (a key term linking much of these ideas together is נוח, e.g. 1 Chron. 22.9; 28.2).

There is a similar paradox here. There is no need for a census in order to verify Israel's military capability, for Israel is called into being and sustained by the LORD himself. Yet, as I shall argue, a census not only may, but must, be held, not to verify Israel's military capability but to verify that the people pays all that it owes to God. It is striking that in 1 Chron. 21.3, 5, 6 the Chronicler introduces three key terms from the Torah for the first time in his work to make clear that David's failure lies in the ritual realm (i.e. in the realm of Israel's formal relationship with God): not only the root אשם (v. 3),[10] but also פקד (vv. 5f.)[11] and תעב (v. 6).[12] It is the second of these, פקד, that will mostly occupy attention below.

9.   1 Chron. 17.4 'It is not *you* who will built me [the] House to reside in, [5] because I have not resided in a house since I brought up Israel...[10]...a house is what the LORD shall build for you...[12] (your descendant) will build [me] a House...[14] [and I will establish him in my House and in my Kingdom for ever].'

10.   Again in 2 Chron. 19.10 (2×); 24.18; 28.10, 13 (3×); 33.23, all in independent Chronicles material.

11.   The root פקד occurs in Chronicles twenty times in all: 1 Chron. 21.5*, 6; 23.11, 24; 24.3, 19; 26.30, 32; 2 Chron. 12:10*; 17.14; 23.14*,18*; 24.11; 25.5; 26.11; 31.13; 34.10*, 12, 17*; 36.23* (all, except those marked *, in independent Chronicles material). The significance of the use in 1 Chron. 21 is somewhat obscured by the fact that the Chronicler suppresses in v. 2 an occurrence of the root already present in the parallel in 2 Sam. 24.2 (though he does add in v. 6 a use not in the parallel in 2 Sam. 24.9).

12.   Again 2 Chron. 28.3*; 33.2*; 34.33; 36.8, 14 (all, except those marked *, in independent Chronicles material). For parallels in the Torah for אשׁמה, cf. e.g.

I have to confess that it was only in connection with subsequent narratives in the Chronicler's work that the full import of the use of the root פקד, here almost casually introduced, became clear to me, and that thus the paradox between 1 Chronicles 21 and 1 Chronicles 27 was resolved. In particular, it is in connection with the narrative of Joash's plan to renovate the Temple in 2 Chron. 23.16–24.14[13] that, for the first time, the significance of פקד is expounded by being brought specifically into relation with Mosaic legislation (2 Chron. 23.18; 24.6, 9).[14] A brief consideration of that passage is, therefore, necessary.

At first sight, it seems wholly laudable that Joash should 'conceive the notion' of 'renovating' the Temple (2 Chron. 24.4). It seems equally unexceptionable that he should have 'gathered' the priests and the Levites to enlist their support for the project (קבץ, v. 5, the Chronicler's key term for securing the unanimous support of Israel, e.g. 1 Chron. 11.1). All the more puzzling, then, that, initially, the Levites should do nothing to expedite the matter.[15]

Lev. 4.3; 5.24; 22.16; for חעב, cf. e.g. Lev. 18.22; 20.13.

13. 2 Chron. 23.18 'Jehoiada entrusted the charge (פקדה) of the House of the LORD [into the hands of the Levitical priests...24.4...it was in Joash's mind to renovate the House of the LORD. [5] So he gathered the priests and the Levites and said to them, "Go out to the cities of Judah and gather silver from all Israel...annually. You expedite the matter yourselves." But the Levites did not do so.] [6] So the king summoned Jehoiada the chief and said to him, "Why [have you not enjoined (דרש) on the Levites to bring from Judah and from Jerusalem the levy of Moses (משאת משה)...to the Tent of the Testimony?"...[8] Then the king gave command and they made] a chest and put it in the [gate of] the House of the LORD...[[9] They made proclamation throughout Judah and Jerusalem to bring to the LORD the levy of Moses (משאת משה)...upon Israel in the wilderness...[11] When it was time to bring the chest to the direction (פקדה) of the king under the authority of the Levites—] when they saw that the silver had accumulated, the king's secretary and the [person appointed (פקיד) by] the high priest would come...[12] he [the king and Jehoiada] would give it to the clerk of works in charge of the maintenance (עבדה) of the House of the LORD...'

14. The reference to 'the Tabernacle of the Lord which Moses made in the wilderness' in the census narrative in 1 Chron. 21.29 is, therefore, of high significance (cf. again, in the same context, 1 Chron. 22.13).

15. The Chronicler chooses his language deliberately in v. 4, 'it was in Joash's mind to renovate the Temple', in order to signal the problem of tension between king and Levites. עם לב is precisely the expression used for David's plan to build the Temple in the first place (1 Chron. 22.7; 28.2; contrast 2 Chron. 29.10), which was immediately modified by the word of the LORD through the prophet Nathan.

It is only when Joash summons the chief priest Jehoiada to confront him with the inactivity of the Levites, and with Jehoiada's own failure as leader of the Levites to impress upon them the necessity for action (v. 6), that the truth of the matter dawns on Joash.

The appropriate legislation is contained in Exod. 30.11-16:

> [12] When you [Moses] take a census (נשׂא ראשׁ) of the Israelites, of those to be mustered (לפקדיהם), each of them must give an atonement-payment (כפר) for his life to the LORD, when they are being mustered (בפקד אתם), so that no plague (נגף) may strike them when they are being mustered (בפקד אתם). [13] This is what each one who is entered among those mustered (על־הפקדים) must pay: half a shekel...as a levy (תרומה) to the LORD. [14] Each one who is entered among those mustered (על־הפקדים), of twenty years of age and older, shall pay the LORD's levy (תרומה). [15]...to make atonement (כפר) for your lives. [16] You shall take the atonement (כפר) silver from the Israelites and apply it for the maintenance (עבדה) of the tent of meeting; it will be a reminder on behalf of the Israelites before the LORD to make atonement (כפר) for your lives.

Chronicles applies this legislation.[16] When the people are mustered for military service, the muster as sacral act must be carried out in accordance with these regulations (cf. Num. 31.48-54). War is not being glorified: military service is only legitimate within the sacramental context of fighting the LORD's battles as the LORD's host. Killing on the field of battle is an inevitable consequence of war; but taking the life of another human being immediately warrants the payment of life for life (cf. Gen. 9.5-6; Num. 35.33). Only the necessary sacral preparation for war as the LORD's war can avert that inevitable forfeiture of life by those who take life. It is that sacral preparation that the legislation in Exod. 30.11-16 provides: the half-shekel given by all is the indemnity laid up as a perpetual reminder before the LORD for the life of '*you* all', that is, not just of the combatants but of the community at large on whose behalf the host sallies forth and which might suffer because of the blood shed by the host.

The Chronicler thus uses in 2 Chron. 23.16–24.14 vocabulary and ideas that are fundamental to his purpose. The upkeep of the Temple is

---

Joash in his impulsiveness is a new David; Jehoiada is to Joash as Nathan was to David.

16. It is striking that the words for the king's 'charge' and the official 'charged' by the chief priest, which are used in 2 Chron. 24.11, come from the same root (פקד) as the word for 'those mustered' in Exod. 30.12.

not a matter of the Levites going about like itinerant tax-gatherers: it is, as Joash now realizes, a matter of the required rendering to God of the indemnity by the entire community (cf. 2 Chron. 34.9). The Temple thus maintained becomes 'a memorial for Israel before the LORD': the visible expression of the petition by the people for the sparing of their lives and of the acceptance by God of that petition. This payment, by which Israel acknowledge their vulnerability before God and dependence upon him, is one of the 'holy things' that symbolize the dedication of the whole of life to God. It is thus the absolute responsibility of Israel to bring these offerings to the Temple *themselves*. This is but the rendering to God of what is due to him and is to be done not *by* the Levites but *under* their supervision and monitoring.

This legislation in Exodus is concerned precisely with atonement, the maintenance of the oneness between community and God which will otherwise be broken even by acts of necessary bloodshed. These rites of atonement are not, thus, in response to actions already committed; they are not retrospective to restore what has already been disturbed. They are, rather, precautionary, prospective measures, which anticipate the possibility of bloodshed. They are prophylactic rites of atonement which have to be observed, as the people set out to war, in order to maintain the existing oneness of Israel with God.[17]

Another case in point is Amaziah's mustering of the army in 2 Chron. 25.5-10.[18] Amaziah draws up Judah ('and Benjamin' is now added) in traditional order as citizen army 'by fathers' houses', under their military leaders, 'the captains (שׂרים) of thousands and captains of hundreds'. The use of the technical term פקד leads deep into the theological issues raised by Amaziah's action. The troops at Amaziah's disposal, sallying forth in principle as the LORD's sacramental host, turn out to be 300,000. By the legislation in Exodus 30, a force of 300,000

17. The term 'prophylactic atonement' is used by A. Schenker in connection with 2 Sam. 24 (*Der Mächtige im Schmeltzofen des Mitleids: Eine Interpretation von 2 Sam 24* [OBO, 42; Göttingen: Vandenhoeck & Ruprecht; Freiburg: Universitätsverlag, 1982], p. 17).

18. [2 Chron. 25.5 'Then Amaziah gathered Judah and lined them up by fathers' houses, by captains (שׂרים) of thousands and captains of hundreds…He mustered (פקד) them from the age of twenty and above and found them to be 300,000 crack troops advancing as a host (צבא)…⁶ He hired from Israel 100,000 warriors with 100 talents of silver. ⁷ But the man of God came to him and said, "O king, let not the host (צבא) of Israel go with you, for the LORD is not with Israel (all the Ephraimites)".']

would pay 50 talents of silver,[19] and that sum should be devoted to the maintenance of the sanctuary. It is precisely double this payment that Amaziah proposes to misapply in hiring 100,000 troops from the North. No wonder the unnamed 'man of God' is outraged (v. 7). The reason that the North must not go with Amaziah is that the LORD is not 'with' them (the 'messianic' significance of the apparently commonplace preposition, 'with', has already been noted in connection with the 'Immanuel' prophecy in 2 Chron. 32.7-8; see above, p. 130). There is but one sovereign LORD and the Davidic king is his sole representative and agent on earth; the host led by the Davidic king is the sacramental representation on earth of the cosmic hosts that the LORD has at his disposal. The North, as a schismatic and apostate kingdom, has forfeited meantime its status of belonging to that people; its 'host' is a non-power, alliance with which can only bring disaster on Amaziah.

In the light of these later incidents, David's fault in the matter of the census in 1 Chronicles 21 becomes clear, I think. A muster is legitimate and necessary. David's אשמה is to neglect the preliminaries necessary to the muster of the host of Israel, which involve both Levites and Tabernacle. As the sequel is about to show, the catastrophic consequences of the neglect of this legislation is the 'plague' (מגפה, vv. 17, 22, from the same root as נגף in Exod. 30.12) which befalls the people. Because these prospective, prophylactic rites of atonement have been ignored, rites of retroactive atonement—the repairing of the relationship damaged through that failure—have now to be brought into operation, as 1 Chron. 22.1 makes clear. It is through that neglect and its consequences that David's reign is brought into direct association with the Chronicler's overall theme of guilt and atonement based on the legislation on מעל, the infringement of the LORD's prerogatives and the possibility of atonement, in Lev. 5.14–26: 'so shall one be forgiven for committing any one of all the acts which one may do and thereby incur guilt (יעשה לאשמה)' (Lev. 5.26; cf. Lev. 22.14-16).

The consequences for David himself are equally catastrophic. He irretrievably loses status: whereas in 1 Chron. 16.2 he acts as highpriest in the dual high-priestly roles of sacrifice and blessing, he is now

19. For the calculation of the number of shekels to the talent, see Exod. 38.25-26. There those mustered amount to 603,550. At a half-shekel redemption per head they should contribute 301,775 shekels. What they contributed is defined as 100 talents, 1775 shekels. Therefore, 100 talents = 300,000 shekels; 1 talent = 3000 shekels.

debarred from access to the altar. David's loss of status is mirrored in Zadok's rise: whereas heretofore Zadok has been but a member of the king's entourage, he is soon to be anointed at the same moment as Solomon himself is anointed as David's successor.[20]

In the light of these observations, the interpretation of two other passages in Chronicles' presentation of David's reign may be illuminated.

1 Chronicles 27.1-15 introduces the census of the people, and the approved manner of conducting it. Within the overall design of Chronicles, 1 Chron. 27.1-15 can now be seen as the deliberate contrast to Joab's aborted census in 1 Chronicles 21 (hence the cross-reference in 1 Chron. 27.23, 24). It is not that this is now a legitimate census as opposed to that illegitimate one;[21] it is that the first ought to have been conducted as the second is.

The paragraph opens:

> [As for the (ordinary) Israelites: with regard to their numbering (מספר), the heads of households and the captains (שׂרים) of thousands and hundreds and their supervisors were the ones who were assisting the king with regard to the whole matter of the divisions, each of which came on duty and went off duty, a month at a time, throughout all the months of the year. Each division had 24,000. [2] Over the first division for the first month was Jashobeam..., and over his division were 24,000...[3] Among the descendants of Perez was the leader of all the captains of the hosts (צבאות) for the first month.][22]

The people are counted by teams of their heads of families and army commanders, that is, by the civil and military leaders, under supervisors: it is each of these teams that amounts to 24,000.[23] For each of the 12 months of the year there is thus a matching 'division' of 24,000

20. For the change in Zadok's status, cf. the sequence 1 Chron. 12.28; 16.39; 24.3, 6, 31; 29.22.

21. Contrast the quotation from Kelly, above.

22. NRSV, 'This is the list of the people of Israel, the heads of families, the commanders..., and their officers who served the king in all matters concerning the divisions..., each division numbering twenty-four thousand', is, I think, misleading: it seems to imply that the whole people are in 12 divisions of 24,000: but the resulting figure of 288,000 is far too small (cf. 1 Chron. 21.5 and the number 300,000 raised by Amaziah from Judah and Benjamin alone, above). NRSV is obliged to translate '*in* his division' in the subsequent verses (vv. 2, 4-5, 7-15) where the Hebrew consistently says 'over'.

23. Cf. NEB.

civil and military leaders and supervisors.[24] Over each division is a high official or, in the case of the first three, his assistant or deputy. Naturally, the total number of the people is not recorded (cf. v. 23).

The precise purpose of the roster of duties is not made explicit. In a similar organization under Solomon in 1 Kgs 4.7-19 (not used by Chronicles), Israel is divided into 12 districts, each with the responsibility of maintaining the royal court for one month.[25] But this is a case where it is vital that ideas characteristic of Samuel–Kings are not allowed to print through to Chronicles. While here too the supervisors are in office for only one month in the year, in Chronicles no districts are specified; it is the whole country that is being served by changing teams. The coincidence of the figure of 24,000 between the divisions of these officials and that of the Levites in 1 Chron. 23.4 is striking: the officials here must be regarded as, so to speak, 'lay Levites', working in the service of the king in parallel to the sacral work of the Levites. Just as in the sacral sphere Israel is in a perpetual state of sanctification through the rendering of all dues required through changing teams of Levites (1 Chron. 26.29-32), so in the secular sphere every military and social duty to the LORD and to his anointed is honoured. It is through this organization of lay leaders that Israel is enabled to bring its due offerings to the sanctuary. Israel is the 'LORD's host' (cf. vv. 3, 5) in a state of perpetual mobilization. This, then, accounts for the huge number of supervisors: 2000 per tribe per month, in order to ensure the steady response from the whole nation throughout the year. The exact figures of the supervisors and the scale of social engineering involved speak of a highly theoretical system; Chronicles writes at an ideological level and the nightmare of organizing such a civil and military service in practice does not concern him.

One final passage where this interpretation may have an impact on understanding is 1 Chron. 15.22. The role of the official named in this passage is unclear: ['Chenaniah, the leader of the Levites in lifting; he instructed in lifting because he had/imparted understanding (מֵבִין)']. The word 'lifting' (מַשָּׂא) has several possible meanings. NRSV, for example, translates it 'music', that is, the lifting of the voice (cf. its recurrence in v. 27 in a context dominated by 'singers' and its frequent use of prophetic utterance, e.g. 2 Chron. 24.27; Isa. 13.1–23.1). If so,

---

24. Cf. 1 Chron. 23.4, 6 for the 'divisions' and 'supervisors' of the Levites.

25. A similar picture in Chronicles of a lavish royal court might be derived from a passage such as 2 Chron. 32.27-29.

the specific sense may be the actual words sung to the accompaniment of the music, the liturgy itself (as in 1 Chron. 16.8-36). Alternatively, since the word משא is used specifically in the context of bearing the ark in 2 Chron. 35.3 (in which context the word מבין, 'have/impart understanding', recurs), that is a very likely meaning for it here: the actual lifting of the ark itself is under the supervision of the chief porter (cf. v. 27, where, however, the text is problematical).

But yet a third possible meaning of משא has to be seriously entertained, namely, 'levy' (cf. the related noun משאת in connection with Joash's plans to renovate the Temple in 2 Chron. 24.6, 9, noted above). If this Chenaniah is the same as the individual mentioned in 1 Chron. 26.29,[26] who was in charge of overseeing the contributions of the laity country-wide (the 'outside works' as opposed to duties at the gates of the Temple detailed earlier in 1 Chron. 26), then the reference here is to this levy (it is striking that a near namesake recurs in 2 Chron. 31.12-13[27] with similar duties). It would be appropriate that, at this solemn moment of the muster of the people to accompany the bearing of the ark into Jerusalem, the capitation tax for the prospective, prophylactic rite of atonement should be levied to avoid a recurrence of the breaking-out of the LORD as in 1 Chronicles 13.

To conclude: David's census is, on this argument, linked to what I believe is the basic theme of the Chronicler's work. Chronicles is concerned to portray Israel's vocation to holiness, that is, to the rendering to God of all that is due to him. The primary definition of what is due to God is provided by the Torah and the primary model of ensuring the rendering of that duty is provided by the Levites (cf. the centrality of the Levites in the midst of the people in the genealogies in 1 Chron. 2–8). Chronicles as a post-monarchic work is concerned to portray the

---

26. [1 Chron. 26 (on the Levitical Temple gate-keepers and treasurers) [29] 'To the Izharites belonged Chenaniah and his sons, (appointed) for the works outside (the Temple) as supervisors and judges over Israel. [30] To the Hebronites belonged Hashabiah... (appointed) over the muster (פקדה) of Israel on the west side of the Jordan for all the works (מלאכה) of the LORD and for the service (עבדה) of the king.'] The key term פקד occurs also in 1 Chron. 26.32.

27. [2 Chron. 31.11 'Hezekiah gave orders to prepare the chambers in the House of the LORD...[12] They brought in the levy (תרומה), and the tithes and the holy things...Over them as leader was Cha/onaniah the Levite, his brother...[13] [and ten others]...appointed (פקידים) under the direction of Cha/onaniah and his brother...by appointment (מפקד) of Hezekiah the king and Azariah the leader of the House of God.']

monarchy as failure. In the process, the maximum that can be stated in favour of the monarchy is stated: it is viewed in terms of the highest possible theology of monarchy, that monarchy is the sacramental expression of the reign of God himself (cf., e.g., 1 Chron. 28.5). But monarchy is not above the Law: three times David himself, ideally the high-priest of his people, is portrayed as infringing the sphere of the holy: in his attempt to bring the ark into Jerusalem (1 Chron. 13); in his proposal to build a Temple (1 Chron. 17); and now, climactically, in the census of the people (1 Chron. 21).

The key position of 1 Chronicles 21 is now clear, I should argue. David is mustering his army (for this specialized sense of מנה in v. 1, cf. 1 Kgs 20.25). The sequence of 1 Chronicles 21 after the account of David's wars in 1 Chronicles 18–20 now takes on an ominous note. The necessity for these prophylactic rites of atonement on behalf of the army as it fights the wars of YHWH has been made only too clear by the three previous chapters where no detail has been spared of the bloody nature of David's subjugation of the neighbouring peoples. This final failure, the omission of the necessary prospective rites of atonement, is, accordingly, brought into direct association with the construction of the altar of sacrifice on the site of the Temple and with the planning for the building of that Temple. The Temple was meant to be the place of rest of the ark: the sacramental symbol of the pacification of the world by the LORD's sacramental host under its sacramental leader. But access to that ark as focus of Israel's worship in the holy of holies can only be by the altar. If David will not observe the prospective, prophylactic rites of atonement, designed to maintain unbroken the existing relationship, he must observe the rites of retrospective, retroactive atonement to heal the breach in the relationship caused by his own action. It is thus by this chapter, the hinge of his presentation of the reign of David, which contains David's climactic act of failure in the realm of the holy, that the Chronicler binds the reign of David, and the ensuing rule of the royal House of David, into his overall schema of guilt and atonement in his presentation of Israel's life.

Summary

From Joab's reply in 1 Chronicles 21 three objections to David's census might be inferred: it *can* not, it *need* not, and it *ought* not to be held. The latter objection might be held to be based on three theological principles: the LORD can save by few or by many; trust may not be replaced by knowledge; Israel is by divine promise uncountable.

However, such objections are undercut by 1 Chronicles 27, where a census is in fact held. The key term for resolving the paradox is פקד, as expounded in 2 Chron. 23.16–24.14 (cf. Exod. 30.11-16): when the people are mustered for military service, an idemnity must be laid up as a reminder before the LORD as a prophylactic rite of atonement (cf. 2 Chron. 25.5-10). The point of a census is not to check Israel's military capability but to verify that Israel pays all that is due to God (cf. the figure of Che/a/onaniah in 1 Chron. 15.22; 26.29 and 2 Chron. 31.12-13).

By means of 1 Chronicles 21, which describes David's climactic failure in the realm of the holy, the Chronicler binds the reign of David, and the ensuing rule of the House of David as failure, into his overall schema of guilt and atonement in his presentation of Israel's life.

Part III

LOOKING THROUGH THE GATEWAY:
APPLYING THE ANALOGY TO THE PENTATEUCH

Chapter 7

REACTIVATING THE CHRONICLES ANALOGY IN PENTATEUCHAL STUDIES, WITH SPECIAL REFERENCE TO THE SINAI PERICOPE IN EXODUS*

In the heyday of the classical literary criticism of the Pentateuch, it was customary to appeal to the analogy of Chronicles in support of the Documentary Hypothesis.[1] In the modern age, when there is lively debate about method in the interpretation of the Hebrew Bible, not least in the Pentateuch,[2] it may be apposite to look again at the Chronicles analogy.

There are pragmatic reasons that make Chronicles a convenient, if daunting, starting-point in the study of the Hebrew Bible. In a time of some scepticism about the reliability of reconstructions of origins,[3] it is the final, summated, form of the material as it palpably stands in the Hebrew Bible at present that provides the interpreter with some kind of solid ground. Chronicles, being at, or near, the end of the Hebrew Bible canon, presents itself as an obvious candidate for such a place to begin. It is, furthermore, helpful to start study with the canonical form of the text, for that is the common ground on which interpreters of all viewpoints can meet.

But, thanks in particular to the widespread existence of parallel sources, especially in Samuel and Kings, Chronicles also provides a valuable case study in critical method. If one wishes to appreciate Chronicles in its present form, not only in its aesthetic and affective

*   Originally published in *ZAW* 99 (1987), pp. 16-37. Reprinted with some corrections and adjustments.

1.   E.g. Carpenter and Harford-Battersby, *Hexateuch*, I, pp. 11-13.

2.   E.g. the review by A.H.J. Gunneweg, 'Anmerkungen und Anfragen zur neueren Pentateuchforschung', *TRu* 48 (1983), pp. 227ff.; 50 (1985), pp. 107ff.

3.   E.g. Thompson, *Historicity*.

function but also in its intentional and referential,[4] one has soon to make a decision about the genre, nature and purpose of the literature. In its final form, with its mass of historically undifferentiated materials, Chronicles is not to be understood as a work of historiography or as a presentation of any of Israel's religious institutions as they ever existed at any one time but, rather, as a theological essay more akin to *midrash*.[5]

Chronicles, further, establishes the propriety of the traditional critical questions about source, authorship, date and historicity. While the work must, ultimately, be fully appreciated in and for itself in its final form, that is, at the synchronic level, this appreciation does not invalidate inquiry into origins. It is, in part, only through the investigation of what the Chronicler has done with his underlying sources that understanding of the intention of his work is attained. Diachronic study of the growth of the material, though subsidiary and ancillary, highlights the distinctive features of Chronicles: it is complementary to synchronic.

Furthermore, of prime significance though the finally redacted form of the work may thus be, its validity is not to be absolutized to the exclusion of that of its sources. In using materials that are paralleled in other books of the Hebrew Bible, the Chronicler (or, at least, the final compilers and canonizers of Scripture) has no intention of abrogating or suppressing these earlier forms. There is here a point of hermeneutical importance: within the canon of the Hebrew Bible, earlier forms live on side by side in continuing validity and complementarity with later because of the consciousness that, short of the eschaton, there is no final form, theologically speaking. This side of the goal, the route retains its importance. Redaction is fundamentally a hermeneutical activity concerned with the receiving and reconceiving of continuingly valid tradition in all the relativities of new historical circumstances. Chronicles is, thus, a hermeneutical, as well as a theological, essay.

If, then, one wishes to lay an exegetical basis for methodology in Hebrew Bible criticism, an obvious place to begin must be Chronicles. It stands clearly at the meeting point of methodologies: it can be read synchronically in order to elucidate the theme and purpose of the final redaction; it can be read genetically and diachronically in order to trace

---

4.   For a clear—and entertaining—discussion of issues behind this phrase, see J. Barton, *Reading the Old Testament* (London: Darton, Longman & Todd, 1984).

5.   As I have argued in Chapter 4.

the origin and history of the materials used in the final redaction. The
continuing existence of earlier sources (e.g. Samuel–Kings) enables
earlier phases of the material to be appreciated, each in its own individual and potentially still valid intention. Chronicles thus provides
something of a controllable case study for methodology in Hebrew
Bible criticism. In this chapter, I am seeking to re-examine that case
study and to reactivate the analogy which it may provide for editorial
procedures that may lie behind other passages in the Hebrew Bible, in
particular, the Sinai pericope in Exodus 19–40, where they are now
obscured because of the more thorough integration of sources and
redaction.[6]

1. *The Literary-Critical Analogy*

The old use of the Chronicles analogy in Pentateuchal studies was to
provide literary-critical support for the Documentary Hypothesis. On
the basis of Chronicles, I should firmly align myself with those who
regard literary criticism, in the form in which it has been conventionally understood in Hebrew Bible research, as, so far as it goes, an
entirely legitimate enterprise. If one were to analyse the books of
Chronicles where they are parallel to Samuel–Kings and divide the
material into sources, 'C' for the Chronicler's own material and 'SK'
for that derived from Samuel–Kings, one would frequently get a picture
of an editor working with what at first sight, at any rate, appears to be a
scissors-and-paste technique, combining sources in blocks, verses, half-
verses and even smaller elements in a way precisely similar to, indeed,
on occasion, still more complex than, that envisaged by the most acute
of the old-time literary critics in the Pentateuch. One example, 1 Chron.
21.1-8, which could be reduplicated in comparable terms many times
over, must suffice:

---

6.   A draft of this chapter was read at the Summer Meeting of the Society for
Old Testament Study, 1986, under the title, '"Der Schluß liefert den Schlüssel":
The Application of a Principle to Exodus' (i.e. Chronicles, in date at or near the
conclusion of the canon, provides the interpretative key for earlier parts). The
pleasingly alliterative German I owe to a conversation with Hans Walter Wolff,
who, naturally, bears no responsibility for the case presented here; it expresses his
view of the function of the last verses in the book of Jonah for the interpretation of
that book.

SK	1_bab_* 2_aai_*		2_ac_*	2_bb_*	3_aab_*_c_*	3_ba_*
1 Chron. 21	----------------	----------	--------	--------	-------------	--------
C	1_a_*	2_aaii_b*	2_ba_		3_ad_	3_bb_

SK	4_a_* 4_bab_* 5_a_*_b_*			8_aa_*_b_ci		8_b_
1 Chron. 21	------------------------	-----	----	-------------	-------	------
C		6	7*	8_a_cii		

To suggest that this method of interweaving written sources is an alien imposition by the modern Western study-based critic onto the ancient biblical text[7] is simply not true. If any critic had proposed on the basis of 1 Chronicles 21, without the benefit of the SK parallel, an analysis as complicated as this, he would have been laughed out of court, manifestly wrongly.

But the analysis of this and other examples also shows clearly enough that the concept of an editorial conflation of two pre-existing literary 'sources' or 'documents' is not entirely adequate. The asterisks signal a degree of cross-contamination between the two supposed 'sources' that virtually defies tabulation; they are an external indication of a scale of editorial intervention that greatly exceeds a merely passive harmonizing activity that is subservient to prior tradition. The Chronicler has indeed had SK as a document in front of him but he has so radically reconceptualized and modified that document, selecting, abbreviating, expanding, rearranging and reformulating it, that it has largely lost in his work its independent documentary character. Further, his own material, C, is more than a 'document' interwoven with another pre-existing document: it represents not merely a substantial amount of intercalated new material, but, rather, a totally new framework and groundwork within which the modified SK is received and, indeed, significantly reconceived. To say that C is both source and redaction, as one conventionally would, does scant justice to the achievement of the writer, who under new theological impulse has presented a thesis, which, while it is formulated in continuity with received tradition, radically extends the content of that tradition. One may guess

---

7. Cf., e.g., R.K. Harrison, *Introduction to the Old Testament* (London: Tyndale, 1970), p. 522: 'It seems only proper to conclude that the composition of the Pentateuch followed contemporary scribal and compilatory patterns, and was not the result of redactional manipulation of artificial documentary sources.'

that the author belongs to the Levitical school, whose office it is to expound Scripture with a hermeneutical flair that combines faithfulness to tradition with the independence and freedom of theological creativity.

The hypothesis prompted by Chronicles is, thus, that elsewhere in the Hebrew Bible, in particular in the Pentateuch, there is an analogous phenomenon. The Levitical school, receiving and reconceiving pre-existing sources, has, in similar sovereign freedom, presented a new synthesis of tradition and innovatory theological reflection. There is, indeed, the lively possibility that both C and P, to retain the conventional siglum for the assumed final redaction of the Pentateuch, are nearly related to one another both in time and in authorship.

2. *The Analogy of the Fundamentally Theological Character of the End-Redaction*

Following the approach outlined at the beginning of this article, one may apply the Chronicles analogy first of all to the Sinai pericope in its final form. At this level is there a statement being made synchronically which is analogous in character, content and method to that of Chronicles?

As I have argued elsewhere,[8] Chronicles presents an account of preexilic and exilic Israel that is primarily theological rather than historiographical in intention. Already in the genealogical section in 1 Chronicles 1–9 the theme of the work is set forth: Israel's vocation to holiness amid the world of the nations. This theme is expressed by means of a stylized presentation of the materials. Using an arrangement of the tribes that is unique to himself, the Chronicler portrays the ideal mechanism whereby Israel's vocation to holiness can be fulfilled: the tribes of Israel are disposed symmetrically around the tribe of Levi, whose custodial function is to preserve and monitor Israel's state and practice of holiness (1 Chron. 5.27–6.66).

This symmetry in the presentation of the tribes of Israel as disposed around the Levites in the midst invites comparison with the stylized arrangement of the tribes in the account of the camp in the wilderness in Numbers 4 and suggests a *prima facie* ground for the legitimacy of the analogy. The distribution of the root *qdš*, from which 'holiness' and

---

8.   See Chapter 4.

related words are derived, with 'centres of gravity' in both Chronicles and the Sinai pericope as a whole (Exod. 19.1–Num. 10.10),[9] gives further *prima facie* evidence for the legitimacy of the analogy in terms not simply of the character and method of the material but also of its substance. The thesis is strengthened that the Sinai pericope comprises material that is primarily theological in character, that a central feature within this theological material is Israel's vocation to holiness, and that the method of expressing this theme includes the stylized presentation of the material in symmetrical form.

An obvious example of such arrangement of material for theological purpose is provided by the immediate external context of the Sinai pericope. Exodus 15.22–18.27 and Num. 10.11–36.13 provide an outer framework whereby Sinai is placed centrally as the focal point of the whole wilderness wandering period. In that framework there is a pattern of recurrent motifs disposed in a relatively symmetrical fashion: for example, the miracles of the quails (Exod. 16.13; Num. 11.31-35), manna (Exod. 16.14-31; Num. 11.6-9) and water from the rock (Exod. 17.1-7; Num. 20.2-13); the arrival of Jethro (Exod. 18.1-12) and the introduction of Hobab (Num. 10.29-32); the appointment of assistants for Moses (Exod. 18.13-27; Num. 11.16-17, 24-30). A dominant thread throughout is the 'murmuring of the people' (Exod. 15.24; 16.2, 7-9, 12; 17.3; Num. 14.2, 27, 29, 36; 16.11; 17.6, 20, 25).

That the primary character of this framework material, at least in the Exodus part, is theological rather than historiographical is clear from a number of considerations. The chronology stated is inadequate for the events recorded: between the fifteenth of the second month (Exod. 16.1) and the first day of the third month (Exod. 19.1), there are the incidents recorded in Exodus 16, which require at least one week (Exod. 16.27), leaving the final week of the second month for the journey 'by stages' from the Wilderness of Sin to Rephidim (Exod. 17.1), the miracle of the striking of the rock there (Exod. 17.1–7), the daylong battle with Amalek (Exod. 17.8-16), which took place the day after the choice of troops (v. 9), the building of an altar in commemoration of the victory on at least the following day (v. 16), the visit of Jethro (Exod. 18) involving a sacrificial meal at the Mountain of God (vv. 5, 12), at least a day during which Moses sat in tribunal from

---

9.   Of the 775 relevant occurrences of the root, some 261 are in the Sinai pericope of Exod. 19.1–Num. 10.10 (cf. some 80 in Chronicles).

morning to night (v. 13), with the consequent appointment of the judges on, presumably, another occasion (vv. 24-25), and the journey from Rephidim to Sinai (19.1-2).

That this material is not primarily historiographical is indicated also by its presupposition of institutions that, in the light of later enactments in the Sinai pericope, were not yet in existence. This is particularly the case with the manna that is to be 'placed before YHWH...before the testimony' (Exod. 16.33-34). 'Before YHWH' implies the Tabernacle, yet to be specified in Exodus 25–31, let alone constructed; it is the Decalogue, only to be revealed in Exod. 20.1-17, which is the 'testimony' (Exod. 31.18; 34.28).

I should suggest that, on occasion, at least in the Exodus part of the framework of the Sinai pericope, as in other cases in the narrative in Exodus 12–13 to be noted below under §4, long-standing institutions are couched in narrative form and are given additional warrant by association with the exodus from Egypt and the period of the wilderness wandering. This must be true of the Sabbath narrative in Exod. 16.23-36 (cf., too, departure from any historical account of the incident itself in vv. 35-36). It may be true of other incidents also, especially the selection of the judges in Exod. 18.13-27 (cf. the frequentative tense of the verbs in v. 26).

What is true of the external framework of the Sinai pericope holds also for its internal arrangement, not least in Exodus 19–40. Symmetry is again strikingly in evidence: the seven chapters, Exodus 25–31, which provide the specification for the Tabernacle, are followed by the six, 35–40, which recount in significantly repetitive terms its construction. This recapitulation is not some regrettable priestly prolixity glorying in insignificant detail for its own sake. Their very mass and repetitiveness suggest that to the mind of the redactor these passages, whatever the sensibility of the reader, mark the true climax of the narrative. The goal of the narrative is not the covenant at Sinai but the Tabernacle in the midst, the form of the divine presence indwelling in the centre of his people and the location where the holy people express their sanctity of life.

This ideal of holiness is also expressed in the Sinai pericope hierarchically through the symmetry of the social pyramid. As, for example, in 1 Chronicles 2–4 the House of David is set at the apex by means of the symmetrical arrangement of successive groups of the House of

Judah,[10] so hierarchy within the community at Sinai is indicated by the disposition of the people at the holy mountain (e.g. Exod. 24): Moses the mediator with sole access to the cloud of theophany and revelation; Joshua his successor in close attendance; thereafter Aaron, head of the priesthood to be, and Hur, grandfather of the craftsman of the Tabernacle (?; cf. Exod. 31.2); while the representative elders are near the top, the young men with the people are at the bottom.

The theological analogy between Exodus and Chronicles holds even further. Both recognize that the ideal stated is the ideal marred. The Chronicler records that Israel has made many false starts and aborted restarts. Though Reuben is the first-born (1 Chron. 2.1), Judah now stands in first position (1 Chron. 2.3–4.23). Within the supplanting House of Judah the first three sons are removed. Then arises Achar guilty of the archetypal sin of *ma'al* (1 Chron. 2.7), the violation of the holy (cf. Lev. 5.14-26), which provides the Chronicler with the key thematic term of his whole work, both in the genealogies (1 Chron. 2.7;

10. The use of symmetry in 1 Chron. 2–8:
     (a) Conventional sequence 2.3-4

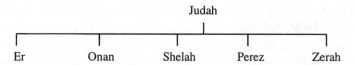

     (b) Ideological sequence 2.5–4.23

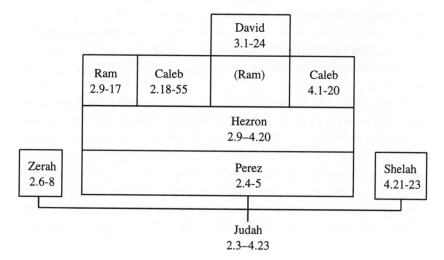

5.25; 9.2) and in the histories, from Saul (1 Chron. 10.13-14) down through the post-Solomonic kings of Judah beginning with Rehoboam (2 Chron. 12.2) to Zedekiah (2 Chron. 36.14). So in Exodus the ideal form of the relationship between God and Israel, the 'holy nation' (Exod. 19.6), is no sooner sealed in covenant (Exod. 24), and the form of the divine indwelling presence specified in the Tabernacle, the locus where Israel's holiness will be expressed (Exod. 25–31), than Israel is guilty of the apostasy of the golden calf (Exod. 32–34).

If the Chronicles model is applied, it may even be suspected that this is an eschatological statement. It is a fundamental error, I believe, to read Chronicles as the first part of a historical work which continues in Ezra–Nehemiah. Chronicles, rather, presupposes Ezra–Nehemiah, as can be most clearly seen, perhaps, by the use of Nehemiah 11 in 1 Chronicles 9. It is a theological reflection on the fact that, though 'the Return' has, historically speaking, taken place culminating in the work of Ezra and Nehemiah, the definitive return, 'the Return' properly speaking, depends on an act of atonement for Israel's *ma'al* in which God alone has the initiative and for which Israel waits maintaining meantime under Levitical instruction what form of holiness it can. Thus in Exod. 24.1, 9 an ominous note is sounded by the redactor of the final form of the Sinai pericope: the presence on the mountain of Aaron's two sons Nadab and Abihu, rebels to be. As the Chronicler notes that the priesthood is not saved from exile by the rites of their own altar (1 Chron. 5.27-41 records the names of Nadab and Abihu and takes the line of the priesthood only as far as Jehozadak, high-priest at the time of the exile), so the redactor in Exodus shows that the priesthood is implicated to the utmost degree in the apostasy of the people in the golden calf incident in chs. 32–34, the ultimate consequence of which, it is hinted, is to be exile (Exod. 32.34). As in 1 Chron. 5.27–6.66 and 9, so in Exodus 32 the Levites are exalted in rank above the Aaronic priesthood.

The symmetry of the presentation of the Tabernacle in the Sinai peri-cope in Exodus has, thus, added significance. The primal ideal of the form of the divine indwelling presence revealed in the first 40 days on the mountain (Exod. 24.18) is matched after the apostasy by the second 40 days on the mountain (Exod. 34.28), which are to issue in Leviticus in the specification of the sacrificial system, with its climax in Leviticus 5 in the laws of *ma'al* and its atonement, and the 'Holiness Code' of Leviticus 17–26. The Tabernacle, the half-sized Temple in the wilderness, is not, then, merely the retrojection of the Second Temple into the pre-settlement period for the purposes of warrant. Its orientation is to the writer's present 'in exile' and to the future he awaits: it is the form of the divine presence now in the wilderness, the 'wilderness of the nations' as Ezekiel 20 puts it, as the writer awaits that definitive future settlement in the land, which can only come about through the act of God himself; it is the mode of spiritual life in the Diaspora in the period of the unrealized ideal of 'The Return'. It is tempting to find in Ezekiel's *miqdāš mᵉ'aṭ* (Ezek. 11.16) a reference to this theological wilderness Tabernacle. No less than the Chronicler, and, one might add, the Deuteronomist, the writer in Exodus envisages himself and his people as poised in the wilderness on the eve of the settlement as an eschatological event. The P document's very chronology, dating the exodus in the 2666th year after creation, that is, ⅔ through an age of 100 generations of 40 years,[11] would already suggest an eschatological statement.

As the Chronicler's work is fundamentally ideological, a theological essay that is inalienably eschatological in its orientation, so too is that of the final redactor of the Sinai pericope. In both it is only through the recognition of the theological and hermeneutical intention of the author that coherence can be imparted to what is in terms of Israel's history and its history of religion nonsensical and in literary terms chaotic.

3. *The Analogy of a Presupposed Deuteronomistic Edition*

The discussion thus far has considered the Chronicles analogy insofar as it suggests that the primary objective of the interpreter must be to do justice to the theological intention of the final editor which he is seeking to express synchronically by his incorporation of traditional sources into a new literary formulation. The analogy, however, prompts the further, diachronic, question: if, as is palpably the case, the Chronicler in the greater proportion of his work presupposes and reformulates the earlier Deuteronomistic History, especially Samuel–Kings, is there evidence that in the Sinai pericope in Exodus a prior Deuteronomistic edition of the material has likewise been presupposed and incorporated in suitably modified form?

---

11. Observation attributed by Carpenter and Harford-Battersby, *Hexateuch*, I, p. 126, to Gutschmid and Nöldeke.

Genetic-diachronic questions have been dominant in criticism since its beginnings, prompted in large measure, one may imagine, by the no doubt very laudable aim of approximating as closely as possible to, if not actually recovering, the original form of the tradition uncontaminated by later accretion, or perhaps, even, an original underlying event. In such an approach, it is natural that one should seek to maximize the evidence for the existence of early sources, J and E, or of their precursors or subdivisions, G, L, N, or whatever, and for the written or oral transmission of the constituent units of tradition.[12]

It has been widely held that source D is virtually confined to the book of Deuteronomy. Given the already great complexities in the identification of J and E and their precursors, this view on the confined nature of D may have been reinforced by some subconscious relief that at least that level of additional complexity has been removed. But if one approaches Exodus from the end of the growth process, then one is equally curious to know if there is evidence that would support a hypothesis not simply of deliberate final redaction but also of pre-final-stage redaction. As the Chronicler's work is itself a complementary theological version of Israel's history to that of the Deuteronomist, especially in Samuel and Kings, which the Chronicler freely exploits for his own purpose, is it possible that the final theological editor of Exodus has similarly freely exploited a pre-existing theological edition of Exodus in the Deuteronomistic mould, an edition that, in the light of the Deuteronomistic History, is likely to be dominated by the covenant theme? Almost merely to pose the question in relation to Exodus 19–40 is to answer it in the affirmative.

To my mind, the most suggestive initial material for identifying such a redaction is Exod. 23.20–33. The presence of Deuteronomic phraseology in this passage has frequently been pointed out; the parallels to Deuteronomy 7 seem to be particularly close.[13] But that this is more than just a Deuteronomic insertion at the end of Exodus 23, is indeed, rather, evidence of a Deuteronomistic recension, seems to me to be suggested by the rather clear way in which the passage is picked up in the Deuteronomistic History in Judg. 2.1-5. The relationship between

12. E.g. O. Eissfeldt, *The Old Testament: An Introduction* (Oxford: Basil Blackwell, 1965); G. Fohrer, *Introduction to the Old Testament* (Nashville: Abingdon Press, 1968).

13. E.g. J.P. Hyatt, *Exodus* (NCB; London: Oliphants, 1971); Childs, *Exodus*, *in loc.*

the two passages is established not simply by the coincidence of vocabulary,[14] but by the corresponding key function that they both discharge within their contexts: Exod. 23.20-33 is the coda to the Book of the Covenant (Exod. 20.22–23.33); Judg. 2.1-5 is the coda to the account of the settlement in the land (Josh. 1.1–Judg. 2.5). Further, Exod. 23.20-33 functions in a way similar to Deuteronomy 27–28. As the code in Deut. 12.1–26.15 is succeeded by a paraenetic section promising the blessing of the covenant on an obedient people and threatening the curse of the covenant on a disobedient people, the blessing and curse being then demonstrated in the ensuing Deuteronomistic History, so the code in Exod. 20.23–23.19 is bound by the Deuteronomist into his presentation of covenant and of the course of the history of Israel as dominated by the blessing and curse of the covenant by this passage, Exod. 23.20-33, and its counterpart, Judg. 2.1-5.

While Exod. 23.20-33 provides a *prima facie* case for a Deuteronomistic redaction of Exodus, there are many other passages in the Sinai (or, rather, at this stage in the history of redaction, the Horeb) pericope that suggest the same conclusion. The key series of passages, I should suggest, is Exod. 24.12-18; 31.18–34.35 (i.e. all of the remainder of the Sinai pericope in Exodus after 24.11, omitting the passages on the specification and construction of the Tabernacle in Exod. 25.1–31.17; 35.1–40.38, which are generally attributed to the P-writer). The striking phenomenon is the almost verbatim correspondence between the 'backbone' of this series, 24.12*, 18b*; 31.18*; 32.7, 8a, 9, 10, 15a*, 19b, 20*; 34.1, 4*, 28, which defines the sequence of events and structure of the narrative, and the account in Deut. 9.7–10.11 (specifically, 9.9, 10, 12-15, 17, 18a, 21a; 10.1a, 2a, 3abb, 4a). There are other passages in the Horeb pericope reminiscent of this account in Deuteronomy (Exod. 32.11-14; cf. Deut. 9.18-20, 25-29; Exod. 32.15b-19a; cf. Deut. 9.16; Exod. 34.28a; cf. Deut. 9.18abcd), while still others are strongly Deuteronomic in colouring (Exod. 32.30–33.23*).[15] While the

14. Especially 'the angel' (Exod. 23.20, 23; Judg. 2.14), *šmʿ bqwl* (Exod. 23.21; Judg. 2.2), *grš* (Exod. 23.28-29; Judg. 2.3), *yšby hʾrṣ* (Exod. 23.31; Judg. 2.2), *krt bryt l* (Exod. 23.32; Judg. 2.2), *hyh l lmwqš* (Exod. 23.33; Judg. 2.3).

15. The articles by J. Vermeylen ('Les sections narratives de Deut 5–11 et leur relations à Ex 19–34') and C.T. Begg ('The Destruction of the Calf [Exod 32,20/ Deut 9,21]'), which had every promise of relevance to the argument of this paper, in N. Lohfink (ed.), *Das Deuteronomium* (BETL, 68; Leuven: Leuven University

question of the priority of which form—the narrative in Exodus or the speech in Deuteronomy—is primary may be insoluble, the plain fact would seem to be that both are Deuteronomic.

Occasionally the history of redaction is as clear in Exodus as it is in Chronicles. As the extant SK text attests the text received by the Chronicler and modified for his purpose, so on at least three occasions a text still extant in Deuteronomy enables the reconstruction of the text of the D-writer in Exodus, which the P-writer has received and reconceived for his purpose. (1) In Exod. 32.20b, Deuteronomy's rite (Deut. 9.21) of washing away of guilt by the flowing stream (in the Sinai Peninsula in May/June?!)—cf. the rite in Deut. 21.4 (involving an *'eglâ*!; cf. the *'ēgel massēkâ*, Exod. 32.4; Deut. 9.14)—has been replaced by a rite reminiscent of the trial by ordeal in Num. 5.24 in connection with the wife suspected of *ma'al* against her husband, a particularly significant reminiscence in view of the theme of the Chronicler's work and its possible relation to P. (2) In Exodus 34 at the end of both vv. 1a and 1b the references to the construction of the ark of the covenant in the parallel in Deut. 10.1b, 2b, 3a*a* have been suppressed not only because P gives elsewhere his account of the construction of the ark (Exod. 25.10-22; 37.1-9) but in order to impart to the occasion of the giving of the second pair of tablets a sanctity comparable to that of the first (Exod. 19.11b*b*[Sinai]-13,[16] 18, 20-25, which I should thus regard as P). (3) The ordination of the Levites in Deut. 10.8-9 has been transposed to the end of the golden calf incident (Exod. 32.25-29) and their role has been transformed in the process from that of bearers of the ark of the covenant into that of YHWH zealots; the relative status of Levite, priest and people in this chapter is again comparable to that in Chronicles and finds here its explanation.

That this redaction is justifiably to be regarded as not simply Deuteronomic but Deuteronomistic is indicated by the verbatim correspondence between Exod. 32.4b, 8b and 1 Kgs 12.28b*cd* and echoes of

Press/Peeters, 1985), noted in *ZAW* 98 (1986), pp. 140-41, were not available to me at the time of writing. I have engaged with part of Vermeylen's argument in Chapter 12, nn. 1 and 25; Begg returns to the subject in 'The Destruction of the Golden Calf Revisited (Exod 32,20/Deut 9,21)', in Vervenne and Lust (eds.), *Deuteronomy and Deuteronomic Literature*, pp. 469-79, to defend the position against Van Seters that Deut. 9.21 is dependent on Exod. 32.20, and not the reverse.

16. Not 19.10-16a*a*, as in the original version of this chapter, in the light of the argument of Chapter 9 and of Renaud's observation noted in Chapter 10, n. 10.

1 Kgs 12.32 in Exod. 32.5 ('altar', 'festival'). The narrative of the golden calf is, I believe, fundamentally an aggadic *midrash* on the breach of the second commandment. At the very moment of the constitution of the people of God on the exclusive terms of the covenant with YHWH, the people are guilty of apostasy in the prototypical form of the golden calf. This apostasy is reproduced through all the subsequent history of Israel, the particular antitype of which is, precisely, the golden calves of Bethel and Dan set up by Jeroboam at the founding of the Northern Kingdom, as recorded in the Deuteronomistic History. As the first unity of the people with their God and with one another is destroyed at the mountain by the golden calf, so their subsequent unity under the Davidic House is destroyed at Bethel and Dan by Jeroboam's golden calves.

But if an extensive Deuteronomic/Deuteronomistic edition of the Horeb pericope is, thus, to be recognized, then, it seems to me, Exod. 34.17-26 is to be seen in a new light. Whereas traditionally in literary criticism the parallels between Exod. 34.17-26 and 23.12-19 are held to provide evidence for the existence of two parallel sources (be they J and E, respectively, or some other independent fragments of tradition),[17] from the perspective of possible Deuteronomistic redaction the often close similarity of language in the two passages suggests, rather, deliberate repetition by the Deuteronomist. If one discounts 34.17 and the legislation on firstlings (34.19-20b*a*, which may in fact be the more original text; cf. the preservation of only the last phrase of 34.20b*b* in 23.15b), which have no parallels in 23.12-19, and the similarly unparalleled homiletic explanation in 34.23b*b*, 24, of the 76 words remaining 57 (or more than 75 per cent) are identical. There are here not parallel sources but largely identical materials deliberately repeated. The reason for such a repetition in a Deuteronomistic redaction would not be hard to find: it is the editor's theological purpose to express the long-suffering mercy of God that the covenant which ought to have been abrogated by the people's apostasy in worshipping the golden calf is reaffirmed on identical terms but now in transformed circumstances. The choice of the parallel material is particularly significant. Exodus 34.18-26 reproduces the end of the legislative part of the Book of the Covenant; 34.17 resumes the second commandment of the Decalogue,

17. Cf. Wellhausen's attribution to J, which L. Perlitt, *Bundestheologie im Alten Testament* (WMANT, 36; Neukirchen–Vluyn: Neukirchener Verlag, 1969), pp. 203ff., cites and with which he critically engages.

which, of course, in the Deuteronomic recension of the Decalogue in
Deut. 5.8-10 is part of the first commandment. That is, Exod. 34.17-26
picks up the beginning of the Decalogue and the end of the Book of the
Covenant to mark by a kind of merismus (in this case, totality indicated
by extremes) the entire contents of Decalogue and Book of the Covenant on the conjoint basis of which the covenant was made (Exod. 20.1–
23.19). Is not this Deuteronomistic shorthand for saying that the
covenant unilaterally abrogated by Israel is remade on precisely the
same terms? These observations are perhaps confirmed by the fact that
Exod. 23.13 seems already to mark a conclusion and that thus Exod.
23.14-19, the part mainly reproduced in Exod. 34.17-26, appears to be
a second conclusion to the Book of the Covenant, which links immediately with 23.20-33, a section I have already identified as Deuteronomistic.

In summary, the attribution of materials in 24.12-18; 31.18–34.35
would be somewhat as follows:[18]

18. The ultimate artificiality of such tabulation must again be stressed. In line
with remarks in §1 above, it should be said that 'D' and 'P' do not represent
sources. Rather 'D' represents the remains of one theological edition (the D-
writer's), which has been incorporated into a new theological edition (the P-
writer's). Since the P-writer may quote, and write in the manner of, the D-writer, it
may on occasion be virtually impossible, where external evidence is lacking, to disentangle the two (e.g. in ch. 33). The D-writer may, in turn, be incorporating earlier
material (e.g. the allusions to the Decalogue and B in ch. 34). The possibility of a
literary, oral and transmission history before the D-writer's edition is no more ruled
out here (see §5 below) than in DtrH.

A few points of detail may be given in substantiation of this attribution of
material:

24.12   *lḥt h'bn*, Deut. 5.22; 9.9a, etc.; *htwrh whmṣwh*, Childs, *Exodus*,
         p. 499, cites 2 Kgs 17.37, i.e. Dtrc.;
24.13   *yhwš' mšrtw*, Deut. 1.38; 3.21, 28, etc.; Josh. 1.1-9, i.e. D/Dtrc.;
         hr h'lhym = *ḥrb*, Exod. 3.1;
24.14   opens with inversion similar to 24.1; *zqnym*, cf. 24.1, 9; *ngš*, cf.
         24.1; 34.30, 32, therefore same edition;
24.15-18a some Dc, colouring: *h'nn*, Deut. 4.11; 5.22; 31.15; *kbwd*, Deut.
         5.24 (but both in Exod. 40.34); *'š*, Deut. 4.24; 9.10, 15; but on the
         other hand, *syny*, 'the seventh day', and the resumption in Exod.
         34.29-35, with the occurrence there of *syny*, *'dt* (v. 29), *'dh*
         (v. 31), point to P; 15a is then a redactional resumption (after the
         pluperfect of 14) of 13b, as is 18ab before the re-emergence of D
         (hence redundant repetition of 'Moses' in 18);

```
D       12*–13          18b*     18aa          18ac*b       1–15aab*b   16–20a
ch. 24  --------------------- 31 ---------------------- 32 -----------------------
P                 14–18a*                 18ab                               20b


D       21–24        30ab–34    1 – 17        19abcb          1
ch. 32  ------------------------ 33 ------------------------- 34 --------------
P                  25–30aa      35          18.19aa       20–23           2–3


D       4aa          4abii*          4baiib.5–28
ch. 34  --------------------------------------------------------
P                  4abi      4acbai                     29*–35
```

From this vantage point, and on the basis of similar arguments from parallels between the Deuteronomic accounts of the theophany and covenant-making at Horeb (especially Deut. 4.11-13; 5.1–5, 23-33) and those in Exodus, the following approximate attribution of the materials

24.18b	cf. Deut. 9.9b;
31.18	verbatim Deut. 9.10a (with adjustment from speech to narrative), with P amplifications, 18ab (cf. *syny*), and *lht h'dt*, 18ac;
32.15a	gives a good example of the possibility of one-word adjustment by P: the virtually verbatim coincidence with Deut. 9.15 (with, again, adjustment from speech to narrative) is altered by the change of *hbryt* to *h'dt*;
32.15b-18,	which have no parallel in Deut. 9–10, still have Dc. echoes: 16, *hmktb*, cf. Deut. 10.4; 17, Joshua; 18, root *ḥlš* used in association with Joshua in Exod. 17.13;
32.21-24	has no parallel in Deut. 9–10 but resumes the events of 32.1-4;
32.30ab-34	picks up the atoning function of the rite of pouring the dust on the flowing stream suppressed by P in 32.20b; for *kpr* in 30, cf. the rite in Deut. 21, v. 8; 34a, the angel of 23.20-33; Jdc. 2.1-5 reappears; 34b, reminiscent of the vocabulary of Jer/DtrJer. e.g. Jer. 5.9;
32.35	finds no mention in Deut. 9–10 and contradicts preceding verses;
33.1-5	cf. 32.34; Deut. 10.11; 1, cf. 32.7, 13; 2, cf. 23.20-33; 3 and 5, cf. 32.9, 10;
33.6-11	the *'hl mw'd* occurs in Deuteronomy only in 31.14-15; there is a close relationship of this passage to Num. 12, especially vv. 4, 5, which is indirectly alluded to in Deut. 9.22-24 (cf. comments below under §5); for 11a, cf. Deut. 5.4; 34.10; 33.12–17, 19 picks up 32.34 and is resumed in 34.5-9; 33.18, 19aa, 20-23 may be intended as correction of 33.11.

of the remaining narrative sections of the Horeb pericope (Exod. 19.1–20.1; 20.18-21; 24.1-11) can be attempted.[19]

D		2b-11ab*		14-17		19		1.18–21	
ch. 19	--- 20 ---------24--------
P	1–2a		11b*–13		18		20–25		1–2

D	3-4	5ac–8	
ch. 24	----------------------
P		5aab	9–11

A particularly far-reaching example of Deuteronomistic redaction may be found in the Book of the Covenant itself in the manner in which a basic law-code combining *ḥōq ûmišpāṭ* has been transformed into a covenant document by means of the addition of a framework of *dābār* and *miṣwâ*. The structure of the Book of the Covenant is fairly plain to see:[20]

19. Again a few points of detail to substantiate the attribution of materials may be given (the tabulation in 19.11-16 and 24.3-8 is simplified from the original version; see n. 16 and Chapter 8, n. 14):

19.3-8(9?) is widely accepted by commentators as Dc.; cf., e.g., Hyatt, *Exodus*, and Childs, *Exodus*, *ad loc.*;

20.18-21 has affinities with the Dc. account of the theophany, especially in Deut. 5.22-27; for *nsh* (v. 20), cf. Deut. 8.2, 16; related material in Exod. 19.16abcb, 17, 19 must then also be Dc.; the remaining verses in Exod. 19 with their concepts of hierarchy, purification and the accompaniments appropriate to revelation (for the latter, cf. 34.2-3) are appropriately assigned to P;

20.1-17 was, no doubt, present in the D-writer's edition but has undergone P revision, especially in the Sabbath commandment;

24.1-11 may be assigned using similar criteria: 1-2, 9-11, with the emphasis on hierarchy, derive from P (see below §5); Nadab and Abihu occur otherwise in P contexts; the covenant on the plain may be largely D; the rather awkward *prym* at the end of v. 5 may be an accusative of specification to make clear that the sacrificial animals used were those appropriate for rites of national atonement and consecration; cf. Lev. 4.

20. While the terminology for the varieties of legal and covenantal stipulations chosen in the text has a fair possibility of reflecting strict usage, the Hebrew Bible is notoriously imprecise in its application of technical terms. Cf., e.g., '*ḥqq*', *TDOT*, V (1986), pp. 139ff.

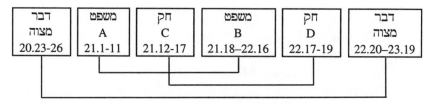

There are two blocks of casuistic *mišpāṭ* material formulated in the
third-person indicative style (A 21.1-11; B 21.18–22.16) and two
blocks of apodeictic *ḥōq* material formulated in third-person participial
style (C 21.12-17; D 22.17-19). These have been intercalated in the
sequence A–C–B–D as a law-code, *ḥōq ûmišpāṭ*, perhaps already in the
pre-Deuteronomistic stage. This law-code has then been set within the
framework of second-person address, either in the singular (*dābār*) or
plural (*miṣwâ*) (20.23-26; 22.20–23.19). The identification of this
framework as Deuteronomistic, at least so far as its formulation is concerned, depends on the observation that virtually the whole of the
Covenant Code in Deuteronomy 12.1–26.15 is cast in precisely this
second person imperatival *dābār* and *miṣwâ* form, even though much of
the Deuteronomy Covenant Code material is fundamentally analogous,
and to a limited extent parallel, to the *ḥōq ûmišpāṭ* material in the Book
of the Covenant (cf. Deut. 12.1). Whereas the Deuteronomist has been
content merely to provide the inherited, traditional, law-code in the
Book of the Covenant with a covenantal framework, in Deuteronomy
itself the whole law-code has been transformed into a Covenant Code.
Consequently, the Deuteronomistic editor may not only have provided
the name, the 'Book of the Covenant' (Exod. 24.7), for the preceding
law-code but appears also to have placed that law-code within a
covenantal framework.

The identification of such a large-scale Deuteronomistic redaction in
Exodus 19–40 under the theme of covenant might then lead to the proposal that all notions of covenant in this section are to be attributed to
the Deuteronomic school. This is a conclusion that I, personally, would
resist, but in order to consider it a further question has to be raised.

4. *The Relation of the Sinai Pericope in Exodus to Historical Events*

To place the genetic question of the historicity of the narrative in the
forefront of critical attention, whether in Chronicles or in Exodus, is to
obscure the ideological nature of the writing; yet to ignore the question

of historicity may be to overlook the artificiality of the construction. A number of preliminary points can be made that make it unlikely that the Sinai pericope in Exodus as it stands should be read as a straightforward transcript of a series of historical events (cf. already, remarks on the historicity of the week before the arrival at Sinai in §2, above). These points are only of value if they serve to expose the essential character of the narrative as theological essay rather than historiography; otherwise they are cheap and demeaning. They should not be construed as intended to detract in any way from the validity of the narrative as a theological statement; they are, in fact, beside the point. Indeed, the possibility may be entertained that, as in Chronicles, obviously non-historical materials have been consciously incorporated into the narrative in the full awareness of its true nature and intention as essentially theological. As the account of a series of miraculous and supernatural events, it is not to be rationalistically dissolved into a series of mundane historical happenings. The narrative, like the narrative of the escape from Egypt, is deliberately cast in the form of a miracle in order to signal the fact that it is a theological statement.

Such preliminary points would include the following. If Mount Sinai is given its traditional identification as Jebel Musa in the south Sinai Peninsula, it is located in an area that can today sustain a Bedouin population of only some 3000;[21] there are indications from flora and fauna that climatic conditions have been unchanged since the Chalcolithic age.[22] It is impossible that two to three million Israelites should have encamped before Sinai for a year, not to mention the sustaining of this number of people for the 40 years in the wilderness. The repeated stiff climb of the ascent now marked by the 3750 steps from St Catherine's Monastery to the summit of Sinai in midsummer heat would have been unendurable for the 80-year-old Moses. Recent archaeological research can find 'no relics from the Exodus' and no trace of Israelite occupation at Kadesh-barnea (Num. 12.26, etc.) before

---

21, Cf., e.g., M. Har-El, *The Sinai Journeys: The Route of the Exodus* (San Diego, CA: Ridgefield, 1983), p. 115.

22. Orally from Mr Avner Goren, Resident Archaeological Staff Officer of the Israeli Department of Antiquities in Sinai for a dozen years after the Six-Day War, during the Sinai excursion organized on the occasion of the International Congress on Biblical Archaeology, Jerusalem, April 1984. For financial assistance from the Carnegie Trust for the Universities of Scotland enabling me to participate in the Congress and its associated activities I here record my thanks.

the tenth century;[23] no material earlier than the Persian period has been recovered at the sites usually identified as Migdol and Baal-zephon (Exod. 14.2).[24]

The genre of the narrative as theological essay and the probability that in the final stages of its history it has passed through two redactions, the 'covenant' redaction of the D-writer and the 'holiness' redaction of the P-writer, do not lead me to be optimistic that a historical event lying at the base of the narrative will be recoverable by conventional literary-critical methods. Those who are capable of interpreting the exile, which they are presently experiencing, as a symbolical wilderness can hardly be expected to provide precise details of a geographical wilderness of a millennium earlier. Even further, however, in content the narrative concerns institutions, the three institutions of theophany, law and covenant, each of which possesses the qualities of timelessness and pervasiveness, rather than the character of a punctual historical event.

The situation in Exodus 19–40 is akin to that in Exodus 11–15. The genre of Exodus 11–15 is religious institution articulated in narrative form, in that case the three institutions of Passover, unleavened bread and firstlings.[25] As the exodus becomes the focal point of reference for these three institutions, which had in origin nothing whatever to do with Egypt or escape from Egypt, so it becomes in turn, through a kind of theological shorthand, the justification for all manner of institutions and practices: for example, Sabbath (Deut. 5.15), circumcision (Josh. 5.9), just weights and balances (Lev. 19.36). This articulation of institution in narrative form is in terms of experience, the resources for expressing that experience being drawn not simply from historical events but also from common lore: for example, in the first nine plagues or, in the Sinai pericope, in the description of the theophany at Sinai in terms of volcanic eruption. 'Historicization', which would imply the focusing of institution in terms of concrete historical incident, is thus too narrow a term.

This couching of institution in narrative form in terms of the multifarious lore of experience brings with it further stylization. Narrative

---

23. R. Cohen, *Kadesh-barnea: A Fortress from the Time of the Judean Kingdom* (Jerusalem: The Israel Museum, 1983), p. v.

24. E. Oren, 'Ancient Military Roads between Egypt and Cana'an', *Bulletin of the Anglo-Israel Archaeological Society* (1982), p. 20.

25. See Chapter 3; Chapter 9 extends the textual base to Exod. 1.1–24.11*.

requires linear progression from beginning, through development, to denouement. It requires thematic coherence and consistency in the presentation of the *dramatis personae*. I should thus regard the figure of Moses as a necessary literary creation (though not necessarily purely fictional) arising from the exigencies and impetus of the narrative. As Ezra of the 12-month ministry (Ezra 7.9; Neh. 8.2; 9.1; Ezra 10.9, 16-17) binds together as link-man the presentation of the 100 or 140 years of the return from exile, or Joshua, the Ephraimite, the conquest as part of the Deuteronomistic construction of events, so Moses, the Levite, whoever he was historically, dominates and integrates the whole presentation of exodus and Sinai in the book of Exodus. Historical actualities, as is their wont, so one may imagine, were vastly more complex. If Exodus 11–15, despite its apparent references to contemporary Egyptian history, is essentially ahistorical or suprahistorical, then, *a fortiori*, how much more is Exodus 19–40 with its purely inner-people-of-God reference? If the exodus is a secondary focus for institutions, how much more Sinai? Experiences and practices of all kinds are secondarily referred to Sinai, however intrinsically congenial a focus it may be, not primarily derived from Sinai.

What, then, of the historicity of Exodus 19–40? Because of their institutional character, I think that it is implausible in the nature of the case to look for one historical event underlying theophany, law-giving and covenant. One is tempted to regard Sinai as the location required by the constraints of the narrative: between an exodus from Egypt and an entry into the land where else in a self-consistent narrative of Israel's origins could the people-creating covenant-making and law-giving take place? If the legal corpus in Exodus 20–23 grew, as I believe it did, over an extended period of time and is, therefore, only secondarily associated in the form of a punctual event with Sinai, may not also covenant, which has its own complex history of development, be equally secondarily related to Sinai? And as for theophany, ought one not to look for it in association with established sanctuaries, or, perhaps, with a travelling ark and its tent-shrine, rather than in some non-locatable place? When I dutifully made the ascent of the traditional Mount Sinai, the Israeli guide[26] pointed out that the very non-existence of a fixed Jewish tradition about the location of Sinai suggests that

26. See n. 22.

there has been a deliberate avoidance of localization, lest such a locality becomes a mere religious fetish (cf. the 'loss' of the tradition about the location of the grave of Moses, Deut. 34.5). The mountain of Sinai, that is, of the vast indefinable terrain between the Egypt of the exodus and the Canaan of the conquest, is a literary device in the context of the book of Exodus. As an immemorial centre of pilgrimage, inherently impressive in its awesome landscape, Sinai congenially provides the lore for the portrayal of Israel's origins.

But the fact that the narrative lacks specific historicity does not mean that there is no underlying history. Is the covenant at Sinai, for example, merely an invention of the Deuteronomistic 'covenant' redaction? It may be, in the particular form in which it is now expressed in the Sinai pericope, but I should certainly wish to suggest that the notion of covenant as such was not the invention of the Deuteronomic school. Appeal does not have to be made to the Hittite Vassal Treaty to substantiate the fact that covenant was an institution that was commonplace in the world of Israel's origins.[27] It is clear from the nature of the case that the institution of covenant as the means of creating a bond that transcends the tie of blood was required as soon as two family groupings combined to form a larger unit or as soon as relations requiring the regulation of pasture and watering rights were entered into by pastor and peasant. Covenant thus belongs to the immemorial fabric of society. It is basically a socio-economic term describing contractual relations entered into by two parties before their respective God or gods as witness and sanction. It is the development of this essentially horizontal, inter-human, concept into the vertical, God–man, concept, so that covenant is now no longer *before* God(s) as witness and sanction, but *with* God as partner, which may well be the work of the Deuteronomistic school as a response to Assyrian overlordship. It is certainly notable how covenant is used in Deuteronomistic passages as an instrument of exclusivism (e.g. Exod. 23.23-33). While, thus, this is the concept of covenant now to be found in the Sinai pericope in Exodus, it marks the evolution of an institution the origins of which go back to the earliest stages of the formation of Israel as a people. In that sense the Sinai narrative is historical.

---

27. D.J. McCarthy, *Treaty and Covenant* (AnBib, 21A; Rome: Biblical Institute Press, 1978), pp. 18ff.

5. *The Pre-Deuteronomistic History of the Material*

These observations suggest that the present literary form of the narrative does not arise from the amalgamation of variant traditions of one underlying historical event or series of historical events, as generally assumed on the classical Documentary Hypothesis, but from the casting into quasi-historical narrative of shared commonplace institutions, which have in origin nothing exclusively, or even much, to do with Sinai, and the subjecting of that narrative to successive theological redactions. If institutional practices do lie at the base of the material, it may be a fundamental error to assume that their tradition will include an external scaffolding of historical events: institutions are the bearers of their own inner history. A working hypothesis must be that this literary task was accomplished by successive generations of the Levitical school of the teachers of Israel using the multifarious lore of shared common experience. It is the universal knowledge of theophany, law and covenant at myriad high-places, shrines and centres throughout the land, now definitively interpreted in terms of covenant and holiness, which underlies the present unitary narrative and provides a common set of presuppositions. Deuteronomic centralization of institution is, then, matched by this Levitical literary integration of a common heritage of religious and social practice; the one sanctuary of the one God of the one people, however ideally conceived, is served and supported by the one Scripture.[28]

Within the Sinai pericope there may well be, therefore, reminiscence of shared ancient convention now cast into literary form. It is the verisimilitude of common experience of theophany, law and covenant, secondarily referred to Sinai, that is here given literary form and subjected to heavy theological qualification in the double redaction of covenant and holiness. The antiquity and complexity of the growth of Israel's legal institutions and their relationship to wider ancient Near Eastern practice are here simply assumed.[29] There is space to illustrate the thesis of the casting of immemorial practice into literary form only in connection with covenant and theophany.

28. R.E. Clements, *God's Chosen People* (London: SCM Press, 1968), pp. 89ff.
29. Cf., e.g., S.M. Paul, *Studies in the Book of the Covenant in the Light of Cuneiform and Biblical Law* (VTSup, 18; Leiden: E.J. Brill, 1970).

I should look for a reminiscence of ancient convention behind 24.9-11: the communal meal, the *zebaḥ šᵉlāmîm*, in the hilltop sanctuary in the presence of Deity, shared by the representative elders of the local community. The scene is at that level reminiscent of, for example, the Jacob–Laban covenant in Gen. 31.44-54 and the communal sacrifice blessed by Samuel in 1 Sam. 9.12-24 (is it mere coincidence that the *qᵉrû'îm* of 1 Sam. 9.13, 22 reappear as tribal representatives in Num. 1.16; 26.9?). But such a scene has nothing specifically to do with Sinai. It is, indeed, virtually bypassed by D in his democratic covenant ceremony at the foot of the mountain where Israel as such is 'a kingdom of priests, a holy nation' (19.6). It is P, with the concept of hierarchy as the appropriate mode of expressing the transcendence, and yet the presence, of God, who reintroduces the pyramid of Moses, priesthood and the 70 elders (the original Sanhedrin? Cf. *Sanh.* 1.6), with the laity resolutely barred from approach. Exodus 24.2b indicates that P already knows D's view of the people at the foot of the mountain, though for D only Moses, accompanied by Joshua, has access to the mountain itself.

Theophany's institutional counterpart is the shrine. In my view, the passage reflecting the earliest view of theophany in the Sinai pericope is 33.7-11. It seems plausible to suggest that such a tent-shrine belongs to Israel's nomadic origins.[30] A tent-shrine seems to be embedded also in the early history of the monarchy (e.g. 2 Sam. 6.17; 1 Kgs 1.39). But that 33.7-11 presents merely the verisimilitude of ancient institution rather than a tradition deriving by historical line of transmission from that very institution itself is suggested by the intriguing place 33.7-11 seems to occupy in the development of the Deuteronomic corpus. That the passage may be Deuteronomic is indicated by the coincidence of language with Deut. 31.14-15. Further, it reflects a specific incident known to the Deuteronomist. The specific incident, the historical character of which need not be discussed here, is that recounted in Numbers 12: the challenge of Aaron and Miriam to Moses' authority at a location between Kibroth-hattaavah and the sending-out of the spies. The vocabulary of Num. 12.4-5 and the ideas of Num. 12.8 are reflected in Exod. 33.7-11. That this narrative of another of Aaron's misdeeds was at least known to the Deuteronomist, if it is not itself Deuteronomic, is clear from the reference to its geographical context in the snatch of the wilderness itinerary included in Deut. 9.22-24 in Deuteronomy's

---

30. B. Rothenberg, *Timna* (London: Thames & Hudson, 1972).

account of the events at Horeb in Deut. 9.7–10.11 already alluded to above in §3 as providing the 'backbone' of the Sinai pericope. Thus, even when a specific incident is available (Num. 12) and is known to the Deuteronomist (Deut. 9.22-24), it is merely its resources of vocabulary that are exploited here in a generalized account of a religious institution which recasts the past tense of narrative into the frequentative tense of habitual action (including even the unlikely repetitive 'he used to call it'). In literary form Exod. 33.7-11 is thus, even on its own terms, not the description of historical events but a verisimilitude of such events expressed in the form of institutional practice.

In the Sinai pericope, therefore, there is not presupposed one underlying historical event or series of events and one primary tradition of that event or series of events, whose ramified forms have now been brought by redactional activity into literary coherence, as on a traditional literary-critical hypothesis. The literary coherence does not reflect the integration of one shared complex of historical events but the integration of a shared set of institutions cast by the Levitical school into a definitive narrative form, which has passed through at least the two redactional stages marked by the D-writer and the P-writer. It is thus wholly appropriate that the entire Sinai pericope in Exodus is set within the framework of a single liturgical year with its implied round of religious institutions and observances: 19.1, 'on the first day of the third month after the exodus...'; 40.17, 'on the first day of the first month of the second year the Tabernacle was set up', not forgetting the burlesque of the New Year Festival in 32.5.[31]

6. Summary

Thanks to the existence of parallel texts, Chronicles provides a case study in redactional method. Read synchronically, it is an eschatological theological essay presenting a 'holiness' redaction of Israel's history, complementary to the earlier DtrH 'covenant' redaction. The existence of the complementary double redaction of Israel's history prompts the hypothesis of a similar complementary double redaction in the Sinai pericope in Exodus 19–40. There is sufficient evidence of a 'holiness' redaction matching Chronicles (cf. alone the distribution of

31. The association with the Autumn Festival is suggested by such factors as the parallel with Jeroboam's New Year Festival in 1 Kgs 12, the *ḥg lyhwh* (cf. Hos. 9.5), and the concern with atonement in the sequel (especially 32.30-35).

the root *qdš*). Equally, an underlying 'covenant' redaction can be detected both in the narrative sections and in the framework of B. After the recognition of these two editions, the interpreter is free to explore genetic questions: in particular, the relationship of the material to historical events. The material is seen to be the verisimilitude of the commonplace institutions of theophany, law and covenant, cast into narrative form in terms of lore of many kinds and secondarily referred to Sinai.

Chapter 8

THE DECALOGUE AND THE REDACTION OF
THE SINAI PERICOPE IN EXODUS*

I

Problematical though they undoubtedly are, parallel passages afford the
literary critic as secure a basis for the analysis of texts and for the interpretation of their redactional intention as can be found in the Old Testament. The critic should also begin, where possible, with the latest text
and proceed from the known to the unknown.

In Chapter 7, I argued on the basis of the parallels between Deut.
9.7–10.11 and Exod. 24.12-18*; 31.18–34.35* (and in the light of
Chronicles//Samuel–Kings) for a double theological redaction of the
Sinai pericope in Exodus 19–40, first by the 'D-writer' using the category 'covenant', followed by the 'P-writer' using the category 'holiness'. I suggested that 'on at least three occasions a text still extant in
Deuteronomy enables the reconstruction of the text of the D-writer in
Exodus, which the P-writer has received and reconceived for his purpose' (p. 154). The texts in question are Deut. 9.21//Exod. 32.20, Deut.
10.1-3a*a//Exod. 34.1 and Deut. 10.8-9//Exod. 32.25-29. A fourth
instance which I had in mind, but which an already over-full article did
not give scope to examine, is the Decalogue. The substantial parallels
between the two versions of the Decalogue in Deut. 5.6-21 and Exod.
20.2-17 invite the application of the same method and present a crucial
test case for it: can it be shown that Deuteronomy provides evidence of
the version of the Decalogue that the P-writer had before him in the D-
writer's prior edition of Exodus 19–40 and which he 'received and
reconceived' for his purpose?

The Decalogue, however, cannot be considered in isolation from the
rest of the Sinai pericope. Already associated with it, at least *prima*

* Originally published in *ZAW* 100 (1988), pp. 361-85, now lightly edited and
made uniform with this collection.

facie, is, among other texts, the reference to 'the ten words' in Exod. 34.28b. Here, too, there is a parallel text in Deuteronomy (Deut. 10.4a). In this case, I shall argue, the comparison between the two texts again clarifies the redactional history of the Exodus passage. But on this occasion there is an added level of interpretation: the 'D-writer', Dtr (i.e. the Deuteronomist), has here not simply transcribed his D source (i.e. Deuteronomy) but has himself extended it. While for D the Decalogue, written by the finger of God on the two tablets of stone, stands in the forefront as the basis of the covenant at Horeb (though the revelation of other 'commandment, statutes and ordinances' through Moses is recognized), for Dtr in Exodus the written basis of the original covenant and of the renewed covenant is the Decalogue plus the Book of the Covenant (B).

Exodus 34.28b, 'he wrote upon the tablets the ten words, the words of the covenant', is a notorious *crux interpretum*: who wrote 'the ten words' upon the tablets and what did these 'ten words' comprise? If it is Moses who wrote, as the context at first reading seems to imply, then can the 'ten words' be the Decalogue, which is elsewhere written by God (e.g. Deut. 9.10)? If the 'ten words' are not the Decalogue, then must a second Decalogue be sought? A comparison of Exod. 34.28b with the parallel text in Deuteronomy within their respective contexts (Exod. 34.1, 4, 27, 28//Deut. 10.1-4a*ab* [9.18]) provides an answer—I should suggest the definitive one—to these questions.

Quite apart from the particular interests of D and P revealed in these texts (the ark of the covenant in Deut. 10.1b, 2b, 3a*a*; in Exod. 34.2-3 the emphasis on hierarchy, ritual preparation and purity), it is obvious that the two texts reflect diverging D and Dtr conceptions of the basis of the covenant.

In the wider account in Deut. 9.7–10.11 of the making of the covenant at Horeb, its breaking in the golden calf incident and subsequent remaking, the only terms of the covenant stated are the Decalogue, recorded on two tablets of stone: 'stone tablets, the tablets of the covenant' (9.9; cf. 9.11, 15, 17); more fully, 'YHWH gave me the two stone tablets, written with the finger of God; what was upon them was in accordance with all the words which YHWH spoke with you on the mountain from the midst of the fire on the day of the congregation' (9.10); for the remaking of the covenant, on the second identical set of tablets (10.1) were inscribed the same words as on the first set (10.2), the Decalogue in identical form and as delivered on the first occasion

(10.4). The same conception is expressed in Deut. 5.2-22: while the sequel in Deut. 5.27, 31 states that, in addition, 'the commandment, the statutes and the ordinances' were communicated to Moses during the 40 days and nights on the mountain for transmission by him to Israel (the impression is oral transmission, but written need not be excluded), the ten words spoken on the mountain from the midst of the fire, cloud and gloom in the direct hearing of Israel and written on the two tablets by God himself constituted the terms of the covenant (so again Deut. 4.9-13).

This conception of the basis of the covenant is reproduced in Exod. 34.1, where the language is identical to that of Deut. 10.1 (with due allowance made for the fact that Exodus is couched as narrative in the third person, while Deuteronomy is framed as reminiscence in the first person). Exodus 34.4 also, though with some material attributable to the P-writer (a*b**cbai*), is very close in wording to Deut. 10.3a*bb*. Given this virtual identity of language, which is only a small part of the parallels in the non-P 'backbone' of the Exodus Sinai pericope to Deut. 9.7–10.11 (Chapter 7, p. 153), it is not unreasonable to identify a similar identity between Exod. 34.28b and Deut. 10.4a*ab*. If so, the writer is God and the 'ten words' are none other than the Decalogue. A close association with Deuteronomy is confirmed by Exod. 34.28a: the motif of Moses' 40-day-and-night fast on the mountain is found in connection with both the remaking of the covenant in Deut. 9.18a*bcd* (cf. 10.10a*c*) and the making of the original covenant in Deut. 9.9b*bcd*; 9.11a).

It may be doubted whether Dtr intended to convey anything different in Exod. 34.28b—that, exceptionally, Moses was the writer of the 'ten words' and that the 'ten words' were other than the Decalogue.[1] Rather, into his accurate transcription of his D source, he has incorporated the wider conception of the written basis of the covenant, as it was originally made and as it was renewed, which is evident in his edition of Exodus 19–24*; 31.18–34.28*.

---

1. For a recent contrary view, see A. Phillips, 'The Decalogue: Ancient Israel's Criminal Law', *JJS* 34 (1983), p. 8 n. 33; Exod. 34.28b represents an insertion by the Pentateuchal editors imposing the Dtr view that the Decalogue was the sole law given at Sinai upon the 'Proto-Deuteronomic' view that the Decalogue + B, written on tablets by Moses, constituted the basis of the renewal of the covenant. So also his 'A Fresh Look at the Sinai Pericope', *VT* 34 (1984), pp. 39-52, 282-94.

So far as a comparison with the D account of the events at Horeb is concerned, the anomaly lies in the preceding verse, Exod. 34.27, which has no parallel in Deuteronomy: Moses himself is to write 'these words', which are the basis of the remade covenant. This anomaly arises from the somewhat different Dtr conception of the basis of the original covenant and of the renewed covenant. As I have argued (Chapter 7, p. 158), in the Dtr version of the making of the original covenant at Horeb in Exodus 19–24, the old law-code Exod. 20.23–23.19, reformulated by Dtr as the Covenant Code and written by Moses himself, stands in the forefront as the basis of the covenant. By allusion to the opening of the Decalogue and sermon upon it in Exod. 34.5-17 and by citation of the end of B in tolerably complete form (more than 75 per cent; Chapter 7, p. 155) in Exod. 34.18-26, the writer wishes to state that the covenant is remade on identical terms. 'These words' in Exod. 34.27 thus correspond to 'all the words of YHWH' in Exod. 24.4a*ab*; like them, they do not refer to the Decalogue as inscribed 'by the finger of YHWH' on the two tablets but to B, the basis of covenant as written by Moses. This basis of the covenant and of the renewed covenant written by Moses could, naturally, have contained besides B a transcription of the Decalogue; logically, in the light of the contention about the structure and purpose of Exod. 34.5-26 given above, this must be so, though one may doubt whether such a mundane historicist question even occurred to Dtr. (See also the discussion in Chapter 1, p. 30.)

In connection with the question of who wrote what, YHWH or Moses, the Decalogue or B, one further verse in the Sinai pericope in Exodus has to be taken into consideration. Whereas Exod. 34.28b//Deut. 10.4a (cf. Exod. 31.18*//Deut. 9.10) envisages YHWH himself as inscribing the Decalogue, while Exod. 34.27; 24.3-4 records Moses as writing B (if not B + a copy of the Decalogue), Exod. 24.12 moves the other way in suggesting that both Decalogue and B were inscribed by YHWH! Here again, I should argue, the state of affairs is clarified by the parallel, Exod. 24.12//Deut. 9.9:

Exod. 24.12   ויאמר יהוה אל משה עלה אלי ההרה והיה שם
ואתנה לך את לחת האבן והתורה והמצוה אשר כתבתי להורתם:

Deut. 9.9a   בעלתי ההרה
לקחת   לוחת האבנים לוחת הברית אשר כרת יהוה עמכם

Once more, the text in Deuteronomy permits the reconstruction of the original Dtr text of Exodus, which has been modified by P. In the light of Deut. 9.9a; Exod. 24.12b (Dtr) may well have read:

ואתנה לך את לחת האבן לחת הברית אשר כרתי עמם:

Deuteronomy 9.9a*biic* has been suppressed, rather as Deut. 9.11 has not been reproduced in Exod. 24.12-18 + 31.18; as Deut. 9.15b has been modified in Exod. 32.15a; and as the ark (of the covenant) has been suppressed in Exod. 34.1. The hand of P is clear in the verb *yrh* (hi) (cf. Exod. 35.34; Lev. 10.11; 14.57); D uses *lmd* (pi) (cf. Deut. 4.14; 6.1). The remainder of Exod. 24.12b*bc* may be a P pastiche of D/Dtr (as I indicated in Chapter 7, n. 18): the awkward syntax of 12b*b* can thus readily be explained. It is P's concern to include *tôrâ* and *miṣwâ*, as well as D's Decalogue, as the content of revelation at Sinai, which has occasioned this singular reading in the text of Exod. 24.12b.

If this argument is sound, then it has significant implications for certain reconstructions of the history of the Decalogue and even, in so far as the issues are connected, of the history of Pentateuch. If in the light of the D parallels the 'ten words' of Exod. 34.28b are none other than the Decalogue, then the search for another decalogue in Exod. 34.17-26 is fruitless and should be abandoned, as, indeed, the citation there of the end of B already indicates. Nonetheless, given the enormous weight of scholarly opinion that has supported the eliciting of a decalogue from Exod. 34.17-26, some engagement with that view is required. Because the angle of approach adopted here concerns the two main final stages of the history of the redaction of the Sinai pericope, it is not necessary to engage directly with the consideration of origins and earlier history typical of literary and form criticism.[2] Rather, I shall limit discussion to more recent work, especially to the account of the history of the redaction of the Decalogue and of the Sinai pericope by F.-L. Hossfeld,[3] which has attracted significant attention and precipitated lively debate.[4]

---

2. The role of Exod. 34.17-26 in classic Wellhausenian literary criticism, whereby J's 'cultic Decalogue' is recovered there as opposed to E's 'ethical Decalogue' in Exod. 20.1-17, or its instrumentality in the defence of the earliness at least of the form of the Decalogue by, e.g., Mowinckel and, by Rowley, of its content, has been repeatedly presented; cf., e.g., the review by J.J. Stamm and M.E. Andrew, *The Ten Commandments in Recent Research* (SBT, 2.2; London: SCM Press, 1967); E. Nielsen, *The Ten Commandments in New Perspective* (SBT, 2.7; London: SCM Press, 1968).

3. *Der Dekalog: Seine späten Fassungen, die originale Komposition und seine Vorstufen* (OBO, 45; Freiburg: Universitätsverlag; Göttingen: Vandenhoeck & Ruprecht, 1982).

4. E.g. B. Lang, 'Neues über den Dekalog', *TQ* 164 (1984), pp. 58-65; more critically, C. Levin, 'Der Dekalog am Sinai', *VT* 35 (1985), pp. 165-91;

II

The thesis I am propounding is that the final form of the Sinai pericope in Exodus represents a P-revision of an underlying Dtr-edition which can on occasion be restored by comparison with appropriate passages in Deuteronomy. The Decalogue is a case in point: the Decalogue in Deuteronomy 5 enables the *Vorlage* of the Decalogue which P has finally edited in Exodus 20 to be reconstructed. The first part of Hossfeld's argument—the priority of the recension of the Decalogue in Deuteronomy 5 to that in Exodus 20—seems, at first sight at any rate, highly congenial to my view. The most significant elements, in my judgment, of that extensive first part[5] will be presented in this section.

Hossfeld's subsequent argument leads, however, in a significantly different direction to mine. Whereas I should contend that the D-Decalogue, or something very like it, was part of the Dtr-*Vorlage* of Exodus which was re-edited by P, Hossfeld argues that, while it is indeed a P-revision of the D-Decalogue which is to be found in Exodus 20, it was P himself who was responsible for fitting this Decalogue into Exodus 20 for the first time. The earlier Dtr-edition of Exodus, he maintains, knew no Decalogue in ch. 20 but only B in chs. 20–23 as the basis of the covenant and defined the *Privilegrecht/*'ten words' in 34.12-26 (which do *not* reproduce the classical Decalogue) as the basis of the renewal of the covenant. In view of this development of his argument, it is scarcely surprising that Hossfeld should seek to maximise the evidence for the priority of the D-recension of the Decalogue over that in Exodus. The appraisal of the development of Hossfeld's argument is reserved for §III.[6]

Hossfeld's discussion proceeds from a sound basis—a synoptic comparison of the versions of the Decalogue in Exod. 20.2-17 and

A. Graupner, 'Zwei Arbeiten zum Dekalog, *VF* 31 (1986), pp. 87-89, *idem*, 'Zum Verhältnis der beiden Dekalogfassungen Ex 20 and Dtn 5', *ZAW* 99 (1987), pp. 308-29. I am indebted to the Editor of *ZAW* for access to the latter at page-proof stage.

5.   Hossfeld, *Der Dekalog*, pp. 21-162.

6.   To prevent confusion, I shall confine the term 'Decalogue' to the traditional 'ten commandments' of Exod. 20/Deut. 5. In referring to the individual commandments the Roman numerals I–X will be used, in accordance with the system of counting the commandments in Exodus.

Deut. 5.6-21, in which he seeks to do justice to *each* version in its own right. By means of a minute and subtly nuanced analysis, combined with a formidable engagement with the scholarly literature, he presents a forceful series of arguments for the priority of the version in Deuteronomy—or, at least in some cases, for the non-compelling nature of the arguments for the priority of the version in Exodus:

1. I and II in Exod. 20.3, 4-6 appear together as *one* commandment in Deut. 5.7-10. Following Zimmerli, Hossfeld argues that the D-form is primary because the prepositional phrase 'to them' in the present II (Exod. 20.5; Deut. 5.9) refers to the 'other gods' of I. In order get a referent for this prepositional phrase, Exod. 20.4, having disjoined I and II, has to add the conjunction 'and' in the phrase '...image *and* any likeness...', which Deuteronomy simply reads asyndetically, '...image, *that is*, any likeness...' The Exodus form thus prohibits prostration before and worship of *idols*, while the Deuteronomy form is concerned with the worship of *other gods* (cf. Deut. 4.19; 30.17). The combination of the verbs 'prostrate oneself before' and 'worship' with idols—and in that order—occurs only in exilic/postexilic contexts, especially DIsa (44.15, 17; 46.6).[7] Hossfeld might have noted that the originality of the conjoining of I and II as in Deuteronomy is supported by the fact that *s^e tûmâ* is not inserted until after II in Exod. 20.6/Deut. 5.10 in the MT.[8]

2. (a) In the enumeration of the generations at the end of II, Exodus 20.5 uses an asyndetic form 'visiting the iniquity of fathers upon sons, *that is*, upon those of the third generation and upon those of the fourth generation'. Deuteronomy uses a polysyndetic form: 'visiting the iniquity of fathers upon sons *and* upon those of the third generation and upon those of the fourth generation'. Hossfeld argues that there was an older system of reckoning the generations whereby the father was included and the 'third generation' therefore meant 'grandson' (Exod. 34.4; Job 42.16), as opposed to the exilic/postexilic system whereby the father was excluded and it therefore meant 'great-grandson' (Gen. 15.16/Exod. 6.13-25; 2 Kgs 10.30/15.12). Deuteronomy with its

---

7. Hossfeld, *Der Dekalog*, pp. 21-26.

8. Hossfeld's pupil C. Dohmen (*Das Bilderverbot* [BBB, 62; Frankfurt: Athenäum, 2nd edn, 1987], pp. 213ff.) supports his *Doktorvater*'s conclusion on the basis of a study of the history of the prohibition of the worship of idols using such texts as Exod. 32; 20.23; 34.17; Lev. 19.4; 26.1; Deut. 4.16-18, 23, 25; 27.15. He argues that the incorporation in the D Decalogue of II within I as a *special* case is earlier than the distinguishing of it as a *separate* case in the Exodus Decalogue.

polysyndeton corresponds to the older method. The change in Exodus is explained on the assumption that the later reckoning was now current: it was now no longer possible to have a series fathers–sons–those of the third generation, when the latter meant 'great-grandsons'. 'Sons' had now to be understood more generally as 'descendants', which the following asyndetic phrase then defines appositionally, 'that is, those of the third generation (= great-grandsons) and those of the fourth generation (= great-great-grandsons)'.[9]

(b) 'His commandments' at the end of II in Deut. 5.10 marks the transition from YHWH's direct speech in the first person singular to the speech of a spokesman for YHWH referring to him in the third person singular. The change to 'my commandments' in Exodus is a redactional easing of the reading.[10]

3. (a) As for IV, Hossfeld accepts the view of Meinhold and others that the identification of 'the seventh day' and 'Sabbath' is late preexilic. Formerly, Sabbath was full-moon day.[11]

(b) He is further surprised[12] that the appropriate inference has not been drawn in scholarship from the observation (already to be found in part in Wellhausen) of the presence of Deuteronomic language in the Sabbath Commandment, especially the list of participants (cf. Deut. 16.11).[13] The phrase 'YHWH your God' and its consistent use four times in IV in Deuteronomy as opposed to once in Exodus, with substitution of 'YHWH' in Exodus's independent aetiology of Sabbath observance, suggests the priority of the Dc form.[14]

(c) 'And your ox and your ass' (Deut. 5.14) is not regarded as a later addition: the pairing already occurs in B (Exod. 23.12). Rather, Exod. 20.10 represents a reduction: for P 'and your cattle' is the sufficient term for domesticated animals (Lev. 25.6-7 [not 26.6-7, as he says]; Gen. 1.24-26.[15]

9. Hossfeld, *Der Dekalog*, pp. 26-32.

10. Hossfeld, *Der Dekalog*, p. 276.

11. Hossfeld, *Der Dekalog*, p. 38 n. 73.

12. Hossfeld, *Der Dekalog*, pp. 43-44.

13. A convenient list of the D/Dtr-terminology in the Decalogue as a whole is to be found in K. Koch, *The Growth of Biblical Tradition* (London: A. & C. Black, 1969), pp. 46-48.

14. Hossfeld, *Der Dekalog*, p. 39.

15. Hossfeld, *Der Dekalog*, p. 46.

(d) The motivation for 'commemorating' (the term implies cultic observance) the Sabbath in Exod. 20.11 is related to the P account of creation in Gen. 2.2-3.[16]

4. In the phrase in V, 'that your days may be long', 'days' is the subject of the verb (rather than the person 'that you may prolong your days') as only twice elsewhere in the Hebrew Bible, both in Deuteronomy (6.2-3; 25.15; so H. Kremers).[17]

5. The expression for 'false witness' in IX in Deut. 5.20 is not necessarily later than that in Exod. 20.16, since it parallels the 'false rumour' in B (Exod. 23.1a [following Holzinger]).[18] Compare Hos. 10.4; 12.12. The Exodus form has broken the connection between IX and III, in order to protect the divine name from implication in any improper use.[19]

6. (a) The combination of Deuteronomy's last two commandments (Deut. 5.21) into the single X in Exod. 20.17 is a consequence of the division of Deuteronomy's first commandment into two in Exod. 20.3-6 and must, therefore, be equally secondary.[20] Again the occurrence of $s^e t\hat{u}m\hat{a}$ at the end of Deut. 5.21a and its omission at the corresponding place in Exod. 20.17 might have been noted.

(b) The substitution in Exod. 20.17 in the first phrase of X of the same verb that occurs in the second phrase and the change in the order of the first two items are equally explained by the need in Exodus to integrate the tenth as a single commandment. In the process 'house' has changed in meaning from 'homestead' in Deut. 5.21 to 'house' as mere object along with others; it cannot mean 'family' since 'sons and daughters' are omitted and other objects not belonging to the family as such are included.[21]

Hossfeld's argument has been subjected to close examination by Levin and, especially, Graupner.[22] Levin begins with the general point that, since in editing canonical texts omission is not permitted, the shorter text (i.e. Exodus) must be the more original. It is indeed striking

16. Hossfeld, *Der Dekalog*, pp. 41-42.
17. Hossfeld, *Der Dekalog*, p. 64.
18. Hossfeld, *Der Dekalog*, p. 75 n. 239.
19. Hossfeld, *Der Dekalog*, pp. 85-86.
20. Hossfeld, *Der Dekalog*, p. 124.
21. Hossfeld, *Der Dekalog*, p. 95.
22. See n. 4. The discussion of Graupner's argument is based on his 1987 article 'Zum Verhältnis'.

that, apart from the differences in IV, Exodus has only 2 semantically significant additions (II, X, both waw) against 13 in Deuteronomy (7 waw [II, IV, VII–X], 6 more substantial [3 in IV, 2 in V, 1 in X]). Of the specific comments on points listed above the following selection may be made:

(1) The 'and' in Exod. 20.4 may be explicative, 'that is'. There may thus be no difference between the Exodus and Deuteronomy forms.[23]

(2) Exodus's list of generations in II is to be explained as a rather maladroit abbreviation of Exod. 34.7 (where, by the figure of speech of *anadiplosis iterata*, which Hossfeld himself [p. 29] recognizes, 'those of the third generation' = 'grandsons'): the omission of the 'grandsons' of that text means that 'sons' in Exod. 20.5 have to be interpreted as descendants of the third and fourth generations; that is, actual 'sons' are omitted![24]

(3) There is nothing in the argument from inconsistency between 'YHWH your God' and 'YHWH': the latter is explained by the change from address to narrative.[25] Both Sabbath aetiologies are in any case secondary, so that no conclusions about priority can be drawn.[26]

(4) The motivation of V is indeed dependent on passages in Deuteronomy but these link the fate of the individual to that of the community ('...upon the land...') and some presuppose an actual experience of exile (e.g. Deut. 17.20). It is, therefore, late.[27]

(5) It is accepted that *'ēd šeqer* (Exodus) and *'ēd šāw'* (Deuteronomy) are synonymous. But the Exodus formulation is a fixed phrase of (presumed) antiquity (e.g. Ps. 27.12; Prov. 6.19).[28]

(6) Graupner regards the status accorded the wife in X as providing the strongest argument overall for the priority of the Exodus edition of the Decalogue.[29] Had the D-form come first, with its honorific position of the wife before and apart from the household, it is inconceivable that deterioration in status would have followed. Levin may be right that

23. Graupner, 'Zum Verhältnis', p. 314.

24. Levin, 'Der Dekalog am Sinai', pp. 171-72.

25. Graupner, 'Zum Verhältnis', p. 316.

26. Levin, 'Der Dekalog am Sinai', p. 172; Graupner, 'Zum Verhältnis', pp. 316-18.

27. Levin, 'Der Dekalog am Sinai', p. 167.

28. Graupner, 'Zum Verhältnis', pp. 319-20.

29. Graupner, 'Zum Verhältnis', pp. 321ff.

priority of the form of X in Exodus is easily defensible:[30] 17a is the
original short command; the second asyndetic 'thou shalt not covet'
provides an appositional exposition of 'house' = 'household'; Deuteronomy's 'field' is thus intrusive in a list that otherwise expounds
'household'. But why are 'children' not then mentioned?

The argument is finely balanced. Levin's opening premise—that priority must always be conceded to the shorter text—cannot be granted in
an absolute way: Chronicles, for example, abbreviates Samuel–Kings
(cf., e.g., 2 Sam. 24.4-7 with 1 Chron. 21.4).[31] One should also be
aware of the drift of Levin's argument: he is searching for the 'core' of
the Sinai pericope in a radically reduced Decalogue of six commandments.[32] Graupner's arguments more than once end with a 'not-proven'
verdict; they also leave the delimitation of ten commandments in Exodus uncertain. In my view, the fact that the arguments seem so evenly
balanced can hardly be accidental. Exodus 20 is a lightly edited P-
version of a Dtr-Decalogue (the lateness of the motive clause for the
Sabbath in Exod. 20.11 is not an issue between these protagonists). The
form of the Decalogue in Deuteronomy has undergone limited expansion from that once located in DtrExodus 20; it is about ten per cent
longer than the present text of the P-Decalogue. The substantial agreement between the forms of the Decalogue in Exodus 20 and Deuteronomy 5 shows how modest P's revision was (fully 80 per cent of the
Decalogue in Exodus = that in Deuteronomy). It is hardly surprising
then that the evidence for the priority of the Dtr-form of the Decalogue
over the D-form (or vice versa) is so ambiguous! The question is highly
marginal and largely wrongly put.

As far as the second part of Hossfeld's thesis is concerned,[33] namely,
that the Decalogue was not in the Dtr-redaction of Exodus 19–40 but
was only placed there by P, there is one recurring feature arising from
his synoptic comparison, which, in my view, already casts doubt: the
thrice-repeated reference back to some promulgation of a commandment, 'As YHWH your God commanded you' (in III, Deut. 5.12, cf. 15;
in IV, 5.16). As Hossfeld himself states, the phrase does not occur in
Exodus 20 because of the relative position of the Decalogue there:

30. Levin, 'Der Dekalog am Sinai', p. 168.

31. Cf. C. Dohmen, 'Dekalogexegese und kanonische Literatur', *VT* 37 (1987),
pp. 81-84.

32. Levin, 'Der Dekalog am Sinai', pp. 188-89.

33. Hossfeld, *Der Dekalog*, pp. 163-213.

since in Exodus it now appears as the first promulgation, there is no place for a reference to a prior promulgation. But if there is a reference to a prior promulgation in Deuteronomy 5, then that prior promulgation is most naturally to be sought in the Dtr-version of the Decalogue in Exodus 20 underlying the present P-version and acting as its *Vorlage*. Deuteronomy is, after all, couched in the form of a reminiscence of a series of events, the original form of which must be presupposed. Hossfeld has to avoid this conclusion by suggesting that III is based on B and the *Privilegrecht* (Exod. 23.12; 34.21a). IV is less directly accounted for on the basis of B (Exod. 21.15, 17). Nonetheless, the D-forms of II and IV would be more naturally accounted for on the assumption that there already was a Decalogue in Exodus 20 to which to appeal. That there *was* such a Dtr-recension of the Decalogue in Exodus 20 is suggested by Deut. 4.23, a further backward reference to an earlier promulgated law. The warning against *pesel tᵉmûnat kōl* can appeal to neither B nor *Privilegrecht* for neither contains either *pesel* or *tᵉmûnâ*. The prior promulgation is most naturally sought in II of the Dtr-Decalogue in Exodus (cf. Deut. 5.8), where both words not only occur but occur in apposition (though the form of the apposition in Deut. 4.23 is probably more original than the extant text of II). At this point in the narrative in Deuteronomy that Dtr-Decalogue can only be found in Exodus 20. With this initial doubt about Hossfeld's position already in mind, I turn now to defend my thesis against the second part of his argument.

III

While Hossfeld's argument for the priority of the D-form of the Decalogue over that in Exodus may provide some support for my contention that the primary form of the account of the making of the covenant between Israel and YHWH in the wilderness in Exodus 19–40 is a Dtr one parallel to the Horeb account contained in Deuteronomy 4–5 and 9.7–10.11, of which the P-writer's account is a second edition, his appreciation of the material the P-writer had to hand in the Sinai pericope in Exodus 19–40 is very different from mine. On the one hand, he affirms the existence of the J and E narrative sources and the Jehovist redaction of these sources (i.e. R^{JE}, referred to below simply as JE) in some such form as is traditional in literary criticism and accepts that these provided the basis for the Dtr redactional work. On the other, he

denies the presence of the Decalogue in the Dtr-edition of Exodus 19–
40. The second part of the account of Hossfeld's work must, therefore,
operate on two fronts: it must seek to evaluate the strength of his arguments for attributing materials to J, E and JE and, thus, for finding the
presence of such sources in addition to D and P; it must, in particular,
weigh the evidence for his contention that the Decalogue was only
finally inserted in Exodus 20 by P. In dialogue with Hossfeld's exposition of his view, I should like to see if the alternative position for which
I have argued in Chapter 7 can be maintained and can now include the
Decalogue within it, namely: the P-redactor of the Sinai pericope had
before him an already existing Dtr-redacted Horeb pericope in Exodus,
which also included the Decalogue in its D-form.

It may be helpful to begin with a concerted statement, drawn from
several parts of his work, which sets out Hossfeld's view of the stages
in the growth of the Sinai pericope. Not every chapter is fully analysed
by him.

J	—	the theophany, 19.20a
	—	the sacrifice, 24.4ac*d*b.5*
	—	the promise of covenant, 34.2, 4a*b*b, 9a, 10a
E	—	the theophany at Sinai, 19.2b, 3ab*a**, 17, 19; 20.20a*aii*b*cb*, 21
JE	—	theophany, 19.16b, 18b*b*, 20b, 21, 23, 25
	—	J's covenant reinterpreted as covenant with Moses; basis = *Privilegrecht*, 34.10b, 11a, 12-26*, 27*
Dtr	—	overture reinterpreting JE's theophany by 'covenant', 19.3b*a**, 4-8
	—	B (already edited), 20.22a*a*, 24-26*; 21.1; 21.2–23.33*, as basis of covenant written by Moses, 24.3a*ab*, 4a*ab*
	—	J's sacrifice reinterpreted as a rite of covenant-making, 24.6-8
	—	JE's covenant reinterpreted as renewal of Horeb covenant: *Privilegrecht* termed 'second Decalogue' ('first Decalogue' = Deut. 5.6-21), 34.1, 4a*ab*, (9b,) 11b, 17, 27b*bii*, 28
P	—	Dtr's overture reworked to heighten role of Moses, 19.3b*b*, 9
	—	JE's theophany rounded off, 19.(22,) 24
	—	Decalogue introduced from Deut. 5, 20.1–19, 20a*ai*
	—	definition of relationship between Decalogue and B, 20.22a*b*.b
	—	B provided with new framework, 20.23; 22.30; 23.13
	—	theophany, 24.1, 2, 9-11
	—	adoption of Dtr's conception of *Privilegrecht* but with reference to Decalogue, 34.29

Hossfeld's analysis may be laid out diagrammatically:

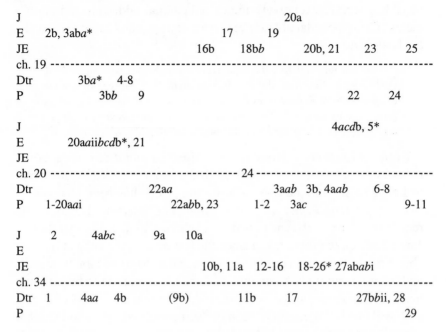

19.2-9: Hossfeld finds here a basic text (E) that has undergone two redactions (Dtr and P).[34]

2b-3ab*a*: 2b marks the beginning of the E Sinai narrative:[35] it is to be separated from 2a on grounds of (1) the repetition of the verb 'encamped'; (2) the new definition of the subject of the verb 'Israel' after three verbs in the verse without such definition; (3) the contrast between this subject 'Israel' and 'the sons of Israel' in vv. 1 and 3b*b*; and (4) the construing of that subject as a singular. 3ab*a* is also to be ascribed to E.

Perhaps a general point should be made at the outset. Hossfeld draws an analogy between Exod. 19.3-9 and the Book of the Covenant:[36] as B has, in his view, undergone a Dtr- and a P-redaction, so too this passage. I find the analogy unconvincing: there is a radical difference in character between a law-code, the essence of which is to grow and develop over the centuries, and a narrative which may be constructed ad hoc. Even more significant is the extent of the presumed original

34. Hossfeld, *Der Dekalog*, pp. 185ff.
35. Hossfeld, *Der Dekalog*, p. 168.
36. Hossfeld, *Der Dekalog*, p. 185.

text. B is a substantial pre-existing text which, even on Hossfeld's view of it, has received relatively minor redactional additions and adjustments; E, the postulated basic text here, is slight and inconsequential. In ch. 19 it runs,

> [2b]Israel encamped before the mountain, [3]while Moses went up to God. God called to him from the mountain (, saying?). [17]Moses brought out the people to meet God from the camp and they took their places at the foot of the mountain. [19]The sound of the trumpet increased exceedingly, while Moses was speaking and God was answering him with a voice.

Even on his theory, Hossfeld is obliged to admit two redactional adjustments within the 15 words of 2b-3a: in 2b P has added in 'there' to link with his itinerary in 1-2a; in 3b*a* 'God' has been changed to 'YHWH' by Dtr. In my view it is simpler to attribute 1-2 to P: the repetition of the verb 'encamped' is explained by the fact that 2a is a parenthesis on the route taken since the last note on the subject in 17.1; 2b continues the narrative of 1.[37] The variation 'sons of Israel'/'Israel', with consequential plural/singular verb, is too imprecise to be diagnostic: BDB, for example, gives the statistics for the use of 'sons of Israel' as 328 P, 49 E, 25 J, 25 D.[38] Similarly, I should assign 3 to Dtr: that Moses 'went up' is noted in Deut. 9.9; 'the mountain' is a recurrent Dc usage.[39]

3b*b*–9: Hossfeld endorses the view of a substantial presence of Dtr but limits that to vv. 4-8.

In 3b he finds traces of a three-part commissioning formula, which occurs more clearly at 20.22: (1) introduction to a divine speech ('YHWH called to him from the mountain saying'); (2) the command to communicate that speech ('Thus you will say to the House of Jacob and declare to the sons of Israel'); (3) the communication of the YHWH's direct speech itself to Israel ('You...'). He finds the closest analogy to this three-part formula in P, for example, Lev. 20.1-2; 21.1, to cite the most unambiguously P of the examples he adduces.[40] There are parallels to this in the prophets, except that in their case the messenger formula, 'Thus says YHWH', is expected at the beginning of the third part. It is omitted in the case of Moses because Moses is so identified with

37. I should now assign 19.1-2a to P, 19.2b to D. See Chapter 1, p. 40; Chapter 7, n. 19; and Chapter 11.
38. BDB, p. 120.
39. BDB, p. 249.
40. Hossfeld, *Der Dekalog*, p. 177 n. 72.

YHWH that YHWH can speak directly through him to the people. A prophet can only report what YHWH has said to him.

By contrast, in Dc and Dtrc literature the second part of the above formula is missing (e.g. Deut. 2.9, 17): that is, Moses is addressed on a par with the people.

On the basis of these observations, E, already modified by Dtr in 3b*a* by the substitution of the divine name 'YHWH', has received in 3b*b* a P-expansion (the second part of the commissioning formula) in order to heighten Moses' mediatorial role. This is confirmed, in Hossfeld's view, by the slight tension between 'say' in 3b*b* and 'speak' + 'words' in 6b and by the parallelism 'House of Jacob/sons of Israel', since the first of these recurs in the Pentateuch only in Gen. 47.27 (= P^S).

At the outset it must be noted that because of his hypothesis that the insertion of the Decalogue in Exod. 20.1-17 is due to P, Hossfeld is obliged to argue that the reference to the Decalogue in 20.22b (the third part of the commissioning formula) must also be attributed to P. It would clearly strengthen that argument if the second part of the commissioning formula were also attributable to P.

The argument, I find, is unconvincing. (1) There is a difference in the third part of the commissioning formula in Lev. 20.1-2; 21.1: the address to the people is couched objectively in the third person; here they are addressed fraternally by Moses in the second person. (2) In this respect there is a parallel to the Lev. 20.1-2; 21.1 formulation in Ezek. 33.27—not surprisingly in view of the often-remarked affinity between H and Ezekiel. There are parallels, however, to the second-person formulation in Jeremiah (23.37; 45.4), the affinity of which to Deuteronomy is equally noted. (3) The omission of the messenger formula can be accounted for on the basis of the D theory of Moses' position as prophet *par excellence* (Deut. 18.15-22; 34.10). (4) Even on his own terms Hossfeld undermines his case by noting that the threefold commissioning formula occurs in Deut. 1.42; 2.2, 4.[41]

The argument from the parallel 'House of Jacob/sons of Israel' is weak since Perlitt, on whom Hossfeld here depends, points out that the phrase 'House of Jacob' occurs by itself in the eighth-century prophets and in parallelism in the sixth/fifth (e.g. Jer. 2.4; 5.20; Ezek. 20.5).[42]

19.9 Hossfeld also ascribes to P. 9b provides the matching outer framework by picking up the second verb of 3b*b* but integrates the new

---

41. Hossfeld, *Der Dekalog*, p. 177 n. 72.
42. Perlitt, *Bundestheologie*, pp. 169-70.

information of 9a into 4-8 by resuming 8b. The purpose of 9a is to heighten the mediatorial role of Moses. The argument is again not compelling. The Dtr language of 9b is admitted. The vocabulary of 9a is D ('cloud', Deut. 5.22: *dibber* + *'im*, 5.4), as Hossfeld himself points out.[43]

19.20–20.21: Hossfeld shares the common view that the Decalogue in Exod. 20.2-17 is only loosely connected to its context.[44] It has a two-part introduction, 'Moses came down to the people and said to them. God spoke all these words, saying' (Exod. 19.25–20.1). The first part of this introduction is clearly inconsequential; the second lacks an indirect object. Hossfeld solves the problem by assigning each of the two parts of the introduction to a different hand, JE and P.

19.25 belongs to JE material which begins at 19.20. 'Moses came down' (19.25a) corresponds to the imperative 'go down' of 19.21, which, in turn, depends on YHWH's summons to Moses to go up in 19.20b. But 19.20-25 is not all of one piece: the imperative 'go down' is repeated in 21 and 24; 22 and 24, concerning the status of the priests and Aaron, interrupt the sequence. Hossfeld accordingly assigns 20b, 21, 23, 25 to JE and the remainder to different P-redactions. 19.25 is JE's bridge from the J-material of 19.20a to the E-material of 20. 20a*aiibcd*b, 21. 20.20-21 (without the opening formula 'and Moses said to the people'), which does not logically answer the request of the people in 20.19,[45] provides the direct speech expected after 19.25.

P, however, wishing at this climactic moment of theophany to introduce the Decalogue from Deuteronomy 5, as the direct address of God and his word *par excellence*, has reformulated 19.25 by means of the new introduction 20.1.

The attribution of 20.1 to P is, in Hossfeld's view, confirmed by a number of observations:

- The relationship between 19.25b and 20.1 is similar to that between the two clauses in Lev. 1.1, another example of P's redactional work, where the first contains an undefined subject and the indirect object (as in 19.25b) and the second supplies the definition of the subject (as in 20.1).

---

43. Hossfeld, *Der Dekalog*, p. 174.
44. Hossfeld, *Der Dekalog*, pp. 164ff.
45. Hossfeld, *Der Dekalog*, p. 172.

- The second clause is similar to P's stock formula for introducing legislative material (e.g. Lev. 4.1 and frequently).
- The use of the indefinite *'eʾlōhîm* for God points to P rather than E, which uses *hāʾeʾlōhîm* (cf. 19.2b-3, 17, 19; 20.20-21). P uses *'eʾlōhîm* in contexts of direct, non-mediated, address, from Gen. 1.1 to Exod. 6.2.

Just as P has introduced in 20.2-17 a suitably edited Decalogue from Deut. 5.6-21, so he introduces in 20.18-19 an appropriately modified account of the events of the theophany and the people's reaction from Deut. 4.33; 5.4, 25-27; 18.16. There is, however, a turn of phrase in 20.19 not typical of Deuteronomy which suggests a later redactor: *šāmaʿ*, by itself meaning 'to commit oneself to obey'.

20.20aαi is a redactional link with 19.25b supplied by P.

I should offer the following comments on Hossfeld's arguments. 19.20-25 can perfectly well be read as a unity: to have 25 follow 23 makes Moses descend despite his protestation that descent is unnecessary. The second imperative 'go down' in 24 is resumptive after Moses' protestation in 23. There is in any case a redundancy in 23b: the instruction to set bounds around the mountain and to sanctify it has already been given and carried out in 10-13 (not analysed by Hossfeld).[46] I should regard the redundancy as part of P's device to bring in and emphasize the clear hierarchy Moses–Aaron–priests–people at the mountain. This matter of hierarchy, which is the reason for Moses' descent, is not continued by P until 24.1, 2, which is deliberately couched as a resumptive in the pluperfect tense: 'Now to Moses he had said, "…" Moses alone was to go up to YHWH…; the people were not to go up with him.' The execution of this command is then recorded in 24.9-11. Hierarchy is thus in the forefront of P's intention in order to complement covenant and Decalogue which were already present in his *Vorlage*, not introduced by him.

The attribution by Hossfeld of 20.18-19 to P and of 20.20-21 (apart from the opening formula) to E is debatable (in any case Hossfeld regards 20.20b as secondary).[47] I should prefer to assign the whole section, 20.18-21, to Dtr. The whole passage hangs together describing the fear of the people at the theophany on the mountain (21a, 'stood at a

---

46. Hossfeld, *Der Dekalog*, p. 169 n. 31.
47. Hossfeld, *Der Dekalog*, p 170 n. 35.

distance', uses the same vocabulary as 18b*b*); the portrayal of the theophany, the reaction of the people and the request for the mediatorial role of Moses correspond to the account in Deut. 5.4-5, 22-31, as Hossfeld himself establishes, and link back to the account of the preparations for the theophany, the account of it and of the reaction to it in 19.16a*bc*b, 17, 19, which, equally, I should assign to Dtr. 20.1 fits within this framework and introduces the Decalogue at precisely the same point as in Deuteronomy 5. Hossfeld's argument for the insertion of 20.18-19 by P is but an extension of his conviction that the Decalogue has been inserted by P. The turn of phrase by which he seeks to establish this point seems to me to be very marginal: the abbreviation of the series *šāma'* + *'āsâ* in Deut. 5.27 to *šāma'* alone in 20.19 is hardly a considerable argument.

As for the missing speech at the end of 19.25, more likely is the suggestion (dismissed by Hossfeld as one of the 'solutions not to be taken seriously' ['keine erstzunehmenden (*sic*) Lösungen']⁴⁸) that the words in the P-narrative, as I should identify it, no doubt communicating the message of 19.24a*bb* in direct speech, have been suppressed in the transition to 24.1.

The appeal to Lev. 1.1 seems strained: apart from more minor differences, Lev. 1.1a does not have the verb 'and he said' left hanging in the air without the necessary direct speech, but has a phrase complete in itself 'and he called to Moses'; Lev. 1.1b does not have the cognate accusative construction, 'spoke...words', which is perfectly Dc. (Deut. 31.1) and provides the title for the Decalogue current in D (Deut. 5.22). It is remarkable that Hossfeld can write, 'In the use of the title the redactor shows himself a true disciple of Deuteronomy, which can make *d*ᵉ*bārîm* a technical term for the Decalogue',⁴⁹ without drawing the conclusion that 20.1 may be attributed directly to Dtr.

The attribution of '*ᵉlōhîm* in 20.1 to P is arbitrary, given the occurrence of precisely this form three times in the Dc account of the theophany and revelation at Horeb (Deut. 5.24-26; 9.10; it is unlikely that at least the first of these is merely appellative, as he says⁵⁰). The attribution of the *hā'ᵉlōhîm* passages (19.3, 17, 19; 20.20-21; 24.11) to E is

---

48. Hossfeld, *Der Dekalog*, p. 165.

49. 'Im Gebrauch des Titels zeigt sich der Redaktor als treuer Schüler des Deuteronomium, das die *d*ᵉ*bārîm* zum terminus technicus des Dekalogs machen kann'; Hossfeld, *Der Dekalog*, p. 167.

50. Hossfeld, *Der Dekalog*, p. 17.

not consistently (he assigns 24.11 to P, as I do), nor, in my view, convincingly, carried through (see above on 19.2-9).

B (20.22–23.33):[51] (1) A key passage is in the opening verse of B, 'you yourselves have seen that from the heavens I have spoken with you' (Exod. 20.22b). Hossfeld does not deny that this must refer to the immediately preceding revelation of the Decalogue. But, because, in his view, it was only by P that the Decalogue was inserted at the beginning of Exodus 20, this passage must also be assigned to P. The supporting argument cannot be said to be strong. Hossfeld is obliged to note that the phrase 'you yourselves have seen' recurs in 19.4, which he along with many others attributes to Dtr; the fact that in 19.4 the phrase is followed by *ᵃšer* ('what [I did]') and not the *kî* of 20.22 'that [I spoke]' is determined not by varying sources, as Hossfeld maintains, but by the varying object clause. He has already pointed out himself[52] that the rather rare idiom *dibber* + *'im* used here is precisely that used in the key D-accounts of the revelation of the Decalogue in Deut. 5.4 (not 6.5 as he states); 9.10. He is impressed by the fact that here God speaks 'from the heavens', whereas in Deuteronomy it is 'upon the mountain from the midst of the fire', and argues that this more transcendental account of revelation accordingly attests a reuse by P of the Deuteronomy material. This sharp distinction cannot be maintained: Deut. 4.11 links both conceptions, 'you stood at the foot of the mountain while the mountain was burning with fire into the heart of the heavens ...' Hossfeld himself cites Deut. 4.36.[53]

(2) Hossfeld identifies P in the first part of the same verse, Exod. 20.22a, or, at least, in 20.22a*b*. The argument here is again based on the similarity of the formulation in 20.22 to the standard way in which revelation to Moses is described in P, already discussed under 19.3b.

(3) Hossfeld identifies the hand of P within the body of B at 20.23, 22.30 and 23.13.[54] I should not deny that this is at least a theoretical possibility and for the purposes of the present argument its presence or absence is neutral. Nonetheless, the arguments even here are not compelling. 20.23 (punctuation emended!) he regards as P because of the prohibition in the second-person plural, which continues 20.22, and the chiastic arrangement (cf. Lev. 19.4; 26.1). But, if the argument about

---

51. Hossfeld, *Der Dekalog*, pp. 176ff.
52. Hossfeld, *Der Dekalog*, p. 174.
53. Hossfeld, *Der Dekalog*, p. 179.
54. Hossfeld, *Der Dekalog*, pp. 183ff.

the previous verse collapses, then the ground for 20.23 is undercut. The alternation of second-person singular and second-person plural in Deuteronomy is in any case notorious. Nor is it clear to me why chiasmus should be regarded as the prerogative of P: compare, for example, Deut. 12.3a in a similar context of prohibition of idol-worship. The opening of B after the prologue of 20.22 with a reminiscence of the first commandment of the Decalogue in its D-form speaks, rather, for the hand of Dtr. Exodus 22.30a is indeed reminiscent of H, though the emphasis of holiness is Dc (but in the form *'am qādôš*, e.g. Deut. 7.6, not *'anᵉšê qōdeš* as here). Exodus 23.13, which is a comprehensive summarizing injunction isolated within the passage 23.12-19 and without a parallel in the corresponding passage 34.18-25, is nonetheless sufficiently Dtrc with its emphasis on 'paying heed' (cf. 23.21) and 'alien gods' (e.g. Deut. 18.20).

24.1-11:[55] 1-2. Hossfeld recognizes that these verses interrupt the natural connection of 24.3 with B and that they are related to 9-11.

3-8. In continuity with his identification of Exod. 20.1 as an insertion by P for whom 'words' are the technical term for the Decalogue, Hossfeld identifies the phrase 3ac, 'and all the ordinances', as a necessary addition by P to include B as the basis of the covenant.

The issues here are finely balanced. Approaching the question from a different angle, I also have attributed 3ac to P. As I have argued in §1 above in connection with 34.27-28, Dtr regards the covenant as originally made and then remade on the basis of 'these words' written by Moses, which are primarily B but include by implication the Decalogue. 'All the words of YHWH' would then be for Dtr a term sufficient to embrace all the foregoing revelation, Decalogue and B. It is possible that P then, knowing from D that 'words' is the technical term for the Decalogue, has inserted 'and all the ordinances' picking up the title of 21.1 applied by extension to the whole of B. It is not, however, impossible that Dtr himself should have taken this step.[56]

The remainder of 3-8 Hossfeld apportions between J and two Dtr-redactions. 4acdb.5* is the narrative source J. There is an older Dtr-redaction in 3.4aab (cf. 19.7 and, for parallel examples of Moses' writing, Deut. 31.9, 22, 24-26)[57] and a more recent one in 6-8, identified by the repetition of the assent of the people in 3b and 7b which is

55. Hossfeld, *Der Dekalog*, pp. 190ff.
56. A view that I should now more emphatically hold. See Chapter 1, p. 29.
57. Hossfeld, *Der Dekalog*, p. 192 n. 149.

expressed in different terms ('do' in the first, 'do and hear' in the second; the latter omits the reference to unanimity).

Again I find it difficult to find here an isolated fragment of a narrative source, which has not featured in the Sinai pericope since 19.20a, running somewhat as follows:

> 19.20a YHWH descended upon the mountain of Sinai to the top of the mountain. 24.4acdb He arose early in the morning and built an altar at the foot of the mountain, with twelve pillars according to the twelve tribes of Israel. 5 He sent the young men of the sons of Israel and they offered holocausts and sacrificed peace-offerings of bulls to YHWH.

Nor can I see that the 'repetition' between 3 and 7 is any different from that implied between the first oral assent of the people in 19.8 (accepted as Dtr by Hossfeld) and either of the more formal assents in 24.3-7. As in 20.19a the loss of one of the pair 'hear'/'do' does not seem to me to be significant.

I therefore adhere to my division of the material between Dtr and P. The commonly observed uniqueness of the rite of sprinkling of blood, whereby the covenant is sealed, makes the attribution to sources hazardous. Nonetheless, blood-rites at the altar would congenially belong to the circle of P's institutions. Hossfeld actually refers to analogous rites of application of blood to individuals for sanctification or purification (Exod. 29.20-21; Lev. 8.23-24, 30; 14.14-25),[58] all presumably P! The communal meal of the peace-offering as an act of covenant-making is the verisimilitude of a long traditional custom (Chapter 7, p. 165). The making of the covenant in terms of 'these words' (8b) fits the Dtr presentation of covenant on the basis of Decalogue plus B (24.3; 34.27-28). 4ac ('he arose early in the morning') matches 34.4abi, one of the two phrases in 34.4 not in the parallel in Deut. 10.3, which may, therefore, be plausibly assigned to P.[59] The 'young men' of 5ab may be a deliberate contrast to the 'old men' in 24.1-9 and thus part of P's hierarchical arrangement at the mountain.

9-11: Arguing initially on contextual grounds, Hossfeld recognizes 9-11 and its related introduction 1-2 as stemming from P: this material complements covenant with a vision of the transcendence of God,

58. Hossfeld, *Der Dekalog*, p. 192 n. 156.

59. But, in the light of the argument in Chapter 9 below, about the chronology of Passover within the D-version, I should now firmly attach the blood-rite in 24.6 to the D-version (see also Chapter 1, p. 46) and withdraw the view that 24.4ac should be assigned to the P-edition.

which links with material far beyond the confines of the Sinai pericope in Exodus and reaches its true climax in the inauguration of the sacrificial cult by Aaron in Leviticus 9. In Lev. 9.1 a similar group of people are involved (Moses, Aaron, his sons and the elders); Lev. 9.23-24, the vision of the glory of God, possesses a similar function in context. This relatively late date is substantiated by such detailed observations as the genealogical material (Nadab and Abihu only in P-material, Exod. 6.23; 28.1; Lev. 10.1-5; Num. 3.2-4: 26.60-61)[60] and the typology of the prophetic vision, where the closest parallel is seen in Ezek. 1.27-28.[61]

The argument of Hossfeld is here entirely compatible with my view of the P-writer's theological theme (Chapter 7, §2). The connection with prophetic vision seems to me to be fully justified. The analogous description of theophany in Ezek. 1.26; 10.1 might be added. There may also be a link between the term for the seventy elders here (*'ᵃṣîlîm*, 11) and the account in Num. 11.17-25 of the apportionment of some of spirit of Moses to the seventy elders so that they prophesy, where the verb 'to apportion' (*'āṣal*) is specifically used. While it is tempting to relate *'ᵃṣîlîm* to the Arabic *'aṣl* 'foundation, base, stock' used metaphorically for 'rank, nobility' (*AEL*), and while that might provide one with a 'scientific' etymology, there can be little doubt that the popular etymology of the Hebrew Bible connects the word with *'eṣel* 'beside', that is, those associated in rank with Moses because sharing the endowment with the prophet spirit.

34.1-29:[62] ch. 34 neatly focuses the issues of the debate.

Hossfeld distinguishes between J, JE and Dtr in 1-28 (his attribution of 29 to P is non-controversial[63]). Central to this distinction is the attribution of 10. 10a he assigns to J: the people are recipients of a promissory covenant; they are passive witnesses of 'wonderful deeds' done 'before' them; the longer, older, form of the first-person singular personal pronoun is used. 10b cannot be from the same source since the people are now actively involved in a demand to obey because of the 'fearful deed' done 'with' them; the shorter form of the first-person singular personal pronoun is used.

---

60. Hossfeld, *Der Dekalog*, p. 201 n. 206.
61. Hossfeld, *Der Dekalog*, p. 197.
62. Hossfeld, *Der Dekalog*, pp. 204ff.
63. Though it represents the reformulation by P of an underlying D-text (Chapter 12, n. 7).

But if 10b is not J, then, he argues, neither is it Dtr. This is shown by the role of Moses. Here Moses is identified with the people, representing them as the covenant partner with YHWH (cf. Deut. 5.2-3). Elsewhere, he is the mediator between the covenant partners, YHWH and the people (Exod. 24.8; Deut. 4.13-23; 9.9; 31.16). Still later, he is identified with YHWH over against the people (Deut. 28.69; 29.9-14). On this typology the passage is 'proto-D'. This Hossfeld finds confirmed by the language of 11a: *šāmar* in the qal is used where D would use the niphal; in D the object of *šāmar* is a noun not a noun clause; in D the subject of the participle 'am commanding you' is Moses, not YHWH. This material he accordingly identifies as JE introducing the *Privilegrecht* in 12-26 (11b, with its list of pre-Israelite inhabitants of the land, is acknowledged to be Dtr). This opening framework element thus provided by JE for the *Privilegrecht* is matched by the closing framework element of 27ab*a*b*i*: the linguistic indications here are neutral but the role of Moses as covenant partner representing his people corresponds to 10b.

Hossfeld agrees that the presence of Dtr is unambiguously attested by the correspondence of 1, 4a*a*b, 28 to Deuteronomy 9–10. 27b*b*ii is secondarily added (its secondary character is indicated by its exceptional position *after* 'covenant', instead of before as in Exod. 23.32; Jer. 31.31) to emphasize that the covenant is with Israel. Dtr ingeniously but somewhat disingenuously[64] left the subject of the verb 'and he wrote' ambiguous, knowing of the tension between his own view of the basis of the covenant and that of JE. He adds 17 to the *Privilegrecht* (the reformulation of his own II in the light of 32.31).

Again I find the identification of J and of JE both unconvincing and unnecessary. The narrative source J is once more at best an inconsequential fragment:

> 2 Prepare yourself for the morning. Come up in the morning to the mountain of Sinai. Present yourself for me there on the top of the mountain. 4 Moses arose early in the morning and went up to the mountain of Sinai as YHWH had commanded him. 9a He said, 'If I have found favour in your eyes, my Lord, may my Lord go in our midst'. 10a He said, 'Behold I am about to make a covenant. Before all your people I will do wonderful things which have not been done throughout the whole earth and among all nations.'

---

64. 'Schon trickreich'; Hossfeld, *Der Dekalog*, p. 209.

The detailed defence of the presence of J is not compelling: the 'promissory covenant' is not early (Jer. 31.31!), 'wonderful things' occur in DtrH (Josh. 3.5; Judg. 6.13) and in Jer. 21.2 (DtrJer?); the longer form of the first-person singular personal pronoun occurs some 56 times in Deuteronomy (*VTC*). Where 1-4 is not Dtr, I should prefer to find P ('Sinai', hierarchy, purity).

Nor is the defence of the presence of JE, as opposed to Dtr in my view, any more successful. The fundamental point here must be the recognition of Hossfeld himself that Dtr, given the necessary adjustment from narrative to personal reminiscence, is using Deut. 10.1-5 verbatim in 34.1, 4ab, 27b. But if this recognition is accorded here (specifically Deut. 10.1aab, 2a, 3abb), why is it not accorded in 24.12a, 18b, 31.18 (specifically Deut. 9.9-11)? Hossfeld, without detailed discussion, insists in regarding the latter verses as containing the JE understanding of the tablets and presumably envisages that they were inscribed 'by the finger of God'. The contents of these tablets, which, I believe, are in reality the Dtr conception, he has to find in the *Privilegrecht*. This *Privilegrecht* itself is defined as 12-26. But the passage is clearly composite: 12-16 is discursive both in structure (e.g. 15a resuming 12ab) and in content (warning interspersed with prohibition in highly Dtr style; e.g. for 13 cf. Deut. 7.5; free reminiscence of II in 14); 18-26 have substantial parallels to Exod. 23.12-19. Hossfeld himself is constrained to admit the hand of Dtr in 17. Even if one were prepared to admit the existence of JE and the *Privilegrecht* for the sake of the argument, one can hardly see why the leaving ambiguously open of the subject of 'and he wrote' in 28b assists in the combining of the JE and Dtr views of the basis of the covenant: the issue is then not who wrote but what was written. Hossfeld says that Dtr regarded the *Privilegrecht* as 'the second decalogue': there is no evidence in the text that it was so regarded; he gives no indication about what the 'ten words' were in 12-26. As regards the overall Dtr redaction of the Horeb pericope, is it likely that, having recognized the *Privilegrecht* as 'the second decalogue', but having displaced it as the basis for the covenant in favour of B, Dtr would then have modestly left out his own Decalogue?

Hossfeld's supporting arguments for the existence of JE on the basis of 'proto-Dtr' ideology and language virtually concede the point that it is a matter here of a Dtr-recension as such. He finds a close parallel to the role of Moses in Exodus 34 as covenant partner representing the people precisely in Deut. 5.2-3! The uncharacteristic qal of *šāmar*

(11aa) is immediately followed by the characteristic Dtr niphal (12aa) (both qal and niphal occur in Deut. 4.9). It is true that in Deuteronomy Moses is generally the subject of 'am commanding you' (11ab) but to find God as subject is not unparalleled (Deut. 26.16). The qal imperative of *šāmar* followed by a noun can be found in DtrH (1 Kgs 8.25).

IV

In the light of the foregoing discussion I can find no compelling reasons for diminishing the role of Dtr in the Sinai pericope in favour of either 'JE' or P. I should maintain that, as is indicated by Exod. 34.27-28; 24.3-4, it was Dtr who was responsible for incorporating the Decalogue and B as the basis of the covenant at Horeb (19-24*), for developing the golden calf incident as the occasion of covenant-breaking (31.18*; 32*) and for defining the basis of the renewed covenant as, once again, the Decalogue and B (34*).

The Decalogue presents a test case for the correctness of the contention that the Sinai pericope in Exodus 19–40 has passed through Dtr and P redactions. I find it entirely satisfactory to interpret it in accordance with the theological and hermeneutical principles laid down in Chapter 7. As the themes 'exodus' and 'Sinai' act as the secondary points of reference for the justification of practices of all kinds, ritual, legal and social, so the clauses of the Decalogue serve as focal points at which Israel's theological affirmations and the consequences derived from them are concentrated in sharp clarity.

The Decalogue is a quintessential expression of Israel's faith but not in any inert way. The preservation of the parallel recensions in Exodus and Deuteronomy and the overlaying of these recensions in Exodus, not to mention the resonances that arise from the varied origins of the individual clauses of the Decalogue themselves, impart the rich texture to its content and provide the necessary, and necessarily paradoxical, framework for the interpretative task. There is here a statement of the summation of tradition but also of the preservation of varieties of tradition in complementary relationship. The sum does not exclude the continuation of the parts. This is already a statement of non-finality, of the continuity of a self-enriching tradition in search of fresh articulation, of an eschatological orientation awaiting fulfilment.

Overlaid recensions suggest the appropriateness of a synchronic approach; parallel recensions suggest the appropriateness of a diachronic approach. Insofar as the Decalogue represents a collection at a specific point in time, F. Crüsemann legitimately identifies the theme of the Decalogue as the 'preservation of freedom'.[65] Insofar as the Decalogue is preserved in parallel recensions, Dohmen is right to object to any such theological reductionism, to which the selection of one theme threatens to subject the interpretation of the individual elements in their origin and growth:[66] the diachronic axis is preserved and must have justice done to it. Insofar as the parallel recensions point to Israel *in via*, Lang appropriately quotes from Crüsemann to draw attention to the hermeneutical task and to hint at the eschatological orientation: the Decalogue does not present us with

> a simple matter of universality and general applicability, of a timeless ethic or general morality. It does not equally address everyone in every situation. It cannot be regarded as the sum or quintessence of OT or biblical ethics. That is historically impossible and theologically problematical.[67]

Hermeneutics belongs intrinsically to the character of the Decalogue in its biblical sources.

It is against such a perspective that the contributions of Hossfeld and others can be evaluated. Hossfeld's intention of appreciating each recension of the Decalogue on its own terms is thoroughly commendable. It rescues the interpreter from the attempt to search for an *Ur*-Decalogue on the basis of a literary critical reductionism to the lowest common denominator; under the benign influence of E. Gerstenberger,[68] it abandons the form-critical reductionism to a series of similarly formed prohibitions. Instead, the variant forms of the Decalogue are seen as responses to changing historical and social conditions. One has reservations only with the account of the literary history and redactional intention thus perceived as reflected in the varying recensions.

Hossfeld's insistence on the need to appreciate each recension in its own right has impeded the perception that there are actually *three* Decalogues involved. *Both* the Deuteronomy and Exodus recension are dependent on a prior composition. Both have late features, most clearly

---

65. F. Crüsemann, *Bewahrung der Freiheit: Das Thema des Dekalogs in sozialgeschichtlicher Perspektive* (Kaiser Traktate, 78; Munich: Chr. Kaiser Verlag, 1983).

66. Dohmen, *Bilderverbot*, p. 211 n. 441.

67. Lang, 'Neues über den Dekalog', p. 64.

68. E. Gerstenberger, *Wesen und Herkunft des 'apodiktischen Rechts'* (WMANT, 20; Neukirchen–Vluyn: Neukirchener Verlag, 1965), pp. 77ff.

the references to an earlier promulgation in IV and V in Deuteronomy and the reason for Sabbath observance in Exodus. Both may have features earlier than those contained in the other (the combination of I and II in Deuteronomy?, Exodus as the shorter text?). Certainly there is a very substantial degree of identity between the two and both are impregnated with language that is characteristic of Deuteronomy. These features are readily accounted for on the assumption that there are three Decalogues: (1) a Dtr-Decalogue in the Horeb recension of Exodus 19–40, cited as (2) in Deuteronomy, with perhaps as little as the cross-references added, and to be identified with the help of that Deuteronomy version as underlying (3), the P-version in the final Sinai recension of Exodus 19–40.

In my view, because of his preoccupation with 'JE' and the *Privilegrecht* Hossfeld has not done full justice to the theological creativity of Dtr.[69] One need not doubt that, as in the case of B, so in the case of the Decalogue, preliminary collections were adopted and adapted. I find convincing the derivation of VI–VIII from the infinitive absolute series in prophetic denunciation in Hos. 4.2 mediated through Jer. 7.9 from which possibly I and IX also derive.[70] One may equally recognize wisdom influence in the form and content of such prohibitions: insofar as wisdom reflects an elementary capacity of the human mind to order and arrange experience and deduce precepts therefrom, the prophets must have shared it as one of their presuppositions in a perfectly general and instrumental way. But I doubt whether preliminary compilations of elements of the Decalogue can be assigned to named sources such as 'JE' any more successfully than can B.

The actual historical circumstances of the D-recension, the threat and experience of deportation, have been well sketched by Hossfeld.[71] But appreciation of the dynamism of the theological response is heightened

---

69. Still less has justice been done on Levin's literary attempt ('Der Dekalog am Sinai', pp. 183ff.) to find the 'embryonic cell' of the Sinai pericope in the Decalogue, which he thinks is referred to in Exod. 24.3. One wishes to know what the growth medium was of this cell, i.e. the theological and hermeneutical intentions of those who produced it within a wider redactional framework.

70. Levin, 'Der Dekalog am Sinai', pp. 169-70.

71. Despite Crüsemann's strictures about Hossfeld's return to the pure literary historical approach of the nineteenth century, which ignores the socio-historical context (*Bewahrung*, p. 14); Hossfeld (*Der Dekalog*, p. 282) is as aware of the need for further work on the history of redaction as is Crüsemann (*Bewahrung*, p. 100 n. 174).

if the Decalogue is seen as already part of the Dtr presentation of the covenant in Exodus 19–34: the promises of the covenant once made, then broken, but now remade with the people 'in the wilderness', that is, in the typological wilderness of exile, will be eschatologically realized in the land towards which they are imminently expecting to set out. Only thus can the full pathos of this collection be appreciated. In a context of exile,[72] liberation and freedom are affirmed: the confession of the nature and action of the God of Israel in the prologue is echoed in faith in the motive clauses of IV despite all the evidences of contemporary history to the contrary (as once from Egypt, so now in the observance of the Sabbath is that true liberation, which is the earnest of liberation to come). Duty towards God and man is defined in terms of the freedom of the negatively formulated stipulations I–III, VI–X and of the absolute restrictiveness of the two positively formulated injunctions IV and V. These latter are laid side by side in order to express in the most ultimate way but also in the way most accessible for a people in exile the terms of their fundamental obligations to God and to humankind and the means for carrying them out in order to preserve identity and community. In the context of collapse of all other institutions, cultic and non-cultic, Sabbath and parents are left as the sole means of imparting the truths and values of tradition. In VI–X there is the pathos of the appeal to standards and reciprocal responsibilities within the covenant community, within a context of the bitter experience of expropriation of the property of the soldier long absent on war or of the exile, hope or even desire for whose return has been given up by so-called compatriots. This is the creed of a people 'in exile'. It is, however, like Deuteronomy itself, eschatologically orientated: V ends with the eschatological promise in the inceptive participle 'the land, which YHWH your God is *about* to give you'. Hope for the future is expressed in the mythopoeic terms of 'settlement'. Such, I believe, are the outlines of the Dtr-formulation of the Decalogue already present within the covenant framework in the 'Horeb' recension of Exodus 19–40.

This 'covenant' recension is complemented by the P-recension with its overall emphasis on holiness articulated through hierarchy. Hossfeld may be right that the very phrase 'to sanctify it' in IV is the contribution of the redactor of the Pentateuch (cf. Exod. 20.11).[73] It may well be

72. Cf. Lang, 'Neues über den Dekalog'.
73. Hossfeld, *Der Dekalog*, p. 248.

that the P-recension of the Decalogue reflects the growing urbanism of the postexilic period (the suppression of 'field' in X)[74] and the continuing violations of social order reflected in Malachi and Nehemiah. But still more significant is the theological background of the consciousness of a 'return' from exile that in fact turned out to be but a partial return (cf. Chronicles' call to preserve holiness as the form of life pending the definitive Return). It may be the P-writer's answering zeal to do further justice to the sole deity of his God that has prompted the separation of I and II. It is through Israel's participation in the 'rest' of God at creation that the means of proleptically anticipating that rest in the 'land' of YHWH is provided (IV). Here the eschatology of P and of the Chronicler lies close at hand. Within this awesome perspective the social dimension of a man's marriage and his possessions falls into its proper place (X).

It is by appeal to its roots in the prophetic, wisdom and Levitical past, to its double recension in Exodus and Deuteronomy and to its overlaid recension in Exodus that the interpretation of the Decalogue is shielded from theological reductionism. To draw attention to the hermeneutical task of the community of God's people en route towards the eschatological fulfilment of promise is as far as the *Alttestamentler, qua Alttestamentler*, can go. But in the contemporary undertaking of that task the *Alttestamentler, qua* human being, will have his own ideas.

Summary

The Decalogue provides a test case for the hypothesis advanced in Chapter 7 of a redaction of Exodus 19–40 first by Dtr and then by P. The thesis, that underlying the present P-recension of the Decalogue in Exod. 20.2-17 there is a Dtr-recension, as is already implied by Exod. 34.27-28; 24.3-4, and which is recoverable from Deut. 5.6-21, is defended within the context of a discussion of recent scholarship, especially the work of F.-L. Hossfeld and selected responses to it.

---

74. Hossfeld, *Der Dekalog*, pp. 125ff.

Chapter 9

THE TWO THEOLOGICAL VERSIONS OF
THE PASSOVER PERICOPE IN EXODUS*

In Chapters 7 and 8 above,[1] I have sought to argue that passages in the
book of Exodus, especially in the Sinai pericope in Exodus 19–40, have
passed through two final processes of theological redaction which I
have termed the 'D-version' (because of its intimate relationship to
Deuteronomy and the wider Deuteronomistic History) and the 'P-edition' (retaining the traditional label for the latest 'document' of the
Pentateuch, recognized here, however, not merely as 'source' but also
as redaction, rather as the Chronicler is both 'source' and 'redaction' in
relation to the Deuteronomistic History).[2] In this chapter[3] I should like
to apply this hypothesis to the Passover pericope in Exodus, especially
Exodus 12–13.

It may be helpful, first, to recapitulate briefly the argument so far.
The book of Deuteronomy, more broadly, the Deuteronomistic History,
provides a text parallel to material in the book of Exodus which enables
a pre-P Deuteronomistic text to be recovered in the book of Exodus

*   Originally published in R.P. Carroll (ed.), *Text as Pretext* (Festschrift
R. Davidson; JSOTSup, 138; Sheffield: JSOT Press, 1992), pp. 160-78, here reproduced in slightly edited form.

1   See also my *Exodus*, pp. 73-86.

2.   On this as on other topics it is impossible within the confines of this chapter
to give other than eclectic reference to the scholarly literature. The question of
'source' versus 'redaction' is discussed with special reference to Exodus by W.H.
Schmidt, 'Plädoyer für die Quellenscheidung', *BZ* NS 32 (1988), pp. 1-14. Interest-
ingly enough, even such a doughty defender of 'sources' as Schmidt concedes
('Plädoyer', p. 13) that a redaction especially interested in the Mosaic traditions and
standing in close relationship to Deuteronomy and DtrH exists in Exodus and that
the question of its extent remains open.

3.   The substance of this chapter was read as the Presidential Address to the
Society for Old Testament Study, London, 3 January 1990.

which was subsequently re-edited by the P-writer. The matter may be put statistically. There are 719 verses in Exodus 19–40. The material on the Tabernacle (Exod. 25.1–31.17; 34.29–40.38, i.e. 463 verses) I am willing with many others to ascribe to P. I should assign a further 32 or so verses in chs. 19, 24 and 32 to P (approximately 19.11*-13, 18, 20-25; 24.1-2, 9-11, 14-17; 32.25-29, 35; 33.18, 20-23; 34.2, 3), giving some 495 verses all told. Of the remaining 224 verses, approximately 116 are taken up by the Decalogue and the Book of the Covenant (Exod. 20.1-17; 22.1–23.19), which are likely to have had an independent history. There thus remain only 108 verses which are neither P nor Decalogue nor B. What is the affiliation of these verses? Almost one-third of them have verbal correspondences, in some cases identity, with material in Deuteronomy (especially the 'backbone' of the material, Exod. 24.12, 18; 31.18; 32.7-10, 15, 20; 34.1, 4, 28//Deut. 9.7–10.11) and/or the Deuteronomistic History (for the coda of the Book of the Covenant in Exod. 23.20-33, cf. the coda to the conquest narrative in Judg. 2.1-5; for the golden calf in Exod. 32.4, cf. 1 Kgs 12.28). Many of the remaining verses, such as 19.3-9, 20.18-21, 24.3-8 and those in chs. 32–34, are strongly marked with Deuteronomic/Deuteronomistic phraseology. I have also argued that both the Decalogue and the Book of the Covenant have passed through Deuteronomistic redaction.

A good illustration, among many, of how a text of Exodus that has been re-edited by P can be reconstructed on the basis of parallels in Deuteronomy is supplied by Exod. 34.1-4//Deut. 10.1-3:

Exod. 34.1, 4	Deut. 10.1-3
¹ ויאמר יהוה אל משה	¹ בעת ההוא אמר יהוה אלי
פסל לך שני לחת אבנים כראשנים	פסל לך שני לוחת אבנים כראשנים
	ועלה אלי ההרה
	ועשית לך ארון עץ:
וכתבתי על הלחת	² ואכתב על הלחת
את הדברים	את הדברים
אשר היו על הלחת הראשנים אשר שברת:	אשר היו על הלחת הראשנים אשר שברת
	ושמתם בארון:
	³ ואעש ארון עצי שטים
⁴ ויפסל שני לחת אבנים כראשנים...	ואפסל שני לחת אבנים כראשנים
ויעל אל הר...בידו שני לחת אבנים:	ואעל ההרה ושני הלחת בידי:

After due allowance is made for the fact that Exodus is couched as third-person narrative and Deuteronomy as first-person reminiscence, there is word-for-word correspondence between the outer frameworks of these two texts. I should suggest that the explanation for this identity is that both come from the same source (as one would argue in the case of Samuel–Kings//Chronicles—or Jer. 52, or Isa. 36–39//Kings), namely, D. On this hypothesis the reason for the suppression of the remaining D-material in Exod. 34.1-4 becomes clear: it concerns the ark of the covenant. Since P has already given the specifications for the ark of the testimony in Exod. 25.10-22 and is about to record the construction of it in accordance with these specifications in 37.1-9, it is superfluous to mention it once more here. This suppressed material has been replaced by matter reflecting P's preoccupation with ritual purity and hierarchy. Deuteronomy 10.1-3, however, permits the recovery of the pre-P text that once stood in Exod. 34.1-4.

The interplay between the two final recensions of the book of Exodus thus illustrated preserves an element of the dialectic and paradox which are an essential feature of biblical interpretation. The recognition of these two synchronic redactions in diachronic tension is not simply a matter of the interpreter's preference and presupposition, but is the identification of an element that is objectively present in the text and only an interpretation that recognizes at least that degree of complexity can begin to claim to be inductively and phenomenologically describing the text as it stands.[4]

---

4.   As the somewhat polemical tone of that last paragraph hints, this approach has to maintain itself against alternatives on either side. On the one hand, there is synchronic, 'final form', interpretation, of which J.I. Durham's *Exodus* (WBC; Waco, TX: Word Books, 1987) is a recent example. His view is that Exodus is a 'one-track book...theologically single-minded', predicated on the theology of the Presence of YHWH (*Exodus*, p. xxiii). The dangers here, in my opinion, of under-description are not unconnected with understating the evidently composite character of the book of Exodus. On the other hand, my approach has recently been explicitly criticized as insufficiently differentiated by, especially, C. Dohmen of the 'Münster school' of Pentateuchal criticism, in F.-L. Hossfeld (ed.), *Vom Sinai zum Horeb* (Würzburg: Echter Verlag, 1989). Dohmen remarks that by my approach the complexity of the text is 'eher verschleiert denn erklärt' (*Sinai*, p. 28 n. 37). My response would be that it is difficult enough already, even with the help of the control of the D/DtrH material, to establish with tolerable certainty the penultimate, pre-P version of the D-school, let alone repose any confidence in more far-reaching hypotheses about origins and developments. Dohmen's ingenious analysis is, in my view, beyond verification and he should not be surprised if few follow him. Within the Sinai pericope he finds seven redactional stages: J, E, Je, three Deuteronomic and P. The J account of the theophanic encounter between YHWH and Moses on the mountain (a couple of verses in ch. 19 [20, 25a] and parts of half a dozen in 34

I turn now to apply this hypothesis to the first part of Exodus, especially to the Passover pericope in chs. 12–13. The D-legislation for the observance of the Passover in Deut. 16.1-8 must provide one of the most critical—even, at first sight, insuperable—hurdles for the theory that there is a Deuteronomic/Deuteronomistic text in Exodus 12–13, underlying the final P-edition. The idiosyncratic features of the Passover legislation in Deut. 16.1-8, as opposed to other liturgical calendars in the Hebrew Bible including Exodus 12–13 (material conventionally attributed to B in Exod. 23.14-17 and 34.18-24; and to P in Exod. 12.1-14, 43-49; Lev. 23.5; Num. 9.1-14; 28.16; 33.3; cf. Josh. 5.10-11; Ezek. 45.21; Ezra 6.19-22), scarcely need emphasizing: in D the Passover lasts not just for one night but for one night plus seven days, thus annexing to itself the festival of unleavened bread; the rite is observed not in homes throughout the land but in the one sanctuary in the one place which YHWH will choose; the rite thus resolutely associ-

---

[1aa, 2*, 4a*, 6aa*, 8a, 10a]) is veiled in wordless mystery (Moses goes up the mountain, comes back down and makes a promissory covenant). E adds that the theophany was at least accompanied by God's speech, though the content is not recounted (Exod. 19.19). Je introduces the tablets (Exod. 24.12*; 31.18*; 32.19) but they are blank: they are the public attestation of the occurrence of the theophany; the phrase *luḥōt 'eben* is a plural of *Gattung* and not a plural of number. The original D-text (<Je) also has blank tablets, though it now understands them in the sense of a genuine numerical plural (*luḥōt 'ᵃbānîm*). D, in the interests of the prohibition of images in the second commandment, introduces the inscription on the tablets of the Decalogue as the basis for the covenant. Meantime in Exodus, Exod. 34.10-26 contains the legal corpus of the *Privilegrecht* (Je), written (v. 27), but not on the tablets. A late D-editor is, therefore, responsible for Exod. 34.1b, which understands that Moses wrote the *Privilegrecht* on the tablets. That the tablets are 'two' is first stated in Deut. 9.10, which derives from R^P. The competition between Decalogue (introduced into Exod. 20 for the first time by P) and *Privilegrecht* is finally resolved in P in the ambiguities of Exod. 34.28.

Quite apart from the highly speculative nature of this reconstruction, it is precisely Dohmen's failure to use the Deuteronomy parallels as control that makes him fail to see that, for example, Exod. 34.28b corresponds directly with Deut. 10.4a and that the subject of 'he wrote' is YHWH, thus undercutting much of his argument.

Nonetheless, on the biblical principle of interpretation, *'îš lᵉpî 'okᵉlō* ('each according to his capacity'), slightly whimsically derived from this very section of Exodus (12.4; cf. 16.18) as the original title of this paper, I should resolutely defend the right of a Durham and a Dohmen to pursue their contrasting methods of interpretation, however unsatisfactory I find them both to be.

ated with the cultus of the central sanctuary is given the sacrificial terminology, *zebaḥ*, and follows sacrificial practice—the victim is not
only a kid or lamb of the small cattle but may also be chosen from the
large and is boiled, not roasted. If, as I should be disposed to believe,
Josiah's Passover is represented as carrying out this Deuteronomic legislation (2 Kgs 23.3, 21-23; 2 Chron. 35.1-19), then the JPSV translation
of 2 Kgs 23.22-23 correctly conveys the revolutionary, indeed unique,
character of the Deuteronomic observance:

> Now the passover sacrifice had not been offered in that manner in the
> days of the chieftains who ruled Israel, or during the days of the kings of
> Israel and the kings of Judah. Only in the eighteenth year of King Josiah
> was such a passover sacrifice offered in that manner to the LORD in
> Jerusalem.[5]

That translation points up the challenge of whether the D-legislation
in Deut. 16.1-8, with its revolutionary observance of the Passover,
enables a similarly revolutionary Deuteronomic text to be recovered in
Exodus 12–13, which has subsequently undergone substantial
modification at the hands of the P-editor. At first sight, the recovery of
such a text seems a forlorn hope. I have few grounds for dissenting
from the prevailing view that Exodus 12, even read with the best will in
the world, shows little sign of D. I should indeed regard the legislation
on Passover in Exod. 12.1-13, 21-28, 43-50 (and on unleavened bread,
vv. 14-20) as an almost purely P composition[6] (though it may itself

---

5.   The question of the pre-Josianic history of the development of the institution of Passover need not be pursued here (see, e.g., J. Van Seters, 'The Place of the
Yahwist in the History of Passover and Massot', *ZAW* 95 [1983], pp. 167-82, for
some discussion and bibliographical leads). I should be inclined to the view that
there is such a history but it may be that, in the light of the discussion in the text
below, the necessary sources for tracing that history are lacking in the Hebrew
Bible: if Exod. 12–13 is a reworking by P of Deuteronomic/Deuteronomistic material and B has passed through Deuteronomistic redaction, then Deut. 16.1-8 may be
the earliest literary source. The fact that that source itself may be composite may
bespeak complex prehistory not only of the literary formulation but of the institution itself. But for the latter we are dependent on educated guesses about inherent
probabilities and the plausibilities arising from anthropological parallels (such as
are adduced by, e.g., J.B. Segal, *The Hebrew Passover* [The School of Oriental &
African Studies; London Oriental Series, 12; London: Oxford University Press,
1963]; Henninger, *Les fêtes de printemps*).

6.   Cf., e.g., Van Seters, 'The Place of the Yahwist', pp. 172-75. F. Kohata
(*Jahwist und Priesterschrift in Exodus 3–14* [BZAW, 166; Berlin: W. de Gruyter,

have undergone development—e.g. v. 19 repeats v. 15): for example, the prominence of Aaron beside Moses in vv. 1, 28, 43, 50; the dating by the Babylonian calendar, vv. 2, 18; the reference to Israel as an *'ēdâ*, vv. 3, 6, 19, 47; v. 12b uses the same vocabulary as Num. 33.4b; for the requirement to observe on pain of death, vv. 15, 19, cf. Exod. 31.14; Lev. 7.20. The P (or, at least, non-D) character of much of Exodus 12 is, I think, fairly non-controversial. I shall, however, return to Exodus 12 below.

But what, then, of Exodus 13? I should like to present an argument that Exod. 13.3-7[7] contains an original Deuteronomic/ Deuteronomistic text attested by Deut. 16.1-8 in which the Passover has been suppressed by P—because it has already been dealt with in quite other terms by P in Exodus 12—just as the ark was suppressed in Exod. 34.1-4.

Once again it may be helpful to lay out the two texts to reveal where the parallels occur:

Exod. 13.3-7	Deut. 16.1-8
3 ויאמר משה אל העם	1
זכור את	שמור את
	חדש האביב ועשית פסח ליהוה אלהיך
היום הזה אשר	
	כי בחדש האביב
יצאתם ממצרים מבית עבדים כי בחזק יד	הוציאך יהוה אלהיך ממצרים לילה
הוציא יהוה אתכם מזה	
	2 וזבחת פסח ליהוה אלהיך צאן ובקר
	במקום אשר יבחר יהוה לשכן שמו שם
ולא יאכל חמץ	3 לא תאכל עליו חמץ
4 היום אתם יצאים בחדש האביב	
5 והיה כי יביאך יהוה אל ארץ	
הכנעני ...	
ארץ זבת חלב ודבש ועבדת את העבדה	
הזאת בחדש הזה	
6 שבעת ימים תאכל מצות	שבעת ימים תאכל עליו מצות
	לחם עני כי בחפזון יצאת מארץ מצרים

1986], p. 267 n. 31) provides a convenient account of the attributions that have been proposed for Exod. 12.21-28 running all the way from N to P.

7.   M. Caloz ('Exode, xiii, 3-16 et son rapport au Deutéronome', *RB* 65 [1968], pp. 5-62) subjects the passage to analysis assuming the correctness of the attribution of materials in the Tetrateuch to sources proposed in O. Eissfeldt, *Hexateuch-Synopse* (Leipzig: J.C. Hinrichs, 1922) ('Exode', p. 9)—which, to a significant degree, is the very point at issue.

Exod. 13.3-7 (cont.)   Deut. 16.1-8 (cont.)

...

ששת ימים תאכל מצות 8

וביום השביעי עצרת ליהוה   וביום השביעי חג ליהוה

אלהיך לא תעשה מלאכה

מצות יאכל את שבעת הימים 7

ולא יראה לך חמץ

...ולא יראה לך שאר בכל גבלך 4   ולא יראה לך שאר בכל גבלך

Is Exod 13.3-7 basically a Deuteronomic text that has been re-edited
by P? There are a number of unevennesses in Exod. 13.3-7 which
provide the *prima facie* case that it has at least undergone editorial
adjustment:

1. The addressees are masculine plural in vv. 3-4 but masculine
   singular in vv. 5-7 (and thereafter).
2. Verse 3b is a legislative snatch abruptly introduced and
   equally abruptly abandoned.
3. Verse 4, 'today you are going out in the month of Abib', is
   lame: its five words provide two definitions of time that are
   not coordinate with one another.
4. According to v. 6, only the seventh day is a *ḥag*, a pilgrimage
   festival; there is no such festival elsewhere in the Hebrew
   Bible.
5. Verse 7a has unusual syntax: the feminine plural subject is
   followed by a masculine singular verb;[8] the adverbial accusative of time, 'for the seven days', is introduced by the *nota
   accusativi*, '*et*.[9]
6. There is repetition in v. 7b.

While it may thus be recognized that this passage has undergone
editorial adjustment, can a basically Deuteronomic/Deuteronomistic
text within it be recognized? It is certainly strongly marked with
Deuteronomic phraseology: v. 3, 'house of slaves' (cf. Exod. 20.2);
'strength of hand' as applied to YHWH (frequent in Deuteronomy,
e.g. 3.24; 4.34; 5.15; 6.21); v. 5, the list of the pre-Israelite population
(cf. Exod. 23.23). There are verbal reminiscences of the legislation of

---

8. GKC 121.b regards the construction as an impersonal passive with preceding object. One notes a similar construction in Exod. 12.16, 48 (P).

9. But cf. Lev. 25.22; Deut. 9.25; BDB notes the construction as 'very rare'.

Deuteronomy 16 in the specifically legislative material in vv. 3b, 6-7 (cf. Deut. 16.3a, 4a, 8).

Can it even be argued that the Deuteronomic text of Deut. 16.1-8 provides materials for the restoration of an underlying Deuteronomic text in Exod. 13.3-7 which has been subsequently modified by the P-editor?

The text is, I submit, explicable from this point of view. Since P has already given his legislation for the Passover in Exodus 12, the Passover has been rigorously excised from this passage and the text has now been transformed from one on Passover into one on the festival of unleavened bread. This is arguable on grounds of parallels and of differences.

1. Parallels. Apart from close correspondence in Exod. 13.3//Deut. 16.1, there are four almost exact parallels: Exod. 13.3//Deut 16.3; Exod. 13.6//Deut. 16.3; Exod. 13.6//Deut. 16.8; Exod. 13.7//Deut. 16.4.

2. The main differences are accountable on the assumption that P is deliberately reusing D-material for its own purposes:

   a. *pesaḥ* of Deut. 16.1, 2, has been suppressed—P has dealt with it in Exodus 12.

   b. The 'over it [sc. *pesaḥ*]' has consequently been omitted in Exod. 13.3, 6.

   c. The whole of Deut. 16.2 has been suppressed, since it insists on the centralization and culticization of the festival.

   d. For similar reasons most of Deut. 16.4 and all of Deut. 16.5-7 has been omitted. The omission of this material has facilitated the transposition of Deut. 16.8.

   e. The plural address in Exod. 13.3-4 matches the plural P has already used in Exodus 12. The singular address of Deuteronomy 16 is resumed in Exod. 13.5-7.

   f. In Exod. 13.3b a new title referring to unleavened bread has been constructed in place of the suppressed Passover. The verbal form has been changed into the impersonal passive (the singular address of the D-form would not in any case suit P's plural address). It is, however, singularly inadequate as a title for the festival of unleavened bread (cf. Exod. 23.15//34.18, for the appropriate form of the legislation, *'et ḥag hammaṣṣôt tišmōr*).

g. In Exod. 13.6 *ʿₐṣeret* has been replaced by the anomalous *ḥag*. In the P conception, Passover cannot have a seventh day to be solemn assembly: *ʿₐṣeret* in P is otherwise used of the eighth day of Tabernacles (e.g. Lev. 23.36).

h. The inconsequential Exod. 13.4 represents the turning into plural address of remnants of Deut. 16.1.

i. Exodus 13.5a is pure Deuteronomic and may have belonged to the underlying D-version (although it could be P-reuse of Deuteronomic clichés). *ʿₐbōdâ*, however, in v. 5b looks like P (Num. 4.23, etc.).

j. Exodus 13.7a is an adaptation of Deut. 16.8a, with, again, the adjustment of the direct address of D's singular verb into P's impersonal passive of legislation.

k. Exodus 13.7bα appears to be a doublet reusing *ḥāmēṣ* from the new title in v. 3b.

The correctness of the hypothesis that an original D-version of the Passover has been suppressed in Exodus 13 by P in preference for his own version in Exodus 12 can be confirmed when we return to consider the latter chapter. Two series of observations on the legislation for the Passover in Exodus 12 can now be made.

1. The general P-character of the material in Exodus 12 has already been conceded. But, if this is the P-legislation on the Passover, how does it relate to the earlier D-legislation (whether that legislation be found only in Deut. 16 or in Exod. 13 as well)? It is presumably intended to correct and, to a degree, to supersede D's practice. That this is so is indicated by the fact that there are indeed verbal citations and material reminiscences, but made in such a way as to make clear that the relationship between P and D is mainly one of polemical correction of D by P. The polemical element centres, naturally, on the P-conception of Passover as a *domestic* rite, with its victim taken from the small cattle, roasted whole over the spit, as opposed to D's sanctuary rite, where the immolation of the victim is formally linked to the sacrificial system of the cultus in terminology and in practice. The elements, which P found objectionable, are those listed particularly in Deut. 16.2, 5-7; thus P in Exodus 12 emphasizes the domestic, non-cultic nature of the observance throughout and provides aetiology for the observance and for the term itself in v. 13; it specifies the choice of the victim from the small cattle (v. 3); it synchronizes the slaughter as *bên hāʿarbayim* (v. 6), rather than D's *bāʿereb kᵉbôʾ haššemeš* (Deut. 16.6); it uses the

not specifically cultic verb *šāḥaṭ* for the slaughter of the victim, not *zābaḥ* (vv. 6, 21); it prohibits the boiling of the victim (v. 9); so far from returning to their tents in the morning, Israel are forbidden to leave their houses all night (v. 22b). The pilgrimage festival of unleavened bread is distinguished from Passover (vv. 14-20).

Besides these polemical corrections, there are, however, verbal and material reminiscences: the eating in haste, *bᵉhippāzôn* (although Deut. 16.3 speaks of *leaving* in haste) (v. 11b); v. 12a*bc* resembles 13.15a*bc*; v. 15a resembles material in 13.6 and v. 25a resembles 13.5, although the plural verb characteristic of P is used (v. 25b introduces the P-expression *ᶜᵃbōdâ*; cf. v. 26b); v. 26a appears to introduce the D-motif of instruction of the son, except that here again the plural is used, and the verb is *'āmar* not D's *šā'al*; v. 27a*a* retains the Deuteronomic phrase (including *zebaḥ* of the Passover!) but the remainder with the domestic aetiology must be P. These polemical corrections and verbal and material reminiscences may suggest that still more of the material in the D-legislation for Passover in Deuteronomy 16 was originally present in the D-version of the Passover that lay before P in Exod. 13.3-7 and stimulated his revision: specifically, at least Deut. 16.3b*ab*, 4b, 7. A plausible reconstruction of the original D-text of Exod. 13.3-7, based both on the parallels to Deut. 16.1-8 in Exod. 13.3-7 and on the polemical corrections by P in Exodus 12, is thus as follows:

ויאמר משה אל העם שמור את חדש האביב ועשית פסח ליהוה אלהיך
כי בחדש האביב הוציאך יהוה אלהיך ממצרים לילה:
והיה כי יביאך יהוה אלהיך אל ארץ הכנעני...ארץ זבת חלב ודבש
וזבחת פסח ליהוה אלהיך:
לא תאכל עליו חמץ שבעת ימים תאכל עליו מצות
ולא יראה לך שאר בכל גבלך שבעת ימים:
ששת ימים תאכל מצות וביום השביעי עצרת ליהוה אלהיך:

2. If the legislation on Passover and unleavened bread in Exodus 12.1-28, 43-50 thus belongs to P, then it is subsequent to the D-version. If it is omitted as an insertion subsequent to the D-version and based upon it, then the remaining material should close up faultlessly. In my view, Exod. 12.29-36 does indeed continue directly from Exod. 11.1-8 as the execution of the threatened tenth plague.[10] As in the other nine plague scenes, so here in the tenth there is no break in the pre-P version

10. So, many (with variations) from J.F.L. George (1835, cited by J.W. Rogerson, *Old Testament Criticism in the Nineteenth Century: England and Germany* [London: SPCK, 1984], p. 67) to Van Seters, 'The Place of the Yahwist'.

between the threat to Pharaoh and the Egyptians and the carrying-out of that threat.

The inclusion of the P-material in Exodus 12, on the contrary, introduces elements of incoherence and incongruity into the narrative. According to the P-scenario, Israel are saved from the tenth plague because they are celebrating Passover in their houses. But why should Israel have been thought to have been under any threat from the tenth plague, when, like the other nine, it was meant to impress *Egypt* and to force them to let Israel go unscathed? Why should it have been necessary for Israel to take special precautions against a plague from which they had already been promised immunity (Exod. 11.7: the verb *hiplâ* has already been used in connection with the fourth and fifth plagues in Exod. 8.18; 9.4, without implying any action on Israel's part)? There is the further incongruity between the selection of a *yearling* ram/kid as victim (Exod. 12.5) and the *first-born* of Israel for which it was meant to be the means of protection.[11] Contrariwise, this incongruity is removed when the intrusive P-material in Exod. 12.43-51 is removed and the tenth plague of the death of the first-born of Egypt is brought into immediate relation, not with the Passover, but with the offering of the first-born of Israel in Exod. 13.1-2. In the light of these considerations I should argue that before P there was no material in Exodus 12 on the Passover; the Passover legislation was confined to ch. 13.

To summarize thus far: the D-version had no Passover material in Exodus 12. Rather, its Passover regulations were to be found in ch. 13 in reformulation of the material on unleavened bread. The P-edition has suppressed this Passover in ch. 13 and, instead, has inserted its regulations on the Passover in ch. 12 with the incorporation of vast new materials of its own and polemical reuse of fragments of D-material. What is the significance of these phenomenological observations for the understanding of the Passover in the D-version and in the P-edition, respectively?

In order to understand the significance of the Passover pericope in the D-version, one has, I believe, to widen the area of discussion significantly beyond Exodus 12–13. Before we can consider its significance we must establish its extent. A basic clue is provided here by the

---

11. The (inconsistent) classical view is expressed by Noth, *History of Pentateuchal Traditions*, p. 67: the Passover is derived from an indigenous rite against 'the Destroyer', the object of whose attack was the fertility of man and beast, especially the first-born 'because they were so highly valued'. Cf. Heb. 11.28.

Deuteronomic chronology. Why does the D-writer define the Passover as lasting for one night plus seven days? What does he envisage as happening during the octave (or, should one say, the heptad?) of the festival?

D and P have radically differing views of the chronology of events that took place following the exodus—and of the related question, the itinerary that the Israelites followed.[12] In the final edition of the itinerary in Exod. 12.37-42; 13.17–19.2 we have an abbreviated form of the P-route itemized in Num. 33.1-15: it takes Israel six weeks or more to march from the Red Sea to Sinai, from the wilderness of Shur to the wilderness of Sin and the wilderness of Sinai via the stopping-places of Marah, Elim, Massah, Meribah and Rephidim (cf., e.g., Exod. 16.1; 19.1). By contrast, Deuteronomy knows nothing of any such itinerary *before* Horeb: Deut. 1.6 begins the review of events with Israel already at Horeb (cf. Deut. 4.34-35, which passes immediately from plagues and exodus to Horeb). Incidents that Exod. 15.22–19.2 portrays as taking place *before* Sinai, Deuteronomy presents as occurring *after* Horeb. Thus in Deut. 1.9-18 Moses appoints judges to help him rule the people *after* the instruction to depart from Horeb (so Num. 11.16-30); the parallel appointment in Exod. 18.13-26 takes place *before* Sinai. In Deut. 9.22 the enraging of YHWH at Massah takes place *after* Horeb between Taberah and Kibroth-hattaavah, the post-Horeb location of which is confirmed in Num. 11.3, 34; Massah, however, is located *before* Sinai in Exod. 17.7. For Deuteronomy, Meribah is 'Meribath-kadesh' (Deut. 32.51; 33.2), which, however, is located 11 days *after* Horeb (cf. Deut. 1.2), whereas in Exod. 17.7 again Meribah is placed *before* Sinai. This variation between D and P in the chronology and itinerary of the journey leading up to Horeb/Sinai corresponds to their divergent overall conceptions: for D, Kadesh-barnea is the starting-point for 38 years' wandering in the wilderness (Deut. 2.14); for P, it is reached only towards the end of the 40 years' wandering (Num. 33.36-38).

What effect has this divergence between the D and P conceptions of chronology and itinerary had on the formation of the Exodus narrative of the route from Red Sea to Horeb/Sinai, especially in Exod. 15.22–19.2? I should suggest that we have a situation similar to that in Exodus 12–13: the P-editor, using materials available to him in the earlier

12. For a standard account, cf. Davies, *The Way of the Wilderness* (but see the discussion of the topic in Chapter 1, pp. 37-42; Chapter 11).

D-version (in this case actually in Num. 11–21), has radically recast
that version according to his own conceptions. In the D-version of
Exodus there was *no* material in *this* location between Exod. 15.22 and
17.16 and in 18.13-26: the D-version had virtually only Exod. 18.1-
12,[13] the account of the rendezvous at the mountain of God in
fulfilment of the promise in Exod. 3.12. This does not mean that some
of the remaining material in Exod. 15.22–19.2 is not strongly marked
with D-characteristics (especially in Exod. 17–18) or that all the
material therein is the creation of P. Rather, P as editor has drawn on
D-material already lying to hand in Numbers 11–21 and has transposed
and refashioned it for his own purposes (the clearest example is Exod.
17.6, where YHWH stands on the rock on Horeb—the D-term for P's
'Sinai'—which Israel is not to reach until ch. 19!). This provides an
example of why redaction criticism is essential. It is totally misleading,
as it is in ch. 12, to try to divide Exod. 15.22–19.2 into 'sources', as in
the old literary criticism. One must work here with the concept of
redaction: there was scarcely any D-'source' material present *in this
context* in the D-version of Exodus; yet D-material has been reused
here from elsewhere in the P-edition of these chapters.

What impact, then, do these findings have on our understanding of
the D-concept of the octave of the Passover? I should suggest that the
following is a possible reconstruction of D-chronology of the one-
night-plus-seven-days period of the festival. After the night of the
escape from Egypt, Israel passes in three days directly to Red Sea and
Horeb: compare the speed implied by Exod. 19.4, 'I have carried you
on eagles' wings and brought you to myself'; compare, too, Moses'
request of Pharaoh that he lead Israel on a three-day journey into
wilderness (Exod. 3.18; 5.3; 8.23; [15.22 is a context edited by P]) to
hold a *ḥag*, a pilgrimage festival (Exod. 5.1; 10.9) with flocks and
herds, to sacrifice (*zbḥ*) to YHWH (cf. the Deuteronomic concept of the
Passover). For three days they prepare themselves at Horeb (Exod.
19.10-11*, 15-16); on the third of these, that is, the sixth day of the
Festival, YHWH reveals the Decalogue directly in the sight and hearing
of the people (Exod. 20); Moses writes the remainder of the revelation,
the Book of the Covenant, overnight and on the following day (Exod.
24.4), that is, the seventh of the festival, the covenant is formally concluded. That is why in Deut. 16.8 the last day of the festival of

13. Even this minimal survival has been abandoned in Chapter 11, below. The
fulfilment of the promise in 3.12 is contained in Exod. 19–24 (D).

Passover is called an *'aṣeret*, a 'solemn assembly'. The Passover pericope in the D-version of Exodus thus runs forward to Exod. 24.8 (Exod. 24.12 begins the next section of the D-presentation, Moses' 40 days and nights on the mountain).

Where, then, does the D-version of the Exodus Passover begin? The Passover pericope in the D-version also has strong links with the Exodus narrative preceding ch. 12. To appreciate this we have once more to return to Deuteronomy, to the legislation on the Passover. It is striking that, in Deuteronomy, the legislation on the Passover in Deut. 16.1-8 is immediately preceded in Deut. 15.19-23 by the legislation on the presentation of firstlings, precisely the institution that provides the envelope around the Passover in Exod. 13.1-2, 11-16. Not only so; firstlings–Passover in Deuteronomy are immediately preceded by the legislation on the release of Hebrew slaves (Deut. 15.12-18). In this sequence, the release of Hebrew slaves–firstlings–Passover which reflects the D-legislation, it seems to me, we have the fundamental clue for understanding not only the extent of the D-version of the Passover pericope in Exodus but also its theology.[14]

The relevance of the three sections of Deut. 15.12–16.8 in providing structural elements that give coherence to the narrative in Exodus 1–15 is, I should submit, readily apparent.

1. The legislation on the freeing of Hebrew slaves in Deut. 15.13 (*kî tᵉšallᵉḥennû ḥopšî mēʿimmāk lō tᵉšallᵉḥennû rêqām*) provides two key thematic terms for the Exodus narrative, the verb *šillaḥ*, 'release', and the adverb *rêqām* coupled with the negative *lō'*, 'not empty-handed'. The verb *šillaḥ*[15] recurs in every chapter from Exodus 3–14, 40 times in all (Exod. 3.20; 4.21, 23 [2×]; 5.1, 2 [2×]; 6.1, 11; 7.2, 14, 16, 26, 27; 8.4, 16, 17, 24, 25, 28; 9.1, 2, 7, 13, 17, 28, 35; 10.3, 4, 7,

---

14. For diverging studies of how DtrH is modelled on D as the casting of law into narrative, see G. Braulik, 'Die Abfolge der Gesetze im Deuteronomium 12–26 und der Dekalog', in N. Lohfink (ed.), *Das Deuteronomium* (BETL, 68; Leuven: Leuven University Press/Peeters, 1985), pp. 252-72; 'Zur Abfolge... Deuteronomium 16,18–21.23: Weitere Beobachtungen', *Bib* 69 (1988), pp. 63-91. The suggestion of C. Carmichael (*Law and Narrative in the Bible* [Ithaca, NY: Cornell University Press, 1985], as in his earlier *The Ten Commandments* [Oxford: Oxford Centre for Postgraduate Studies, 1983]) that the laws are formulated in response to issues raised in the narratives seems to me to be precisely the opposite of the actual process so far, at least, as Exodus is concerned.

15. Other verbs 'to release', e.g. *g'l, grš, hwṣy', hwšyʿ, hṣyl, pdh*, might have been used.

10, 20, 27; 11.1 [2×], 10; 12.33; 13.15, 17; 14.5 [some of these reused in P-contexts]). But the all-pervasive theme is not just the freeing of the Hebrew slaves: they are not to be freed empty-handed. Thus, although *rêqām* occurs only once in Exodus 1–15 (at 3.21), that occurrence is highly significant inasmuch as it is in the context of the first occurrence of *šillaḥ*:

> I will stretch out my hand and smite the Egyptians with all the miraculous deeds which I shall perform among them. Then they will release you. I will give this people favour in the eyes of the Egyptians so that, when you go, you will not go empty-handed.

The phrase 'give favour in the eyes of the Egyptians' recurs in 12.36 (cf. 11.2-3) in the context of 'spoiling the Egyptians', so that, in my view, the traditional interpretation whereby the spoiling of the Egyptians is understood as compensation for the years of the slaves' work in accordance with the Deuteronomic law in Deut. 15.13-14 is fully justified.[16]

2. An even more fundamental idea is provided by the legislation on firstlings. The true focus of the D-version of Exodus 13 is not Passover but the dedication of the first-born. The pre-eminence of the offering of firstlings is made clear in Exod. 13.1-2, where it is communicated as direct word of God. The instruction for the ensuing one-night-plus-seven-day Passover is reduced in status as Moses' own instruction. This dedication of the first-born in connection with Passover is another of the revolutionary features of the Deuteronomic reformation. It was not simply the Passover that was centralized; the centralization of the cult, that is to say the abolition of the local sanctuaries, also involved centralization of the offering of the firstlings. These could now no longer be offered as in B on the eighth day after birth at the local sanctuary; D, accordingly, has to make provision for their offering yearly in connection with the Passover. This revolutionary step provides the occasion for no-doubt revolutionary theological reflection. The word *bᵉkôr*, 'first-born', is equally a thematic term of Exodus 1–15 (4.22, 23; 11.5 [4×]; 12.29 [4×]; 13.2, 13, 15 [4×] [12.12 is reused by P] are the relevant occurrences). The first occurrence in the context of 4.21-23, with the key word *šillaḥ* also occurring three times, thus sets the scene for the whole D Passover pericope:

16. Cf. D. Daube, *The Exodus Pattern in the Bible* (London: Faber & Faber, 1963), pp. 22-23, 50-54.

YHWH said to Moses, 'When you go back to Egypt, all the wonders which I have put in your power you will work in Pharaoh's presence. But I will harden his heart and he will not release the people. You will say to Pharaoh, "This is what YHWH has said: 'Israel is my son, my firstborn. I have said to you, "Release my son so that he may serve me." But you have refused to release him. Therefore I am about to slay your son, your firstborn'"'.'

These words contain all the ingredients of the following D-narrative down to Exodus 13: the focus is the dedication of Israel to YHWH as YHWH's son in the person of their first-born sons dedicated in association with the Passover. In contrast to the illogicality of the P-edition where the plague narrative culminates in the Passover, the concept of Israel as YHWH's first-born in the D-version provides the logic for the culminating tenth plague and the link with the whole plague cycle: if Egypt will not let Israel, YHWH's first-born, go free, then they will be forced to release them at the cost of their first-born. The concept of Israel as YHWH's son is, of course, Deuteronomic (Deut. 14.1).

This cycle of ideas may explain the enigmatic narrative in Exod. 4.24-26, the incident in the wayside inn when YHWH attempts to kill Moses, which immediately follows the passage I have just cited. It is at the cost of the dedication of his first-born son through circumcision that Moses is saved. It is fitting that the leader of the people who are dedicated as YHWH's first-born by the dedication of their first-born should himself be dedicated by the dedication of his first-born.[17]

3. On this argument the whole span of Exod. 1.1–24.8 insofar as it is Deuteronomistic must be taken together as the D Passover pericope. Under the heading of Passover, understood in the revolutionary sense of a one-night-plus-seven-day festival, and interpreted in the light of the equally revolutionary association with it of the dedication of the firstlings, the D-writer has linked together the themes of the Hebrews as YHWH's sons, redeemed from slavery, dedicated as his first-born and bound in a relationship to him of awe, which is sealed in the formal tie of covenant. The Passover on this conception is Israel's annual sacramental actualization and participation in these truths; it is not merely an apotropaic rite lest Israel suffer the same fate as the Egyptians nor is it merely a celebration of liberation.

17. B.P. Robinson ('Zipporah to the Rescue: A Contextual Study of Exodus iv 24-6', *VT* 36 [1986], pp. 447-61) associates the blood with that of Passover.

One may well ask what the gains are of recovering this D-layer in
Exodus 1–24. I should suggest there are at least three. (1) There are
phenomena here that have to be explained. There are varieties of witness to what the Passover was, the interrelationship of which has to be
clarified. The biblical text is in contradiction about the extent and character of the Passover. The canon has at times, and certainly here, a
curiously jagged, dialectical character, which cannot be ignored.
(2) This D-layer in Exodus provides the narrative accompaniment to
the law of Deut. 15.12–16.8, and especially of 16.1-8, which otherwise
hangs suspended in the air without rationale. The Deuteronomic legislation in Deut. 15.12–16.8 is reproduced in narrative form in the D-version of Exodus 1–24 (as, one suspects, much of the Deuteronomistic
History reproduces in narrative form other parts of the D law-code, e.g.
Deut. 17 on the judges period and the monarchy). (3) Even if all this
analysis were entirely false, it may still have brought into clearer focus
one aspect of the narrative—the importance of the concept of Israel as
YHWH's first-born, which otherwise tends to be lost in the presentation
of the Passover in the final form of the text. There are cases when the
danger is that the final form of the text in its obliterative power is *less*
than the sum of its parts, if these parts are not given due weight in and
for themselves.

The significance of the Passover for the P-edition is the significance
of the Passover in the familiar 'final form' of the text, of the text 'as it
stands'. As such, it is probably superfluous to try to say anything further on it. However, the recovery of the prior edition of the text in the
D-version does enable a number of distinctive features of the P-edition
to be highlighted.

For P, there can be no question of the Passover pericope culminating
in a covenant ceremony at the mountain of God, as D's does in Exodus
24. As far as P is concerned, Israel has been a covenant-people since
the patriarchs (Exod. 6.4), with the sign of covenant engraved on their
flesh through circumcision (Gen. 17). The experience at the mountain
of God is, rather, that of the revelation of Torah. The need for that revelation of law is highlighted by the insertion by P of the six-weeks of
murmuring in the wilderness between exodus and Sinai in Exod.
15.22–19.2; it is anticipated by a promulgation of חק ומשפט in 15.25
and by the appointment of judges in 18.13-27. While for D the Passover pericope culminates in a formalization of the relationship between
God and people in covenant in Exodus 24, P ends the Passover

pericope in Exodus 12 and drives a wedge of rebellion in the wilderness between Passover and the revelation of Torah. In its final form, the Passover pericope is thus now no longer about God's gracious deliverance of Israel, his responsive covenant partner-to-be. It is much more restricted: Passover is an independent one-night festival with its own significance, rather than, as in the D-version, an all-encompassing framework within which all manner of institutions and affirmations are gathered. The emphasis is now on the celebration of, and sharing in, the act of freeing by Yahweh and of sparing his own people; observance of it is, indeed, the precondition of sharing in that deliverance, not as in D a memorial of it.

D, no doubt addressed to a generation newly in exile, stresses the deliverance of God and the eager responsiveness of the people. It is only after the covenant has been concluded that the rebellions begin which explain the long years in the wilderness. Even after the first rebellion of the golden calf, the relationship is intact and the covenant can be remade on identical terms. P, written deep in the postexilic period, is, by contrast, profoundly pessimistic about the realizability of covenant obedience in life as it presently is. In the wilderness, the metaphorical, all-encompassing wilderness of this world, there is a profound alienation between God and his people. In order to attain D's covenantal ideal of 'a kingdom of priests and a holy nation' (Exod. 19.6; cf. Deut. 14.1-2), the life of holiness has now to be spelt out in Torah: it is only through the hierarchy of priest and Levite that Israel can be instructed in holiness and its practice of holiness can be enabled and monitored.

This development has profound implications for the celebration of Passover. It is removed from the week-long celebration of the temple cultus as an all-encompassing rite of national commitment and becomes a one-night domestic rite. The round of annual festivals as part of the priestly and Levitical rites of holiness in the temple now far transcends the sphere of practice of the laity. The P-edition has, thus, driven a wedge between the lay rites in the home and the national priestly rites in the temple. Even the offering of firstlings disappears from view as an annual focus of dedication of Israel as Yahweh's first-born expressed through the dedication of their own first-born: in Numbers 18 it is submerged as part of the emoluments of the priesthood (offered monthly, Num. 18.16?). The domestic Passover is separated from the temple festival of unleavened bread. The two poles of worship—intimacy and objectivity, accessibility and inaccessibility—are, thus, now institutionally separated. P recreates religious intimacy in his development of the Passover as a household rite, a robust intimacy which affirms the unity of the family and solidarity with the neighbour. But the other pole of religion, the sense of awe at the unapproachable mystery God, is now institutionalized in the rites of the temple with its hierarchy of holiness, which are detached from Passover and attached to Unleavened Bread and the other pilgrimage Festivals. P has radically polarized the practicable domestic aspects of religion and the unattainable holiness expressed through the temple cult.

Chapter 10

THE DEUTERONOMISTIC CYCLES OF 'SIGNS'
AND 'WONDERS' IN EXODUS 1–13*

1. *Posing the Question*

A series of observations suggests that interconnections exist between
chapters in the second half of the book of Exodus and the
Deuteronomistic corpus.[1] If such interconnections exist in the latter part
of the book, is it possible that there may be similar connections in the
opening chapters of the book with texts in the Deuteronomistic corpus?
The focus in this chapter will be in particular on the so-called plague
cycle in Exodus 7–12. The context is, however, delimited in the title as
Exodus 1–13 to signal my conviction that the plague cycle is not a
separable narrative but has been conceived as integral to a wider whole.

Interconnections that may be observed between Exodus and the
Deuteronomistic corpus include the following:

1. There are cross-references between Exodus and DtrH. The best
recognized is, perhaps, that between the golden calf incident (Exod.
32.4) and Jeroboam's golden calves at Bethel and Dan (1 Kgs 12.28;
2 Kgs 17.16);[2] there is also, I believe, the link between the coda to the
Book of the Covenant in Exod. 23.20-33 and the coda to the conquest

---

* This chapter represents a revised and expanded version of the essay originally published in A.G. Auld (ed.), *Understanding Poets and Prophets* (Festschrift
G.W. Anderson; JSOTSup, 152; Sheffield: JSOT Press, 1993), pp. 166-85. The presentation has been simplified by the omission of tables. As explained in Chapter 1,
some refinement of content (especially the significance of the phrase יד חזקה as
referring specifically to the last 'plague') has been introduced in the light of further
engagement with the text. An appendix on 14.1–15.21 has been added.

1. See Chapters 7–8.

2 . For a guarded discussion (but not, I think, including the important reference
in 2 Kgs 17.16), one might refer to R.W.L. Moberly, *At the Mountain of God*
(JSOTSup, 22; Sheffield: JSOT Press, 1983), pp. 162-71.

narrative in Judg. 2.1-5 (see Chapter 7). But there would appear to be similar cross-references in chs. 1–14: the rare term, מסכנות, for the storehouses that Pharaoh built (Exod. 1.11), coincides with that for those that Solomon built (1 Kgs 9.19;[3] cf. the anti-Solomon polemic of the Deuteronomic legislation on the monarchy, Deut. 17.14-20); the carrying-up of the bones of Joseph (Exod. 13.19) links not only with Gen. 50.25 but also with Josh. 24.32; long ago, de Vaux argued that one of the narratives of the crossing of the Sea in Exodus 14 was modelled on that of the crossing of the Jordan (Josh. 3–4).[4]

These cross-references are too significant to be regarded as merely sporadic glosses: they suggest deliberate editorial work. Indeed, they suggest joint-editorial work: DtrH is not simply quoting a pre-existing source, for the plural reference in the golden calf incident ('These are your gods, O Israel, which brought you up out of the land of Egypt') suggests that the primary focus lies with the Kings passage, in the light of which the Exodus passage is being written up, just as, on de Vaux's argument, priority lies with the narrative of the crossing of the Jordan rather than with that of the crossing of the Sea.

2. There are parallels between Exodus and the book of Deuteronomy itself. These parallels in language and phraseology, many of which have long been noted,[5] again suggest that the phenomenon is not simply a matter of sporadic glosses but of deliberate editorial design. In particular:

(a) Deuteronomy provides material that enables the reconstruction of a pre-P text in Exodus (for example, Exod. 13.3-8*//Deut. 16.1-8; Exod. 34.1-4*, 27-28*//Deut. 10.1-4,[6] not to mention the Decalogue, Exod. 20.2-17*//Deut. 5.6-21).[7]

(b) Material in Exodus is the narrative counterpart to reminiscence in Deuteronomy (e.g. in the making and, especially, the renewal of the covenant in Exod. 24.12-18*; 31.18–34.28*//Deut. 9.7–10.11)[8] and is occasionally referred to as such, as in connection with the revelation of

---

3.   Apart from five passages in Chronicles, including the parallels to the Kings passage, מסכנות occurs nowhere else in the Hebrew Bible. The root סבל is also of significance between the two passages (Exod. 1.11, cf. 1 Kgs 5.29; 11.28).

4.   *Histoire*, I, pp. 361-64.

5.   Cf., e.g., Hyatt, *Exodus*.

6.   See Chapter 9.

7.   See Chapter 8.

8.   See Chapter 7.

the Decalogue, where the cross-reference is specific ('as the LORD your God commanded you', Deut. 5.12, 16, referring to Exod. 20.8*, 12; cf. Deut. 4.23).[9]

(c) Perhaps even more significantly, material in Exodus provides the narrative counterpart to legislation in D. This is particularly the case with the Passover: the 'octave' of the revolutionary D-Passover of Deut. 16.1-8 can be found in Exodus in the night of expulsion, the three days' pilgrimage into the wilderness 'to sacrifice' (Exod. 3.18, etc.) and the three days' preparation at Horeb (Exod. 19.10-11*, 14-16),[10] culminating in the solemn covenantal assembly on the seventh day (Exod. 24.3-8). Indeed, the narrative sequence in the penultimate edition of Exodus 1–24 matches the sequence of the legislation in Deut. 15.12–16.8 as a whole (release of Hebrew slaves, offering of first-born, Passover).[11] That observation permits the deduction that, if a Passover narrative can be reconstructed in Exodus that matches the unique Passover of D, then that narrative must be highly specifically Deuteronomic not only in content but also in date.

All of this raises the question whether a Dtr version of the 'plague cycle' can be reconstructed in Exodus 7–12. Is there reminiscence of the plagues in Deuteronomy? And is there a narrative in Exodus that corresponds to that reminiscence?

2. *The Deuteronomistic Model of the Conditions of Israel's Life in Egypt*

In order to establish whether there *was* a Dtr version of the plague cycle in the penultimate edition of Exodus, one must first construct the model of the D/Dtr view of the conditions of Israel's life in Egypt and of the means of their deliverance from it and then apply that model to Exodus.

Deuteronomy contains a number of references to Israel's experience before, during and immediately following the exodus.[12] A range of

9. See Chapter 8, p. 178.

10. Renaud (*La théophanie du Sinaï*, pp. 92-93) helpfully draws attention to the parallel in the motif of 'sanctification' in Josh. 3.5; 7.13-14 [i.e. DtrH].

11. See Chapter 9, pp. 211-14.

12. The list comprises Deut. 1.30; 3.24; 4.20, 34, 37, 45, 46; 5.6, 15; 6.12, 21, 22; 7.8, 15, 18, 19; 8.14; 9.7, 12, 26, 29; 10.19, 21, 22; 11.2, 3, 4, 10; 13.6, 11; 15.15; 16.1, 3, 6, 12; 20.1; 23.5; 24.9, 18, 22; 25.17; 26.5, 6, 7, 8; 28.27, 60; 29.1, 2, 24; 34.11, 12. The list attempts to include all the references to Israel's Egyptian experience; but some are quite marginal to the issue.

vocabulary is used, some perhaps specific, some general.
One of the most comprehensive of these is Deut. 4.34:

הנסה אלהים לבוא לקחת לו גוי מקרב גוי במסת
באתת ובמופתים ובמלחמה וביד חזקה ובזרוע נטויה
ובמוראים גדלים

In this verse there would appear to be a general term מסת, which in
context must mean something like 'demonstrations of power'. It is
cognate with the main verb, נסה, and is then spelt out (as is indicated by
the lack of the conjunction ו before באתת) in a list of six items: 'has ever
a god demonstrated his power to come to take for himself one nation
from the midst of another—by demonstrations of power, i.e. [1] by
signs and [2] by wonders and [3] by war and [4] by a strong hand and
[5] by an outstretched arm and [6] by great acts of terror?'[13]

Other passages repeat these terms and add others:

11.2-4 provides a new general term, מוסר, the discipline of the
LORD, which is then spelt out: '[7] his greatness [גדל], [4] his strong
hand[14] and [5] his outstretched arm, and [1] his signs and [8] his deeds
[מעשים], which he performed in the midst of Egypt, to Pharaoh...';

26.8: '[4] by a strong hand and [5] by an outstretched arm and [6] by
great terror and [1] by signs and [2] by wonders';

29.1-2: '...everything which the LORD did...in the land of Egypt to
Pharaoh, and to all his servants, and to all his land: i.e. the great
demonstrations of power...i.e.[15] [1] the signs and [2] those great wonders';

34.11-12: '...[1] all the signs and [2] the wonders which the LORD
sent him to perform in the land of Egypt to Pharaoh and to all his servants and to all his land and...[4] all the strong hand and [6] all the
great terror...';

---

13. Deut. 7.18-19 poses a problem to regarding מסת as the general term of
which the remainder is the specification. There the general phrase appears to be
'what God did' (v. 18). The following phrases then appear to be the specification:
המסת הגדלת which your eyes saw *and* [1] the signs and [2] the wonders and [4]
the strong hand and [5] the outstretched arm with which the LORD brought you
out...' (v. 19). *BHS* cites textual evidence to question of originality of the italicized
and. If it is not original, then מסת remains the general term of which the following
is the specification.

14. Cf. again the textual evidence cited in *BHS*.

15. Once again there are textual variants; cf. *BHS*.

Jeremiah 32.21: '...[1] by signs and [2] by wonders and [4] by a strong hand and [5] by an outstretched arm and [6] by great terror'.

The heaping up of expressions, some dozen in all including the general and the particular, is striking.[16] It suggests that there is at least a *prima facie* case that a multifaceted process is being alluded to; it also prompts the question whether different aspects of that process are being described by these terms.[17]

The vocabulary employed in the Deuteronomistic model[18] may now be applied heuristically to the text of Exodus to determine whether there are matching usages there.[19] Two points in particular will be

16. The list of descriptive terms is less complete in other contexts; items may be substituted by other terms. Thus, 1.30 [3] 'war' is the focal term; 3.24: [7] 'greatness' (without acts of terror; so 9.26), [4] strong hand, [8] deeds, [9] might [גבורה]; 4.37 [10] great strength [כח גדל] (9.29); 5.15 pairs '[4] strong hand and [5] outstretched arm'; 6.21 [4] strong hand alone (so 7.8; 9.26); 9.29 [5] stretched-out arm alone; 6.22 [1] signs and [2] wonders, great and grievous on the Egyptians, on Pharaoh and on all his house; 10.21: '[7] the great things and [cf. 6] these fearful things' [נוראת]; Judg. 6.13, 'wonderful deeds' [נפלאת]; cf. also Josh. 24.5, 'struck' (נגף); Josh. 24.7, 'smote' (נכה); 1 Sam. 6.6, 'sported' (עלל).

17. This is questioned by B.S. Childs, 'Deuteronomic Formulae of the Exodus Traditions', in B. Hartmann *et al.* (eds.), *Hebräische Wortforschung* (Festschrift W. Baumgartner; VTSup, 16; Leiden: E.J. Brill, 1967), pp. 30-39 (e.g. p. 32: 'Nowhere in Deuteronomy is there a specific identification of the signs and woners with the plagues'). That may be so; but, if my argument is correct, it provides another example of the necessity for reading Deuteronomy and Exodus reciprocally. Cf. the discussion of the reciprocal reading of Deut. 4–5 and Exod. 19–24 in Chapter 1, pp. 29-33.

18. I am aware of the distinct possibility of the composite nature of Deuteronomy and that a diachronic factor has to be taken into consideration in its interpretation as discussed in, e.g., A.D.H. Mayes, *Deuteronomy* (NCB; London: Oliphants, 1979), pp. 29-55. But the recurrence of these relatively few and conventionalized expressions across Deuteronomy may justify the conclusion that at least in this regard the Deuteronomic view is relatively consistent across any layers that the book may contain.

19. The relevant verses turn out to be 1.10, 13, 14, 16, 21; 2.2, 5, 6, 11, 12, 23, 24, 25; 3.2, 3, 4, 6, 7, 8, 9, 10, 11, 12, 13, 14, 15, 16, 17, 19, 20, 21; 4.1, 4, 5, 9, 10, 13, 14, 15, 17, 18, 21, 23, 28, 30, 31; 5.1, 2, 9, 11, 15, 16, 18, 19, 21, 22; 6.1, 3, 5, 6, 7, 8, 9, 11, 13, 26, 27; 7.1, 2, 3, 4, 5, 6, 9, 10, 11, 14, 16, 20, 22, 26, 27, 28, 29; 8.1, 2, 3, 4, 5, 7, 9, 11, 13, 14, 16, 17, 19, 20, 22, 24, 25, 27, 28; 9.1, 2, 5, 6, 7, 8, 13, 14, 15, 16, 17, 19, 20, 21, 27, 30, 34, 35; 10.1, 2, 3, 4, 5, 6, 7, 8, 10, 11, 12, 13, 14, 15, 20, 23, 24, 26, 27, 28, 29; 11.1, 3, 6, 8, 9, 10; 12.12, 13, 17, 23, 25, 26, 28, 30, 31, 33, 35, 36, 38, 39, 41, 42, 50, 51; 13.3, 4, 5, 7, 8, 9, 11, 13, 14, 15, 16, 17,

explored: whether the passages in Exodus in which this vocabulary is embedded should be identified on other grounds as Deuteronomistic; and whether there is a specialized use of this vocabulary to denoted specific aspects of Israel's deliverance. But to establish a Deuteronomistic version in Exodus further argumentation is required. A mechanically compiled list of vocabulary is in itself unable to distinguish between original use and reuse by a subsequent editor or editors. To establish the extent of any Dtr-version one would have to consider two additional factors: (1) passages already identified in Exodus 1–13 as the narrative counterpart to the D-legislation on slaves, first-born and Passover (see Chapter 9); (2) any further vocabulary and thematic connections required for the sake of narrative coherence.

Do, then, any parts of the Dtr-model of Israel's experience in Egypt match any of the materials narrated in Exodus 1–13; in particular, do any of these terms refer specifically to the 'plague narrative' in 7.14–12.36?

In the focal statement, Deut. 4.34, the phrase most likely to refer to the cycle of plagues is אתת ומופתים.[20] The amplifications of Deut. 4.34 in other parts of Deuteronomy suggest that there is indeed a certain specialization in Deuteronomy's vocabulary. Deuteronomy 34.11 is relatively clear: האתות והמופתים are performed *in* the land of Egypt. So too is Deut. 11.3, where the אתות ומופתים '*in the midst* of Egypt' are separated from the action at the sea by the conjunction at the beginning of v. 4. Can this model then be applied to Exodus 1–13? Does there occur there material that corresponds to D's אתות ומופתים?

18, 19. For the compiling of these data I am indebted to I. McCafferty, temporary part-time research assistant in my department in 1990–91.

20. This is expressly denied by J. Van Seters, 'The Plagues of Egypt: Ancient Tradition or Literary Invention?', *ZAW* 98 (1986), pp. 31-39: 'Deuteronomy does not know of any plagues tradition but makes reference to the "signs and wonders" that God did in Egypt in a very general way. Only in the latest development of the exodus tradition are "signs and wonders" restricted to the plagues' (p. 35). For Van Seters the plagues were developed in Exodus by his exilic J from the curses in Deuteronomy. The connection between the curses in Deuteronomy and the plague cycle in Exodus seems to me, however, far from self-evident: there is an overlap of only three: V, VI and VIII (Deut. 28.21, 27, 35, 38); and in any case in Deuteronomy these are a threat to Israel.

3. *The Distribution and Use of* אתות *and* מופתים *in Exodus 3–13*

It is indeed clear that there is a concentration of אתות material in Exodus 3–4 concerning Israel and Moses (3.12; 4.8, 9, 17, 28, 30) and of מופתים material announced in 4.21 concerning Egypt. But whereas in the earlier chapters there is a clear distinction between the two—the אות (3.12–4.30) is a sign of reassurance to Israel and the מופת (4.21) is a portent publicly worked in Egypt, a 'plague' (so 11.9-10)—in later chapters the two are indiscriminately used: in 7.3 they are combined to describe the action of YHWH in Egypt; in 7.9 מופת no longer refers to a plague proper but to a public demonstration, a 'sign' worked to convince the Egyptians; in 8.19 (plague IV) and 10.1-2 (plague VIII) אות is used of the plagues. How is one to account for this strict use of אתות and מופתים as virtual technical terms in chs. 3, 4 and 11 and this more indiscriminate use in chs. 7–10? The next step must be to establish the affiliation of these blocks of material.

4. *The Affiliation of the Distinctive and of the Indiscriminate Uses of* אתות *and* מופתים *in Exodus 3–13*

It seems to me that good grounds can be adduced for regarding Exod. 3.1–6.1,[21] where אתות and מופתים are distinctively used respectively of 'signs' as regards Israel and 'wonders' as regards Egypt, as a consistently Dtr edition. For example:

21. To go no further back. I should argue on grounds of narrative coherence that much of the remaining material in Exod. 1–2 is Dtr, since it provides the necessary background for what follows: e.g. Pharaoh's command to slay the sons of the Israelites—and that would include the first-born—sets the scene for the theme of the offering of the first-born which dominates the presentation down to ch. 13. The argument from narrative coherence can be backed up by the use of stock Dtr expressions: the descendants of Jacob as 'seventy souls' (1.4; cf. Deut. 10.22); in 1.11-12 the repeated use of the verb ענה (cf. Deut. 26.6-7). 'Hebrew' in 1.15 is to be a consistent theme (e.g. 7.16; 9.1) and echoes the D-legislation on the release of Hebrew slaves in Deut. 15.12 (cf. Jer. 34.9). The 'storehouses' for Pharaoh (1.11) have already been mentioned in the text above. Nonetheless, there are P-materials: in particular, the echo of Gen. 1.20; 9.7 in 1.7; the harsh treatment of slaves in 1.13-14 echoes the legislation in Lev. 25.43-53; the covenant with the patriarchs (2.24; cf. 6.5; Gen. 17), with its sign of circumcision already engraved on the flesh of the males within the community, matches the necessary lack of emphasis on covenant in the P-edition of Exod. 19–34.

(a) 3.1 'Horeb', Deut. 1.2, etc.

(b) 3.6-7 YHWH, the God of the fathers, seeing affliction and hearing the cry, Deut. 26.7. 'Taskmasters' recurs in the Pentateuch only again in 5.6, 10, 13-14; but the finite verb נגש occurs in the Pentateuch only in Deut. 15.2-3, in connection with the sabbatical year of release of debts, a suggestive location, given the use of the pattern of Deut. 15.12–16.8 in Exodus 1–24 as a whole.

(c) 3.8 'to deliver from the hand of the Egyptians', Judg. 6.9; 'to bring up', Deut. 20.1; cf. Judg. 11.13; the 'good land', Deut. 1.25; 8.7; 'flowing with milk and honey', e.g. Deut. 26.9, with the list of indigenous population, e.g. Deut. 7.1.

(d) 3.9 'seen the oppression', Deut. 26.7.

(e) 3.10 'bring out', Deut. 4.20 (cf. Deut. 4.45); Jer. 31.32; so vv. 11, 12.

(f) 3.12 אות, the twin focus of this argument, see §3 above for use in Deuteronomy; so 4.8, 9, 17, 28, 30; 'send', Josh. 24.5; so again 3.13, 14; cf. 3.20; עבד as key term in association with 'serving the LORD, 4.23; 5.9, 18; 7.16, 26; 8.16; 9.1, 13; 10.3, 7, 8, 11; 12.31 (contrast 14.12; all D-passages as is argued below; 10.24, 26 is reuse by P).

(g) 3.13-14 'name' theology, highly characteristic of D/DtrH, e.g. Deut. 12.11; 1 Kgs 8.43.

(h) 3.14-17 repeats in large measure the vocabulary of 3.6-10.

(i) 3.18 presupposes the chronology of the seven-day D-Passover and uses זבח, the sacrificial terminology of the centralized cultus, for it.

(j) 3.19 יד חזקה, Deut. 4.34; Jer. 32.21. Cf. 'my hand', v. 20. It is striking that in Exodus יד חזקה seems to refer specifically to plague X (6.1; cf. 13.3, 9, 14-16), an important observation which confirms the possibility that not just אתות and מופתים but also other items in the D-vocabulary have specific reference. (The parallel term in Deuteronomy, זרוע נטויה, which does not figure in Exod. 1–13, may refer specifically to God's action at the sea; cf. Exod. 15.6, 12, 16. מלחמה, which likewise does not occur in this connection [contrast 1.10; 13.17] in Exod. 1–13, may also refer to the action at the sea; cf. Exod. 14.25; 15.3.)

(k) 3.20 נפלאתי, Judg. 6.13; שלח begins the key thematic series of 'freeing of the Hebrew slaves', which casts the legislation of Deut. 15.12-13 into narrative form.

(l) 3.21-22, 'not empty-handed', has its fulfilment in the plague X narrative (11.2-3; 12.35-36).

(m) 4.1-17 contains the series of three further אתת and, besides continuing the thematic vocabulary introduced in ch. 3 ('send' vv. 4 [2×], 13 [2×], 'God of the fathers' v. 5, play on root עבד v. 10), introduces new thematic terms: 'believe' (vv. 1, 5, 8, 9; so again v. 31, 14.31, cf. 19.9 and 2 Kgs 17.14), שמע בקול (v. 1, so again 5.2, cf. 19.5; 23.21-22, Deut. 1.45 etc.; cf. שמע לקול vv. 8-9 [already in 3.18]), Moses' staff (v. 2, so again vv. 4, 17, 20; 7.12, 15, 20 [plague I]; 9.23 [plague VII]; 10.13 [plague VIII]; 17.9), which will be instrumental in working the אתת (v. 17), 'mouth' (vv. 10, 11, 12, 15, 16), 'teach' (vv. 12, 15; which, while it is typically a P-word, is found in Deut. 17.10-11; 24.8; 33.10). Aaron enters the narrative for the first time at v. 14 and is required for the sequel in vv. 27-31 (not to mention the 'golden calf' incident in Exod. 32; cf. Deut. 9.20; 10.6; 32.50).[22] Verse 15 picks up the divine name of 3.14.

(n) 4.18-20: the reference to Moses' staff as 'the staff of God' is a novelty, but emphasizes the link between Moses as agent and God as sender (cf. 10.12-13, where Moses' deeds shade into YHWH's deeds, just as YHWH's words shade into Moses' words in 7.17; 9.3; 11.7-8, and as the acts of Moses and YHWH are equated in 10.12-13). This lack of distinction between God's instrumentality and word and Moses' instrumentality and word fits with the D-understanding of Moses as prophet, indeed as prophet *par excellence* (Deut. 18.15-18; 34.10-12). Compare, too, Moses' role as intercessor (8.4-5, 24-25; 9.28; 10.17).

(o) 4.21-23 introduces the series of מופתים, the cycle of 'wonders' which is the joint topic of this discussion. Again all the indications are that this passage belongs to the D-version. The verses are replete with D-terms, especially שלח, vv. 21, 23 (2×); בכור, vv. 22, 23, which anticipate precisely plague X, the crucial plague for the D-presentation, as noted above. The plural מופתים signals that, however, more than one plague is now to be expected in the D-cycle of wonders.[23] The passage

22. The role of Aaron has to be carefully evaluated: in ch. 4 he appears merely as spokesman for Moses to the Israelites. In ch. 5 he appears in vv. 1-5, 20-21 as joint-spokesman with Moses to Pharaoh (though it is clear by the reversion to the singular in 5.22–6.1 that, essentially, it is Moses alone who is God's spokesman). In 7.2 it is Aaron alone who is to speak to Pharaoh. It will be argued below (in common with many commentators) that 7.2 is P-material. While it would be neat to argue that the role of Aaron as joint-spokesman to Pharaoh in ch. 5 is also to be attributed to P, this would involve a fairly extensive excision or modification of text and seems to me, on balance, too complex an operation to be convincing.

23. The sole instrumentality of Moses here contrasts with the role of Aaron as

resumes the thematic root עבד (v. 23; cf. 3.12) and introduces new thematic terms 'harden the heart' (v. 21)[24] and 'refuse' (v. 23; cf. 7.14, 27; 9.2; 10.3, 4).

(p) 4.24-26, the redeemer redeemed, fits, as I have argued elsewhere,[25] appropriately into the Dtr-version of Exodus since it involves

wonder-worker in 7.1-13 (P, as will be argued below).

24. In my view, none of the three terms used for the 'hardening of the heart' is clearly diagnostic of D or P: they are all D-terms, which may be reused by P (for difference of language not necessarily implying difference of source, precisely in this connection but following a rather different argument, see J. Kegler, 'Zu Komposition und Theologie der Plagenerzählungen', in E. Blum *et al.* [eds.], *Die hebräische Bibel und ihre zweifache Nachgeschichte* [Festschrift R. Rendtorff; Neukirchen–Vluyn: Neukirchener Verlag, 1990], p. 58 n. 8). The evidence is as follows:

1. (a) חזק, the verb used here in the piel, of YHWH as subject hardening the heart of Pharaoh, recurs in plague VIII (10.20) (D) but also in plagues VI (9.12) and IX (10.27) (P) and in the summary on the 'plagues' in 11.10 (P reusing D, as will be argued in the text below). Cf. the use in 14.4, 8, 17, again all P, as is argued in the appendix to this chapter.

    (b) The qal of the same root, with the heart of Pharaoh as subject, occurs in P-passages (7.13, 22; 8.15; 9.35). But the qal is used in a D-passage of the hand of the Egyptians urging the Israelites to leave their country (12.33), which picks up the expression יד חזקה in the D-passages 3.19; 6.1. Cf. hiphil of Pharaoh maltreating Israel (9.2 [D]).

2. כבד is the other major root used in connection with 'hardening of the heart': the qal (subject 'Pharaoh's heart') is used in 9.7 (cf. the adj. also of Pharaoh's heart in 7.14; both D); the hiphil (subject 'Pharaoh', object 'his own heart') occurs in 8.11 (P), 28 (D); 9.34 (D); the hiphil (subject 'YHWH', object 'Pharaoh's heart') occurs in 10.1 (discussed in text below).

3. The verb הקשה (subject 'YHWH', object 'Pharaoh's heart') is used in 7.3 (P, though it is a perfectly good D term—cf. Deut. 2.30; cf. Exod. 13.15 [D], where the subject is 'Pharaoh', object 'his own heart').

If one were to insist on these uses as being diagnostic of different sources, as in traditional literary criticism, then one might be forced to some such conclusion as that of R. Friebe, *Form und Entstehungsgeschichte des Plagenzyklus Exodus 7,8–13,16* (ThD dissertation; Halle-Wittenberg, 1967), p. 75. While correctly, in my view, detaching the plague cycle in origin from the Passover, she also refuses to relate it to the first-born, interpreting it, rather, as arising from the confession of God's intervention to deliver Israel from Egypt and the answer to the associated question, 'how?' In her view, then, 4.21-23 is to be attributed to the final redactor who has combined materials from the two major sources, J and P (p. 109).

25. *Exodus*, p. 109; Chapter 9, p. 213.

the sparing, by the dedication of his own first-born through circumcision, of the leader of the Hebrew slaves who are released at the cost of
the first-born of Egypt, and who are themselves about to be dedicated
through the dedication of their first-born.

(q) 4.27-31 fulfils 4.14-17, using the appropriate vocabulary; it
resumes thematic terms ('mountain of God', v. 27, cf. 3.1; 'elders of
Israel', v. 29, cf. 3.16; 'believe', v. 30, cf. v. 1; 'visit', v. 30, cf. 3.16;
13.19; 20.5; 'see the oppression' v. 31, cf. 3.7) and introduces a new
one ('fell down and worshipped', v. 31, cf. 12.27 [D reused by P];
34.8).

(r) 5.1–6.1 recounts the initial attempt of Moses and Aaron to secure
the release of the Hebrew slaves (cf. the thematic verb שלח in vv. 5.1-2
[3×] and 6.1). It alludes to Passover according to D-conceptions (a pilgrimage feast, 5.1; cf. the 'three days' in 5.3 as in 3.18; the sacrificial
terminology, 5.3, 8, 17). Thematic terms are resumed: שמע בקול (5.2),
'cry' (5.8, 15), play on the root עבד (5.9, 11, 15, 16 [2×], 18, 21),
'deliver' (5.23), יד חזקה (6.1 [2×], where it is used with the omission of
the parallel זרוע נטויה, as in Deut. 3.24; 6.21; 7.8; 9.26; 34.12). It introduces the new thematic term 'drive out' (6.1), which is to be resumed
in the introduction to plague X in 11.1.

(s) In 5.1–6.1 there are other anticipations of the plague cycle. As
there, so here, Moses functions as archetypal prophet, introducing the
command to release Israel with the 'messenger formula'. Pharaoh's
response, 'I do not know YHWH', anticipates the purpose of the
מופתים—the demonstration and acknowledgment that YHWH is God
(7.17 [plague I]; 8.6 [plague II], 18 [plague IV]; 9.14, 29 [plague VII];
11.7 [plague X]; cf. 10.7). The title, 'the God of the Hebrews' (5.3),
suits well the nature of Exodus 1–13 as the narrative counterpart of the
D-legislation on the release of Hebrew slaves.

(t) The remainder of ch. 5 is prolix. But, interpreted as anticipation of
the plague narratives to come, the passage contains some significant
features, pre-eminently a burlesque on the commissioning of the agent
to carry out the LORD's bidding, in this case the overseers on behalf of
the Pharaoh. As the plague narratives contain in principle five scenes—
the commissioning of Moses by YHWH, the delivery of the message,
including the messenger formula followed by an inceptive participle,
the execution of the message, the reaction to the execution and the
outcome, prefaced by Moses' intercession—so here: vv. 6-9 are the
commissioning; vv. 10-11 the delivery of the message including the

messenger formula and inceptive participle; vv. 12-14 the execution; vv. 15-21 the reaction; vv. 22–6.1 the outcome, prefaced by Moses' intercession. Two points in particular mark the foreshadowing of the plague narratives: Pharaoh's words in v. 18, לכו עבדו, anticipate precisely his command in plagues IX (10.24; but this is P reuse of D, as will be argued below) and X (12.31); the bitter words of the despairing Israelite marshalls, הבאשתם את ריחנו בעיני פרעה ובעיני עבדיו (v. 21), are the counterpart to the action of YHWH in 11.3: ויתן יהוה את חן העם בעיני מצרים (cf. 12.36).[26]

While, thus, I regard 3.1–6.1 as an uninterrupted Dtr-composition, 6.2–7.13, on the other hand, where the very specific purposes of the אתות and מופתים are confused, seems to me to represent a P-composition, reusing, in part at least, D/Dtr-elements. But, on quite other grounds than this confusion in the use of אתות and מופתים, 6.2–7.13 is widely recognized by the commentators as a P composition.

One may append the following observations:

(a) There is non-continuity: 7.14 resumes 6.1.

(b) As conventionally in literary criticism, 6.2-13 can be regarded as offering an alternative resumption of 2.25, parallel to 3.1–6.1 (v. 5, for example, picks up 2.24).

(c) 6.29–7.7 is represented as Moses and Aaron's first interview with Pharaoh in contrast to ch. 5.

(d) 6.30 introduces the role of Aaron as 'prophet' for Moses and miracle-worker, which stands in contradiction to 4.13-17, 27-30. In ch. 4, Aaron is to be spokesman for Moses to the people (a role that fits with Aaron's presumptuous arrogation to himself of that role in Exod. 32), while Moses speaks directly to Pharaoh and performs the מופתים; in 7.1-13, by contrast, Aaron is spokesman for Moses to Pharaoh, is endowed with a hitherto-unheard-of miracle-working staff like Moses' (v. 9), and performs the מופת in competition with the Egyptian magicians (vv. 9-12); vv. 7, 9 and 12, in particular, with their statement that

---

26. Vocabulary items are compatible with, or diagnostic of, D/Dtr provenance: the potential threats from plague or sword (v. 3) are particularly characteristic of (the Dtr editing of) Jeremiah (14.12; 21.9; 27.8, 13, etc.); the thematic terms 'burdens' (vv. 4, 5; cf. related terms in 1 Kgs 5.29; 11.28); 'taskmasters' (vv. 6, 10, 13-14; so already 3.7); 'each day's assignment daily accomplished' (vv. 13, 19; 1 Kgs 8.59; 2 Kgs 25.30) and the highly characteristic D-word 'marshalls' (Deut. 1.15; 16.18, etc.). 'Standing ready to encounter them' (v. 20) anticipates 7.15; cf. 9.13.

Israel is yet to acknowledge and obey, stand in tension with 4.31, which speaks of the believing submission of the Israelites.

(e) There is distinctive language, for example, אני יהוה (6.2, 6, 7, 8, 29; 7.5; cf. 7.17; 8.18; 10.2; 12.12; 29.46; 31.13 and some 52 instances in Leviticus; the phrase does not occur in D, except once in conjunction with ידע [Deut. 29.5]; the phrase is especially characteristic of Ezekiel [87 instances]); הקים ברית (6.4; cf., e.g., Lev. 26.9); perhaps עבד in the hiphil (6.5, used already in 1.13-14 in association with פרך, which recurs in the Pentateuch only in Lev. 25.43, 46, 53); גאל (6.6) is used of the human avenger of blood in Deut. 19.6, 12—the metaphorical use for YHWH is typical of Second-Isaiah; שפטים (6.6) recurs in 7.14; 12.12 and Num. 33.4 in the Pentateuch (probably all P-passages) and is characteristic of Ezekiel (ten instances); the idiom נשא יד (6.8) is found seven times in Ezekiel (though once in poetry in Deuteronomy [32.40]); מורשה (6.8), though occurring in Deut. 33.4, is typical of Ezekiel (seven instances); the genealogical material in 6.14-25; the usage, 'hosts' for Israel as a whole (6.26, as opposed to Israel as an army, e.g. Deut. 20.9), seems, again, to be typical of P (so again 7.4; 12.17, 41, 51 and, especially, Numbers, e.g. 33.1). In 6.28-29 it is as though Moses and Aaron had not yet encountered Pharaoh, yet the whole of ch. 5 has just recounted that first meeting. The chronological data in 7.7 too are likely to stem from P.

The contours of a hypothesis are beginning to emerge: where אתות and מפתים are used as technical terms, the D-version is in evidence; where they are indiscriminately used, it is the P-edition. Does this hold true for the narrower plague cycle beginning in 7.14? The first step must be the identification of P-passages by means of the themes and vocabulary of 6.2–7.13, for example, those referring to Aaron as agent of מופת, to his wonder-working staff, and to his competition with the Egyptian magicians.

On this basis it is likely that the short plagues III (8.12-15) and VI (9.8-12) should be identified as P (for ויחזק לב פרעה [8.15; cf. 9.12], cf. 7.13; for שמע אל [8.15; 9.12], cf. 6.9; for כאשר דבר יהוה [8.15; 9.12], cf. 7.13). This is confirmed by the striking formal point that in both there is a bare plague, with neither the commissioning of Moses to deliver a message of command, accusation and announcement of the impending act by God nor the delivery of such a message (one or other of these elements invariably occurs in plague narratives I–II, IV–V,

VII–VIII, X). In the retrospect in 9.15 in plague VII, it is not plague VI
that is being referred to but V.

On similar grounds, plague IX must fall under suspicion (cf. the formulation נטה יד על [10.21-22], which echoes 7.6, and has recurred in
7.19; 8.2 [also, however, 9.22; 10.12]). Most significant is the vocabulary for Israel's rite in the desert in 10.26: whereas the D/Dtr-material
has been using the D-Passover terminology of חג and זבח (e.g. 3.18;
10.9), here it is the priestly terminology עבד that is being used (cf., e.g.,
12.25-26; 13.5). That observation may then clear Moses of disingenu-
ousness when, in the same verse, he says to Pharaoh, 'For our part, we
do not know how we shall serve YHWH until we get there'. On the P-
scenario the legislation on sacrifice and festival is given on Sinai and
has not yet, therefore, been revealed. Compare, too, Moses' request to
Pharaoh that *he* furnish him with the necessary sacrifices (9.25). In
addition, Pharaoh's prohibition in 10.28 on Moses' seeing him again
contradicts 11.4-8, where Moses is once more in Pharaoh's presence
(so, explicitly, 11.8b).[27]

The remaining seven-plague cycle (I–II, IV–V, VII–VIII, X) can be
defended as belonging to the D-version (retouches by P will be noted
below). Many of the thematic terms already recognized in chs. 3–4 are
now resumed. For example:

(a) שׁלח of freeing slaves 3.20 in plagues I (7.14, 16), II (7.26, 27;
8.4), IV (8.16, 17, 24, 25, 28), V (9.1, 2, 7), VII (9.13, 17, 28, 35), VIII
(10.3, 4, 7, 10, 20) and X (11.1 [2×], 10; 12.33; reused also in IX
[10.27]).

(b) 'Not empty-handed' (3.21-22) is fulfilled in plague X (11.2-3;
12.35-36).

(c) Moses' staff (4.2, 4, 17, 20) recurs in plagues I (7.20), VII (9.23)
and VIII (10.13).

(d) Pharaoh's 'I do not know YHWH' (5.2) is made the reason for
plagues I (7.17), II (8.6), IV (8.18), VII (9.14, 29) and X (11.7).

(e) 'God of the Hebrews' (3.18; 5.3) is picked up as a thematic term
in plague I (7.16) and plague V (9.1).

(f) מאן is picked up as a thematic term from 4.23 in 7.14, 27; 9.2;
10.3, 4 in plagues I, II, V and VIII.

---

27. In Ps. 78.43-51 it is precisely these three plagues, III, VI and IX, that are
missing, though the material on the remainder is somewhat rearranged and
re-expressed.

Further characteristics can be noted in the individual plagues, which suggest Dtr affiliation:

(a) I. For D associations of ידע with YHWH (7.17), cf. Deut. 29.5; for שׁית לב (7.23), cf. Deut. 11.18.

(b) II. For the root נגף (7.27), cf. Josh. 24.5; משׁארת (7.28) occurs in the Hebrew Bible only in 12.34; Deut. 28.5, 17; העתיר (8.4-5) is now introduced as a thematic term, recurring in 8.24-26 (IV), 9.28 (VII) and 10.17-18 (VIII); for 'he hardened his heart' (8.11), cf. 1 Sam. 6.6.

(c) IV. For the new thematic term הפלה (8.18 [IV]; 9.4 [V]: 11.7 [X]), cf. 33.16;

(d) V must also, I think, be regarded as Dtr, being replete with now-familiar thematic terms.

(e) VII. While there are several parenthetical sections that interrupt the standard pattern of the plague narratives (the retrospect in vv. 14-16, the instruction to the Egyptians and response of many of them in vv. 19-21 and the definition of the season of the year in vv. 31-32, which provides the necessary explanation, however, for the vegetation about to be destroyed in plague VIII), none of the vocabulary needs be denied to a Dtr-version.

(f) VIII. Once again, the vocabulary may be regarded as, in the main, fully compatible with a Dtr-version (cf. the frequent references back to plague VII; vv. 5, 12, 15 link plagues VII and VIII closely together).

(g) X, as already mentioned above, is the essential plague in a Dtr plague cycle, reflecting the sequence of Deut. 15.12–16.8 concerning the freeing of the Hebrew slave 'not empty-handed' in association with the offering of the first-born and the celebration of the Passover. The key term בכור, already announced in 4.22-23 recurs in 11.5 (4×); 12.29 (4×).[28] But even in this plague, relatively replete with D/Dtr-phraseology though it is, things may not be all that they appear. I have reservations about 11.9-10, the summary on the preceding מפתים, in particular. On the observation above, that יד חזקה refers specifically to plague X and thus that plagues I–II, IV–V, VII–VIII constitute a separate block of six מפתים in the D-version, such a summary would not be out of place in the D-version (though perhaps we should expect it to precede

28. Other typical D/Dtr-expressions are the stress on eyewitness/personal experience ('eyes' 11.3 [4×]; 12.36; cf. Deut. 3.24; 4.34; 10.21; 29.2); 'great' (11.3, 6; 12.30; cf. Deut. 3.24; 6.22; 10.21); זעקה/צעקה (11.6; 12.30; cf. Deut. 26.7); variations of the root עבד (11.3, 8; 12.30, 31; cf. Deut. 6.21; 7.8; 26.6); the verbs יצא (11.8; 12.31; cf. Deut. 4.20, 45) and עשה (11.10; 12.35; cf. Deut. 3.24).

11.1). But 12.29 joins happily with 11.8 and one could well see how P, having once introduced the heavily polemical correction of D's concept of the Passover into 12.1-28, linking plague X now with Passover rather than, as in D, with the offering of the first-born, draws, so to speak, a line under the plague cycle by introducing a summary. If so, he has done his work rather subtly, for he correctly uses the D-word מופת (and עשׂה and שׁלח). There are, however, some disturbing elements for such a D-version: the inclusion of Aaron as an agent of מופת with the use of a plural verb (v. 10), the use of the idiom שׁמע אל (v. 9), which, while it is abundantly attested in D (Deut. 3.26; 4.1; 9.19, etc.), occurs in Exodus 1–15 again only in 6.9; 7.4 (the idiom is otherwise שׁמע ב/ לקול [4.1, 8-9, etc.]) and the terminology for the hardening of the heart in v. 10bα is characteristic rather of P (cf. n. 24). Perhaps the safest conclusion would be that 11.9-10 represents the reuse by P of largely D-material.

The confusions that remain within the plague cycle, in particular for the present purpose with regard to אתת in 8.19 and 10.1-2, can be attributed to P:

(a) I. 7.19: cf. the further opening formula and how the 'waters of the Nile' (v. 17) have become all the waters throughout all the land of Egypt, including those in every container (so v. 21b)—which contradicts v. 24; the plural verb and 'and Aaron' in 7.20aα (cf. singular verb in 20aβ); 7.22 (cf. 7.13; in addition, v. 23 would be redundant after v. 22).

(b) II. 8.1-3: the role of Aaron and the parallel to 'all the waters of Egypt' in 7.19; perhaps the last phrase of 8.11a and 11b (cf. 6.9; 7.13).

(c) IV. 8.19: where אות is used as a portent to Egypt as in 7.3 thus diverging from the regularity of the D-usage. Assuming the soundness of the text,[29] there are reasonable grounds for holding that the verse belongs to the P-edition: it repeats 8.18; it uses the word פדות, the termination of which is conventionally regarded as a mark of late Hebrew[30] (though it mirrors the use of the verb פדה in 13.13, 15; Deut. 7.8; 9.26, etc.).

(d) VII. 9.35aαb (cf. 7.13 and the repetition of 9.34b). 9.25bβ, which contradicts 10.5bβ, may be a secondary heightening.

29. Cf. apparatus in *BHS*.

30. Again assuming the text is in order; cf., e.g., G.I. Davies, 'The Hebrew Text of Exodus viii 19: An Emendation', *VT* 24 (1974), pp. 489-92.

(e) VIII. In 10.1, 2 there are two divergences (vv. 1bβ, 2aγb) from the regularity of the pattern laid down in chs. 4–5: אתות, not מפתים, is used of the plagues; the point of the plagues is that Israel, not Egypt, may believe (cf. 6.12 contrasted with 4.31). These divergences are shared precisely with the P-material in 7.1-13. There is no overwhelming reason to deny the rest of the passage to D (e.g. for התעלל, cf. 1 Sam. 6.6), even if one were to suspect that the hand of P is considerably more influential, reusing as in 11.9-10 elements of D. Factors that suggest the wider presence of the hand of P include the use of the shorter form of the first-person singular personal pronoun 'I'[31] and the instruction of the children in 2a (cf. 12.26-27, where it is secondary).[32] All of these materials are contained within an explanation to Moses of why he is being sent (vv. 1b-2) which is unique in the plague cycle. The D-version may then have run 1a, 3aαii (reading ויאמרתם; cf., e.g., the opening of II in 7.26). In v. 20a there is again P-formulation.

In sum, the identification of 7.1-13 as P, backed up by less direct indications, requires the identification of 8.19 and 10.1b-3aαi as P. With the exclusion of plagues III, VI and IX and 8.19 and 10.1b-3aαi as P, a coherent picture emerges of Dtr-cycles of 'signs' and 'wonders' in the penultimate version of Exodus 1–13.

5. *The Reason for the Difference between the D-Version and the P-Edition in the Matter of 'Signs' and 'Wonders'*

The isolation of the D/Dtr-material throws into relief certain thematic elements.[33] Already in the D-version, there are clear interconnections

31. The statistics for Exodus are אני 36× (2.9; 3.19; 4.21; 6.2, 5, 6, 7, 8, 12, 29, 30; 7.3, 5, 17; 8.18; 9.14, 27; 10.1, 2; 11.4; 12.12; 13.15; 14.4, 17, 18; 15.26; 16.12; 18.6; 22.26; 25.9; 29.46; 31.6, 13; 33.16, 19; 34.10), 15× in definitely P-contexts. The longer form אנכי, conventionally regarded as earlier, 21× (3.6, 11,12, 13; 4.10, 11, 12, 15, 23; 7.17, 27; 8.24, 25; 17.9; 19.9; 20.2, 5; 23.20; 32.18; 34.10, 11), none in a definitely P-context. But אני with the perfect of the verb, as here, is paralleled in D-contexts, e.g. 3.19. The perfect hiphil of כבד may well be D, as in 8.11aγ (cf. note 24); 10.1bα seems deliberately to resume 9.34b (D).

32. Chapter 9, p. 207.

33. Many excellent observations on the contributions of the two main editions of the plague cycle (though attributed to 'two main tradition-complexes...corresponding roughly to *JE* and *P*'), are made by M. Greenberg, 'The Redaction of the Plague Narrative in Exodus', in H. Goedicke (ed.), *Near Eastern Studies in Honor of William Foxwell Albright* (Baltimore: The Johns Hopkins University Press, 1971), pp. 243-52.

between the plagues and preceding materials, making it clear that the
'plague cycle' should not be separated off as an independent composition but is integral to a much larger whole.[34] For the present purpose,
there is an אתות section in 3.11–4.17, where the word is used for a number of signs given to Moses to show to Israel in order to overcome all
doubts both in himself and in his people. Equally, in 4.21-23 מופתים is
used of the plagues, terminology that is accurately picked up in the
summary in 11.9-10. These two series of אתות and מופתים are locked
together by the demonstration of the אתות to Israel in 4.27-31. In the D-
version, Israel is already responsive to the אתות in 4.31, as YHWH's
potential covenant partners; the מופתים are reserved for the Egyptians.
By contrast, the P-edition, as in its version of the Passover and in its

---

34. It may be instructive to contrast at this point a recent account of the 'plague
cycle' along more traditional literary-critical lines—that of L. Schmidt, *Beobachtungen zu der Plagenerzählung in Exodus vii 14–xi 10* (Studia Biblica, 4;
Leiden: E.J. Brill, 1990). In the plague cycle as delimited in the main in the title of
his work, Schmidt finds there is no E-document, only J, JE, P and R[Pch]. J describes
four *Erzwingungswunder* ('compulsion wonders', I, II, IV, VIII, the latter including
11.8b). JE expands these to six *Schauwunder* ('demonstration wonders'; seven,
with the death of the first-born; I, II, IV, V, VII, VIII, X). P recounts five
Schauwunder (including Aaron's staff, 7.8-13, plus I, II, III, VI, concluding with
11.9-10). R[Pch] begins again at 7.14—he describes ten plagues (including the death
of the first-born): to reach this figure, he constructs the ninth plague.

Quite apart from the, to my mind, questionable procedure of beginning with the
hypothetical earliest document, 'J' (no one knows who 'J' or 'E' or 'JE' were, but
Deuteronomy certainly exists and provides the starting-point for proceeding from
the known to the unknown), the following are the principal weaknesses of
Schmidt's reconstruction, in my view: the inclusion of Aaron's wonder in 7.8-13
within the plague cycle proper in P (it is merely reusing D's technical term מופת
loosely in 7.9 as it has loosely used D's technical term אות in 7.3); the separation
across two versions between the word and act of God and those of Moses in 7.16;
the quite arbitrary separation off of 11.8b and attachment of it to plague VIII and
the equally arbitrary separating off of 11.9-10 and attachment of it as the conclusion of P's cycle to the end of VI in 9.12; the slicing in half of plague X by the
omission of 12.29-36; above all, the admission of uncertainty over the attribution of
11.2-3, which precisely leads the discussion beyond Schmidt's separation of the
'plague narrative' from the wider context of Exodus and links it to the whole cycle
of the narrative presentation of D's legislation on the release of Hebrew slaves,
Israel's offering of the first-born and celebration of the Passover. Even if such ana-
lytical scholars as L. Schmidt are right—and there is, I submit, no way of knowing
that—it would affect the completeness but not necessarily the at least partial rightness of my conclusion.

insertion of the cycle of 'murmuring in the wilderness' *between* exodus and Sinai,[35] is much more pessimistic about Israel: the people are not immediately responsive but still require to be convinced (6.7, 12). They even require a מופת as an אות to persuade them (10.2). They are spared from the climactic plague, not because they are already set apart in Goshen as God's people long poised ready for freedom, but because they have participated in the prophylactic rite of the Passover.

6. *Summary*

As in connection with other parts of Exodus (especially the 'octave' of the Passover, the Decalogue and the making and renewal of the Covenant), so with regard to the so-called 'plague cycle' in Exodus 7–12 materials in Deuteronomy and, more widely, the Deuteronomistic corpus provide a reminiscence that enables the reconstruction in Exodus of a corresponding narrative. These materials gathered from the D-model of Israel's experience of life in Egypt, coupled with the reconstruction of the Dtr Passover 'octave' in Exodus and considerations of narrative coherence, suggest that there is a Dtr-cycle of 'signs' (אתות) in Exodus which refers specifically to the attestation of YHWH's beneficent purpose towards his people and the authentication of Moses' status (3.1–4.31[6.1]). A further Dtr-cycle of 'wonders' (מופתים) refers to the six punitive acts (so-called 'plagues' I, II, IV, V, VII and VIII (7.14–10.20*) by which the Pharaoh's heart is simply made the more obdurate. It is only by the final 'blow' (11.1), the demonstration of the LORD's יד חזקה, that the Pharaoh is coerced into releasing Israel (11.1-8; 12.29-36). The two cycles of אתות and מופתים are connected by motifs such as Moses' staff, which figures in 'plagues' I, VII and VIII and links back to Exodus 4, and are interlocked by Exod. 4.21-23, which introduces the מופתים, and Exod. 4.27-31, which records the execution of the אתות. יד חזקה (3.19; 6.1; 13.3, 9, 14-16) provides a still wider framework motif. Together these are only part of a still wider whole, the מלחמה of YHWH: the demonstration of his מוסר, מסות, נוראות, נפלאות, his גדל, גבורה and כח גדול, by which he is to bring Israel into being as his chosen, loved, covenanted and possessed people. This penultimate version (the 'D-version') was subsequently modified in the final edition (the 'P-edition'). It is only in the P-edition, with the insertion of the Aaron narrative in 6.2–7.13 and the reuse there and in 8.19

35. Chapter 9, pp. 214-16.

and 10.1b-3aαi of D's technical terms אתות and מופתים in less precise
fashion (not to mention the long insertion in 11.9–12.28 which bisects
Dtr's climactic demonstration of YHWH's יד חזקה), that Israel ceases to
be the immediately believing, responsive potential covenant-partner
and becomes the less readily impressed, potentially recalcitrant object
of YHWH's redeeming purpose.

Appendix: Exodus 14.1–15.21

For completeness, a discussion of Exodus 14.1–15.21, which does not
figure elsewhere in this collection, is appended.

In the light of the discussion of itinerary and chronology, especially
in Chapters 11 and 12 below, I have no hesitation in assigning 14.1-4,
9b to P: v. 2 = station 4 in Num. 33.7-8, which locates the sea of the
crossing in the Eastern Delta, as opposed to the Red Sea of Deut. 11.4
= station 7 in Num. 33.10 (suppressed by P in the matching narrative in
Exod. 16.1 in the interests of presenting a harmonized version with D).
These two views of itinerary have already figured in Exodus: 12.37-42;
13.20 for P; 13.17-19, 21-22 for D. 'Encamping at the Sea' in v. 9a
matches v. 2b and thus suggests that the whole of v. 9 should be
assigned to the P-edition.

Links with v. 4 later in the chapter enable further P-materials to be
isolated. In v. 4, the point of the P-narrative is indicated: the LORD will
harden the heart of Pharaoh in order to 'get glory' and to win the
acknowledgment of the Egyptians. This is echoed in vv. 8 (where the
'high hand' matches Num. 33.3), 17, 18. The acknowledgment by the
Egyptians matches the motive in 10.2 (identified above as a P-addition).

It is striking that in vv. 21-22 there are two diverging views of the
means whereby Israel crosses the sea: on the one hand, in v. 21a it is by
means of 'a strong east wind' (cf. Exod. 10.13 [D]) with which the
LORD drives the sea back so that Israel crosses on חרבה (for the word,
cf. Josh. 3.17; 4.18 [DtrH]); on the other hand, in vv. 21b, 22 it is
because the sea is 'split' that Israel crosses on יבשׁה, with a 'wall' (חמה)
of water to right and left (contrast Josh. 3.13, 16 where the waters are in
a 'heap' [נד]). The violent figure of the 'splitting' of the sea matches
the cosmic significance of the occasion in P's presentation (cf. Ps.
74.12-15; and P's motif of the confrontation with the gods of Egypt,
Exod. 6.6; 7.4; 12.12). For P the conflict is one of ideology: it is within
the waters of their own Nile that the Egyptian host perishes, in order

that the LORD's power be acknowledged. Verses 21b-22, in turn, link
with vv. 16aβii, b, 23, 27b, 29. The double instrumentality of Moses'
hand and staff in v. 16aαβi, as opposed to the single instrumentality of
hand in vv. 21, 26, may suggest the presence of P in v. 16aα as well.

There are good grounds for considering much of the remainder of the
presentation as D. As before, the parallels in Deuteronomy and DtrH
provide useful evidence:

Deut. 11.4:

ואשר עשה לחיל מצרים לסוסיו ולרכבו אשר הציף
את־מי ים־סוף על־פניהם ברדפם אחריכם ויאבדם יהוה עד
היום הזה:

Cf. Josh. 24.6-7:

וירדפו מצרים אחרי אבותיכם ברכב ובפרשים:
ויצעקו אל־יהוה וישם מאפל ביניכם ובין המצרים ויבא עליו
את־הים ויכסהו:

From these reminiscences, it is already clear that P on occasion reuses
D-material (as, e.g., in Exod. 12.21-28; so here in v. 4, רדף אחרי [and
vv. 8-9], and [חיל [מצרים; v. 9, סוס, רכב, פרשים [cf. v 26. for a D-con-
text]). It is likely, therefore, that there will be room for continuing
uncertainty about the precise delimitation at the margins of P as a new
edition of D (see comment on the tabulation of D and P in Chapter 7).
It may be suspected that v. 7 is also P: it repeats the Pharaoh's 'taking'
of his forces already dealt with in v. 6, and elaborates on their numbers
and rank. But with v. 10, 'the Israelites cried to the LORD', we are in
the realm of Josh. 24.7; so again v. 15 (cf. Exod. 3.9 [D, as argued
above]). The parallel of the despair of the people in vv. 10-15 with
Exodus 5 (e.g. v. 21) suggests that the whole of that passage should be
taken as D (for 'present oneself' in the LORD's presence, v. 13, cf.
Exod. 19.17 [D]; Deut. 31.14). The LORD fighting for his people (v. 14;
so v. 25b) corresponds to part of the D-vocabulary of God's action on
behalf of Israel (Deut. 1.30; 4.24, noted as item [3] in §3, above).

Verses 19-21a are replete with D-motifs: 'the angel of God' (cf. 3.2;
23.20; 33.2); the pillar of cloud (13.21-22; 33.9-10; cf. Josh. 24.7, but
with different vocabulary); for the 'pillar of fire' as well as 'cloud',
v. 24, cf. 13.21; Deut. 1.33. It is possible that v. 25a should be assigned
to P (cf. the ending ות-, usually reckoned a feature of late Hebrew, on
כבדת, though the word itself is a *hapax* in biblical Hebrew).

The returning waters (cf. Josh. 4.18) and the instrumentality of
Moses' hand in vv. 26-27a match the scenario in v. 21 ('the midst of

the sea', however, in v. 27b picks up the P-version in v. 23, as noted above). The 'covering' of the Egyptians by the returning waters (v. 28) matches the vocabulary of Josh. 24.7. The 'salvation of the LORD' in v. 30 picks up the vocabulary of v. 13 (so also the 'seeing' in v. 31). The dead Egyptians on the edge of the Red Sea (v. 30) mark the final release of Israel from slavery and the definitive setting of the boundary beyond which Egypt cannot pass (cf. v. 13b and the view expressed in Deut. 11.4b; contrast the cosmic significance of the Sea in P). The D-version closes with the 'belief in the LORD and in Moses' (v. 31), which resumes Exod. 4.1-9, 31 (cf. 19.9 [D]). The יד גדולה (to be distinguished from the יד חזקה, which, as argued above, refers to the final 'plague') picks up the Deuteronomic term for the LORD's 'greatness' (Deut. 3.24; 10.21; 11.2, noted as item [7] in §3, above). 'Fearing the LORD' contrasts with the earlier fearing of the Egyptians, vv. 10, 13, and equally echoes the Deuteronomic term for God's actions, 'his acts of terror' (Deut. 4.34; 26.8; 34.12; Jer. 32.21 [cf. Deut. 10.21], noted as item [6] in §3).[36]

It is to be noted how perfectly the action fits into the D-scenario of a three-day journey into the wilderness (3.18, etc.): the day after the night of escape, the Egyptians pursue; it is during all the following night that the east wind drives back the sea and at dawn on the second day (cf. v. 24), then, that Israel sees Egypt dead on the seashore. It is on the third day that Israel reaches Horeb.

In all likelihood, the Song in Exod. 15.1-19a was already present in the D-version (cf. the 'songs' in Deuteronomy 32–33). The end of v. 1 reflects Deut. 11.4; the term 'Red Sea' is used for the location of the crossing in v. 4; there is further use of the vocabulary of the crossing of the Jordan in Joshua 3–4 (DtrH) in v. 8 (the 'heap' in which the waters of the sea stood up echoes Josh. 3.13, 16; cf. Exod. 14.21, 26). The internal references confirm a relatively late date, compatible with the exilic D-version.[37] Though the initial topic is the drowning of the

---

36. With this analysis of Exod. 14 assigning vv. 1-4, 7-9, 16a*b, 17, 18, 21b, 22-23, 25a?, 27b, 29 to the P-edition and the remainder to the D-version there may be contrasted, e.g. M. Vervenne's attribution to P of vv. 1-4, 8ab, 9b*, 10a, 11-12*, 15-18, 21abc*d, 22-23, 26, 27ab-d*, 28ab, 29, 31* (Vervenne works by clause in his subdivision of verses; 'The Sea Narrative Revisited', *Bib* 75 [1994], p. 85 n. 13).

37. Cf. M.L. Brenner, *The Song of the Sea: Ex 15:1-21* (BZAW, 195; Berlin: W. de Gruyter, 1991).

Egyptians in the sea (vv. 1, 4, 5, 9, 10), and the deliverance of Israel at the sea (v. 8), the hymn goes on to celebrate God's subsequent acts: his guidance of his people through the wilderness (vv. 12-15), the conquest under Joshua (v. 16; cf. Exod. 23.27; Josh. 2.9 for the 'dread' that will fall on the indigenous population); and the climax of the choice of Jerusalem at the time of David (vv. 13, 17).

Many of the themes of the Jerusalem tradition of theology, as expressed in the prophets of Jerusalem, particularly Isaiah, and in the liturgy of the Jerusalem Temple as reflected in the Psalms, are utilized in this hymn. In structure the poem would be perfectly at home in the Psalter. Its title 'a song' (v. 1) is one of the commonest in Psalms; the term 'hymns' (v. 11) corresponds to one of the two main categories of Psalm. It begins with an exhortation of the Psalmist to himself in the collective first person, 'Let me...' (cf., e.g., Ps. 101.1). It switches from hymnic celebration of the LORD, who is spoken of in the third person in vv. 1-5 and in the conclusion in v. 18, to direct address of God in the second person in the thanksgiving of vv. 6-17 (cf. the structure of, e.g., Ps. 48). There is coincidence of language: for example, v. 2a is the same as Ps. 118.14; for vv. 2b and 18, cf. Ps. 145.1-2.

There are also striking parallels in form and vocabulary with Isaiah of Jerusalem: for example, the exhortation in the first person in v. 1 is used in Isa. 5.1; v. 2a is found also in Isa. 12.2b; 'majesty' (v. 7) is a term for God in Isa. 2.10, 19, 21.

These coincidences with expressions of the Jerusalem tradition of theology cannot be accidental. As the 'Melchizedek' theology of the priest-kings of God Most High of pre-Israelite Jerusalem (cf. Gen. 14.18-20; Ps. 110.4), which echoes the ancient Canaanite mythologies of, for instance, the recognition of the kingship of the victorious god through the exposure of the powerlessness of his rivals,[38] was polemically adopted by David and the Davidic House after their conquest of Jerusalem and provided a theological basis for their rule, so this Jerusalemite tradition of theology is exploited once more (cf. the myth of the conflict between Baal and Sea[39] which re-echoes throughout this song) to provide theological resources for the development of a creative apologetic response to the challenge and threat of rival theological systems, this time of the Babylonians under the guise of Egypt. It is

38. Cf. Johnstone, 'The Sun and the Serpent'.
39. Cf. J.C.L. Gibson, *Canaanite Myths and Legends* (Edinburgh: T. & T. Clark, 2nd edn, 1978), pp. 37-45.

through the appropriation of such language and concepts that the themes of the universal sovereignty of the LORD (vv. 5, 8b), the incomparability of the LORD among the gods (v. 11), and the eternal reign of the LORD (v. 18) are here developed.

But that version is now placed within a framework supplied by the P-edition: v. 19 as summary ties the song into its context by picking up the vocabulary of ch. 14 (for v. 19b, cf. 14.22, 29). In vv. 20-21, the traditional role of women as those who greet the returning victorious army with tambourines, dance and song (cf. 1 Sam. 18.6) is recalled. Miriam is called 'prophetess', rather as in 1 Chron. 25.1 the musicians in the Temple are said 'to prophesy'. The first line of Moses and Israel's song (Exod. 15.1) is cited, but with one modification: as sung by leaders of public praise, the first word is now turned into an imperative, 'Sing to the LORD'.

With all the qualifications that 'P' cannot be separated from 'D' as 'source', but rather 'receives and reconceives' it as a new edition sometimes in polemical correction, as ChrH does DtrH (cf. Chapter 7), and is thus on occasion closely and inextricably intertwined with it, nonetheless an indicative diagram of the attribution of materials in Exod. 1.1–15.21 may be appended (see opposite).

As is about to be argued in Chapter 11, no such diagram is possible for Exod. 15.22–19.2: while there is abundant D-material in that section, it all represents reuse by P from other contexts.

Summary of Attribution of Material in Exod. 1.1–15.21
to the D-version and P-edition

```
D     1-6   8-12   15-22    1-22           1 — 1
ch. 1 ----------------------2-------------3----6------7--------------------
P      7    13-14            23-25         2 — 13


D     14-18      20aβ-21a      23-29           4*-11aαβ
ch. 7 -------------------------------------8-------------------------------
P        19-20aα      21b-22          1-3              11aγb-15


D    16-18  20 — 7        13-25bα       26-34     35aβ
ch. 8 -------------9--------------------------------------------------------
P      19            8-12         25bβ          35aα        35b


D    1a    3aαii-19   20b        1-8                 29-36
ch. 10 ----------------------------11---------------12------------------
P     1b-3aαi      20a    21-29          9-10*    1-28*     37-51


D    1-19   21-22      5-8  10-15                  19-21a
ch. 13 --------------14-----------------------------------------------------
P      20          1-4    7-9    16a*b, 17, 18        21b, 22-23


D    24    25b-27a   28     30      —     19a
ch. 14 ---------------------------------15--------------------------------
P        25a?      27b    29                 19b-21
```

Chapter 11

FROM THE SEA TO THE MOUNTAIN. EXODUS 15.22–19.2:
A CASE STUDY IN EDITORIAL TECHNIQUES*

Texts in Deuteronomy/DtrH enable the reconstruction of a pre-P version of sections of Exodus, I have argued in earlier chapters.[1] This

* Originally published in M. Vervenne (ed.), *Studies in the Book of Exodus: Redaction–Reception–Interpretation* (BETL, 126; Leuven: Leuven University Press/Peeters, 1996), pp. 245-63. Résumés of earlier stages of the argument, felt necessary when the article was published independently, have been omitted. The argument has also been slightly revised.

1. See Chapters 7, 8 and 10 above. While I am grateful to J. Van Seters for comment on my analysis of Exod. 34.1-3* in the article reproduced as Chapter 7 above (*Life of Moses: The Yahwist as Historian in Exodus–Numbers* [Kampen: Kok/Pharos, 1994], p. 324 n. 17), I should wish to insist that the other elements of the thread of the narrative in Exod. 24.12*, 18*; 31.18*; 32.7-20* are also taken into consideration as part of a wider argument. If one is approaching the analysis of the Pentateuch by 'subtraction' from the final version using the D-work as instrument, as I am attempting to do (see Chapter 1, n. 9), there is no obvious room for Van Seters' exilic J-source. I am attempting the analysis in the manner of a new archaeologist tackling a much-excavated site: a fresh sounding must be made with as few preconceptions as possible. (I am thinking of an actual instance: when O. Pelon took over the excavation of the eastern part of Enkomi, Cyprus, from C.F.A. Schaeffer in 1971, he would remark of Schaeffer's 'Sol V', which had become the main stratigraphical reference point of the previous four decades of excavation, merely, 'Quel sol cinq?' In terms of Pentateuchal criticism, approaching the matter once more from the surface levels, one might equally ask, 'Quel J?', and, for that matter, 'Quel E? Quel JE?') But it is clear on approaching the Pentateuch that there is a final 'level' from which material in Deuteronomy diverges (e.g. the position of Kadesh-barnea in the wilderness wandering—in years 1/2, according to Deut. 2.14; in year 40, according to Num. 33.36-38; the duration of the Passover—one night, according to Exod. 12; one night plus seven days, according to Deut. 16.1-8). It is, therefore, appropriate to inquire whether there is, or has been, material matching that divergent Deuteronomic tradition in other parts of the Pentateuch and, if there is, to label it with some kind of Deuteronomic siglum.

chapter proposes to test the thesis in a further area—the account of the
itinerary (and its related chronology) of the Israelites from the sea to
the mountain in Exod. 15.22–19.2. It will be argued that on this topic
the situation is rather different from that in most other areas of Exodus:
while elsewhere P is editing D-material already present in the given
context, here, in its wide-scale transposition of D-material, P's technique is closest to that which has already been observed in Exodus 12.[2]

Can, then, a pre-P version of the journey from the sea to the mountain be recovered in Exod. 15.22–19.2 with the help of the D-work?

I

The first, possibly surprising, observation is that Deuteronomy provides
no information about the route through the wilderness from the sea to
the mountain. There are no data on the route *before* Horeb in, for
example, Deut. 1.6–3.29, even though it, by contrast, provides abundant material on the route *after* Horeb all the way to Moab. The sole
possible exception in Deuteronomy is 9.7: 'Remember, do not forget,
how you enraged the LORD your God in the wilderness: from the day
since you came out of the land of Egypt until you have come to this
place you have been rebelling against the LORD.' This might be taken
to imply that from the first day after the exodus there was rebellion in
the wilderness, including even on the way from the sea to the mountain,
matching precisely the account in Exod. 15.22–19.2. But it is relatively
clear that the *vav* at the beginning of Deut. 9.8 is not the mere conjunction 'and', '*And* at Horeb you enraged the LORD', any more than it is,
thrice over, at the beginning of Deut. 9.22, '*And* at Taberah *and* at
Massah *and* at Kibroth-hattaavah', and at the beginning of Deut. 9.23,
'*And* when the LORD dismissed you from Kadesh-barnea'. For each of
these places is *within* the wilderness itinerary, not additional to it; the
vav is, therefore, in each case, explicative, '*Namely*, at Horeb'.[3] The list
specifies the (signal) places in the wilderness where the recalcitrant
behaviour of Israel was in evidence and, notably, thus begins *after* the
arrival at the mountain.

---

2. See Chapter 9, above, pp. 209-10, where the issue of the significance of
itinerary and chronology is given preliminary consideration.
3. GKC 154 *a* N (b), though not citing this passage.

II

It is not at all surprising, therefore, that the material on the itinerary from the sea to the mountain, from, indeed, Exod. 12.37 to Exod. 19.2, has no counterpart in Deuteronomy. Rather, that Exodus material corresponds in names and in their sequence almost precisely to the consolidated itinerary of Numbers 33 (the numbers correspond to those of the first 12 staging-posts of the itinerary in Num. 33.3, 5-15): (1) Raamses (Exod. 12.37); (2) Succoth (Exod. 12.37); (3) Etham (Exod. 13.20); (4) Pi-hahiroth (Exod. 14.2); (5) Marah (Exod. 15.23); (6) Elim (Exod. 15.27); (8) The wilderness of Sin (Exod. 16.1); (11) Rephidim (Exod. 17.1); (12) The wilderness of Sinai (Exod. 19.2). The only differences are three omissions in Exodus ([7] the Red Sea [Num. 33.10]; and [9] Dophkah and [10] Alush [Num. 33.12-13], neither of which recurs again in the Hebrew Bible), and one highly significant addition, to be noted in §III, below. The non-D character of the itinerary in Numbers 33 is at once clear from its chronology: the 'day after the Passover' is 'the fifteenth day of the first month' (v. 3); that is, Passover is the one-night affair of Exodus 12, of the final edition of the Pentateuch (cf. the late 'Babylonian' reckoning of the first month in the spring), not the one-night-plus-seven-days Passover of the old 'Canaanite' month of Abib of Deuteronomy 16.

III

The list of places in the itinerary of the Israelites from the sea to the mountain in Exod. 12.37–19.2 presents one crucial addition to that of Numbers 33—the addition of Massah and Meribah (Exod. 17.7). What is the affiliation of this Massah and Meribah material?

Massah occurs in the Pentateuch only again in Deuteronomy (6.16; 9.22; 33.8); only on the third occasion does it appear in association with Meribah. But Deut. 33.8 also stands apart from the other occurrences, in that the reference is to God's 'trying' and 'striving' with Levi in an incident which, if anything, appears to relate to Horeb, Exod. 32.26-29. Meribah recurs in a number of guises: 'the waters of Meribah' in Num. 20.13, 24 (and Deut. 33.8); 'the waters of Meribah of Kadesh in the wilderness of Zin', Num. 27.14; Deut. 32.51.[4] Numbers

---

4.   The question of the affiliation of the other biblical references to Massah in

27.14 refers back to the incident of Num. 20.13 and the whole context (vv. 12-14) is very closely parallel in phraseology to Deut. 32.48.

It is striking that Massah/Massah and Meribah/Meribah are located at different points on the itinerary in different passages. In Exod. 17.7 Massah and Meribah are located *before* Sinai at Rephidim, station 11 of Num. 33.14. In Deut. 9.22 Massah is located *after* Horeb between Taberah and Kibroth-hattaavah; Taberah does not feature in Numbers 33 but Kibroth-hattaavah is defined as station 13 in Num. 33.16. In Numbers 20, Meribah is associated with Kadesh in the wilderness of Zin (v. 1), that is, station 33 of Num. 33.36. Since Massah/Massah and Meribah/Meribah cannot be placed in all three locations, it is likely that one location is primary and that the other two represent secondary use of these place-names. It seems clear that the secondary use is in Exod. 17.7 and Num. 20.13, for in both the place where the action takes place has already been named, Rephidim and Kadesh respectively, and Massah and Meribah/Meribah are brought in as secondary identifications to provide, through play on etymology, incidents of rebellion in the wilderness (Massah, 'the place of trial', on the root of which there is play in Exod. 17.2-7; 'Meribah', the place of strife, on the root of which there is play in Exod. 17.2-7; Num. 20.13). (Though the roots are different, there may also be further play on the Marah of Exod. 15.23 [in another water incident] in the use of the qal of the verb מרה, 'to rebel', in Num. 20.10-24; 27.14, showing still further editorial assimilation of incidents.)

If so, then the primary identification of the location of Massah/Massah and Meribah/Meribah is to be found in Deut. 9.22. There Massah is an independent locality situated between two other independent localities, Taberah and Kibroth-hattaavah. Now, there is no narrative in the Hebrew Bible that identifies the location of Massah, the second of that triad; but there are consecutive narratives that identify the location of the first and third of the triad, Taberah and Kibroth-hattaavah, namely, Num. 11.1-3, 4-34.

We are now in a position to enunciate a hypothesis. Deuteronomy knows of no period of murmuring in the wilderness before Horeb. This corresponds to a number of data: Moses' requests to Pharaoh to let his people go a short journey of three days' duration into the wilderness

Ps. 95.8 and to Meribah in Pss. 81.8; 95.8; 106.32 (the references in Ezek. 47.19; 48.28 concern merely the definition of boundaries) lies outside the scope of this inquiry.

(Exod. 3.18; 5.3; 8.23), the destination of which is the Mountain of God (Exod. 3.12), identified as Horeb (Exod. 3.1). The shortness of the journey corresponds to the speed with which, the LORD states, he has brought his people to himself, Exod. 19.4. I have already argued that there are sufficient grounds for regarding all these passages as Dtr.[5] It also corresponds to the hypothesis that the Dtr version of Exod. 1.1–24.11* represents the casting into narrative form of the D-legislation in Deut. 15.12–16.8.[6] In particular, the three days' journey into the wilderness corresponds to the first three days of the 'octave' of the Passover. On that hypothesis the Dtr-version of the route from the sea to the mountain need include no more than Exod. 15.22a; 19.2b: 'Moses led Israel out from the Red Sea. They came out to the Wilderness of Shur and encamped there before the Mountain of God.'

Instead of the three days of the Dtr-version, the final edition of Exodus has inserted into Exod. 15.22b–19.2a a six-week period (Exod. 19.1) of rebellion in the wilderness before the arrival at Sinai. In order to create this narrative the final editor ('P') has reused material from the Dtr version of events in the wilderness *at and after* Horeb and has transposed them *before* Sinai. One of the most signal of these is the transposition of events at Massah into Exod. 17.7 from its original location in Numbers 11 between the narrative explaining the etymology of Taberah (Num. 11.1-3) and that explaining the etymology of Kibroth-hattaavah (Num. 11.4-34), the framing place-names for Massah in Deut. 9.22.

IV

The argument to establish this hypothesis requires the consideration in detail of the relevant passages in Exodus.

Exodus records four of the stages from the sea to the mountain from the itinerary of Numbers 33: (1) Marah (station 5), 15.22-26; (2) Elim (station 6), 15.27; (3) Midbar-sin (station 8), 16.1-36; (4) Rephidim (station 11), 17.1–18.27.

(1) Marah (station 5; Exod. 15.22-26), Israel reaches after three waterless days, only to find bitter water there. It seems clear that two versions are combined in this passage. The roughness in the two phrases of v. 25b, with their ambiguity about subject and indirect object

5. Chapter 10 above, pp. 224-28, 230-31.
6. Chapter 9, pp. 211-14.

in the first, and about subject and direct object in the second, is ample evidence of editorial activity. Who 'appointed statute and ordinance' to whom in v. 25bα?—the LORD to Moses, or to the people; or Moses to the people? Who 'tried' whom 'there' in v. 25bβ: did the LORD try Moses or did he try the people? or was it Moses who tried the people? or even the people who tried the LORD (or, indeed, Moses)? In the light of v. 26, where the speaker refers to the LORD in the third person, the most likely interpretation in the immediate present context is that Moses is the subject of both and that the people are the indirect and direct objects. Yet that is unlikely since, in the wider context of the Pentateuch, it is either the people who try the LORD or the LORD who tries the people (see below on נסה).

The impression of the composite nature of the text is confirmed by the presence of both P- and D-material. The P-material is recognizable not only in the mention Marah, the fifth station in Num. 33.8 (the only other context in the Hebrew Bible in which it is mentioned), but also in the vocabulary, especially at the beginning of v. 24, where the verb לון is used, elsewhere in this section of Exodus in association with P-vocabulary (e.g. 16.1-2; it does not occur in Deuteronomy [though it does in Josh. 9.18, but perhaps in a P-edited section, cf. עדה]). On the other hand, vv. 25b, 26 are replete with D/DtrH-vocabulary: שׂים חק ומשׁפט Josh. 24.25; 1 Sam. 30.25 (D itself uses the plural, חקים ומשׁפטים, with a variety of other verbs, e.g. למד, 4.5, שׁמע, 5.1, שׁמר, 7.11); while שׁמע לקול יהוה is not found in Deuteronomy (v. 26; but cf. e.g. Gen. 3.17; 16.2), שׁמע בקול יהוה is commonplace in D (Deut. 4.30 and some further 19 times); for עשׂה הישׁר בעיניו, cf. Deut. 6.18 and some four further verses in D; שׁמר with חקים is very frequent (e.g. Deut. 4.40 and some further 18 times in D); מחלה, placed here on Egypt, is used again in Exod. 23.25, the coda to B, and in DtrH in 1 Kgs 8.37; for the LORD as healer, cf. Deut. 28.27-35; 32.39.

The affiliation of other vocabulary in the section, especially in v. 22, is not so clear: נסע is used both in D (e.g. Deut. 1.6) and in P (Num. 33 *passim*), though in neither case in the hiphil as here; the Midbar-shur does not occur elsewhere in the itineraries, being met elsewhere in the Pentateuch only in Gen. 16.7; 20.1; 25.18. It is notable that Shur occurs in DtrH in 1 Sam. 15.7, as the southern boundary of Amalek with Egypt, in a context (v. 2) that makes direct reference to the harassment of Israel by Amalek in the wilderness period in Num. 14.39-45, which, in turn, is directly cross-referred to in Deut. 1.43-44. The 'three days' journey' is not decisive: it is attractive to relate it to the three days' journey of Moses' request to Pharaoh, Exod. 3.18, etc., and that may well be the primary affiliation of the material (cf. Num. 10.33, which also appears to be Dtr, as will be argued below in connection with Exod. 18.1-12). But it is to be noted that the phrase recurs in Num. 33.8, precisely in connection with the journey to Marah: P is thus rein-terpreting the 'three days' of the D-version.

The conclusion to be drawn from these observations is that Exod. 15.22-26, as it presently stands, comes from the hand of the P-editor, who, nonetheless, has used pure D-materials in vv. 25b-26. What is not clear is whether the D-edition had its own version of such an incident during the three-day journey from the sea to the mountain, or whether P has introduced the material here, including his borrowing from extant D-materials but from a quite different context, to suit his own concep-tion of the wilderness wandering as a time of complaining even before Sinai.

One of the cruxes of the question is the force of those enigmatic phrases in v. 25b. It is notable that in Deuteronomy the verb נסה is used in two senses with regard to 'testing' (there are still other uses of the verb in 4.32; 28.56). On the one hand, in 8.2-3, 15-16 (cf. 13.4) it is used of the LORD's testing of Israel to see whether they will be loyal to him or not (cf. Deut. 29.4). Similar examples of testing Israel's devo-tion and resolve are given in Deut. 13.4 (by false prophets) and in DtrH, Judg. 2.22; 3.1, 4 (by the surviving pre-Israelite population). Deut. 33.8 is in line with this usage: there the incident at Massah is understood in terms of the LORD's testing the loyalty of the Levites and this is how the verb נסה is about to be used in Exod. 16.4.

On the other hand, Deuteronomy does know of Israel's testing of the LORD. This is how the verb נסה is used in connection with Massah in Deut. 6.16 (though in 9.22 the incident at Massah is related in terms of the verb הקציף). This is also how it is about to be used in Exod. 17.7. It is this second sense that the P-editor exploits, using the alternative vocabulary, לון (for the first time in Exod. 15.24 and thereafter fre-quently [16.2, etc.]).

In which sense, then, is נסה being used in Exod. 15.25b? The first is the more likely: the subject of neither the preceding nor the following verb is the people. If so, where and when, on the D-scenario, did this testing of Israel by God take place? Unfortunately, Deut. 8.2-6, 14-16, the key reference to God's testing of the devotion of his people, defines neither time nor place. Even the 'forty years'' testing is not decisive, for the 40 years could begin at the sea or at Horeb (just as, for the latter, in Deut. 9.7–10.11 the rebellions begin at Horeb). There would appear to be three possibilities:

(a) During the journey to the mountain. This is what is implied by the final version of Exod. 15.22-26, though there the testing as it now stands appears to be by Israel of God and that may be merely the interpretation of the final editor. It certainly makes sense in context that the first issue should be that of water: if the journey to Horeb takes place in the 'octave' of the Passover, which in the D-scenario includes the consumption of unleavened bread, then the food-supply of Israel in these first days has already been taken care of, but not the drink. But, given the genre of the narrative, it may be an inadmissible extension of logic to ask how the D-writer envisaged Israel's supply of water at this juncture (water at Horeb is just about to be mentioned in 17.6); in any case, there is no reference in vv. 25b, 26 to water, but to freedom from the diseases of Egypt and to health, which do not seem obviously appropriate in context. Besides, to what does the enigmatic phrase 'statute and ordinance' refer? It is only at Horeb that these are about to be revealed.

(b) After the making of the covenant. The question of the loyalty of the people does not arise in any section of Deuteronomy until at or after Horeb (Deut. 1; 9). Most of trials in Deuteronomy 8 belong to the 40-year period as a whole. In that case 'the statute and ordinance' might refer to instruction by Moses at Kadesh-barnea (cf. Deut. 1.20-46), though the phrase is not explicitly used of such instruction there in D (but cf. Deut. 4.1, etc.).

(c) On the sixth day after the exodus on the eve of the covenant. It is notable that, as is stated by Exod. 20.20 (which I have already argued belongs to the D-version),[7] the theophany at Horeb and the revelation of the Decalogue provided an incident when the LORD was testing his people's response ('It is in order to test [נסות] you that God has come—that his fear may be before you, so that you do not sin'). That incident would provide the referent for the 'statute and ordinance'—the Book of the Covenant itself, Exod. 20.22–23.33—about to be written as the basis of the covenant the next day (Exod. 24.4).

7.   Chapter 7, p. 158.

If either of possibilities (b) or (c) is correct, then in Exod. 15.22-26 P has reformulated D-material from an entirely different context to suit its own scenario of rebellious Israel persistently grumbling all the way of the six weeks' journey to Sinai.

(2) Elim (station 6; Exod. 15.27) is passed without incident, apart from Israel's implied satisfaction with the abundant water-supply from the 12 springs, attested by the grove of 70 palm-trees. Elim occurs only in this context and in the itinerary in Numbers 33; D makes no mention of it; it can, thus, be assumed to belong to the final edition.

(3) Midbar-sin (station 8; Exod. 16.1-36) produces a complex incident related to the theme of hunger. As in the incident at Marah, the framework—and, in this case, the bulk—of the material is provided by the P-editor. If one takes certain features as characteristic of the P-editor, then it may be seen that, once again, a core of D-material, which belongs to a quite different context in the D-scenario of the wilderness wandering, has been exploited to produce an entirely novel narrative.

These characteristics are as follows:

- Midbar-sin, like Elim, only occurs in this context and in Numbers 33;
- Israel as עדה;
- the mountain as Sinai;
- the chronological notice of the fifteenth of the second month (v. 1, only the first occurrence of these expressions in the chapter is noted here and below; many recur several times to lend narrative coherence to the whole);
- the root לון (v. 2);
- 'eating food to satiety' (v. 3, cf. Lev. 26.5);
- v. 6 supplies the response to that complaint of the עדה (the 'recognition formula', 'you shall know that I and the LORD your God' is characteristic of P, e.g. Exod. 29.46);
- the narrative proceeds with its own momentum through v. 7 (the כבוד of the LORD is characteristic of the P-work, e.g. Lev. 9.6, 23, but not exclusive to it, cf. Deut. 5.24; the late form נחנו), to v. 12;
- the regulations for the gathering of the manna (vv. 16-30; זה הדבר אשר צוה יהוה v. 16, cf. v. 32 and Lev. 8.5; 9.6, etc.), interweaving תורה (v. 28) and narrative incident to help its enforcement (cf. Lev. 24.10-23; Num. 14.32-36) and culminating in the legislation on the Sabbath, with the characteristic

P-word שבתון (v. 23, e.g. Lev. 16.21), all held within the
framework of the naming of the manna, vv. 15, 31;

- the regulations for the deposit of the manna, vv. 32-34, before
  the עדת (v. 34, cf. Lev. 16.13);
- the data on the עמר (vv. 16, etc., 35), which recurs in the Hebrew Bible only in Lev. 23.10-15.

All these indicators suggest that the chapter comes from a comprehensive P-edition.

Nonetheless, there are also fragments in the chapter of D-material,
especially in vv. 4-5, 13-15, 31 and 35. The words of YHWH in v. 4: 'in
order that I may try (נסה) it [the people] whether…' match the prepon-
derant D-emphasis, that 'food from heaven' is the means of the LORD's
trial of his people's dependence on his word, rather than an impatient
response to their complaints as in P. The phrasing matches the key passage in Deut. 8.3 (cf. 16), though that passage continues, '…whether it
will keep my commandments'; the modification here to '…whether it
will walk in my תורה' one can assume to be an adjustment of the P-
editor.

The material in Deut. 8.2-5, 14-16 provides a tantalizingly brief basis
on which to reconstruct an original D-version. Nonetheless, there are
further coincidences: the phrase 'they said to one another, "It is
manna", for they did not know what it was' (v. 15) echoes 'manna
which you did not know…' (Deut. 8.3, cf. 16); the eating of manna for
40 years (v. 35) corresponds to Deut. 8.2 and to the note on the cessa-
tion of the manna on arrival in the agricultural area in DtrH (Josh. 5.12).

Other phrases are less determinant, though perfectly congenial to the
hypothesis of D-material reused by P: for example, 'I am about to rain
bread for you out of the sky' (v. 4) is most closely paralleled only in
Ps. 78.24, 27,[8] though the idea of 'raining' is found in the Dtr plague
VII (Exod. 9.18); 'the daily amount' (v. 4) occurs in Exod. 5.18 (Dtr),[9]
cf. 1 Kgs 8.59 (DtrH), though it is also used in P (Lev. 23.37); הכין
(v. 5) of preparing food is found in Josh. 1.11 (DtrH).

There is, however, a much wider argument that must now be brought
into play. Incidents in Exod. 15.22–19.2 are paralleled in Numbers,
especially 10.29–11.34; 21.1-3; in particular, the incident of the manna

---

8.   Ps. 78, I have already argued, matches the Dtr seven-plague cycle (Chapter
10, n. 27).
9.   Chapter 10, pp. 227-28.

(and the quails) of Exodus 16 recurs in Num. 11.1-34. The questions of the affiliation of Numbers 11 and of its relation to Exodus 16 must, therefore, be explored. If it can be shown—as I shall argue that it can—that Numbers 11 is essentially a D-composition and, thus, prior to the P-composition in Exodus 16, this would both help to explain the existence of D/Dtr-fragments in Exodus 16 and further support my contention that P has deliberately composed, from pre-existing D-materials in another context, an account of murmuring in the wilderness by Israel before Sinai, where nothing comparable existed in the earlier D-narrative.

The materials in Exodus 16 that particularly resemble those in Numbers 11 are לקט qal (v. 4, on this hypothesis reused in the other verses of this chapter by P [P elsewhere uses the piel, e.g. Lev. 19.9], cf. Num. 11.8), the conjunction of quails with manna (v. 13; cf. Num. 11.31-32, the only other passage in the Hebrew Bible where 'quails' occurs, apart from Ps. 105.40), the association of manna with the falling of dew (vv. 13-14; cf. Num. 11.9) and its comparison to coriander seed (v. 31; cf. Num. 11.7-8).

What, then, is the affiliation of this material in Numbers 11? It is clear that the framework of Num. 10.11–22.1 continues as in Exod. 12.36–19.2 to be provided by stations of the itinerary of the Israelites through the wilderness as summarized in Numbers 33. Thus, Num. 10.12a picks up station 12, Midbar-sinai, from Exod. 19.2a (cf. Num. 33.16); stations 13 (Kibroth-hattaavah) and 14 (Hazeroth) follow in Num. 11.34-35 and thereafter stations 33 (Midbar-zin, Num. 20.1), 34 (Hor-hahar, Num. 20.22), 37 (Oboth, Num. 20.10), 38 (Iyye-haabarim, Num. 20.11), and 42 (Areboth-moab, Num. 22.1). But there are now large gaps in the narrative: stations 15-26, 31, 35, 36, 40 of Numbers 33 do not recur anywhere else in the Hebrew Bible, let alone here, and, as is at once apparent, still more are omitted in the Numbers framework: stations 27-30, 32, 39 (though that is alluded to in the poetic text in Num. 21.30), and 41 (mentioned out of sequence in Num. 27.12-14). The fixed formulae of Numbers 33 ('and they set out from *x* and encamped in *y*') are also much less consistently used. While Numbers 33 provides the general framework and thus enables the final edition of Numbers to present a coherent picture, it is imposed on the materials in a very loose way and allows the incorporation of a multiplicity of narratives. Several of these narratives provide the narrative counterpart to notes in Deuteronomy.

It is at once notable that Num. 11.1-3 is the only other text in the Hebrew Bible besides Deut. 9.22 that mentions Taberah. That is, Num. 11.1-3 provides the narrative counterpart to the reference in Deut. 9.22. The vocabulary of Num. 11.1-3 is fully compatible with a Dtr composition:

- v. 1 אנן only occurs again in Lam. 3.39;
- 'in the ears of the LORD', e.g. DtrH 1 Sam. 8.21;
- 'the anger of the LORD was kindled', e.g. Deut. 7.4, and is compared to burning fire, e.g. DtrJer. 7.20;
- 'the edge of the camp', e.g. DtrH Judg. 7.11;
- v. 2 'cry out to', e.g. Exod. 8.8 in plague II;[10]
- Moses as intercessor, e.g. Deut. 9.20;
- v. 3 the aetiological naming of a place, as in DtrH, e.g. Josh. 5.9; 7.26; Judg. 2.5.

If Num. 11.1-3 thus provides the Dtr aetiological narrative for the otherwise unattested Taberah of Deut. 9.22, then it would not be surprising if Num. 11.4-34 similarly provides the Dtr aetiological narrative for the Kibroth-hattaavah of Deut. 9.22 (the fact that Kibroth-hattaavah is also mentioned in Num. 33.16-17 as the first station of the wilderness wandering after Sinai does not necessarily affect the D/Dtr-character of tradition: P is merely making use of inherited data. If my argument is sound, P has indeed made radical use of this Dtr-narrative: while preserving the place-name Kibroth-hattaavah in traditional position immediately after the mountain, it has transposed the content to its own Midbar-sin.).

Only a sample of the data need be given in this context to suggest that Num. 11.4-34, is overwhelmingly, if not exclusively, a D/Dtr-composition. Numbers 11.4-34 is a complex narrative: the outer framework is supplied by the aetiological narrative explaining the name Kibroth-hattaavah ('graves of craving'). This framework is announced immediately in v. 4 where the motley gathering 'were overwhelmed with craving' (התאוו תאוה) for ordinary food, the fish and the succulent vegetables of Egypt (v. 5), thus picking up the element '-hattaavah' (התאוה), 'craving', in the place-name (v. 34). The 'graves' are those of the victims of the great slaughter inflicted by God on the host. The purpose of the narrative can be understood to exemplify the D-dictum that

man shall not live by food alone but by the ordering of God (Deut. 8.3-
5; 29.4-5): life in the wilderness is the starkest possible statement of
Israel's dependence on God, for there there is no other source of
supply; the divine character of that supply is expressed by hitherto
unknown manna. The craving for ordinary food is thus a failure in
unconditional reliance upon God. (For D's account of the appropriate
way to satisfy these natural cravings once Israel has successfully settled
the land, cf. Deut. 12.20, where the root אוה is again used.)

Other strands are interwoven into the plot, which tie the narrative
still more closely to the D-account. The craving of the people becomes
the occasion of Moses' complaint that the burden of sustaining the
people is intolerable. This complaint is reminiscent of the complaint of
Moses to the people in Deut. 1.9-18: in v. 14 the phraseology, 'I am not
able myself alone to bear...', coincides with Deut. 1.9, 12; the *leitmotif*
provided by the root נשא recurs in vv. 11, 12 (2×), 17 (3×). Now it is to
be acknowledged that the account in Deuteronomy 1 differs somewhat
from that here (as it does from Deut. 9.22): there, there is no hint that
the appointment of judges stems from the rebellion of the people and
the impression is given that the appointment of the judges took place at
the moment of departure from Horeb. But whether these differences
amount to evidence for different stages in the D-tradition must be a
matter for judgment. It is not necessarily so. The differences may
simply be due to the particular emphases of the two accounts: for
Deuteronomy 1 the signal event of rebellion takes place at Kadesh-
barnea; also here the words are spoken by Moses to God rather than
reported to the people—that report to the people in fact follows in
v. 24. (To anticipate the discussion of Exodus 18: it is notable that the
appointment of these judges both here and in Deuteronomy, on the
point of leaving Horeb or soon after, is entirely different from the
account in the final form of Exod. 18.13-26, where it takes place before
Sinai. There are certain coincidences of vocabulary ['not able alone',
v. 18] but the whole can be accounted for as yet another example of the
P-editor recasting the D-tradition for his own purposes: the 70 elders
recur in Exod. 24.1.9; their being termed אצלים in Exod. 24.11 can
hardly be divorced from the use of the verb אצל of the distribution of
the spirit—itself a DtrH-motif, e.g. 2 Kgs 2.25, cf. Deut. 34.9—of
Moses here in vv. 17, 25.)

'Weeping', a further *leitmotif* that runs through Num. 11.4-34 (vv. 4,
10, 13, 18, 20) links the passage with DtrH, especially Judg. 2.1-5 (cf.

Deut. 1.45 for weeping before YHWH as in v. 20). 'The land which YHWH swore to the forefathers', cf. v. 12, is highly characteristic of D (e.g. Deut. 1.8; 7.13).

Other phrases link Numbers 11 with the pre-P version of Exodus (e.g. 'each one at the door of his tent', v. 10, cf. Exod. 33.10; 'find favour in the eyes of YHWH', vv. 11.15, cf. Exod. 33.13; 34.9).[11]

These and more examples (e.g. D-vocabulary items in Num. 11.11, 16, 18) firmly link the parallels in Exodus 16 to Numbers 11, noted above (לקט, the conjunction of quails with manna, the association of manna with the falling of dew and its comparison to coriander seed), into the Dtr version of the wilderness wandering. The relatively isolated character of these parallels in Exodus 16 within a predominantly P-edition suggests reuse by P of pre-existing Dtr-material, which it has both reshaped and relocated.

(4) Rephidim (station 11; Exod. 17.1–18.27) is the setting for three incidents:

    (a)   water from the rock at Massah and Meribah (17.1-7);

    (b)   the battle with the Amalekites (17.8-16);

    (c)   the visit of Jethro and the appointment of judges (18.1-27).

(a) 17.1-7 is the key passage for establishing the hypothesis that the final version of 15.22–19.2 is a P-construction which has created, partly out of D-materials lying to hand elsewhere, a narrative of the complaining of Israel in the wilderness *before* Sinai, where there was none in the pre-P version.

It seems clear that P provides v. 1 (cf. Num. 33.2, 12, 14 for the phraseology and the only other mention of Rephidim in the Hebrew Bible apart from this context; there is room for debate whether the last phrase of v. 1 comes from the D-version, Deut. 8.15; cf. Num. 20.5; 21.5). Verse 3 is similarly P (לון).

The remainder, however, 17.2, 4-7, is an aetiological narrative explaining the double name Massah and Meribah (the association with Rephidim by means of v. 1 is, thus, clearly secondary). In the D-itinerary of Deut. 9.22, Massah occurs between Taberah and Kibroth-hattaavah. The matching narratives for the 'angering' of God at Taberah and Kibroth-hattaavah occur in Num. 11.1-3 and in Num. 11.4-34 respectively. According to the hypothesis, this Massah narrative should originally have been found, therefore, between Num. 11.3

---

11. Cf. Chapter 7, p. 157.

and 4. Is there evidence that it was? It is notable that the first verse, Exod. 17.2, enunciates at the outset the key roots, in this case ריב and נסה, which are to provide (chiastically) the etymology for the place-names Massah and Meribah to be applied in Exod. 17.7, the last verse, precisely as Num. 11.1 enunciates בער, the root of the place-name, Taberah, to be applied in v. 3, and Num. 11.4 enunciates אוה, the root of the place-name, (Kibroth-)hattaavah, to be applied in v. 34. Furthermore—and this is surely a decisive point—the place-name at the end of the section is introduced by the same aetiological formula, 'And he called the name of the/that place *x*' (Exod. 17.7) as in Num. 11.3, 34. There is thus strong evidence on grounds of structure that 17.2, 3-7 originally stood, as Deut. 9.22 suggests, between Num. 11.3 and 4.

There is other evidence for the D-character of Exod. 17.2, 4-7. As has already been noted, it is only in Deuteronomy that Massah is again mentioned in the Pentateuch: Deut. 6.16, where נסה is used in the same sense as here; 9.22; cf. 33.8, where, as here, it is conjoined with Meribah. Other uses of Meribah in Numbers, 20.13, 24; 27.14, provide valuable identification of Meribah with Kadesh-barnea and flashbacks to the earlier action there, as in Deut. 32.51. Their character as flashbacks is indicated by the fact that the references are not fully comprehensible in context: it is only when the disqualification of Moses from entering the promised land is related to Moses' being over-impressed by the people's speciously prudent demand for a reconnaissance of the land from Kadesh in Deut. 1.23 (contrast the somewhat different emphases of Num. 13), that Yahweh's anger also with Moses is explicable.

Still other turns of phrase in Exod. 17.2, 4-7 confirm the D-character of the material: for example, 'the staff with which you smote the Nile' refers to plague I (v. 5),[12] צור as in Deut. 8.15 (as opposed to סלע, Num. 20.8, 10-11) and Horeb in v. 6, and the use of בקרב in v. 7 (P uses בתוך).[13]

Thus, as has been argued above, just as P has used material from Num. 11.4-34 for the construction of Exodus 16, so, in an even more comprehensive fashion it has transposed Exod. 17.2, 4-7 from its

---

12. Chapter 10, pp. 230-32.

13. The last point was made to me orally by R. Achenbach; cf. his *Israel zwischen Verheissung und Gebot: Literarkritische Untersuchungen zu Deuteronomium 5–11* (EurHS, 23.422; Bern: Peter Lang, 1989), pp. 119-20, 264, 277. I am grateful to Dr Achenbach for supplying me with a copy of the above work.

original position between Num. 11.3 and 4, yet kept references to it in Numbers 20–21.

It is probable that in the process of transposition P has relocated the verses on the punitive slaughter of the rebellious people by the Levites from the same incident, as Deut. 33.8-9 indicates, to its present position in Exod. 32.25-29. There it replaces the Deuteronomic view of the appointment at Horeb of the Levites as bearers of the ark (Deut. 10.8-9; see Chapter 12 below). It is striking that the two incidents preserved in Numbers 11 both contain punishment on the people, now for the first time, post-Horeb on the D-scenario, rebellious (Num. 11.1, 33). On this argument, Massah-Meribah would provide a third such incident.

(b) The second incident related to Rephidim, the successful battle with the Amalekites, Deuteronomy knows nothing about; instead it records the defeat of Israel, at first recalcitrant then headstrong, in the offensive from Kadesh-barnea in Deut. 1.44, which is matched, with verbal coincidences, in Num. 14.43-45. The knowledge that there are old scores to pay off against the Amalekites is expressed in Deut. 25.17-19 (cf. DtrH 1 Sam. 15.2). That material is exploited in Exod. 17.14b, again with verbal coincidences. But it would seem that, once again, the P-editor has made use of D-material (and other traditional material in v. 16?) to compose his own narrative (cf. the occurrence of Hur in vv. 10, 12, who is otherwise only known in P-contexts, Exod. 24.14; 31.2, etc.), both here and in his rival version of victory over Amalek in Num. 21.1-3 (Num. 21.1 has verbal coincidences with Num. 33.40, but there would appear to be D/DtrH-phrases embedded in that narrative: e.g. the vow, v. 2, cf. DtrH Judg. 11.30; 1 Sam. 1.11; חרם, v. 2, cf. Deut. 2.34 and frequently; 'YHWH listened to the voice of Israel', v. 3, cf. DtrH Josh. 10.14; the aetiological formula, v. 3, cf. the argument on Exod. 17.7, above).

(c) The third incident, the visit of Jethro and the appointment of judges (Exod. 18.1-27), is even more loosely attached to Rephidim— the place-name is not mentioned at all in the chapter! Other considerations suggest the secondary character of this material in this context. Once again, as in the reference to Horeb in 17.6, there is an anticipation of events only subsequently to be recounted—the arrival at the 'Mountain of God' (v. 5). Elsewhere in Exodus the 'Mountain of God' is identified with Horeb (3.1; cf. other contexts where הר and אלהים are combined, e.g. 3.12; 19.3) and that mountain is not reached until the next chapter. The reference to 'the tent' in v. 7, if that refers to 'the tent of meeting' of Exod. 33.7-11, would be a similar anachronism. If so, a more logical place for the encounter would have been on the eve of departure from Horeb after the events of Exodus 33–34.

Are there other traditions that suggest a more logical order of events? Deuteronomy knows of no such visit of Moses' father-in-law or of Moses' reunion with his wife (who only recurs in Exod. 2.21; 4.25) and family (v. 3b cites Exod. 2.22 for the aetiology of the name of the first son), and thus provides no help in identifying where the encounter might have taken place, but (as mentioned above in the discussion of Num. 11.4-34) does provide in Deut. 1.9-18 an entirely different account of the appointment of the judges. This rather emollient account is supplied with a much more astringent narrative counterpart in Num. 11.4-34, the events at Kibroth-hattaavah. Strikingly, the passage just a few verses earlier, Num. 10.29-32, provides further material on the visit of Moses' in-laws, in this case his brother-in-law, Hobab.

A hypothesis similar to that which has been argued throughout this chapter can account for these phenomena. The P-editor has detached from before Num. 10.29-32 the material on Moses' father-in-law now found in Exod. 18.1-12. He has then radically readapted the material on the appointment of judges of Deut. 1.9-18; Num. 11.4-34.

Detailed observations in support of this hypothesis include the following. Hobab is introduced without any preparation in Num. 10.29. If Exod. 18.1-11 were transferred (back to where they originally belonged as preface to Num. 10.29-32, on this hypothesis), the abruptness of this opening would disappear. This transposition requires that both passages belong to the D-version. There are sufficient indications that this is so: in Exodus 18, beside the links between vv. 2-4 to the earlier narrative of Exod. 2.21-22; 4.25, and the references to 'the Mountain of God' (v. 5) and 'the tent' (v. 7), the vocabulary of v. 8 is typical of DtrH ('on behalf of', Josh. 14.6; Judg. 6.7, etc.; 'the vicissitudes', only again in the Pentateuch in Num. 20.14 in association with D-language [e.g. Deut. 26.5 for v. 15]); v. 12 contrasts with the feasting on the mountain in the presence of God in the P-edition in Exod. 24.11, where the number of participants is restricted to the 70 elders. Exodus 18.27 could form the natural conclusion of Exod. 18.1-12 and the link to Num. 10.29 (a shadow of the presence of Hobab in the earlier narrative may be found in Exod. 18.6, where the text seems to require the advent of a messenger from Jethro to Moses [cf. v. 7 where Moses goes out to meet his father-in-law]).

Numbers 10.29-32 contains such Dtrc. (or at least pre-P) phrases as 'the place which the LORD promised to give' (v. 29, e.g. Gen. 13.14-15; Num. 14.40), 'the LORD has spoken good things concerning Israel' (v. 29, e.g. Josh. 21.45; 23.2-15; 1 Kgs 8.56), 'my land and my birth-place' (v. 30, e.g. Gen. 12.1; 24.4); DtrH (Judg. 1.16) provides the conclusion to the accompaniment of Hobab through the wilderness with the Israelites into the land; the ensuing verse, Num. 11.33, is replete with Dtr-phraseology (e.g. 'the ark of the covenant of the LORD').

By contrast, Exod. 18.11-26 seems to be a P-edition of events. It contrasts both with Deut. 1.9-18 and Num. 11.4-34 in that the initiative now comes from Jethro and not from Moses with the agreement of the people. There is also a similarity of conception of legal consultation to Exod. 24.14.[14] Tell-tale signs of language are the תורות of vv. 16, 20, the verb הזהיר (v. 20), which is highly typical of Ezekiel (e.g. Ezek. 3.17-21), the verb חזה (v. 21, cf. Exod. 24.11). The need for law *before* Sinai on P's scenario has already been recognized in 15.22-26; now in 18.13-26 provision is made for the discharge of justice (for 'statutes', cf. 15.25) and to provide 'rulings' in regulation of the life of the people during Moses' impending absence on the mountain. Nonetheless, there are embedded in the text turns of phrase borrowed from Deuteronomy, especially 'alone', 'able' (vv. 14, 18; cf. Deut. 1.9), 'the leaders of thousands...tens' (vv. 21, 25; cf. Deut. 1.15). This reuse is consistent with a hypothesis of borrowing with polemical purpose of correction.

V

Summary and Conclusion

The detailed study of the text of Exod. 15.22–19.2 supports the hypothesis enunciated at the beginning that the pre-P version of this section of Exodus may have contained no more than Exod. 15.22a; 19.2b: 'Moses led Israel out from the Red Sea. They came out to the Wilderness of Shur and encamped there before the Mountain of God.' The intervening materials have been edited from materials to be found in the D-version in other contexts and supplied with new frameworks by the final editor as follows: 15.22b-26 has been transposed from the context of Exod. 20.20; 16 is a parallel version of Num. 11.4-34; 17.1-7 has been transposed from between Num. 11.3 and 4 (and in the process the material now in Exod. 32.25-29 has been disjoined and relocated);

14. Chapter 7, p. 156.

17.8-16 is a parallel version to Num. 21.1-3; 18.1-12, 27 has been transposed from immediately preceding Num. 10.29; 18.13-26 is a parallel version to Num. 11.10-30.

This thesis seems radical enough without attempting to identify levels and sub-levels within the various materials. It could be argued, for example, that the notes on the itinerary in Deut. 9.22-24 represent a secondary expansion of the material: there is, after all, a clear resumption in v. 25 of v. 18. Yet it must be observed that vv. 22-23 fit the wider structure of the chapter: the acts of enraging signalled by the verb הקציף already in v. 7 and the subsequent itemization of incidents with an initial וב (as in 9.8), even if they are out of chronological sequence and require the cumbersome recapitulation.

The cumulative nature of the accounts of rebellion in the wilderness might also be evidence for growth in the Deuteronomy tradition: Kadesh-barnea alone, in chs. 1–3, the addition of Massah in ch. 6 and Horeb, Taberah, Massah and Kibroth-hattaavah in ch. 9. But it would seem to me over-logical to assume a history of development of the text matching the growing complexity of the presentation of rebellion in the wilderness. After all, within Deuteronomy there is no explicit reference to the sea as place of deliverance until 11.4, though some expressions, especially נוראות, מלחמה, זרוע נטויה (4.34, etc.; see Chapter 10), can be held to imply the action at the sea. I should be prepared to maintain that there is sufficient consistency in the D-presentation for its general unitary character to be affirmed.

There is an analogous question in connection with the P-edition: does variation between two corresponding texts in the final level of the Pentateuch (e.g. the three omissions in the itinerary of Exod. 12.36–19.2, Red Sea, Dophkah and Alush, over against Num. 33, not to mention the more far-reaching omissions in Num. 10.11–22.1) represent an acceptable degree of abbreviation or divergence within the one edition or is it evidence for two stages in the process of the redaction of the final edition? The question is impossible to determine on this set of texts alone, but, in order to avoid the unnecessary accumulation of hypotheses, I should be inclined to the former.

This is not to deny that there may be marginal adjustment within the D-material. For example, Deut. 10.6-7, recording stages in the itinerary that match Numbers 33, is clearly parenthetical to its context and seems to be an attempt to bring D into line with P. The fact that it transposes stations 27 and 28 and appears to relate the death of Aaron with station

27, rather than 34, as in Numbers 33, suggests a maladroit adjustment which could be even later than the P-edition of the Pentateuch. The name Sinai (Deut. 33.2) seems to be further evidence of a post-D edition of the material which takes it in the direction of P.

The material on the itinerary seems to me to provide a rather slender basis for discrimination in the use of the labels 'D' and 'Dtr'. It is presumably appropriate to label the material on the quails in Exodus 16 'Dtr', since quails are not mentioned in Deuteronomy. However, they do occur in the narrative counterpart to Deut. 9.22 in Num. 11.4-34. The fact that the reference to Kibroth-hattaavah in Deut. 9.22 hardly makes any sense without being associated with the narrative in Numbers 11 seems to me to throw doubts, on grounds of coherence, on the ultimate possibility of separating D and Dtr, at least on this point.

As for the radicality of the hypothesis, it must suffice to observe that if, as is demonstrable, there are fundamental differences in the presentation of the wilderness wandering between the final edition of the Pentateuch (the 'P-edition') and Deuteronomy (the 'D-version'), notably in the duration of the Passover and in the location of Kadesh-barnea, yet if that final edition provides the framework of the narrative in both Exodus and Numbers, then it is not at all unexpected that the final edition should have introduced fundamental reorganization into the narrative, not least in Exodus. The way in which the P-editor has freely reorganized traditional material within his own imposed framework is analogous to the way in which he has earlier polemically adjusted the D-version of the Passover in Exodus 12–13:[15] amid a radically reformulated edition remnants of the earlier version are, nonetheless, embedded.

15. Chapter 9.

Chapter 12

FROM THE MOUNTAIN TO KADESH,
WITH SPECIAL REFERENCE TO EXODUS 32.30–34.29*

In the Pentateuch there are two radically different views of the itinerary
of Israel from Mount Sinai/Horeb to Kadesh and of the chronology
associated with that itinerary. On the one hand, in Numbers 33 in the
summary of Israel's wandering in the wilderness, Kadesh (v. 36) is station 33, reached only in the fortieth year after the exodus (the chronology is indicated by the following station, Hor-hahar, v. 37, which is
related in v. 38 to the death of Aaron 'on the first of the fifth month in
the fortieth year of the exodus'; cf. Num. 20.1, 22-29). On the other
hand, in Deuteronomy in the retrospect on Israel's wandering in the
wilderness, Kadesh stands early in the period (Deut. 1.19). The precise
moment of arrival at Kadesh is not made clear in Deuteronomy. But the
year of departure from it may be deduced from Deut. 2.14: Israel's
crossing of the Zered into the territory of Moab took place 38 years
after the departure from Kadesh. Since, according to Deut. 2.7; 8.2, 4;
29.4, the length of the wilderness wandering was 40 years, on the
Deuteronomic chronology the departure from Kadesh must have taken
place in year 2 of the exodus. The length of Israel's stay at Kadesh is
left vague in Deut. 1.46: 'as many days as you spent there'; but the pre-
sumption must be that Israel's arrival at Kadesh took place already in
the first year of the exodus. In the two versions the function of Kadesh
is, thus, entirely different. In the summary in Numbers 33 Kadesh
marks the last point in the wilderness wandering from which the successful advance into the Promised Land is launched in the fortieth year
through the territories of Israel's eastern neighbours; in the retrospect in

    *   Originally published in M. Vervenne and J. Lust (eds.), *Deuteronomy and
Deuteronomic Literature* (Festschrift C.H.W. Brekelmans; BETL, 133; Leuven:
Leuven University Press/Peeters, 1997), pp. 449-67. As in Chapter 11, some abbre-
viation and adjustments to fit this collection have been made.

Deuteronomy, it is the starting-point for the initial attempt in the first year to enter the land directly from the south and, when that failed, for the ensuing 38 years of wandering in the wilderness.

The question that arises is how far these divergent views in Numbers 33 and Deuteronomy 1 on the itinerary and chronology of events between the mountain and Kadesh are represented in the preceding Pentateuchal narrative. In this chapter, the question will be raised especially in connection with the narrative of preparations for departure from the mountain in Exod. 32.30–34.29.[1]

I

It needs hardly to be said that there is a *prima facie* case that an earlier version of the departure from the mountain for Kadesh has been overlaid by a later in the Exodus–Numbers narrative. Departure from the mountain is first commanded in Exod. 32.34 (and repeated in 33.1; cf. 34.9) and the reader expects that command to be obeyed forthwith. But the departure is then delayed by a complex series of incidents, inauguration of institutions, especially the Tabernacle and its rites, and legal enactments, beginning especially in Exodus 35, and only gets under way some 43 chapters later towards the end of Numbers 10. A precise chronology binds together the final version, which is uniform with the

1.   This chapter argues that much further evidence of P's editorial technique of transposing and editing pre-existing D-materials, identified in Chapter 11, is to found in Exod. 32–34 in connection with the narrative of preparations for departure from the mountain.

My angle of approach—transposition and reuse of D-material by P—is frequently so different from that of other interpreters, e.g. J. Vermeylen, 'L'affaire du veau d'or [Ex 32–34]: Une clé pour la "question deutéronomiste"?', *ZAW* 97 (1985), pp. 1-23, or S. Boorer, *The Promise of the Land as Oath: A Key to the Formation of the Pentateuch* (BZAW, 205; Berlin: W. de Gruyter, 1992), esp. pp. 203-325, where elaboration of a basic text is the model used, that running engagement with their views is difficult (see, however, n. 25 below). C. Brekelmans's programmatic study, 'Die sogenannten deuteronomischen Elemente in Genesis bis Numeri: Ein Beitrag zur Vorgeschichte des Deuteronomismus', in P.A.H. de Boer (ed.), *Volume du Congrès: Genève 1965* (VTSup, 15; Leiden: E.J. Brill; 1966), pp. 90-96, has provided me with both confirmation and challenge. M. Vervenne, 'The Question of "Deuteronomic" Elements in Genesis to Numbers', in F. García Martínez *et al.* (eds.), *Studies in Deuteronomy* (Festschrift C.J. Labuschange; VTSup, 53; Leiden: E.J. Brill; 1994), pp. 243-68, provides a sympathetic recent discussion of Brekelmans's programme with valuable bibliographical surveys.

dating of the beginning of the itinerary in Num. 33.3: the Tabernacle is instituted on 'the first of the first month of the second year' (Exod. 40.17); the departure from the mountain takes place on 'the twentieth of the second month of the second year' (Num. 10.11). But beneath this final edition there is room for a much brisker narrative continuing in Num. 10.29 which puts into effect with some urgency the commands to depart from the mountain in Exodus 32–34. The chronology of this version is nowhere explicitly given. But, by inference from a number of passages in Exodus, the departure from the mountain takes place already in the first year after the exodus: after the conclusion of the covenant on the seventh day after the Passover (Exod. 24.3-8),[2] all that is required before the departure is two periods of 40 days, first for inscribing (Exod. 24.18; 31.18) and then for re-inscribing (Exod. 34.1.28) the two tablets of the Decalogue, with only a couple of days in between (Exod. 32.30; 34.4). This chronology fits with the continuation of the narrative in Num. 10.29 which leads, after the incidents of Numbers 11 and 12, to the sending-out of spies to reconnoitre the land 'at the time of the first-fruits of the grapes' (Num. 13.20), that is, early autumn. The correspondences of this earlier version with Deut. 1.6-46; 9.9–10.11 (among other evidence) have led me to propose that it be called the 'D-version'.[3]

II

The sequence of place-names shows, however, how greatly this D-version has been disturbed in the process of the superimposition upon it of the final edition (the 'P-edition').[4] From Deuteronomy the itinerary from the mountain to Kadesh is clear. In Deut. 1.19 that progression is direct and takes place, seemingly, within the first year after the exodus. At all events, the sequel is the unsuccessful attempt to enter the land directly from Kadesh followed by the stay 'for many days' until the second year, as already noted. If one were to add the evidence of Deut. 1.2,[5] it might even be that the length of time envisaged before the arrival at Kadesh from Horeb is 11 days.

2. Chapter 9 above, p. 211.
3. E.g. Chapter 7 above.
4. Chapter 7 above.
5. For the coherence of that passage with the continuation in Deuteronomy, cf. Z. Kallai, 'Where Did Moses Speak (Deuteronomy I 1-5)?', *VT* 45 (1995), pp. 188-97.

Deuteronomy 9.22 adds incident to that journey: between Horeb (Deut. 9.8) and Kadesh (Deut. 9.23) take place the three episodes of enraging the LORD at Taberah, Massah and Kibroth-hattaavah. Since the incidents at Taberah and Kibroth-hattaavah are recounted in Num. 11.1-34 in a passage that is replete with D-terminology, I have argued that that passage provides the narrative counterpart to D's reminiscence (do the 'eleven days' of Deut. 1.2 then relate to the 'three days' journey' of Num. 10.33 to Taberah and include the two further stages of Massah/Meribah and Kibroth-hattaavah?). Further, I have argued that the missing Massah narrative, now found in Exod. 17.2, 4-7, was originally located between Num. 11.3 and 4 but has been transposed by the P-editor as part of his construction of a narrative of rebellion in the wilderness *before* Sinai.[6]

This dislocation is, however, only one of several. It is striking that, in the present narrative in Num. 11.35–14.45, Kadesh itself is virtually suppressed. Whereas in Deuteronomy 1 Kadesh is the centre for activities of many kinds (Moses' initial command to the Israelites to advance into the land of the Amorites to take possession of it; Israel's demurral; the sending of spies; their bringing back a good report reinforced by the grapes of Eshkol; Israel's initial refusal to go up and change of mind; the LORD's angry response that the whole exodus generation would die out before the entry into the land, which explains the ensuing 40 years of the wilderness wandering), in Numbers 11–14 there is mention of Kadesh only somewhat in passing (13.26) in the wake of the mention of Taberah and Kibroth-hattaavah. 'Wilderness of Paran' is the preferred term, which occurs in the Pentateuch only in Num. 12.16; 13.3-26; Deut. 1.1; 33.2. The last occurrence, in parallel to 'Sinai' (in Deuteronomy where, above all, 'Horeb' is expected!) poses the question of the editing of the earlier D-version, including Deuteronomy itself, in the direction of the P-edition. The mention of Kadesh in Num. 20.1 in P-material (cf. the characteristic word there for Israel, עדה), where the arrival is dated in the 'first month', presumably in year 40 after the exodus, relates it to the itinerary of Numbers 33. In Num. 11.35, instead of arrival in Kadesh after Kibroth-hattaavah, as in Deuteronomy 1 and 9, the next station is Hazeroth, that is, station 14 of Num. 33.17. Nonetheless, that this is a secondary adjustment in favour of the itinerary of the P-edition is clear from the way in which Numbers 12–13 resumes the sequence of events expected from Deuteronomy: the

6. See n. 1.

spies return from the reconnaissance of the land to Kadesh in Num. 13.26, just as in Deut. 1.25. The worsting at the hands of the Amorites, only now called Amalekites and Canaanites, follows in Num. 14.40-45 in terms largely identical with those in Deut. 1.43-44. Apart from the explicit mention of Kadesh in Num. 13.26, it seems that for the sake of harmonizing the D-version with the superimposed P-edition, Kadesh has been replaced with 'the wilderness of Paran'.

This virtual suppression of Kadesh from early in the itinerary at the level of the final edition of Numbers is matched by the fact that the departure in the second year is now from Sinai (Num. 10.12); in D it is from Kadesh (Deut. 1.46–2.1).

III

The evidence in Deuteronomy suggests that there is displacement of three further blocks of material in the final edition of Exodus which should lie between the departure from the mountain and the arrival at Kadesh: (1) the arrival of Jethro and Moses' family (Exod. 18.1-12); (2) the appointment of the judges (Exod. 18.13-27); (3) the material on the tent of meeting (Exod. 33.7-11). The first two of these have already been discussed in Chapter 11 above (pp. 257-59), where the argument was that the D-material now embedded in Exodus 18 was originally located as preface to Num. 10.29. Only the third requires some further consideration here.

The note in Exod. 33.7-11 about Moses' customary practice with regard to the tent of meeting interrupts the complex interchange between Moses and the LORD (Exod. 33.1-6 and 12-23). Once again, Deuteronomy gives the clue about the location of the material on the tent of meeting in the D-narrative in Exodus of the departure from the mountain. The text on this occasion is Deut. 10.1-5.[7] During the course of the second period of 40 days and nights on the mountain, Moses

---

7.   Not Deut. 10.1-4 as I had earlier suggested (*Exodus*, pp. 76-77). The point is that the account of Moses' descent from the mountain in Exodus which is analogous to that in Deut. 10.5 ('I turned and came down from the Mountain and I put the tablets in the ark which I had made') has been replaced by the beginning of P's account in Exod. 34.29 ('As Moses came down from Mount Sinai, with the two tablets of the testimony in Moses' hand, as he came down from the Mountain, Moses did not know'; the repetitions in Exod. 34.29 may confirm that it represents the editing of an underlying text).

receives the command not only to fetch two replacement tablets but also to construct the ark to house the tablets about to be inscribed.

While D, as a matter of fact, gives no account of the erection of the tent to receive the ark (the tent is mentioned in D only in Deut. 31.14-15 in the context of Moses' death at the end of the 40 years' wandering; as on other matters—the incidents at Taberah, Massah/Meribah, and Kibroth-hattaavah, for instance, in 9.22—D simply presupposes the existence of the institution), the logic of the D-narrative would be that the erection of the tent follows the construction of the ark, especially once the tablets have been deposited in the ark. Deut. 10.8 (after the intrusive material, 10.6-7, proved as intrusive by its non-use of the pre-vailing second-person address) would confirm this: the Levites were appointed 'at that time', not only 'to carry the Ark' but also to 'stand before the LORD to serve him', a note that implies the existence of a sanctuary. That is to say, in the original D narrative in Exodus, the intrusive information in Exod. 33.7-11 about the pitching of the tent, with its frequentative tense, must follow the D-version of Exod. 34.29, which, reconstructed from the parallel in Deut. 10.5, must have read in some such terms as, 'Then Moses turned and came down from the Mountain and put the tablets in the Ark which he had made'. Exodus 33.7 would then make an appropriate continuation: 'Moses would take a[8] Tent and pitch it for it[9] outside the camp.'

This argument is confirmed by the continuation of the D-narrative from Exod. 34.29 in Numbers 10–12, where there is reference both to the ark (Num. 10.33-36) and to the tent (Num. 11.16, 24, 26, in the context of which some of the same vocabulary as in Exod. 33.7-11 is used).[10] The general material on the tent should precede this narrative: if the ark 'sets out' and 'rests' (Num. 10.35-36), then the tent whence it departs and whither it returns must already have been mentioned. That is, the latest point in the narrative for the insertion of the general mate-rial on the pitching of the tent now located in Exod. 33.7-11 is between Num. 10.34 and 35.

8.   The use of the article as in GKC 126q-s (not citing this passage).

9.   The ark as referent is confirmed on this argument (for note—without endorsement—and bibliography, cf. Childs, *Exodus*, p. 584).

10.   'Descending and speaking', Num. 11.17, cf. Exod. 33.9; 'each one at the doorway of his tent', Num. 11.10 = Exod. 33.10; cf. the recurrence of the tent of meeting in Num. 12.4; the phrase, 'in a pillar of cloud and stood at the entrance to the Tent', is identical in Num. 12.5 and Exod. 33.9.

In summary, in the light of Deuteronomy and the narratives it pre-supposes in Numbers, the procedures of the final editor of Exodus become clear. Just as on the earlier argument on the route from the sea to the mountain P has transposed the Massah/Meribah incident from between Num. 11.3 and 4, so now in consideration of the route from the mountain to Kadesh it would appear that P has transposed from between Exod. 34.29 (in its D-form) and the continuation in Num. 10.29 the material on the pitching of the tent of meeting now to be found in Exod. 33.7-11. That should be followed by the material now in Exod. 18.1-12 on the arrival of Jethro (cf. his entry into 'the tent', Exod. 18.7). The material on the appointment of the judges in Exod. 18.13-27 is a free composition by P reusing materials from the D-version of events at Kibroth-hattaavah on the third stage of the journey from the mountain to Kadesh in Num. 11.11-17, 24-30. The course of events in the D-version of the itinerary from the mountain to Kadesh in Exodus–Numbers was thus: Moses' second period of 'forty days and forty nights' on the mountain (Exod. 32.30–33.6; 33.12–34.29); arrangements for the deposit of the ark in the tent of meeting (33.7-11); the arrival of Jethro (18.1-12); the departure from the mountain and the journey to Kadesh (Num. 10.29–12.16), all insofar as they are not P.

IV

That last proviso opens up a further stage in the inquiry: how far has P modified and adapted not just the sequence of these blocks of the D-narrative but also their content, in particular the content of the first block of material, the account of Moses' second period of 'forty days and forty nights' on the mountain in Exod. 32.30–33.6; 33.12–34.29?

That the P-editor may indeed intervene within the existing blocks of D-material is perhaps clearest in Exod. 34.1-4, 29, as the parallel with Deut. 10.1-5 suggests. Because he deals with the construction of the ark in Exod. 25.10-22//37.1-9, P has removed the ark material from Exod. 34.1b, 29a from the parallel in Deut. 10.1b, 2b, 3aα, 5a and has sub-stituted it with material on Sinai and the sanctity of the mountain.[11] Similarly, P has no need to deal with the matter of the transportation of the ark by the Levites (Deut. 10.8-9), since that is a matter to be

11. See Chapter 7, p. 154; Chapter 9, pp. 199-200.

legislated for in his account of the departure from the mountain in Num. 3.31; 4.5-15. That material is, therefore, suppressed.[12]

These observations open up the possibility of less obvious intervention by the P-editor in other parts of the material. The final form of Exod. 32.30-35, the account of Moses' intercession and related events in association with his second period of 'forty days and forty nights' on the mountain, shows some marked disparities with the 'reminiscence' in Deuteronomy 9. Whereas the Exodus account of Moses' two periods of 'forty days and forty nights' on the mountain records intercession by Moses on both occasions (Exod. 32.11-14 and 32.31-32), the parallel in Deuteronomy records intercession only on the second. But some of the vocabulary of that intercession ('whom you brought out of Egypt with a strong hand. Remember for the sake of your servants Abraham and Isaac' and the motifs, at least, of the land as the goal and the mockery of Egypt if that goal is not attained, Deut. 9.26-29) occurs in Exodus on the occasion of the first 'forty days and forty nights' (Exod. 32.11-13). The version in Deuteronomy is the more logical: Moses cannot confess the sin of the people and engage in intercession for them until he has seen the sin that they have committed. It seems, therefore, that there may be here yet another example of transposition of material by the P-editor: material from Moses' intercession on the second occasion has been transposed in the P-edition into the first in order to develop the second occasion in a different direction. The element of confession is now more strongly marked (v. 31; Deuteronomy admits the guilt of the people somewhat in the bygoing, 9.27b); material not at all in Deuteronomy is introduced—the divine 'book' (vv. 32-33), which in datable texts is late postexilic,[13] and the plague (v. 35). The view of individual responsibility (v. 33) is different from that of guilt extending to 'the third and fourth generation', which appears, reiterated from the Decalogue, in Exod. 34.7, which will be regarded as a D-text below. This may be an example of the polemical corrections introduced by the P-edition to the D-version (as shall be argued in connection with Exod. 33.12-23). Other elements then come into consideration as deriving

12 See also Chapter 11, p. 257.

13. Mal. 3.16; Dan. 12.1; cf. Pss. 56.9; 69.29; 139.16; the idea of 'wiping out' might, on this hypothesis, be reuse by the P-editor from Deut. 9.14, where, however, it concerns wiping out 'their name from under heaven'.

from P, for example, 'atonement' (v. 30): how else before the P-legislation in, say, Leviticus 5, can atonement be effected than through the death of Moses?[14]

As an aside, it may be noted that in P's transposition of D-material into the first period of 'forty days and forty nights' some adjustments have been made, especially in Exod. 32.13, where the order of the elements has been changed and the formula of the promise to the Patriarchs appears in the relatively rare form, 'Abraham, Isaac and Israel' (for the usual—some 20 times in the Hebrew Bible—'...and Jacob';[15] the rarer formulation '...and Israel' occurs only in 1 Kgs 18.36 in an 'Israelite'—i.e. northern—context, and then in postexilic texts, 1 Chron. 29.18; 2 Chron. 30.6; cf. 1 Chron. 1.34).

These data suggest, then, that the P-editor has freely constructed, partly out of pre-existing D-materials especially on the first occasion, the content of Moses' intercession on both the first and the second periods of 'forty day and forty nights' on the mountain. In the second in particular he has thus introduced episodes of divine retribution for which there is no warrant in Deuteronomy 9–10 (for a comparable episode in recognizable P-terms, cf. Num. 17.6-15). It is this reuse of D-material that accounts for the rather bewildering repetitions in the Exodus text as it stands: in particular, the command to depart, with the promise of the accompanying angel (32.34, repeated in effect in 33.1-3). The 'departure' from the mountain introduced by P in 32.34-35 provides the space for his narrative of the plague wreaked in punishment on the people: the angel has now become an avenging angel.

V

If one adheres, then, to the logical order as envisaged in Deuteronomy 9–10, such repetitions are avoided. The sequence of events is as follows: Moses' prayer (Deut. 9.25-29) receives a gracious response from God, which is not stated but is to be assumed from the immediate instructions to hew two new tablets to be inscribed with the Decalogue (and to be deposited for safe-keeping in the ark; Deut. 10.1-4). The

---

14. Cf. the atoning efficacy of the death of the high-priest in Num. 35.25, 28, 32; for atonement in Deuteronomy—but in quite different, specific circumstances—cf. Deut. 21.8.

15. Gen. 50.24; Exod. 2.24; 3.6, 15, 16; 4.5; 6.3-8; 33.1; Num. 32.11; Lev. 26.42; Deut. 1.8; 6.10; 9.5-27; 29.12; 30.20; 34.4; 2 Kgs 13.23; Jer. 33.26.

summary in Deut. 10.10-11 makes the sequence unambiguous: at the end of the second 'forty days and forty nights', the command comes to depart from the mountain. The sequence of the matching D-version in Exodus, that has been so radically rearranged in the P-edition, must then have been: after the D-version of Moses' prayer of intercession at the end of Exodus 32, which is to be restored from Exod. 32.11-14*, the material in Exod. 34.1-28* must follow; only then does the material in Exod. 33.1-6, 12-23* follow the logic of the Deuteronomy version, before the descent from the mountain takes place (Exod. 34.29*) and the arrangements are made for the safe-keeping of the ark in the tent of meeting (Exod. 33.7-11).

After the restoration of Exod. 32.11-14 to its rightful place in Exod. 32.31-35 (and thus eliminating the repetition in v. 34a of the impending instruction to depart of 33.1), the D-narrative continues, then, in Exod. 34.1-4 (with the restoration of the ark material from Deut. 10.1-3 and the elimination of the P-material).

Now follows a Deuteronomistic elaboration in Exod. 34.5-28a. It is entirely appropriate that in preparation for inscribing the Decalogue on the second set of tablets an abbreviated re-run of events in Exodus 19–24 in preparation for the inscribing of the first should take place.[16] Thus vv. 5-9 are the equivalent of Exod. 19.1–20.21*. In v. 5, 'the LORD descends' (cf. 19.11) 'in the cloud' (cf. 19.9); Moses 'takes his stand' (as the people did as they awaited the pronouncement of the Decalogue, 19.17). Everything is predicated on the name, 'the LORD' (vv. 5-6, as in the opening of the Decalogue, 20.2). The significance of that name is elaborated in vv. 6-7 in Deuteronomic terms.[17] Verse 7 quotes almost verbatim from the second 'Word' (but in inverted order; cf. 20.5b, 6). In v. 8 Moses' response is as the people's in 4.31; 12.27.[18]

The ensuing section, Exod. 34.10-27, is held within the framework of the phrase 'make a covenant' (vv. 10, 27) and is, thus, the counterpart

16. Cf. Chapter 7, p. 155.

17. רחום occurs in the Pentateuch only again in Deut. 4.31 in a context recalling the theophany at the mountain; חנון only again in the Pentateuch in Exod. 22.26; 'slow to anger and abounding in mercy' recurs in the Pentateuch only in Num. 14.18, in the context of a passage reminiscent of Exod. 32.11-14/Deut. 9.26-29, in the aftermath of the refusal of guidance into the land, which is the topic of v. 9: guidance into the land is the corollary and test of obedience.

18. Both of which, I have argued (Chapter 9, p. 207; Chapter 10, pp. 227), belong to the D-version.

of the covenant ceremony in 24.3-8. This covenant is concluded on
precisely the same basis as the first—the Decalogue and the Book of
the Covenant (20.22–23.33). Thus there is citation of both the beginning of the Decalogue (v. 14; cf. the Second Word of the Decalogue,
20.5) and the conclusion of the Book of the Covenant (vv. 17-26, cf.
23.12-19; v. 17 again resumes the Second Word of the Decalogue, only
using מסכה for פסל, since that is the term that has been used for the
golden calf in 32.4, 8; cf. Deut. 9.12-16; 2 Kgs 17.16). The stringency
of exclusive worship of the LORD is developed here in covenantal
terms: the covenant with the LORD permits the contracting of no other
covenant, least of all with the people of the land, for among the 'wonderful things' that the LORD is about to do for his people is the driving-
out of these indigenous peoples from the land (v. 11). A covenant with
them would thus negate this action of the LORD; besides, a covenant
with them, sealed by intermarriage (v. 16), would inevitably involve
recognition of their deities. Once again the motif of 'guidance into the
land' is essential to the presentation: the conclusion of the covenant at
the mountain and the departure from the mountain are both part of the
one action, which through the continued guidance of the LORD will
culminate in the possession of the land.

It is natural, therefore, that the next section is dominated by the discussion of the mode of that guidance into the land. Following the
sequence of the reminiscence of Deuteronomy (Deut. 10.11), the next
section should concern dismissal from the mountain and departure to
enter the land from Kadesh. Exodus 33.1 provides precisely that link:
the coincidence between Deut. 10.11 and Exod. 33.1 is sufficiently
close: 'the LORD said/spoke to me/Moses...go...before/and the
people...inherit/to the Land which I swore to their ancestors/Abraham,
Isaac and Jacob to give to them/their descendants.' Further, 33.1 picks
up the issue raised in 34.9, where the LORD is implored to go in their
midst, simply because they are a stiff-necked people. Exodus 33.1-6
develops the counter-argument that this is precisely why the LORD
cannot go in their midst. The sequence of this argument requires ch. 34
to precede 33.1-6. That link is followed in 33.2, 3a by the all-important
assurance of guidance into the land through the angel and of the
preparation for the entry by the driving-out of the resident population:
what had been promised at the conclusion of the original covenant in
23.20-33 (especially vv. 20 and 28, along with the same cautions
against involvement in the cults of the nations, vv. 24, 32-33, such as

have just been given in 34.11-13) is now repeated.

The narrative then takes an unexpected turn. The promise of the angel in the lead turns out to be a second best. The ideal of the direct leadership by the LORD cannot be attained because of the recalcitrance of the people; that recalcitrance would provoke the LORD to destroy them. That withholding of direct guidance is indicated institutionally by the periodic descent of the LORD in the cloud on the tent of meeting. The institutional link between the angel and the tent of meeting must be the ark of the covenant—the physical manifestation of the exclusive bond between Israel and the LORD—carried ahead of the advancing hosts of Israel by the Levites.

The sequel in 33.3b-6 has no parallel in Deuteronomy; nonetheless, it is replete with D-terms.[19] At first sight it might be held that the narrative would flow more smoothly if v. 4 followed v. 5. But the curious to-ing and fro-ing is conditioned by the conception of revelation to Moses on the mountain requiring appropriate action by the people (cf. the multiple ascents and descents by Moses in Exod. 19–20; 24): on this occasion, there has already been the ascent for intercession, the descent to hew the replacement set of tablets and to construct the ark, and the ascent for the reception of the Decalogue and reaffirmation of the Book of the Covenant. Because the instruction to depart includes directions to the people on their appropriate response, the scene twice shifts momentarily to the camp, to return again to the mountain-top, where the final instruction to depart includes the command to place the tablets in the ark (as in Deut. 10.6).

As the sign of their chastened loyalty the Israelites 'go in mourning', the same verb that is to be used of their response to the rebuke of Moses when they refuse to enter the land from Kadesh in Num. 14.39, before their fateful headstrong attempt to storm the land which is recalled in terms similar to Num. 14.40-45 in Deut. 1.41-44. The narrative thus closes with a fine *inclusio*: as the Israelites had been urged 'to spoil the Egyptians' (נצל, 3.22; cf. 12.36) as they escaped from Egypt in triumph, so now they 'despoil themselves' (התנצל, v. 6) in token of their humble submission to the terms the LORD lays upon them. This is the rite by which the renewal of the covenant is sealed (contrast 24.3-8 and the wild Bacchanalian revel in Exod. 32.2-6, 17-19 in honour of the golden calf) on departure from the mountain, Horeb.

19. E.g. 'to consume', vv. 3-5 has already occurred in Exod. 32.10-12; 'stiff-necked', vv. 3-5, in Exod. 32.9; 34.9; Deut. 9.6-13.

At this point a note equivalent to Deut. 10.5a should follow, the descent from the mountain to place the tablets in the ark (which has now been replaced by the P-edition in Exod. 34.29), in order to provide the link to Exod. 33.7-11 and thence, as argued above, to the coming of Jethro and Moses' family (Exod. 18.1-12) which links with Num. 10.29.

VI

This leaves the problematical passage Exod. 33.12-23 to be accounted for. The passage is problematical for a number of reasons. First, it is internally repetitious: 'find grace in the eyes' occurs five times, vv. 12, 13 (2×), 16, 17; cf. 'be gracious', v. 19; there are sixfold variations on the verb 'to know', vv. 12 (2×), 13 (2×), 16, 17. Second, it repeats material from other passages, especially from Exod. 34.5-9: 'find grace in the eyes' recurs in 34.9; 'proclaim the name "YHWH"', 33.19; 34.5; 'YHWH passed in front on him', 34.6, is repeated as 'I will cause to pass in front of you' in 33.19. Yet, third, it contradicts what has gone before: especially v. 12, 'You have not told me what you will send with me', appears to contradict what has just been said in 33.2, and is, in any case, an issue that should have been resolved by that point.

These large-scale repetitions both internal and external (and the downright denial of 33.2 in 33.12aγδ) suggest a process of qualification. There is here material that is characteristic of the D-version (the parallels to 34.5-9, just noted) and of Deuteronomy (especially 'the face of the LORD' [Deut. 4.37] and 'give rest' [e.g. Deut. 3.20] to his people, in v. 14). But there is also material that is characteristic of the P-edition, especially 'the glory of God' (v. 18; not unknown in Deut. [5.24], but especially characteristic of P, cf., e.g., Exod. 40.34-35). The probability is that there is correction here by the P-edition of the earlier D-version, precisely on the nature of the guiding and accompanying presence of God.

That there is here an extended commentary by P on pre-existing material is suggested, further, both by the form of the discussion and its structure. There is an introductory 'quotation' of earlier statements, 'See, you tell me, "Take up this people…"'; 'You have said, "I know you by name and you have found grace in my sight"' (v. 12; for the repetition of the last phrase cf. the D-material in Num. 11.11-15). These would be quotations from, respectively, 33.1 and 34.9. But perhaps more notable is the structure: the 'quotation' from 34.9 occurs twice—vv. 12 and 17. Each, as incidentally the massoretic paragraph-marker makes plain, introduces an independent section: the first, vv. 12-16, is the D-version in the form of quotation; the second, vv. 17-23, is the P-revision of that version.

Some further considerations may be held to justify that contention. In the quoted D-version (vv. 12-16), it is likely that P has, once again, transposed material from its original setting. It is striking that in the original context in 34.9 no reply is given by the LORD to Moses' request for an assurance that he will 'go in our midst'. Instead, the covenantal form of the relationship is immediately and somewhat brusquely developed in vv. 10-27. The material now in 33.13-16 would form an appropriate sequel to 34.9. It not only gives a reply to Moses' question, namely, that the 'face of God will indeed go with his people'. It also creates an appropriate bridge to 34.10-27: the nature of Israel's separateness from 'all the people which are upon the face of the earth' (33.16; the root פלה has been used in the D-version of the plagues in 8.18; 9.4; 11.7)[20] is then defined precisely in terms of the covenant relationship in 34.10-27, which is to be the means whereby Israel is to be separated from the peoples of the land.[21]

The fundamental point that the P-edition wishes to clarify and to correct in the requotation and development of 34.9 in 33.17-23 is that 'no one can see God and live' (v. 20), in contradistinction to the D-version of Moses as the one who spoke 'face to face with the LORD, as a man speaks to his friend' (33.11; cf. Deut. 5.4; 34.10). Therefore, though the presence ('face') of God may go with his people, that presence is represented by 'glory' (v. 18) or 'goodness' (v. 19). Even

20. Chapter 10, p. 231.
21. The theory that 33.13 quotes 34.9 may be extended to suggest that 33.13, indeed, provides a more original version of 34.9. There are unevennesses in the text of 34.9 as it stands. The connection of the 'because' clause in 34.9b with the foregoing is by no means clear: 'Let my LORD go in our midst, because it is a stiff-necked people' and the change from first-person plural 'our midst' to third-person singular 'it' is disturbing. The connection between 34.9bα and 9bβ is also far from clear. 33.14-16 would give a natural continuation to 34.9a; 34.9bα may be derived from 33.3b and has replaced the much more kindly phraseology of 33.13b, 'consider that this nation are your people'. It may be that 33.13a has itself suffered in the process: the last phrase of 13a, 'in order that I may find grace', is unexpected after the first phrase, 'if I have found grace'. Something like 'that I may bring up this people' would be more natural.

Moses is here only permitted to see the undelineated 'back' of YHWH (vv. 20-23).

VII

In summary, in the light of the Deuteronomy model in Deut. 9.18, 25–10.5, 10, 11, the D-version of the preparations to depart from the mountain within the first block of the narrative of the journey from the mountain to Kadesh in Exod. 32.30–34.29, into which the P-edition has interposed quite thoroughly with transpositions and reformulations, would have run somewhat as follows:

- Exodus 32.11-14: Moses' intercession on the second occasion of 'forty days and forty nights', which P has transposed into the first period of 'forty days and forty nights' and replaced with the extant 32.30-35;
- Exodus 34.1.4*: the hewing of the second set of tablets, with the ark material restored from Deut. 10.1aγ, b, 2b, 3aα and P-material removed;
- Exodus 34.5-9a: the gracious response of God to Moses' intercession, supplemented with Exod. 33.13b-16;
- Exodus 34.10-28: the terms of the covenant in Decalogue and Book of the Covenant reaffirmed;
- Exodus 33.1-6: the command to depart from the mountain;
- Exodus 34.29a: reformulated in terms of Deut. 10.5a, 'And Moses turned and descended from the Mountain and put the tablets in the Ark';
- Exodus 33.7-11: the habitual practice of pitching the tent of meeting for the ark;
- an equivalent to Deut. 10.8abα: 'The LORD set aside[22] the tribe of Levi to carry the Ark of the Covenant of the LORD, to stand before the LORD to serve him and to pronounce blessing in his name';
- Exodus 18.1-12, the coming of Jethro, would continue the narrative, linking directly with Num. 10.29.

The basically D/Dtr-character of the material in Exod. 32.30–34.29a is thus reaffirmed. The new element in the argument is the recognition of the substantial intervention of P to rearrange the material, the

---

22. Omitting D's 'reminiscence formula', 'At that time'.

control, as before, being supplied by the reminiscence in Deut. 9.7–10.11.

VIII

P's motives in undertaking the adjustments to the primary D-text of Exodus are plain. P provides a 'restoration of the cult' edition over against D's 'exilic' version. For D the cult has been irretrievably lost and the only remaining institution that can preserve the identity of the people is the covenant, predicated on the sovereign grace of God towards his errant people, represented by his constant presence through his 'angel' to provide guidance. P, by contrast, restores the institutions of the cult to the centre of the life of the people.

The order and treatment of events in the P-edition, in contrast to the D-version, makes that purpose clear. The second occasion of 'forty days and forty nights' in Exod. 32.30-35 is no longer an occasion for the display of the sovereign grace of God (contrast Deut. 10.10b). In the absence of the atonement cult only the death of Moses, the leader, might atone; but, when that proposal is rejected, the people's transgression must be followed by immediate retribution (rather in the manner of Chronicles: e.g. 1 Chron. 28.9bβ).

With the vast insertion of material on the Tabernacle in 25.1–31.17; 35.1–40.38, the material on the tent of meeting must be removed as far as possible from that of the Tabernacle with which it is to be integrated: it is quite literally 'outside the camp' to enable the construction of the Tabernacle in the midst. But, unlike the ark, mention of the tent of meeting cannot be suppressed: while awaiting the construction of the Tabernacle and its inauguration on the first day of the first month of the second year, and the installation of the ark of the testimony therein, an interim sanctuary is required.

Exodus 33.12-23 must correct the 'face-to-face' intimacy of 33.11 between God and Moses in the tent of meeting: the face of God is now his awesome presence; access to God must now be regulated by the degrees of holiness. The unique quality of the encounter between God and Moses is now expressed through P's own narrative of the shining face of Moses in Exod. 34.29-35. After Exod. 34.5-9a the gracious response of God to Moses' intercession is now complemented by emphasis on the sinfulness of the people in 34.9b.

IX

The isolation of P's material and the recognition of his rearrangement of the D-version still leaves a very complex text. The relationship between Deuteronomy (in particular, Deut. 9.7–10.11) and the D-version of Exodus presents the interpreter with a conundrum. On the one hand, the D-version of Exodus 'quotes' from Deuteronomy (with the necessary modification of first-person reminiscence in Deuteronomy to third-person narrative in Exodus, and with due allowance for the fact that Deuteronomy contains also hortatory material in second-person address).[23] The clearest example of this 'quotation' is in Exod. 34.28b where it is only from the parallel in Deut. 10.4 that the subject of the verb 'he wrote' can be established as 'the LORD'. In the light of this, it is probable that other materials in the D-version of Exodus are similarly deliberate utilizations of material in Deuteronomy.[24]

Yet, on the other hand, it is clear that Deuteronomy presupposes the developed narratives of Exodus–Numbers: thus the 'reminiscence' of Deut. 9.12–10.10 requires the vivid details of the circumstantial account in Exodus 32: for example, the casting of the golden calf (vv. 1-6); 9.22 is wholly obscure without its narrative counterpart in Numbers 11 (including the Massah/Meribah narrative now at Exod. 17.2-7). The interruptions in the sequence of events by anticipations and recapitulations are further indication of the dependent character of Deuteronomy: it can assume that the ordered progression of events is made clear from its companion narrative in Exodus and Numbers. Thus, because the reminiscence of Moses' second period of 'forty days and forty nights' on the mountain which already begins in 9.18 separates the anger of the LORD with Aaron (9.20) and the destruction of the golden calf (v. 21) from their immediate connection with the breaking of the tablets (v. 17), they then have to be introduced in 'flashbacks', as indicated by word-order in 9.20-21. The break in the narrative is further exacerbated by anticipated events in 9.22-23 and the

23. 9.7-8, 9aγ, 10b, almost all of 16 (apart from 'I saw' and 'molten calf'), 17 (last word), 18b, 19, 25b; 10.4b, 9.

24. Thus for phraseology in Exod. 24.12-18, cf. Deut. 9.9; for 31.18, cf. 9.10-11; for 32.7-10, cf. 9.12-14; for 32.15, 19, cf. 9.15-17; for 32.20, cf. 9.21; for 34.1, cf. 10.1-2; for 34.4-28b, cf. 10.3-4; 9.9. The particular circumstances of 32.11, 13, cf. 9.26-27; and 32.12-13, 34 as D-material reused and relocated by P have been discussed above.

thread of the narrative has to be resumed by a number of cumbersome resumptions (9.25 resumes 9.18 and is, in turn, resumed by 10.10). Nonetheless, the coherence of the account of events in Deuteronomy and its dependence on the narrative in Exodus–Numbers are clear.

The only solution to this conundrum can be that the Deuteronomy 'reminiscence' and its narrative counterpart in the D-version of Exodus–Numbers are written at the same time and are developed in deliberate interplay with one another. It may thus be a vain hope to try to trace the stages of that interplay.[25] The verbal coincidences between D and Dtr and the general coincidence of the shape of events are still of a large enough scale to warrant the conclusion that they come from the same school but have different functions. The simplified narrative in Deuteronomy 1–11 has presupposed the work of Dtr. Dtr is concerned to give a concerted account of the entire sweep of Israel's history from creation to the exile. Thus, in Exodus–Numbers it is concerned not merely to give a coherent and explanatory account of the period in question itself, the wilderness wandering, but to relate this period to what has gone before (hence the large plus about the renewal of the covenant in identical terms in Exod. 34.5-27) and as foreshadowing

25. For the mutual interpretation of one another by Exodus and Deuteronomy, see now Chapter 1, pp. 29-32. These observations make me doubtful about whether Brekelmans's programme of inquiry into proto- and post-Deuteronomic material (see n. 1 above) can be realized. Nor have I found the criteria of theology and style, which he proposes, to be decisive (e.g. the limitation of the death penalty to the guilty individual, as in Deut. 24.16, might be held to indicate the D-character of Exod. 32.33—but then what of Deut. 5.9?). The decisive criterion is, rather, the distinctiveness and consistency of view about *Realien*, in this instance chronology and itinerary, that enables both the substantially unitary character of the material in Deuteronomy to be affirmed and the D-version of Exodus to be recovered.

The difficulty of applying the criteria of language and theology to distinguish layers within the Deuteronomic movement seems to me to be illustrated by the argument of Vermeylen, 'L'affaire du veau d'or'. Because of his view that the group of Deuteronomic redactors functioned in the period c. 587-520, he is not sympathetic to Brekelmans's programme of search for pre- or proto-Deuteronomic material. But Vermeylen's own attempt to distinguish four Deuteronomic redactions approximately in the years 585, 575, 560 and 525 rests on similar criteria. While he makes many valuable observations, which, however, in my view, merely enable the general Deuteronomic character of many passages in this pericope to be identified, I cannot share his view that one can distinguish no fewer that four D-redactions nor some of his attributions of material (that Exod. 32.15-16 is E, for instance, or that Exod. 33.7-11 is P[S]).

things to come (thus the connection with the break-up of the monarchy in 1 Kgs 12). Deuteronomy, by contrast, is concerned with more limited purposes: to introduce, and to justify the introduction of, another law-code (Deut. 12–26). Once one can see that Deuteronomy 1–4 (11) is not the introduction to DtrH, one is freed to observe the more limited function of these chapters.

Further, the material in Deuteronomy in 1.6-41 and 9.7–10.11 seems almost entirely self-consistent.[26] This consistency resides not merely in language, but, more crucially, in matters of place, time and institution, in particular, the itinerary, chronology and associated events on the journey from the mountain to Kadesh. The question of the unitary or composite character of these chapters of Deuteronomy is thus quiescent as far as this inquiry is concerned. Deuteronomy 9.9–10.11 provides material that lends incident to Deut. 1.6-46 and can be intercalated within it.

What can be demonstrated is that, yet once again, the 'reminiscence' in Deuteronomy enables a coherent pre-P narrative to be recreated in Exodus 32–34. It is by this means that the transpositions and adjustments of the final P-edition of Exodus 32–34 can also be identified and appreciated.

---

26 Only 10.6-7 cannot be reconciled, as discussed at the end of Chapter 11 above (pp. 260-61).

Part IV

THE VIEW BEYOND

Chapter 13

SOLOMON'S PRAYER (2 CHRONICLES 6):
IS INTENTIONALISM SUCH A FALLACY?*

This chapter is written with an uneasy mind and a troubled consciousness. 'Intention' is a term that I find natural to use in pursuit of the
meaning of a biblical text.[1] Yet, I think it is fair to say, there is a widespread impression, at least, that the search for the intention of the
biblical writers is now an outmoded and, indeed, intrinsically suspect
goal in biblical study. This has been focused in general consciousness
by Wimsatt and Beardsley in their identification of the 'intentional fallacy';[2] recent attempts to rehabilitate intentionalism, as by B.S. Childs
in his canonical approach to biblical interpretation, have by no means
won unqualified support.[3] Against the background of debate about
intention in the past decades, is one right to have such an uneasy mind
if one keeps on using the term?

This paper is divided into two sections: section I discusses some general questions; section II considers the matter from the perspective of a
practical example.

I

A recent succinct statement of options, which I take to be typical of
current opinion, is provided by M.I. Wallace. He defines intentionalism
(following Ricoeur) as follows:

*   Originally published in *ST* 47 (1993), pp. 119-33.
    1.   The following reflections are stimulated by a deprecating remark by a col-
league at the heading of the last chapter ('Matters Theological: The Pervasive
Intention')—which was indeed intended to be mildly provocative—in my *Exodus*.
    2.   W.K. Wimsatt and M.C. Beardsley, 'The Intentional Fallacy', repr. in
D. Lodge, *20th Century Literary Criticism* (London: Longmans, 1972), pp. 334-45.
    3.   The merit of Childs's work is recognized by the widespread debate that it
has provoked. For recent discussion, including that of Childs's 'canonical intention',

[T]he author's stated or uncovered intention in writing a text is considered to be the primary criterion for any valid interpretation.

On that he comments:

As works of public discourse, texts are not private extensions of an author's interior life; they are not controlled by the determinate intentions of their authors...What the text means is not equivalent to what the author intended it to mean; hence the question concerning how best to uncover and discern the author's intentions...is beside the point. The point is to interpret the text, not the author, and let the text say something to the reader above and beyond what the author might have intended it to say.[4]

This is contrasted with a dictum of E.D. Hirsch:

All valid interpretation of every sort is founded on the re-cognition of what an author meant.[5]

On that choice I find myself instinctively siding with Hirsch.[6] By 'intention' I mean what the person or persons responsible for the production of the text intended to communicate to the reader through the medium of the written word. The text is referential to theological matters beyond itself. The text has a given sense deliberately and purposefully designed and imparted to it by the original writers. When I read, I am in touch with a rational mind and it is the thought-processes of that

see, e.g., M.G. Brett, *Biblical Criticism in Crisis?* (Cambridge: Cambridge University Press, 1991), esp. pp. 116, 179 n. 14.

4.   M.I. Wallace, *The Second Naiveté: Barth, Ricoeur, and the New Yale Theology* (Studies in American Biblical Hermeneutics, 6; Macon, GA: Mercer University Press, 1990), p. 11. Cf. Wimsatt and Beardsley: 'The poem is not the critic's own and not the author's (it is detached from the author at birth and goes about the world beyond his power to intend about it or control it). The poem belongs to the public. It is embodied in language, the peculiar possession of the public, and it is about the human being, an object of public knowledge' ('Intentional Fallacy', p. 335).

5.   Wallace, *Second Naiveté*, p. 34 n. 21.

6.   It is to be noted that what Wallace says goes considerably further than Wimsatt and Beardsley: while the former talks of 'texts' the latter are speaking specifically about poetry, which they contrast with 'practical messages, which are successful if and only if we correctly infer the intention'. Even if 'practical messages' are themselves the only evidence for what the author was trying to say, they are rational discourses reflecting rational processes: even the words of a poem 'come out of a head, not out of a hat', as they acknowledge. As literary critics, their concern is with 'success as a work of literary art', with 'the worth of the poet's performance' ('Intentional Fallacy', pp. 334-35).

rational mind in producing this text in order to communicate theological belief that I am seeking to reconstruct.

Let me offer an analogy. A number of years ago I was involved in a little epigraphical puzzle—deciphering the shipbuilder's signs on the timbers of a Punic warship found off the coast near Marsala, Sicily.[7] In the attempt to understand the signs there was an intense excitement of reaching across the millennia to reconstruct the thought-processes of an intelligent human being, indeed a highly skilled craftsman, in connection with the construction of a ship. The situation of biblical interpreters is analogous, I think: they too are involved in the attempt to reach across the millennia and reconstruct the rational thought-processes involved in the production of the biblical text. The excitement of encounter with the thought of a rational mind through the medium of writing should surely not be denied the biblical commentator in attempting to understand the rationale of a biblical text. I find the pessimism about reconstructing such intention overdrawn.

It is not my intention to criticize *seriatim* the arguments of Wimsatt and Beardsley about intention; I wish, rather, to focus on a specific biblical text as a practical example. Only a couple of points may be taken up where there seem to be continuing echoes of Wimsatt and Beardsley's work in biblical scholarship: (1) a literary work as a public document; and (2) the question of the growth of meaning of words.

1. The fact that a biblical document has passed through a long transmission history—which I do not dispute—may seem to confirm the public character of that document. There can hardly be said to be *an* author with a coherent point of view; there seems to be a multiplicity of competing voices, no one of which is heard with such clarity as to make it quite unambiguous what it intended. This may heighten the impression that, since no primary intention is recoverable, one reading is as good as another: the authorial intention is—to use the jargon—a readerly construction;[8] reader response rather than authorial intention is

---

7.   W. Johnstone, 'The Signs', in H. Frost (ed.), *The Marsala Punic Ship* (Notizie degli Scavi 1976, 30, Supplement; Rome: Accademia dei Lincei, 1981), pp. 191-240; also W. Johnstone, 'The Epigraphy of the Marsala Punic Ship: New Phoenician Letter-forms and Words', in P. Bartoloni *et al.*, *Atti del I Congresso Internazionale di Studi Fenici e Punici*, III (Rome: Consiglio Nazionale delle Ricerche, 1983), pp. 909-17.

8.   The phrase was used by H. Pyper in the discussion on his paper 'The Implications of Biblical Parody: Texts and Readers "Beside Themselves" ' (Society for

the appropriate avenue of approach to interpretation.

J. Barton in a recent paper gives an extreme example—without, it should be said, committing himself to it—of what one might call readerly construction over against authorial intention.[9] Taking the phenomenon of Q^{e}re and K^{e}tib, Barton explores the possibility that for the Massoretes the traditional text was frequently unintelligible, just so many blobs of ink on the paper. As traditional text it had to be taken with ultimate seriousness but the question of meaning was a matter of the Massoretes' reading. The Q^{e}re is their reading of the text, whatever the original intended to say (indeed, despite the fact that in these cases the original is unrecoverable or makes little or no sense at all).

But is this not to elevate the occasional problem at the expense of the general intelligibility of the whole? The Q^{e}re and K^{e}tib system is extremely peripheral, precisely marginal, one might say: the overwhelming majority of the text was transmitted by the Massoretes unannotated, one must assume because the traditional text made sense to them as it stood. In the vast majority of cases the sense they perceived was the sense transmitted to them, not the sense they imposed on the text.

Indeed, the fact that there is no author in the sense of the recoverability of a named individual but a reinterpreted tradition assented to by the traditionists and consented to by the receiving community may actually serve to constrain the limits of meaning. The text has indeed grown by compilation but it has been promulgated to impart a normative interpretation. The public character of the biblical text is that it is a corporately produced document with a corporately shared interpretation. The intention is thereby not less but more—it is a shared intention. It represents deliberate reshaping of Scripture to produce more Scripture. Current criticism of intentionalism seems to me to pass too quickly from the admittedly unrecoverable 'what the author meant to say' to the arena of public debate about a document with a long history of reception. The narrow channel of tradition seems to me to add definition to the intended meaning of the text and to constrain the freedom of the interpreter. It was the redactors' intention to promulgate authoritative Scripture with an agreed public meaning and to command

Old Testament Study; London, 6 January 1993).

9. 'Canon and Meaning in Judaism and Christianity', Faculty of Arts and Divinity Lecture, University of Aberdeen, 8 March 1993.

assent. It has indeed an openness to the future; but that future orientation does not mean relativity:[10] its aim is to constrain the interpreter
within the channel of its intention. Its future orientation is eschatological: it is not designed to be received in our terms but as the fulfilment
of its own promise; the future is delineated in terms of its own dogmat-
ically rendered past.

The point may be further illustrated in considering inductive and
deductive methods of interpretation. In the interpretation of a specific
text it is possible to approach the question of meaning inductively. One
is patiently submissive to a text, obediently inferring the meaning it
intends us to elicit, allowing it to impose upon us the readers its own
pattern of meaning, as it suggests its own criteria of understanding and
interpretation. It is, of course, also possible to approach the text deduc-
tively. One may bring to the text some prior understanding, some
heuristic questions. The two approaches are illustrated in the rather
brilliant work of D.J.A. Clines, for example, in his commentary on
Job.[11] In the introduction he raises the possibility of feminist, vegetar-
ian, materialist and Christian readings of the book. These, it seems to
me, are deductive, hermeneutical, questions: one brings to the text
one's own agenda—what does the text say about such and such a contemporary issue in which I am interested, for example, environmental
questions? Contrast with that section of the introduction Clines's work
in the body of his commentary: there he is concerned with traditional
exegetical issues. That is, he aims to establish the best meaning of the
text, the meaning that seems most likely, given a whole range of evidence, textual and linguistic. The two approaches need not cancel one
another out but it is space for the inductive for which I am arguing.
When one asks what the Bible says about such and such an issue, then
the interpreter is master and the reasoning is deductive from an exter-
nally applied hermeneutical question. But when one seeks to express
what the Bible says in its own terms, then one is obliged to proceed in
an inductive manner, with internally derived exegetical principles.

When one asks exegetically about the meaning of a text one is, I
submit, wholly dependent on the text itself and in the reading of the
text itself one is in contact with a rational mind that seeks to make

10. Contra the new E.D. Hirsch acclaimed by Brett, *Biblical Criticism*, pp. 24-
25, 124.

11. *Job 1–20* (WBC, 17; Waco, TX: Word Books, 1989).

prescriptive contact with us across the centuries, which seeks to circumscribe, constrain and delimit our understanding. We bring no data; we supply no systems. Our task is the objective description of the phenomena that are there, with completeness and accuracy. Exegesis is a matter of competence, not of preference.

2. A particular development of the argument from the public meaning of a text is Wimsatt and Beardsley's argument from the developing meaning of words. In *Literary Criticism: A Short History*,[12] Wimsatt and his other colleague Brooks cite the following two views, which to a degree express the opposing views in biblical interpretation:

> The original meaning of a word in a great poem is the only one worth attending to. However delightful the meaning arising out of new verbal connotations, such meaning is irrelevant to the author's poem. He must stand by his poem as he meant it (Geoffrey Tillotson).

Contrast:

> One can no more bind within the limits of the author's intention the interactions with new minds of a play or poem that lives on centuries after his death, than one can restrict within its parents' understanding the interrelations of the child that goes forth from their bodies to live its own life in the world (Maude Bodkin).

Wimsatt and Brooks comment:

> Thus, Miss Bodkin, refusing to allow the 'author's intention' to tyrannize over the meaning of the work, recognizes the possibility of a growth of meaning in the constituent elements of a work and therefore a possible development in the meaning of the work itself (p. 715).

Change in sensibility, even in the meaning of words, so the argument goes, opens up new possibilities of meaning unsuspected by the original author.[13] It seems to me that the fact that we are not native speakers of biblical Hebrew conclusively denies us this freedom. A dead, sacred language permits no possibility of such growth and when it takes place, as in the creative philology of the NEB or of Dahood's commentary on Psalms, it is quickly discarded. In translating one naturally assumes that one is to capture the intention of the original. The single most fundamental criterion in judging the excellence of an English version is its

12. London: RKP, 1957, p. 546.

13. Cf. Wimsatt and Beardsley, 'the history of words *after* a poem is written may contribute meanings which if relevant to the original pattern should not be ruled out by a scruple about intention' ('Intentional Fallacy', p. 345 n. 7).

faithfulness to the original, however 'dynamically equivalent' that rendering may be. And exegesis is an extension of translation.

The point seems to me to be well put in unselfconsciously 'common sense' terms by J.W. Wevers in connection with the LXX of Exodus.[14] His appraisal of the quality of the LXX as a translation focuses entirely naturally on the success of the translators in capturing the intention of the original:

> Chapter 25 is an adequate rendering of 𝔐 with only a few departures from the *intent* of the parent text...The translator sought to put the *intent* of his parent Hebrew text into Greek.[15]

Wevers couples the rendering of intention with the point just made about the constraints on interpretation imposed by canonical Scripture:

> I find it difficult to conceive of the Alexandrian community accepting a translation as a canonical text that was illogical, confused and inconsistent. Admittedly, they were not instructed in modern linguistics—but one ought to...presuppose that they knew what they were doing and were aware of rendering normative Hebrew texts with a normative Greek one.[16]

One might add that when attempts are made to modernize the biblical text in favour of some contemporary concern the results are not always happy in literary terms (e.g. NRSV's attempts at inclusive language).

II

It is not my purpose to add yet another theoretical discussion to the many highly competent studies of this question that have been made.[17]

---

14. *Text History of the Greek Exodus* (Mitteilungen des Septuaginta-Unternehmens, 21; Abhandlungen der Akademie der Wissenschaften in Göttingen, Philologisch-Historische Klasse, 3.192; Göttingen: Vandenhoeck & Ruprecht, 1992), my emphasis.

15. Wevers, *Text History*, pp. 121, 125.

16. Wevers, *Text History*, p. 119.

17. E.g. for setting the issue in the context of modern critical theory, Barton, *Reading the Old Testament*; for specific discussion of the issue, N. Watson, 'Authorial Intention: Suspect Concept for Biblical Scholars', *AusBR* 35 (1987), pp. 6-13; *idem*, 'Reception Theory and Biblical Exegesis', *AusBR* 36 (1988), pp. 45-56; W.J. Abraham, 'Intentions and the Logic of Interpretation', *Asbury Theological Journal* 43 (1988), pp. 11-25.

Rather, I wish to defend pragmatically, by the consideration of a specific text, the proposition that something recognizable as the intention of the writers to shape the text in order to give it referential meaning is present and recoverable in the texts of the Hebrew Bible and that its recovery is essential for the understanding of the theological system within which they operate. Constraints are placed on the interpreter by the material itself. These constraints are of such an intellectual character that they can legitimately be described as expressing the intention of those responsible for the production of the text. The text I have chosen—for no better reason than that it is one that I have recently been working on—is 2 Chronicles 6, Solomon's prayer at the dedication of the Temple.

The great advantage of Chronicles is its unreadability. Nobody in their right mind would read Chronicles for pleasure: it is for *midrash*. It is difficult to approach such an unwieldy work with a prior opinion about what it is about. But a host of features suggests that there is before us in the Chronicler (C)'s work not just ink blobs on the paper, a K^{e}tib, of which we have to make what sense we can, our Q^{e}re, but that there is deliberate, inherent design, an intention that it is our task to reconstruct inductively. What else could one call these elements of deliberate design if not the intention of those responsible for framing it? It was their intention that we should appreciate their work and profit from it. There are two main features which I shall comment on: matters of outward form—the arrangement of the material—which display an organizing intelligence; and features of the message which display entirely unexpected elements which that intelligence wishes to communicate.

One may begin at the obvious level of the parallels between C and Kings. C is a masterful manipulator of his underlying Kings source. His radical reformulation of his underlying text needs no belabouring. 1 Kings 1–11 has 434 verses mostly on Solomon; 2 Chronicles 1–9 has only 201. While something like 167 of these are derived from 1 Kings, even these he abbreviates, amplifies, rearranges, modifies. It is probable that he even quotes the earlier source in order to provide a correction. This, I think, is clear in 2 Chron. 6.12-13. The second half of v. 13 repeats almost word for word v. 12 (= 1 Kgs 8.22) but is a virtual commentary on, indeed correction of, it:

> [12] he stood before the altar of the LORD in the presence of all the *qahal* of Israel…[13b]—rather, he stood on it [the platform that he had made in

the concourse outside the inner court where the altar was] and fell on his knees in the presence of all the *qahal* of Israel and spread out his hands.[18]

This is not an isolated occurrence: the same is to be observed in 2 Chron. 7.1 and 8.12. These, like the other modifications, are the high contrivance of a desk-bound commentator with a written text in front of him.

Do these modifications have a rationale? I do not think that the rationale is far to seek. These modifications have the effect of throwing Solomon's prayer at the dedication of the Temple into the centre of his presentation of the reign of Solomon, as the following diagram makes clear:

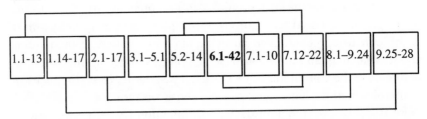

The inner and outer elements framing Solomon's prayer in ch. 6 show quite unambiguous repetitions: 1.14-17, on Solomon's status in Jerusalem, his military might, his prosperity and commercial acumen, has been brought forward and repeated from 9.25-28, its equivalent place in 1 Kgs 10.26-29; an equally unambiguous repetition is 7.1-3, 6 on the sacrifice of dedication which resumes 5.6, 13, 14. Other framework elements show strong interconnections: the relations with Huram of Tyre (2.1-17) is matched by 8.1–9.24, the relations with the nations of the earth including Huram.

The reason for thus throwing the prayer at the dedication of the Temple into central prominence is surely relatively clear. The Temple is the central focus of the whole of C's presentation of Solomon's reign. It provides the temporal framework of the reign.[19] The reign is

18. In the urgency of his correction the last word of the parent text of 1 Kgs 8.22, 'heavenwards', has been broken off in v. 12 and is only brought in at the end of the resumption in v. 13.

19. Thus one need not overpress the evidence to produce an over-neat system in the above diagram: the specifications of the Temple in 3.1–5.1 are too generally significant for the whole section to be reduced to a mere matching structural block.

divided into 2 equal parts of 20 years. The building dominates the first 20 years (chs. 1–7; in 1 Kings it is implied that the Temple begun in year 4 was finished in year 11); the remainder of Solomon's reign is dated to the 20 years after the completion of the Temple (8.1). Thus Solomon's prayer at the dedication of this Temple provides the rationale of the whole reign.

One may draw out just a few features. To set the prayer in context we have to look first a little wider. Perhaps the most telling statement by C in the immediate vicinity is 3.1, where the Temple is given its location. This is not done chronologically as in the famous parallel passage in 1 Kings 6 (the Temple was founded 480 years after the exodus) but topographically: the Temple was founded on Mount Moriah at the site where the LORD appeared to David at the threshing floor of Ornan. That says it all. By the mention of Moriah, David and Solomon's actions are related to Abraham. It is in Abraham that the definitive restart for human history is announced in the argument of C in 1 Chron. 1.27.[20] As it was on Moriah that the archetypal substitutionary sacrifice was provided—the ram caught in the thicket for Isaac—so on Moriah for David, the designated agent through whom God's purpose for humanity was to be realized, atonement was to be offered at the place where the consequences of David's guilt were neutralized—at the place where not only the site but the materials for the burnt-offering were provided by Ornan the representative of the nations of the world (1 Chron. 21).

Solomon's prayer resumes these themes. The main body of the prayer is the petition in vv. 14-42. C in fact provides very few modifications of the parent text in 1 Kings 8, but these modifications are highly significant: vv. 40-42 are mostly C's addition (from a variety of sources, of course, especially Num. 10.33-36 and Ps. 132). The section is thus carefully structured. There is a hymnic opening in vv. 14-15. The petition proper contains seven sections (vv. 22-39). These are surrounded by a double framework, marked by the fourfold repetition of *(wᵉ)'attâ*, '(And) now...'

The chronological notes in 1.18; 7.11, also omitted from the diagram, which again integrate the whole presentation, equally relate all events in the first 20 years of Solomon's reign to the building of the Temple.

20. See Chapter 4.

v. 16 And now, fulfil for your servant David my father what you promised to him
v. 17 And now ... let your promise which you gave to your servant David be confirmed

v. 22 If anyone sins	v. 24 And if your people are smitten	v. 26 When the heavens are re-strained	v. 28 When there is a famine	v. 32 And also unto the foreigner	v. 34 When your people go to war	v. 36 When they sin against you

v. 40 Now, O my God, let your eyes be open ... to the prayer of this sanctuary
v. 41 And now, arise, O LORD God, to your rest; you and your mighty ark. Let your priests, O LORD God, be clothed in salvation, And let your loyal people rejoice in well-being. v. 42 O LORD God, do not reject the face of your anointed ones ...

Once again, deliberate design subserving intended purpose is plain to see. God's purpose on C's perception is the realization of harmony on earth as intended in Adam, through the intermediacy of his people Israel under the agency of his anointed of the house of David. Peace on earth is represented by the laying-up of the ark in the Temple: that which had been the symbol of the invincibility of YHWH on the field of battle has now entered its place of rest. As C has been concerned to portray to this point, all the nations of the world are at peace with Israel and have brought their tokens of recognition of the role of the Davidic house and of the status of Jerusalem.[21]

The threats to this peace through human folly are recognized. It is at once evident how relevant all these petitions are to C's central theme. Most of them are pleas for mercy arising from sin and from situations, especially dispossession of the land, which are the consequences of sin. The distribution of the root 'to sin' itself in C is highly significant: it

---

21. Needless to say this is an eschatological statement, pathos being added by the addition of the phrase 'until this day', 2 Chron. 5.9, where the reference is to the ark itself, not the carrying-poles as in Kings; cf. the eschatological note in the perpetual choice of Jerusalem and David in 2 Chron. 6.6.

has occurred for the first time in 1 Chron. 21.8, 17, in David's confession of culpability in embroiling Israel in sin because of his census. It is David's sin that is instrumental in the inauguration of the whole Temple cult. Apart from the ten occurrences in this chapter and its resumption in 2 Chron. 7.14, the root 'to sin' reappears only in 2 Chron. 25.4; 28.13; 29.21, 23, 24 (2×); 33.19, all of them, except 2 Chron. 25.4, in material peculiar to C. Sin and the eradication of its consequences is what lies precisely at the centre of the rites on the day of atonement (cf. Lev. 16) and thus lies centrally in the whole of C's presentation.

One must draw attention to the ideal implied: the priests, the ministers of atonement are mentioned for blessing, but that is not the ultimate aim of the petition. Atonement is made by the priests for Israel. The true goal is that God's people will enjoy well-being in God's own land. Beyond that even further is the petition that God's agent on earth, the Davidic king, will remain in perfect harmony with his divine king. The twin foci of C's work not least in 2 Chronicles 1–7 are altar and ark; there is a ceremonial way, flanked by ten basins in the court and ten lampstands and ten tables in the nave, which leads from the altar at the point of entry into the inner court to the ark in the holy of holies (2 Chron. 4.6-8): atonement at the altar is only preliminary to the affirmations of the kingship of God.

Many points of detail would call for attention—for example, the petitions envisage a progressively worsening situation for Israel. In the first two, prayer is possible within the Temple itself, beginning from in front of the very altar. In the next two it is a matter of prayer towards the Temple: it is as though Israel, while still allowed access to Jerusalem, is debarred from the Temple itself. In the second last case, Israel seems to be debarred from Jerusalem and can only pray *towards the city and the Temple*. Last of all, Israel is in exile and can only pray *towards the land, the city and the Temple*. A notable feature, given Israel's role on behalf of the nations, is that the Gentiles too are included.

It must suffice to draw attention to the few occasions where C has diverged from his parent text in 1 Kings 8, but which point up his intention:

- v. 16: not, as in 1 Kgs 8.25, that the descendants of David in the royal house should 'walk before me' but should 'walk *in my Tôrâ*'. The whole system of revelation is in place. The

- v. 18: C adds 'Will God truly dwell with Adam on earth': the
  point of the whole presentation from 1 Chronicles 1 is
  involved in the function of the Temple. Compare the univer-
  salist addition of the conjunction 'and' in v. 29.
- v. 19: the 'today' of 1 Kgs 8.28, that is, the once-for-all day of
  dedication, is omitted. The significance of the Temple is
  eschatological and stands for all time.
- v. 22: and the following petitions (except v. 27, presumably by
  oversight; the point is confirmed by C's own material in
  2 Chron. 7.14), God is entreated to hear not statically
  'in' heaven, as in Kings, but dynamically as befits the one
  enthroned invincibly on the ark of the covenant, 'from
  heaven', the macrocosmic counterpart of the Temple.

In order to emphasize again the highly ideological character of C's
writing, let me conclude with just two further examples from the wider
context of Solomon's prayer. These again illustrate the passivity of the
interpreter, for the points C is making are, at first sight at least, entirely
unexpected. One is not aware of being other than totally submissive to
the text, struggling to suppress one's incredulity.

1. The first is the sheer effrontery of C. With incredible insouciance,
Solomon says primly, 'No wife of mine shall live in the house of David
king of Israel' (2 Chron. 8.11). Despite all we have been led to believe
from Samuel and Kings about the sexual proclivities and practices of
David and Solomon, C declares Jerusalem a sex-free zone. He includes
among his list of the building activities of Solomon not just the Temple
but the construction of a house for his wife, Pharaoh's daughter,
outside Jerusalem. This is not because she is a dangerous foreigner but
because sexual activity as such is inappropriate for the approach to God
of his consecrated personnel (cf. Exod. 19.15; 1 Sam. 21.4-5). Arising
from his ideology of holiness as the ultimate vocation of Israel, ritual
cleanness including abstinence from sex is here included in C's presentation. He does not scruple to distort his sources if it will suit his
purposes.

2. The second example concerns the atemporal character of C's
presentation, which entirely overthrows our expectations. If one may
return to the immediate framework of Solomon's prayer, the beginning
of ch. 7 resumes material from ch. 5. It is quite clear from the fractured

Hebrew at the beginning of ch. 7[22] that C intends us to envisage that all the events are taking place contemporaneously.

As was noted above, v. 2 resumes 5.14, v. 3 echoes 2 Chron. 5.13 and v. 6 corresponds to 2 Chron. 5.11-13: this resumption, symmetrically disposed around ch. 6, suggests that the whole process recounted in these chapters of installing the ark, sacrifice and prayer of dedication is being presented as one concerted event. The rather complex structure of vv. 1-4 confirms this impression:

- There are significant modifications of the Kings text. The parallels begin with the first phrase in v. 1, but then break off, not to be resumed until v. 4. (The intervening verses are radically different in the two versions. While C is concerned with the fire and the cloud, Kings recounts Solomon's blessing of the people.)
- Whereas Kings records a series of events, C describes a set of simultaneous circumstances. The first phrase makes that clear: for Kings' 'When Solomon had finished praying' (1 Kgs 8.54), C reads, 'As Solomon was finishing praying'. Similarly the last phrase, v. 4, 'while the king and all the people were sacrificing communion sacrifices before the LORD', is used by C as a conclusion (in the MT of C it marks the end of a paragraph), rather than, as in Kings, the beginning of a new phase of the narrative.
- The tenses of the verbs in the intervening material, all of which is peculiar to C, equally express simultaneous circumstances. Verse 1 breaks off from the construction of the parent text in Kings to resume: 'Now the fire had descended from the heavens...while the glory of the LORD was filling the House.' Verse 3 similarly describes continuing circumstances: 'Meantime all Israel were observing the descent of the fire and the glory of the LORD upon the House.'
- The references to the 'whole burnt-offering and the communion sacrifices' (v. 1, not in the Kings parallel) can only be to what has gone before in 2 Chron. 5.6.

22. This is not the only occasion where C's ideological intrusion into his source causes the breakdown of syntax: 2 Chron. 5.11a, where NRSV even fails to provide a sentence, is another case in point.

All of this contemporaneous presentation is presumably intended to state that the action of God is not in mere response to human initiative; rather, human action is taken up into the divine. Appropriately for the location of the atonement cult, there is a oneness in the action that is wholly expressive of the new relationship with God inaugurated in the dedication of the Temple which God himself has planned and endorsed. The contemporaneousness of the presentation reminds one of the rabbinical dictum *'ên muqdām ûmᵉ'uḥār battôrâ*, 'there is no earlier and no later in the Torah'.[23] In C's presentation we are already in eschatological time with all its possibilities of harmonious simultaneity of observation of all duties.

To sum up, let me return to the epigraphical analogy. I have no idea who the shipbuilder was who constructed the Marsala Punic ship or of what his state of mind was. Mass-production techniques indeed suggest that there was a team of shipbuilders. I have no idea where precisely it was built, though the converging evidence, for example, the ballast stones, the timbers used, the dunnage, not to say the epigraphy itself, all suggests somewhere in the central Mediterranean. But there was a ship; it had a purpose, which is entirely independent of any idea I may have, indeed it is part of the pain of archaeological research that there is but one right answer to the questions about which the material evidence is so ambiguous.

C is a work of corporate intellectual joinery. Collegially produced, it was collegially promulgated to constrain the reader's understanding. Whatever its quirkiness, the text intended to inform and instruct. It seems to me to be natural to affirm that it was intentionally produced to draw the reader into its intention. To be other than submissive in interpretation to the intention embedded in the text is not only incredible arrogance but incompetence. The task of exegesis is to expose the character of the text itself, even its highly alien character, not to short-circuit the hermeneutical process.

---

23. *B. Pes.* 6b. A similar 'timeless contemporaneity' has already been noted in Chapter 4, p. 94, in connection with C's eclectic genealogies. Matching these impossibilities of time are also impossibilities of space, e.g. the incorporation of the furnishings and utensils of the tent of meeting into the new Temple; the courts of the Temple thronged by all Israel and all the officiating clergy at the time when the centre of the inner court has been given over as one vast altar. Ideology has again taken over from physical possibility (e.g. 2 Chron. 5.2; 7.7, 22).

The purpose of this chapter has been to deliver myself from an uneasy mind and a troubled consciousness. In the light of the evidence from C, it seems to me that the opponents of intention have not made out their case. It is misguided of biblical studies to be over-impressed by a theory of interpretation that even within its sphere of origin has now been heavily qualified.[24] To return to Wallace's remark quoted at the outset, 'The point is to…let the text say something to the reader above and beyond what the author might have intended…' At the very least, one has to understand 'what the author intended' before one can consider what might be 'above and beyond'; that intention provides the framework within which the 'surplus' of meaning is to be sought.[25] In C's case that framework is so idiosyncratic that the interpreter can only be left with the consciousness of being submissive to what the text itself says, a content rationally accessible, however unexpected, that can legitimately be called the 'intention' of its editors.

24. See again D. Newton–De Molina symposium, *On Literary Intention: Critical Essays* (Edinburgh: Edinburgh University Press, 1976).

25. Even Childs's 'canonical intentionality' cannot be allowed to override the specifics of the particular text under discussion. His concern is ultimately an ecclesiastical/systematic theological one, to integrate the variety of individual texts into some kind of overall consistency. While I am not unsympathetic to that task, the primary aim of the exegete must be to do justice to the text that is the present subject of discussion within its own self-contained context. It is such obedience which sets on one side considerations of canonical consistency that is, paradoxically, one of the factors in theological creativity.

Chapter 14

JUSTIFICATION BY FAITH REVISITED*

The question of justification by faith is reopened for me—a not altogether welcome occurrence for one whose primary task is that of Heb-
raist rather than theologian—by a sequence of ideas that seem to
emerge from the Hebrew Bible. These begin with issues raised by the
Babylonian exile in Deuteronomy and the Deuteronomistic History.

One of the problems posed by the exile to Israel's theologians must
have been the sheer survival of Israel. At the heart of the Pentateuch
stand law-codes requiring the death penalty for manifold violations. A
good example is the case of the rebellious son (Deut. 21.18-21). The
status of Israel as YHWH's son is familiar to D (Deut. 14.1); it is a key
motif in Exodus 1–15. By every legal precedent, therefore, Israel as
YHWH's rebellious son ought to perish. Why this has not happened is
the question that the exilic theologian faces. Doubtless it is part of
God's transcendent otherness that he can set aside the penalty of the
law which he has himself ordained. But the D/Dtr school add two
points. (1) Largely in D, but also in the framework of the Book of the
Covenant in Exod. 20.22–23.19, they change the formulation from
standard third person of law-code to second-person address of
covenant-code: he/they has become I/Thou. (2) They add the expectation of the eschatological transformation of the human mind and will.
Deuteronomy itself is an eschatological work: it ends with Israel poised
to cross the Jordan and enter the Promised Land. But the clearest eschatological note is contained in the famous 'new covenant' passage in Jer.
31.31-34, in all probability the work of Dtr-editors. Here the eschatology is one of transformation: the law is still valid but 'in that day'
it will no longer be inscribed on stone tablets, as the Decalogue was,
but on the hearts of the people themselves, so that they all individually

*   Originally published in *ExpTim* 104 (1992), pp. 67-71.

will have an immediate, intuitive knowledge of YHWH and his commandments. A similar point is made in Deut. 30.6, where the figure of circumcision of the heart is used.

All this awakens echoes in my mind of the Christian doctrine of justification by faith. Israel has been spared, all undeserving, thanks to the gracious decision of her covenant God. The eschatological hope of Jer. 31.31-34 is well expressed in the Pauline expression that God will not only 'will' but will also 'do of his good pleasure' (Phil. 2.13). Paul uses the figure of the circumcision of the heart (Rom. 2.29).

Yet there are differences between justification in the Hebrew Bible mode and that in at least some expressions of conventional Christian belief, which prompt the revisiting of the doctrine and the posing of the question: if that is what the Hebrew Bible says—Paul's own scriptures, his *proepaggelion*, to coin the word from Rom. 1.2—what can Paul mean? The differences include the following.

1. The first point—for me, the beginning of the posing of the question—is that this justification is *without* faith on Israel's part. There is no indication in the D/Dtr-presentation that Israel is even repentant, let alone obediently trusting in the mercy of God. Indeed, in Dtr's mentor, Hosea, the repentance is on the part of God, not of Israel (Hos. 11). Over against highly subjectivized demands for personal faith as the mechanism whereby justification becomes operative in the life of the individual, familiar in conventional Christianity, the Hebrew Bible stresses the objectivity of God's grace.

2. 'Justification' is, in any case, a highly confusing term (in normal secular usage it means 'being proved right, vindicated'): the law as norm remains valid; there is no hint that Israel are declared innocent or have had innocence, let alone righteousness, imputed to them, as on some traditional formulations.[1] A much wider term is appropriate, for example, the relationship between God and his people; the clichéd rendering of 'justification' as 'right relationship' is at least more normal English and points in the correct direction.

3. The sentence is not cancelled; it is at best mitigated despite unbelief. 'Justification' preserves Israel alive but in the realized hell of the carrying-out of the curses of the covenant contained in Deut. 28.15-68. Once divine mercy has been shown, everything is not made right, as on a traditional Christian formulation such as Henry Francis Lyte's

---

1.   Cf., e.g., Calvin, *Institutes*, III, 14.11-20.

'ransom'd, heal'd, restor'd, forgiven' (against which A.N. Wilson, the formerly hailed 'Christian' novelist, has recently inveighed).

4. Restoration is an eschatological process, not an immediate cancelling of debts. It takes place beyond a pilgrimage back through the desert towards the Promised Land.

Before comparing the Pauline version of justification by faith, we must construct the Hebrew Bible model more fully.

5. 'Justification' is not the badge of an exclusive community who draw a boundary around themselves by their subjective response of faith. The Dtr theologians portray how God's dealing with his people Israel is parallel to his way of dealing with humanity at large. God's grace is even more radical; what is true in the inner circle, the model case of Israel, is true also in the wider, outer, circle for humanity as a whole: remitted capital sentence, mitigated penalty, realized hell, eschatological hope. The configuration of the narrative in Gen. 2.4*b*– 3.24, which portrays the fate of humanity as a whole, exhibits astonishingly close parallels to the fate of Israel as portrayed in D/ DtrH: law, or, rather, prohibition couched in the I/Thou form, designed like the prohibitions of the Decalogue as the safeguard of liberty, with the sanction of death (Gen. 2.16-17). When the prototypical humans disobey, the reversal is in God: the penalty is mitigated (Gen. 3.4). But part of this mitigated penalty is life under the manifold curse: they are ejected from the garden, as was Israel from the land, bearing with them their new burden of universal knowledge and moral responsibility, into the realized hell of the wilderness of this world. Then begins the long eschatological process at the centre of which Israel is placed. In the Hebrew Bible it is thus not only to the believer but to all humanity, even unknowingly and without faith, that God freely offers the process of restoration of the harmonious relationship with himself.

But this is not the last word of the Hebrew Bible on the relationship between God and humanity. The last word of the Hebrew Bible in the final edition of the Pentateuch (P) and its counterpart in Chronicles (Chr) is on the vocation of God's people within the potentially catastrophic condition within which humanity finds himself.

Like D/DtrH, Chr is an eschatological 'exilic' work. Again there is a link between the fate of Israel and the fate of the nations. Israel is set amidst the nations (1 Chron. 1): Israel's constant inclination is to revert to the nations and to suffer inroads from them, rather than to be for the nations what the nations themselves cannot be. Indeed, that is precisely where Israel has ended up—scattered among the nations of the world. But Chr ends—and thus the canon of the Hebrew Bible ends—with the words of Cyrus's edict, 'let him go up', that is, let the exiles return from the world of the nations to the land. The verb belongs to the same root as *ʿaliyyāh*, the technical term to this day for the 'immigration' of the Diaspora to the land. It is not that Chr, writing in the fourth century BCE, is unaware that, historically, in response to Cyrus's edict in 538 and subsequently, there was an 'immigration' as portrayed in Ezra–Nehemiah. But for him that political Zionism was at best a partial return. The definitive 'Return' still awaits the final consummation.

As an 'exilic' work, Chr is thus concerned with how Israel is to survive in the wilderness of this world in the in-between time of waiting for the final consummation. This final edition poses two further questions to the traditional doctrine of justification by faith:

6. The nature of atonement: As DtrH might be considered a *midrash* on the curse of the covenant in Deuteronomy 28, so Chr is a *midrash* on the curse at the end of the Holiness Code (H) in Leviticus 26. The category that both binds Chr together and relates it to Leviticus is that of *maʿal*, conventionally rendered 'unfaithfulness', but essentially 'defrauding' God of that which is his due. It is thus that Chr explains the fact that Israel is in exile. The means for dealing with *maʿal* is the atonement cult, as defined in Lev. 5.14-26. There are two aspects to atonement. First, there is the sacrifice of the guilt-offering: as in every sacrifice in the Hebrew Bible acceptance is not mechanical but depends of the grace of God himself. But, because atonement is for defrauding God of what is his due, the sacrifice is complemented by reparation, physically paying back the fraud with the addition of 20 per cent of the value.

But the payment of reparation can only be achieved in the eschaton. Israel has built up such a scale of debt that the only possible outcome is forfeiture of the land. The eschaton is portrayed in terms of the jubilee when all Israel will return to their land to live as God has intended.

7. The duty of reparation inseparably linked with atonement leads naturally to the question of the relation between 'faith' and 'works'. Chr is concerned to portray how Israel should live now in holiness during the in-between time of waiting for the final consummation. In a word, whereas Dtr is concerned with justification, Chr is concerned with sanctification. Its model is presented already in the genealogical section of the tribes of Israel in 1 Chronicles 2–8: there the Levites are

placed centrally in the midst of the people of Israel. That expresses not simply the centrality of the Levites as the tribe from whom the priests come who officate in the atonement cult. The role of the Levites is also that of teachers. H, including not only ritual laws but ethical laws including the 'golden rule', 'you shall love your neighbour as yourself' (Lev. 19.18), is doubtless a manual of their instruction. It is possible even 'in exile' to anticipate something of this end-time, to begin to realize proleptically the quality of life God intends for his people. Within the utopian vision, there is a practicable ethic.

Chr seems thus to add further qualifications of the traditional understanding of 'justification' to those noted above under Dtr. 'Works' cannot be a matter for self-righteousness, for, for a people in exile, all pretence of rectitude has been stripped away. That they live at all is due to the grace of God. But, thanks to the gracious acceptance by God as expressed through the atonement cult, they are now summoned to live a life of holiness. Personal responsibility is, thus, totally reinstated: there is an absolute requirement to make amends in material terms for the damage for which they are responsible and to live in harmony with the precepts of such codes as H. There is, thus, no polarization between 'faith' and 'works', as on traditional formulations of justification, where the impression is given that actions on the part of humanity are somehow a devaluation of the unmerited grace of God. There is a struggle even in standard textbooks to insist that this justifying faith is not itself a 'work'.[2] In the Hebrew Bible model such contortions are unnecessary.

I propose now to apply these questions that arise from the Hebrew Bible to Paul, the chief New Testament exponent of justification by faith, in order to see how far they elicit response. It is not within my competence to contribute novelties to the interpretation of the New Testament. But it may be that from this perspective added support is given to a particular way of reading the New Testament material (e.g. severely reduced subjectivity in 'faith'; irreversible consequences of actions; non-polarization of 'faith' and 'works'; affirmation of individual responsibility).

It is perhaps appropriate to begin with point 5, the relation between Israel and the nations (where, indeed, the two final 'exilic' editions of the Hebrew Bible begin, cf. Gen. 1–11, 1 Chron. 1). Paul shares with

---

2. Cf., e.g., J.A. Ziesler, *Pauline Christianity* (Oxford: Oxford University Press, 1990), pp. 84-85.

the Hebrew Bible the question of the relationship between Israel and the nations among whom they are placed. Paul, the Jew, is, after all, the 'apostle to the Gentiles' (Rom. 11.13). Galatians 2.3 personalizes the issues: Paul, on his second visit to Jerusalem, the hot-bed of the Judaizers, provocatively parades Titus, the uncircumcised Greek. The specific question is: how can the Gentiles now be affirmed as part of the people of God, given exclusive Jewish claims to that status hitherto?

As for point 1, there is a fundamental objectivity in God's grace in Paul's discussion. All initiative lies with God (cf. the passive voice in Gal. 4.9 or Phil. 3.8-9). The justification is not by human faith but by divine promise. That promise remains though all humanity proves faithless (Rom. 3.3-4; cf. 2 Tim. 2.13). God is the believer. That objectivity is focused in the act of God in Christ ('while we were yet sinners Christ died', Rom. 5.8).

As for point 2, Paul's choice of language—'justification', 'faith'—may be determined by his task as theologian. Paul may be regarded as a classic example of 'doing theology': the theologian caught between tradition (in this case, emerging post-biblical Judaism) and contemporary situation (the question of the Gentiles' status) appeals to Scripture as warrant as he attempts to resolve the tension and articulate appositely the word of God for his time. His warrant for the inclusion of the Gentiles is the figure of Abraham, the 'father of many nations'. Paul focuses the whole Abraham saga on the term 'righteousness'. But that term is shorthand for the relationship itself between God and Abraham.

The obligations of the relationship with God can be expressed in legal terms (though to regard the Torah as merely law is, as we have seen, a distortion). But with the bringing-in of the Gentiles the status of the law, written and oral, becomes a particular focus for discussion. The law is now seen to be a double problem: it has hitherto been the *basis* of self-identity for the Jews as the people of God; as such it is also a *barrier* keeping out the Gentiles. Positively, this barrier has held God's people in being until the fullness of time. But, now that all peoples are to be recognized as the people of God, the 'middle wall of partition' (Eph. 2.14) has to be dismantled, in particular, its three features that most characteristically have separated Jew from Gentile: circumcision, diet, and holy days.

But, if the law is abandoned as the basis for existence as the people of God, is there an alternative basis available for that relationship? Paul, reaching back behind Moses, appeals to Abraham: before the law was promulgated, the call and the promises came to Abraham and he responded in faith; it was that faith, awakened by God, that was accounted to him for righteousness—that gave expression to the right relationship with God. The new basis of the people of God, indeed the recovery of the basis that has always been there, is that prior basis of *faith*. This is first and foremost the objective faith of Abraham—that which has been achieved by *his* response so that all generations *are* blessed in him; he *has* become the father of many nations (Gal. 3.7-9; Rom. 4). The objectivity of the prior grace of God is, thus, continued in the objectivity of the prior faith of Abraham. The Jews by physical descent from Abraham have no choice but to belong to this community (though it is possible for the individual Jew to reject this status). But it now becomes clear that the Gentile has no choice either: Gentiles equally are the offspring of Abraham by promise and by that promise fulfilled in Christ (though they too have freedom to reject their status).[3]

On questions 3 and 4, the continuing baneful effects of past sin despite the mercy of God and the awareness of the long eschatological struggle towards restoration with many a setback may be recognized by Paul in his teaching on the 'law of sin in my members' (Rom. 7.7-25) and in his experience of the all-too-obvious failings of the early Church communities (e.g. the Church at Corinth, with its manifold problems of immorality and litigation). If there is a meagreness in the treatment at this point it is presumably because of the vivid expectation at least in the early Paul of the imminent parousia and his confidence in the perfectibility of the Christian through the work of the Spirit. He is summoning the churches proleptically to realize the eschaton in the new life of the Spirit of the resurrected Christ. Here the Hebrew Bible with its perspective on the long route to restoration has an important contribution to make. One can sympathize with Luther's transposition of Paul's moral perfectibility into the more realistic terms of *simul justus et peccator*, however much a misinterpretation of Paul that undoubtedly is.[4]

---

3.   It is a serious obstacle to understanding the objectivity of the faith of Abraham when the standard UBS edition of the Greek New Testament heads Rom. 4, 'The Example of Abraham'. This is a gross under-translation of v. 1, Abraham as '*progenitor*', and of v. 11, '*father* of all who believe'. For the universalism of this status, cf. Rom. 11.32.

4.   Cf. E.P. Sanders, *Paul* (Oxford: Oxford University Press, 1991), pp. 48-49, 68.

As for point 6, how, then, is atonement effected through Christ? Again the law is undercut by appealing behind it to Abraham. Christ, son of God, is identified as the seed of Abraham (Gal. 3.16). That which has been accomplished in Abraham is that which is now definitively accomplished in Jesus Christ as Abraham's descendant.

How so? The death of Christ on the cross is a scandal under the law (Gal. 5.11; cf. Deut. 21.22-23, 'anyone hung on a tree is under God's curse'). But this scandal becomes a positive advantage: the penalty/ curse cannot affect the 'seed of Abraham' promised before the giving of the law; the resurrection, the raising to life of the man condemned by that law—and thus God's fundamental objective statement of justification—has rendered the law invalid; those condemned/accursed by the law, that is, everybody, can find in him their hope through identification with him in his scandalous death and in his resurrection.

The life of the new people of God can, therefore, be lived only 'in' Christ (Rom. 8.1). The whole process of becoming a new creature is described in a variety of terms—for example, crucified with Christ, baptized into his death—including 'becoming Abraham's seed' (Gal. 3.29) and thus co-heirs with Christ.

7. What, then, of 'works'? It is important to note that Paul's discussion of observance of the law is part of an inner-Jewish debate between Paul the Jewish ex-Jew and his Jewish or Judaizing audience, not an argument about 'works' in general. It seems to me particularly unhelpful to extrapolate from 'salvation by the works of the Law' which Paul was condemning to 'works' in general such as are required for reparation and sanctification. This confusion, which denigrates human action, leads to a number of misrepresentations of the human condition. It ignores the fact the humanity 'driven out of the garden' has knowledge of *good* and evil: human life as it is lived by the vast majority of the human race is not a matter of total depravity; certainly it is a realized hell of potentialities for absolute evil, but it is a punishment mitigated in the mercy of God. It unnecessarily heightens the emphasis on personal faith: if all my actions are corrupt then only by my conscious commitment to Christ can I be invested with that righteousness which makes me pleasing to God.

How, then, is the end-time proleptically realized in Christ? Atonement is not the goal but the means: the end for which humanity exists is not mere reconciliation but the realization of the pattern of living which is expressive of the harmonious relationship with God. Atonement is,

indeed, the expression of the mercy and acceptance of God. But atonement also carries with it the duty of reparation for the damage for
which one is responsible (here again the Hebrew Bible model provides
necessary supplementation: one has to wait till Phlm. 19 for the verb
that the LXX uses in Lev. 5.16 to translate 'pay reparation'!). Before
and beyond atonement lies the vocation to accord God his due in every
dimension of life. This is the practical realization now in terms of contemporary experience of the summation of the end-time when God will
perfectly will and perform in accordance with his intention and
purpose.

In Pauline terms, this vocation is realized through the fruits of the
Spirit of Christ working in those who are in Christ (Gal. 3.2; Rom.
8.11). It is thus that the Law is to be fulfilled. At this point the response
of the individual is crucial: not just subjective faith, personal conviction
of unworthiness and of acceptance by God despite that unworthiness,
but trust, as a descendant of Abraham, in the reliability of God's
promises and *hupakoē*, obedient hearing. In Gal. 5.14 and Rom. 13.9-
10 the focus of life in the Spirit, that is, of sanctification, is precisely,
Lev. 19.18, the fundamental statement of H, as it is in the Gospels. Paul
recognizes the eschatological character of this life in the Spirit (Rom.
8.18-25).

Thus, in my view, E.P. Sanders is nearly right when he says Paul is
about 'getting in and staying in' the people of God.[5] But in the light of
the Hebrew Bible model a better formulation would be 'being the
people of God and realizing that status', in other words, 'becoming
what we are'.

---

5. E.g. *Paul, the Law and the Jewish People* (Philadelphia: Fortress Press,
1983), p. ix.

INDEXES

INDEX OF REFERENCES

OLD TESTAMENT

Genesis		47.27	183	1.14	221
1–11	302	49.15	84	1.15-22	241
1.1	185	50.24	43	1.15	223
1.20	223	50.25-26	21	1.16	221
1.24-26	175	50.25	218	1.18-21	158
2.2-3	176			1.21	221
2.16-17	300	Exodus		1.23-25	241
3.17	247	1–24	24, 25, 214,	2.2	221
4.25	107		224	2.5	221
4.26	82	1–15	211, 212,	2.6	221
9.5-6	133		232, 298	2.9-11	158
12.1	259	1–14	23	2.9	233
13.14-15	259	1–13	22, 217, 222,	2.11	221
14.18-20	239		224, 227,	2.12	221
15.5	130		233	2.21-22	258
15.13	75	1–6	241	2.21	258
15.16	75, 174	1–3	17	2.22	258
16.2	247	1–2	223	2.23	221
16.7	247	1	111, 241	2.24	221, 223,
17	214, 223	1.1–24.11	161, 246		228, 270
17.4-5	107	1.1–24.8	44, 213	2.25	221, 228
20.1	247	1.1–15.21	240	3–14	211
22	104	1.2-4	108	3–4	223, 230
24.4	259	1.4	223	3	23, 48, 82,
25.16	109	1.6	43		223, 225
25.18	247	1.7	223, 241	3.1–6.1	223, 228
31.44-54	165	1.8-12	241	3.1–4.18	23
33.19	21	1.8	43	3.1–4.31[6.1]	235
35	111	1.10	221, 224	3.1	156, 224,
35.23-25	108	1.11-12	223		227, 241,
38	110	1.11	75, 218, 223		246, 257
38.1-5	110	1.13-14	223, 229,	3.2	221, 237
38.3	110		241	3.3	221
38.7	110	1.13	221	3.4	221
46.23	111	1.14-15	22	3.6-10	224

Exodus (cont.)		4	223, 225, 228, 235	4.27-31	225, 227, 234
3.6-7	224			4.27-30	228
3.6	221, 233, 270	4.1-17	225	4.27	227
		4.1-9	238	4.28	221, 223, 224
3.7	221, 227, 228	4.1	221, 225, 227, 232	4.29-31	23
3.8	221, 224	4.2	24, 225, 230	4.29	227
3.9	221, 224, 237	4.4	221, 225, 230	4.30	221, 223, 224, 227
3.10	221, 224	4.5-28	157	4.31	23, 221, 225, 227, 229, 233, 234, 238, 271
3.11–4.17	234	4.5	221, 225, 247, 270		
3.11	221, 224, 233	4.8-9	225, 232		
3.12–4.30	223	4.8	223-25		
3.12	48, 210, 221, 223, 224, 226, 233, 257	4.9	221, 223, 225	4.32	248
		4.10	221, 225, 233	4.34	204
				5	24, 225, 227, 228, 237
3.13-14	224	4.11	225, 233	5.1–6.1	227
3.13	221, 224, 233	4.12	225, 233	5.1-5	225
		4.13-17	228	5.1-2	227
3.14-17	224	4.13	221, 225	5.1	210, 211, 221, 227, 247
3.14-15	23	4.14-17	227		
3.14	221, 224, 225	4.14	221, 225		
		4.15	221, 225, 233	5.2	211, 221, 225, 230
3.15	221, 270				
3.16	221	4.16	225	5.3	210, 227, 228, 230, 246
3.16-17	43	4.17	221, 223-25, 230		
3.16	227, 270				
3.17	221	4.18-20	225	5.4	228
3.18-22	43	4.18	221	5.5	228
3.18	210, 219, 224, 225, 227, 230, 238, 246, 248	4.20	225, 230	5.6-9	227
		4.21-33	24	5.6	224, 228
		4.21-23	212, 225, 226, 234, 235	5.8	227
				5.9	221, 224, 227
3.19	221, 224, 226, 233, 235	4.21	211, 221, 223, 225, 226, 233, 235	5.10-11	227
				5.10	224, 228
				5.11	221, 227
3.20	24, 211, 221, 224, 230			5.12-14	228
		4.22-23	43, 231	5.13-14	224, 228
3.21-22	224, 230	4.22	212, 225	5.13	228
3.21	44, 212, 221, 246	4.23	211, 212, 221, 224-26, 230, 233	5.15-21	228
				5.15	204, 221, 227
3.22	43, 273				
3.24	204	4.24-26	213, 226	5.16	221, 227
4–5	233	4.25	258	5.17	227

Reference	Pages
5.18	221, 224, 227, 228, 251
5.19	221, 228
5.20-21	225
5.20	228
5.21	221, 227, 228, 237
5.22–6.1	23, 225
5.22-61	228
5.22	221
5.23	227
6.1	211, 221, 224, 226-28, 235, 241
6.2–7.13	228, 229, 235
6.2-13	228
6.2	185, 229, 233, 241
6.3-8	270
6.3	221
6.4	214, 229
6.5	221, 223, 229, 233
6.6	38, 221, 229, 233, 236
6.7	221, 229, 233, 235
6.8	221, 229, 233
6.9	221, 229, 232
6.11	211, 221
6.12	233, 235
6.13-25	174
6.13	221
6.14-25	229
6.21	204
6.23	75, 190
6.26	221, 229
6.27	221
6.28-29	229
6.29–7.7	228
6.29	229, 233
6.30	228, 233
7–12	217, 219, 235
7–10	223
7	241
7.1-13	226, 228, 233
7.1	221
7.2	211, 221, 225
7.3	221, 223, 226, 232-34
7.4	221, 229, 232, 236
7.5	221, 229, 233
7.6	221, 230
7.7	228, 229
7.8-13	234
7.9-12	228
7.9	221, 223, 228, 234
7.10	221
7.11	221, 247
7.12	225, 228
7.13	226, 229, 232, 241
7.14–12.36	222
7.14–10.20	235
7.14-18	241
7.14	24, 211, 221, 226, 228-30, 234
7.15	24, 225, 228
7.16	211, 221, 223, 224, 230, 234
7.17	24, 225, 227, 229-31, 233
7.19-20	241
7.19	230, 232
7.20-21	241
7.20	221, 225, 230, 232
7.21-22	241
7.22	221, 226, 232
7.23-29	241
7.23	231, 232
7.26	211, 221, 224, 230, 233
7.27	211, 221, 226, 230, 231
7.28	221, 231
7.29	221
8	241
8.1-3	232, 241
8.1	221
8.2-3	248
8.2	221, 230
8.3	221
8.4-11	241
8.4-5	225, 231
8.4	211, 221, 230
8.5	221
8.6	227, 230
8.7	221
8.9	221
8.11-15	241
8.11	221, 226, 231-33
8.12-15	229
8.13	221
8.14	221
8.15-16	248
8.15	226, 229
8.16-18	241
8.16	211, 221, 224, 230
8.17	211, 221, 230
8.18	24, 208, 227, 229-33, 275
8.19	221, 223, 232, 233, 235
8.20	221, 241
8.22	221
8.23	210, 246
8.24-26	231
8.24-25	225
8.24	211, 221, 230, 233

Exodus (cont.)

Reference	Pages
8.25	211, 221, 230, 233
8.27	221, 226
8.28	211, 221, 230
9.1	211, 221, 223, 224, 230
9.2	211, 221, 226, 230
9.3-9	181
9.3	225
9.4	24, 208, 231, 275
9.5	221, 231
9.6	221
9.7	211, 221, 223, 226, 230, 241
9.8-12	229, 241
9.8	221, 260
9.12	226, 229, 231, 234
9.13-25	241
9.13	211, 221, 224, 228, 230
9.14-16	231
9.14	221, 227, 230, 233
9.15	221, 230, 231
9.16	221
9.17	211, 221, 230
9.18	251
9.19-21	231
9.20	221
9.21	221
9.22	230, 248, 278
9.23	225, 230
9.25	230, 232, 241
9.26-34	241
9.26	232
9.27	221, 233
9.28	211, 225, 230, 231
9.29	227, 230
9.30	221
9.31-32	231
9.34	221, 226, 232, 233
9.35	211, 221, 226, 230, 232, 241
10	241
10.1-3	24, 233, 236, 241
10.1-2	24, 223, 232, 233
10.1	221, 226, 233, 236, 241
10.2	23, 24, 221, 229, 233, 235
10.3-19	241
10.3	211, 221, 224, 226, 230, 233
10.4	211, 221, 226, 230
10.5	221, 232, 272
10.6	221
10.7	211, 221, 224, 227, 230
10.8	221, 224
10.9	210, 230
10.10	212, 221, 230
10.11	221, 224
10.12-13	225
10.12	221, 230
10.13	221, 225, 230, 236
10.14	221
10.15	221
10.17	225
10.19	77
10.20	212, 221, 226, 230, 233, 241
10.21-29	241
10.21-22	230
10.23	221
10.24	221, 228
10.26	221, 230
10.27	212, 221, 226, 230
10.28	221, 230
10.29–11.34	251
10.29	221
11–15	162
11	223
11.1-13	23
11.1-8	207, 235, 241
11.1	212, 221, 227, 230, 232, 235
11.2-3	212, 224, 230, 234
11.2	43
11.3	221, 228, 231
11.4-8	230
11.4	233
11.5	212, 231
11.6	221, 231
11.7-8	225
11.7	24, 208, 227, 230, 231, 275
11.8	221, 230-32, 234
11.9–12.28	236
11.9-10	223, 231-34, 241
11.9	221
11.10	212, 221, 226, 230, 231
12–13	17, 198, 201, 202, 208, 209, 261

Ref	Pages
12	25, 47, 80, 148, 202, 203, 205-208, 210, 211, 215, 242-44
12.1-28	207, 232, 241
12.1-14	201
12.1-13	202
12.1	203
12.2	203
12.3	203, 206, 231
12.4	201
12.5	208
12.6	203, 207
12.9	207, 232
12.10	232
12.11	207
12.12	203, 207, 212, 221, 229, 233, 236
12.13	117, 206, 221
12.14-20	202, 207
12.15	203, 207
12.16	204
12.17	221, 229, 232
12.18	203
12.19	203
12.21	207, 232
12.21(25)-27	23
12.21-28	25, 47, 202, 203, 237
12.21-27	24, 47
12.21-24	25
12.21-23(24)	25
12.22	25, 207
12.23	117, 221
12.24-27	12
12.24	232
12.25-27	24, 25
12.25-26	230
12.25	31, 207, 221
12.26-27	233
12.26	207, 221
12.27	207, 227, 271
12.28	25, 203, 221
12.29-36	24, 25, 47, 207, 234, 235, 241
12.29	25, 212, 231, 232
12.30	221, 231
12.31	221, 224, 228
12.33-34	
12.33	212, 221, 226, 230
12.34	231
12.35-36	23, 43, 224, 230
12.35	221, 231
12.36-19.2	252, 260
12.36	212, 221, 228, 231, 273
12.37-19.2	244
12.37-51	241
12.37-42	209, 236
12.37	76, 244
12.38	221
12.39	23, 221
12.40-41	75
12.41	221, 229
12.42	221
12.43-51	208
12.43-50	202, 207
12.43-49	201
12.43	203
12.47	203
12.48	204
12.50	203, 221
12.51	221, 229
13	25, 47, 80, 203, 206, 208, 212, 213, 223, 241
13.1-19	241
13.1-16	12
13.1-2	208, 211, 212
13.2	212
13.3-16	23
13.3-8	218
13.3-7	203-205, 207
13.3-4	204, 205
13.3	31, 204, 205, 221, 224, 235
13.4	204, 206, 221, 248
13.5-7	204, 205
13.5	31, 204, 206, 207, 221, 230
13.6	204-206
13.7	204-206, 221
13.9	221, 224, 235
13.11-16	211
13.11	221
13.13	212, 221, 232
13.14-16	224, 235
13.14	221
13.15	207, 212, 221, 226, 233
13.16	221
13.17-19.2	209
13.17-19	236
13.17	212, 221, 224
13.19	21, 218, 227
13.20	236, 241, 244
13.21-22	236, 237, 241
13.21	237
14	82, 238, 240, 241
14.1-15.21	17, 217
14.1-4	42, 236, 238, 241
14.2	42, 236, 244
14.4	233, 236, 237

Exodus (cont.)

14.5–15.21	236	14.31	23, 43, 225, 238	16	147, 251, 252, 255, 256, 259, 261
14.5-8	241	15–19	17		
14.5	212	15–17	20		
14.6	237	15.1-19	238	16.1-36	246, 250
14.7-9	238, 241	15.1-5	239	16.1-2	247
14.7	237	15.1	238-40	16.1	39, 147, 209, 236, 244, 250, 253
14.8-9	237	15.2	239, 247		
14.8	236, 238	15.3	224		
14.9	236, 237	15.4	239	16.2	147, 248, 250
14.10-15	237, 241	15.5	239, 240		
14.10	237, 238	15.6-17	239	16.3	250
14.11-12	238	15.6	224	16.4-5	251
14.12	224	15.7	239	16.4	248, 251, 252
14.13-14	23	15.8	238-40		
14.13	43, 237, 238	15.9	239	16.5	251
14.14	237	15.10	239	16.6	250
14.15-18	238	15.11	239	16.7-9	147
14.15	237	15.12-15	239	16.12	147, 233, 250
14.16	237, 238, 241	15.12	224		
		15.13	239	16.13-15	251
14.17	233, 236, 238, 241	15.16	224, 239	16.13-14	252
		15.17	239	16.13	252
14.18	233, 236, 238, 241	15.18	239, 240	16.14-31	147
		15.19-21	241	16.15	251
14.19-21	237, 241	15.19	240, 241	16.16-30	250
14.19	21	15.20-21	240	16.16	250, 251
14.21-22	237	15.21	43	16.18	201
14.21	236-38, 241	15.22–19.22	255	16.23	148, 251
14.22-23	238, 241	15.22–19.2	26, 45, 209, 210, 214, 240, 243, 251, 259	16.27	147
14.22	236, 240			16.28	250
14.23	237, 238			16.31	251
14.24	237, 238, 241	15.22–18.27	147	16.32-34	251
		15.22-26	26, 246, 248-50, 259	16.32	250
14.25-27	241			16.33-34	148
14.25	224, 237, 238, 241	15.22	15, 210, 246, 259	16.34	251
				16.35-36	148
14.26-27	237	15.23	244, 245	16.35	251
14.26	237, 238	15.24	147, 247, 248	17–18	210
14.27	237, 238, 241			17	178
		15.25	214, 246-49, 259	17.1–18.27	246, 255
14.28	238, 241			17.1-7	26, 47, 147, 255
14.29	237, 238, 240, 241	15.26	233, 247, 249	17.1	147, 182, 244, 255
14.30-31	23	15.27	244, 246, 250	17.2-7	245, 278
14.30	238, 241			17.2	255-57, 265
				17.3-7	256

17.3	147, 256-58	18.20	259	19.4	187, 210, 246		
17.4-7	256, 265	18.21	259				
17.5	24, 256, 257	18.22-23	260	19.5	225		
17.6	210, 249, 256, 257	18.24-25	148	19.6	150, 165, 215		
		18.25	259, 260				
17.7	209, 244-46, 248, 256, 257	18.26	148	19.7	188		
		18.27	258	19.8	189		
		18.29	259	19.9	29, 30, 33, 180, 183, 184, 225, 233, 238, 271		
17.8-16	26, 147, 255, 260	18.30	259				
		19–40	144, 148, 159, 161, 162, 166, 168, 179, 180, 193, 195-99				
17.9	147, 225, 233						
17.10	257			19.10-13	185		
17.12	257			19.10-11	210, 219		
17.13	157			19.11-16	158		
17.14	26, 257	19–34	26, 196, 223	19.11-13	19, 154, 158, 199		
17.15	257	19–24	16, 26, 45, 170, 171, 210, 271				
17.16	147, 210, 257			19.11	33, 271		
				19.12-13	33		
18	20, 26, 147, 254, 258, 266	19–20	273	19.13	33		
		19	22, 26, 158, 182, 199, 200, 210	19.14-17	158		
				19.14-16	219		
18.1-27	255			19.15-16	210		
18.1-12	147, 210, 248, 258, 266, 268, 274, 276	19.1– Num. 10.10	147	19.15	294		
		19.1–20.21	271	19.16	30, 158, 180, 181, 186		
		19.1-20.1	158				
18.1-11	258	19.1-2	38, 39, 148, 158, 182	19.17-19	158		
18.2-27	257			19.17	30, 31, 180, 181, 185, 186, 237, 271		
18.2-4	258	19.1	38, 40, 41, 147, 166, 209, 246				
18.5	147, 258						
18.6	233, 258			19.18	33, 154, 158, 180, 181, 199		
18.7	258, 260, 268	19.2-11	158				
		19.2-9	181	19.19	27, 29, 31, 158, 180, 181, 185, 186, 201		
18.8	258	19.2-3	181, 182, 185				
18.11-26	259						
18.12	147, 258	19.2	15, 38, 40, 180, 182, 244, 246, 252, 259				
18.13-27	27, 147, 214, 266, 268			19.20–20.21	184		
18.13-26	48, 209, 210, 254, 259			19.20-25	19, 32, 33, 154, 158, 185, 199		
		19.3-9	29, 182				
18.13-17	33	19.3-8(9)	158	19.20-21	181		
18.13	33, 148	19.3-8	27, 31, 45	19.20	33, 180, 184, 189		
18.14	259	19.3	180, 183, 186, 187, 257				
18.15	33, 258			19.21	180, 184		
18.16	259			19.22	180, 184		
18.18	33, 259, 260	19.4-8	180, 182, 184				
18.19	241						

Exodus (cont.)
19.23   180, 181,
         184, 185
19.24   180, 184-86
19.25–20.1 184
19.25   33, 180, 181,
         184-86
20–24   47
20–23   58, 162, 173
20   17, 22, 173,
         178-80, 184,
         187, 200,
         201, 210
20.1–23.33 31
20.1–23.19 156
20.1-17 27, 148, 158,
         172, 183,
         199
20.1   33, 184, 186,
         188
20.2-17 168, 173,
         184, 185,
         197, 218
20.2   204, 233,
         271
20.3-6   176
20.3   174
20.4-6   174
20.4   174, 177
20.5-6   19
20.5   174, 177,
         227, 233,
         271
20.6   174, 271
20.8   219
20.10   175
20.11   176, 178,
         196
20.12   219
20.16   176
20.17   176
20.18-22 34
20.18-21 27, 32, 47,
         158, 185
20.18-19 185, 186
20.18   27, 29, 30,
         186

20.19   30, 184-86,
         189
20.20-21 184-86
20.20   30, 31, 33,
         180, 185,
         249, 259
20.21   29, 30, 180,
         181, 185
20.22–23.33 14, 30, 153,
         187, 249,
         272
20.22–23.19 298
20.22-26 45
20.22   27, 30-33,
         45, 180, 182,
         183, 187,
         188
20.23–23.19 153, 171
20.23-26 159
20.23   174, 180,
         187, 188
20.24-26 180
21.1-11 159
21.1-3   251
21.1   45, 46, 180,
         188
21.2–23.33 180
21.12-17 159
21.15   179
21.17   179
21.18–22.16 159
22.1–23.19 199
22.17-19 159
22.19   46
22.20–23.33 46
22.20–23.19 159
22.26   233, 271
22.30   81, 180, 187,
         188
23   152
23.1   176
23.12-19 19, 155, 188,
         192, 272
23.12   175, 179
23.13   156, 180,
         187, 188
23.14-19 156
23.14-17 201

23.15   155, 205
23.20-33 11, 19, 21,
         152, 153,
         156, 157,
         199, 217,
         272
23.20   153, 233,
         237
23.21-22 225
23.21   153, 188
23.23-33 163
23.23   153, 204
23.25   247
23.27   239
23.28-29 153
23.28   21
23.31   153
23.32   153
23.33   153
24   20, 22, 26,
         149, 150,
         157, 158,
         181, 199,
         214, 273
24.1-11 158, 188
24.1-9   189, 254
24.1-2   27, 33, 158,
         188, 189,
         199
24.1   27, 150, 156,
         180, 185,
         186
24.2   165, 180,
         185
24.3-8   27, 31, 45,
         46, 158, 188,
         219, 264,
         272, 273
24.3-7   189
24.3-4   158, 193,
         197
24.3   29, 180, 188,
         189, 195
24.4   171, 180,
         181, 188,
         189, 210,
         249
24.5-8   158

Reference	Pages
24.5	27, 158, 180, 181, 188, 189
24.6-8	180, 188
24.6	189
24.7	159
24.8	191, 211
24.9-11	27, 158, 165, 180, 185, 188, 189, 199
24.9	27, 150, 156
24.11	153, 186, 187, 254, 258, 259
24.12-18	33, 153, 156, 168, 172, 218, 278
24.12-15	46
24.12-13	157
24.12	46, 153, 156, 171, 172, 192, 199, 201, 211, 242
24.13	46, 156
24.14-18	157
24.14-17	199
24.14	26, 33, 156, 257, 259
24.15-18	33, 156
24.15	33
24.18	150, 153, 157, 192, 199, 242, 264
25–31	101, 148, 150
25	200
25.1–31.17	153, 199, 277
25.9	233
25.10-22	154, 200, 268
28.1	190
29.20-21	189
29.46	229, 233, 250
30	128, 134, 135
30.7	128, 133, 140
30.11-16	128, 133, 135
30.12	17
31–34	26, 149, 257
31.2	233
31.6	229, 233
31.13	203
31.14	153, 156, 168
31.18–34.35	22, 45
31.18–34.29	17, 218
31.18–34.28	170
31.18–34.28	46, 148, 153, 157, 171, 192, 193, 199, 201, 242, 264, 278
31.18	20, 33, 46, 150, 199, 263, 264, 280
32–34	15
32–33	26, 150, 157, 174, 193, 199, 225, 228, 271, 278
32	157
32.1-15	278
32.1-6	157
32.1-4	273
32.2-6	21
32.2-3	157
32.2	154, 199, 217, 272
32.4	155, 166
32.5	242
32.7-20	33, 34, 44
32.7-14	199, 278
32.7-10	153, 157
32.7	153, 154
32.8	272
32.9	153, 157, 273
32.10-12	273
32.10	44, 153, 157
32.11-14	34, 45, 153, 269, 271, 276
32.11-13	44, 269
32.11	278
32.12-13	278
32.13	157, 270, 278
32.15-19	153
32.15-16	279
32.15	153, 172, 199, 278
32.16-20	157
32.16	157
32.17-19	273
32.18	233
32.19	153, 201, 278
32.20	153, 154, 157, 168, 199, 278
32.21-24	157
32.25-30	157
32.25-29	168, 199, 257, 259
32.26-29	244
32.30–34.29	263, 276
32.30–33.23	153
32.30–33.6	268
32.30-35	34, 166, 269, 277
32.30-34	157, 276
32.30	157, 264
32.31-35	271
32.31-32	269
32.31	191, 269
32.32-33	269
32.33	269, 279
32.34-35	270
32.34	21, 150, 157, 263, 270, 271, 278
32.35	157, 199, 269

Exodus (cont.)

Reference	Pages
33–34	33, 258
33	33
33.1-17	157
33.1-6	266, 272, 276
33.1-3	270
33.1	263, 270-72, 274
33.2	237, 272, 274
33.3-6	273
33.3-5	273
33.3	157, 272, 275
33.4	21, 273
33.5	157, 273
33.7-11	165, 166, 258, 266-68, 271, 274, 276, 279
33.7	267
33.9-10	237
33.9	267
33.10-27	275
33.10	255, 267
33.11	32, 275, 277
33.12–34.29	268
33.12-23	266, 269, 271, 274, 277
33.12-16	275
33.12	274, 275
33.13-16	275, 276
33.13	255, 274, 275
33.14-16	275
33.14	274
33.16	24, 231, 233, 274, 275
33.17-23	275
33.17	274, 275
33.18-19	157
33.18	199, 274
33.19	157, 233, 274
33.20-23	157, 199
33.20	275
34	19, 154, 157, 181, 190, 192, 193, 200, 263, 272
34.1-29	190
34.1-28	190, 264, 271
34.1-6	268
34.1-4	47, 200, 218, 271, 276
34.1-3	242
34.1	153, 154, 157, 168-70, 172, 180, 191, 192, 199, 201, 268, 278
34.2-3	157, 158, 169
34.2	180, 181, 199, 201
34.3	199
34.4-28	278
34.4-4	199
34.4	153, 157, 169, 170, 174, 180, 181, 189, 191, 192, 199, 201, 264
34.5-28	271
34.5-27	279
34.5-26	171
34.5-9	271, 274, 276, 277
34.5-8	19
34.5	271, 274
34.6-7	271
34.6	19, 201, 274
34.7	19, 177, 269, 271
34.8	47, 201, 227, 271
34.9	180, 181, 255, 263, 268, 272-75, 277
34.10-28	276
34.10-27	271, 275
34.10-26	201
34.10	180, 181, 190, 191, 201, 233, 271
34.11-27(28)	21
34.11-16	19
34.11-13	273
34.11	180, 181, 191, 193, 233, 272
34.12-26	173, 180, 192
34.12-16	181
34.12	191-93
34.13	156, 192
34.14	19, 192, 272
34.15	156, 192
34.16	272
34.17-27	19
34.17-26	155, 156, 172, 272
34.17	155, 174, 181, 191, 192, 272
34.18-26	155, 171, 181, 192
34.18-25	188
34.18-24	201
34.18	156, 205, 275
34.19-24	193
34.19-20	155
34.19	275
34.20-23	276
34.20	155, 272
34.21	179
34.23	155
34.24	272
34.27-28	181, 188, 189, 193, 197, 218

34.27	169, 171, 180, 181, 191, 192, 271	5.15	96, 100, 101	23.36	206
		5.16	306	23.37	251
		5.17	100, 119	23.42-43	81
		5.18	99	24.10-23	250
34.28	36, 37, 148, 150, 153, 169-72, 180, 191, 192, 199, 201, 272, 278	5.21-24	100	24.11	111
		5.21	96, 100	25.6-7	175
		5.24	132	25.8-24	125
		5.26	135	25.9	126
		7.1-7	99, 102	25.13	126
		7.20	203	25.22	204
34.29–40.38	199	8.5	250	25.23	126
34.29-35	156, 157, 277	8.23-24	189	25.43-53	223
		8.30	189	25.43	229
34.29	156, 180, 190, 266-68, 271, 274, 276	9	190	25.46	229
		9.1	190	25.53	229
		9.6	250	26	104, 105, 119, 301
		9.23-24	190		
34.30	156	9.23	250	26.1	174, 187
34.31	156	9.24	103	26.5	250
34.32	156	10.1-5	190	26.6-7	175
35–40	101, 148	10.1-3	110	26.9	229
35.1–40.38	153, 277	10.11	172	26.34-35	120
35.25-29	154	14.14-25	189	26.34	120
35.34	172	14.57	172	26.40	96, 104, 119
36.13	147	16	81, 99, 293	26.41	119
37.1-9	154, 200, 268	16.13	251	26.42	270
		16.21	251	26.43	120
38.25-26	135	17–26	150		
40.17	264	18.22	132	*Numbers*	
40.34-35	274	19.4	174, 187	1.2	128
40.34	156	19.9	252	1.16	165
		19.18	302, 306	2	109
Leviticus		19.36	161	3.2-4	190
1.1	184, 186	20.1-2	182, 183	3.12-13	81
4	158	20.13	132	3.31	269
4.1–5.13	99	20.23-26	159	4	146
4.1	185	21.1-11	159	4.5-15	269
4.3	132	21.1	182, 183	4.23	206
4.27-35	99	21.12-17	159	5.2	100
5	100, 115, 150, 270	21.18–22.16	159	5.6	96
		22.1-16	119	5.12	96
5.14-26	99, 115, 117, 135, 149, 301	22.14-16	135	5.24	154
		22.16	132	5.27	96, 100
		22.17-19	159	5.30	104
5.14-16	119	22.20–23.19	159	7	109
5.15-26	102, 104, 113	23.5	201	8.14-22	81
		23.10-15	251	9.1-14	201
		23.26-32	99	10–13	38, 41

Reference	Pages	Reference	Pages	Reference	Pages
Numbers (cont.)		11.5	253	13.26	41, 265, 266
10–12	267	11.6-9	147	14.2	147
10	26, 109, 263	11.7-8	252	14.4	259
10.11–36.13	147	11.8	252	14.18	271
10.11-28	40	11.9	252	14.27	147
10.11-22	252, 260	11.10-30	260	14.29	147
10.11	264	11.10	254, 255, 267	14.32-36	250
10.12	38, 40, 41, 252, 266	11.11-17	268	14.36	147
10.20	41	11.11-15	274	14.39-45	247
10.25	38	11.11	255	14.39	273
10.29–12.16	268	11.12	255	14.40-45	266, 273
10.29-36	26	11.13	254	14.43-45	257
10.29-32	147, 258, 259	11.15	255	16.11	147
10.29	258, 260, 264, 266, 268, 276	11.16-30	209	17.1-7	259
		11.16-17	147	17.6-15	270
		11.16	255, 267	17.6	147
10.33-36	267, 291	11.17-25	190	17.20	147
10.33	248, 265	11.17	267	17.25	147
10.34	267	11.18	254, 255	18	119, 215
10.35-36	267	11.20	254, 255	18.1-12	260
10.35	267	11.24-30	147, 268	18.8-24	100
11–34	265	11.24	267	18.13-26	260
11–21	210	11.26	267	18.16	215
11–15	161	11.31-35	147	18.27	260
11–13	41	11.31-32	252	20–21	257
11–12	33	11.33	257, 259	20	245
11	26, 47, 246, 252, 255, 257, 261, 264, 278	11.34-35	252	20.1	245, 252, 262, 265
		11.34	209, 253, 256	20.2-13	147
11.1-34	252, 265	11.35–14.45	265	20.5	255
11.1-3	245, 246, 253, 255	11.35	38, 40, 41, 265	20.8	256
11.1	253, 256, 257			20.10-24	245
		12–13	265	20.10-11	256
11.2	253	12	157, 165, 166, 264	20.10	252
11.3	26, 209, 253, 255-57, 259, 265, 268	12.4-5	165	20.11	252
		12.4	267	20.12-14	245
		12.5	267	20.13	244, 245, 256
11.4-34	245, 253-56, 258, 259, 261	12.7-8	42, 44	20.14	258
		12.8	32, 165	20.22-29	262
		12.16	38, 40, 41, 265	20.22	252
11.4	26, 253, 254, 256, 257, 259, 265, 268	12.26	160	20.24	244, 256, 257, 260
		13	256	21.1-3	257, 260
		13.3-26	265	21.1	257
		13.20	264	21.5	255
		13.21	41	21.10-13	38, 39
				21.10-11	39
				21.30	252

22.1	41, 252	*Deuteronomy*		2.34	257
26.2	128	1–11	21, 279	3.20	274
26.9	165	1–4	280	3.21	156
26.60-61	190	1–3	18, 260	3.24	219, 227,
27.12-14	252	1	249, 254,		231, 238
27.14	244, 245,		263, 265	3.26	232
	256	1.1	265	3.28	156
28.16	201	1.2	209, 264,	4–5	27, 31, 32,
31.10	109		265		34, 179
31.16	96	1.6–3.29	38, 243	4	30, 32
31.48-54	133	1.6-46	264, 280	4.1	232, 249
32.11	270	1.6-41	280	4.2	12, 69
33	36-39, 41,	1.6	209, 247	4.9–5.33	28
	244-47, 250,	1.8	255, 270	4.9-13	170
	252, 260-63,	1.9-18	209, 254,	4.9	29, 193
	265		258, 259	4.10-13	32
33.1-49	38	1.9	39, 259	4.10	28, 30
33.1-5	209	1.11	129, 254	4.11-13	157
33.1	229	1.12	254	4.11	30, 156, 187
33.2	37, 255	1.14	254	4.12-14	48
33.3-4	41	1.15	228, 259	4.12	28, 30
33.3	38, 201, 236,	1.17	254	4.13-23	191
	244, 264	1.18	254	4.13	28-30, 47
33.4	203, 229	1.19	262, 264	4.14-15	29
33.5-15	244	1.20-46	249	4.14	30, 31, 46,
33.7-8	42	1.23	256		47
33.8	247, 248	1.24	254	4.15	28, 30
33.9	39	1.25	224, 254,	4.16-18	174
33.10	236, 244		266	4.19	174
33.12-13	244	1.30	219, 237	4.20	219, 224,
33.12	255	1.33	237		231
33.14	245, 255	1.37	48	4.23	174, 179,
33.15	38, 40	1.38	156		219
33.16-17	41, 253	1.41-44	273	4.24	156, 237
33.16	40, 245, 252	1.42	183	4.25	174
33.17	40, 265	1.43-44	247, 266	4.30	247
33.36-38	39, 209, 242	1.44	257	4.31	271
33.36	41, 245, 262	1.45	225, 255	4.33	28, 185
33.37	262	1.46–2.1	266	4.34-35	209
33.38-39	41	1.46	262	4.34	30, 219, 220,
33.38	262	2.2	183		222, 231,
33.40	257	2.4	183		238, 260
33.43-44	39	2.7	262	4.36	30, 32, 33,
33.48	41	2.9	183		187
35.25	270	2.14	39, 209, 242,	4.37	219, 274
35.28	270		262	4.40	247
35.32	270	2.17	183	4.45	219, 224,
35.33	133	2.30	226		231

Deuteronomy (cont.)		5.31	30, 31, 46, 48	9.7–10.11	18, 33, 47, 153, 166, 168-70, 179, 199, 218, 249, 278, 280
4.46	219	6	260		
5	31, 47, 173, 178, 180, 184, 186	6.1	46		
		6.2-3	176		
5.1-5	157	6.5	187		
5.2-22	170	6.10	270	9.7-8	18, 278
5.2-3	191, 192	6.12	219	9.7	219, 243, 277
5.4-5	186	6.16	244, 248, 256	9.8	243, 265
5.4	28, 32, 33, 157, 185, 187, 275	6.18	247	9.9–10.11	264, 280
		6.21	219, 227	9.9-11	192
5.5	28, 29, 31, 32, 48	6.22	219, 231	9.9	153, 156, 157, 169-72, 182, 191, 278
		6.24	156		
5.6-21	168, 174, 180, 185, 197, 218	7	177		
		7.1	224		
		7.4	253	9.10-11	278
5.6	219	7.5	192	9.10	153, 156, 157, 169, 186, 187, 201, 278
5.7-10	174	7.6	188		
5.8-10	156	7.8	219, 227, 232		
5.8	179				
5.9	174, 279	7.13	255	9.11	169, 170, 172
5.10	174, 175	7.15	219		
5.12	178, 219	7.18-19	220	9.12–10.10	278
5.14	175	7.18	219, 220	9.12-16	272
5.15	161, 178, 219	7.19	219, 220	9.12-15	153
		7.20	21	9.12-14	278
5.16	178, 219	8	249	9.12	219
5.20	176	8.2-6	248	9.14	154, 269
5.21	176	8.2-5	251	9.15-17	278
5.22-31	186	8.2	158, 251, 262	9.15	156, 157, 169, 172
5.22-27	158				
5.22	47, 156, 184, 186	8.3-5	254	9.16	153
		8.3	251	9.17	153, 169, 278
5.23-33	157	8.4	262		
5.23	30	8.7	224	9.18-20	153
5.24-27	30, 48	8.14-16	248, 251	9.18	153, 170, 276, 278, 279
5.24-26	186	8.14	219		
5.24	250	8.15	255, 256		
5.25-27	185	9–10	157, 191, 270	9.19	232, 278
5.25	30			9.20-21	278
5.27-31	170	9	44, 45, 249, 260, 265	9.20	225, 253, 278
5.27	30, 186				
5.28-33	30	9.5-27	270	9.21	153, 154, 168, 278
5.28-29	32	9.6-13	273		
5.30	30			9.22-24	18, 48, 157, 165, 166, 260

9.22-23   41, 278
9.22   26, 47, 209,
               243-46, 253-
               56, 261, 265,
               267
9.23   243, 265
9.25–10.5   276
9.25-29   48, 153, 270
9.25   204, 278,
               279
9.26-29   44, 269
9.26-27   278
9.26   219, 227
9.27   269
9.29   219
10   22
10.1-5   192, 266,
               268
10.1-4[9.18]   169
10.1-4   47, 218, 266,
               270
10.1-3   168, 199,
               200, 271
10.1-2   278
10.1   154, 169,
               170, 192,
               268, 276
10.2   153, 154,
               169, 192,
               238, 268,
               276
10.3-4   278
10.3   153, 154,
               169, 170,
               189, 192,
               268, 276
10.4   153, 157,
               169-71, 278
10.5   266-68, 274,
               276
10.6-7   34, 260, 267
10.6   225, 273
10.8-9   154, 168,
               257, 268
10.8   267, 276
10.9   278
10.10-11   271

10.10
10.11   46, 157, 272,
               276, 277
10.19   219
10.21   219, 231,
               238
10.22   219, 223
11.2-4   220
11.2   30, 219, 238
11.3   219, 222
11.4   39, 42, 219,
               222, 237,
               238, 260
11.10   219
11.18   231
12–26   211, 280
12   57
12.1–26.15   153, 159
12.1   159
12.3   188
12.11   224
12.20   254
12.32   12, 69
12.38   222
13.4   248
13.6   219
13.11   219
14.1-2   215
14.1   213, 298
14.9-10   30
15   44
15.2-3   224
15.12–16.8   25, 211, 214,
               219, 224,
               231, 246
15.12-23   24
15.12-18   211
15.12-17   44
15.12-13   224
15.12   223
15.13-14   212
15.13   211
15.15   219
15.19-23   44, 211
16   205-207, 244

16.1-8   24, 38, 44,
               46, 47, 201-
               204, 207,
               211, 214,
               218, 219,
               242
16.1   205, 206,
               219
16.2   205, 206
16.3   205, 207,
               219
16.4   38, 205, 207
16.5-7   47, 205, 206
16.6-7   205
16.6   206, 219
16.7   207
16.8   205, 206,
               210
16.11   175
16.12   219
16.18   228
17   214
17.10-11   225
17.14-20   218
17.16   91
17.20   177
18.15-22   183
18.15-18   225
18.16   185
18.20   188
19.6   229
19.12   229
19.16–20.22   28
20.1-19   180
20.1   186, 219,
               224
20.9   229
20.20   180
20.22-23   28
21   157
21.4   154
21.8   157, 270
21.18-21   298
21.22-23   305
23.5   219
24.8   225
24.9   219
24.12   33

Deuteronomy (cont.)

24.16	279
24.18	157, 219
24.22	219
25.15	176
25.17-19	257
25.17	219
25.19	26
26.1-15	100
26.5	219, 258
26.6-7	223
26.6	219
26.7	219, 224, 231
26.8	219, 220, 238
26.9	224
26.16	193
27–28	153
27.15	174
28	301
28.5	231
28.15-68	299
28.17	231
28.21	222
28.27-35	247
28.27	219, 222
28.35	222
28.56	248
28.60	219
28.69	191
29.1-2	220
29.1	219
29.2	219, 231
29.4-5	254
29.4	248, 262
29.5	229, 231
29.9-14	191
29.12	270
29.24	219
30.6	106, 299
30.17	174
30.20	270
31.1	186
31.9	188
31.11-14	34
31.14-15	33, 157, 165, 267

31.14	237
31.15	156
31.16	191
31.18	33, 157
31.22	188
31.23	33
31.24-26	188
32–33	238
32.11-14	34
32.15-18	157
32.15	157
32.21-24	157
32.30-34	157
32.34	157
32.35	157
32.39	247
32.40	229
32.48	245
32.50	225
32.51	96, 244, 256
33.1-5	157
33.2	82, 261, 265
33.4	229
33.6-11	157
33.8-9	257
33.8	69, 244, 248, 256
33.10	69, 225
33.12-17	157
33.18	157
33.19	157
33.20-23	157
34.4	270
34.5-9	157
34.5	163
34.9	254
34.10-12	225
34.10	32, 157, 183, 275
34.10[-12]	33
34.11-12	220
34.11	219, 222
34.12	219, 227, 238
34.19	157

Joshua

1–12	90
1.1–Judg. 2.5	153
1.1-9	156
1.11	251
2.9	239
3–6	82
3–4	218, 238
3.5	192, 219
3.13	236, 238
3.16	236, 238
3.17	236
4.18	236, 237
5.9	161, 253
5.10-11	201
5.12	251
6–7	97
6.9	97
6.18	96
6.19	114
6.24	97
7.1	96
7.11	97, 98
7.13-14	219
7.24-26	96
7.25	120
7.26	253
9.18	247
10.14	257
14.6	258
18	157
18.11-28	112
21.5	111
21.10-42	109
21.45	259
22	96, 111
22.16	96
22.20	96
22.22	96
22.31	96
23.2-15	259
24.5	224, 231
24.6-7	237
24.7	237, 238
24.12	21
24.25	247
24.32	21, 218

Judges

1.1–2.5	90

1.16	259	5.11-25	91	15.5	97
2.1-5	11, 21, 152, 153, 199, 218, 254	6.2-11	91	15.12	174
		6.12-19	91	16.7-9	97
		6.17	165	17	122
2.2	153	11–12	90, 103	17.14	225
2.3	153	13–21	92	17.16	217, 272
2.5	253	23.8-9	91	17.37	156
2.8	43	24	103, 134	18.13–20.11	91
2.10	43	24.2	131	19.35-37	92
2.14	153	24.4-7	178	21.17-18	97
2.22	248	24.9	131	23.3	202
3.1	248			23.21-23	202
3.4	248	*1 Kings*		23.22-23	202
5.4	83	1–11	289	23.29-30	125
6.7	258	1.39	165	23.31–25.30	121
6.9	84, 224	4.7-19	137	24	122
6.13	192, 224	5.29	218, 228	24.15-16	122
7.11	253	6	291	24.18–25.30	31, 37
11.13	224	6.1	75	24.18-20	97
11.18	38, 39	8	291, 293	25.15-16	122
11.30	257	8.1	291	25.30	228
17–18	111	8.22	289, 290	25.37	63
		8.25	193, 293		
Ruth		8.28	294	*1 Chronicles*	
4.18-22	75	8.37	247	1–9	106, 107, 117, 146
		8.43	224		
1 Samuel		8.54	295	1	107, 294, 300, 302
1.11	257	8.56	259		
6.6	231, 233	8.59	228, 251	1.1-4	123
8.21	253	9.19	218	1.1	90, 107, 123
9.1-2	112	9.26	77	1.4	107
9.12-24	165	10.26-29	290	1.10	107
9.13	165	10.28-29	91	1.11	107
9.22	165	11.28	218, 228	1.19	107
12.6	43	12	166, 280	1.24-27	123
12.18	43	12.28	154, 199, 217	1.27	107, 291
15.2	257			1.34	124, 270
15.7	247	12.32	155	1.43	107
18.6	240	14.25	97	2–8	93, 94, 108, 110, 138, 149, 301
21.4-5	294	18.24	103		
30.25	247	18.36	270		
31.1-13	95	18.38	103	2–4	148
		20.25	139	2.1–9.1	116
2 Samuel				2.1-2	108
1.1–		*2 Kings*		2.1	124, 149
2 Kgs 25.30	91	2.25	254	2.2	111
5.1-3	91	10.30	174	2.3–8.40	108, 111
5.6-10	91	13.23	270	2.3–4.23	109, 149

1 Chronicles (cont.)

Ref	Pages
2.3-4	149
2.3	96, 110
2.4-5	124
2.5–4.23	149
2.6–4.23	108
2.6-8	149
2.7	96, 106, 110, 116, 149
2.9–4.20	149
2.9-17	149
2.9-15	124
2.10-16	94
2.18-55	149
2.19-20	94
2.50-55	94
3.1-24	94, 108, 149
3.1-8	108
3.5	124
4.1-20	149
4.1-8	94
4.21-23	110, 149
5.1-2	110, 127
5.17	94
5.20	109, 110
5.22	109, 110
5.25	96, 98, 106, 116, 121, 150
5.26-41	111
5.26	107, 110
5.27–6.66	108, 110, 146, 150
5.27-41	108, 150
6.1-15	109
6.14-42	291
6.16-38	109
6.39	109
6.46	111
7–10	112
7.2	94
7.6-12	112
7.12	111
7.13-40	112
7.40	113
8	113
8.1-27	112
8.28	94, 112
8.29-40	112
8.40	130
9	94, 150
9.1	96-98, 106, 112, 113, 116, 126
9.2-17	93, 94
9.2	93, 94, 112, 113, 126, 150
9.3-34	126
9.3-9	112, 113
9.10-13	112, 113
9.14-34	112
9.26-32	113
9.26	114
9.29-38	112
9.34	112
9.35-44	112
10	95, 106, 113
10.1-14	112
10.13-14	92, 95, 98, 116, 150
10.13	96, 98, 115, 116
11–2 Chron. 36	91
11–2 Chron. 9	103, 117
11–13	107
11	91
11.1–2 Chron. 36.21	91
11.1-9	91, 112
11.1	132
11.11-41	91
12.1-33	66
12.2	130
12.28	136
13	138, 139
13.6-14	91
14	107, 130
14.1-16	91
14.17	107
15–16	103
15.22	137, 140
15.25–16.3	91
16.2	135
16.8-36	138
16.39	136
17	139
17.4	131
17.5	131
17.12	131
17.14	131
18–20	129, 139
18.10-11	101
21–2 Chron. 7	131
21	96, 103, 104, 117, 128, 130-32, 135, 139, 140, 145, 291
21.1-8	144
21.1	129, 139, 145
21.2	130, 131, 136, 145
21.3	103, 117, 129, 131, 145
21.4-5	136
21.4	145, 178
21.5-6	117
21.5	131, 136
21.6	130, 131, 145
21.7-15	136
21.7	145
21.8	145, 293
21.17	135, 293
21.22	135
21.26	104
21.27–29.30	104
21.29–22.1	103
21.29	132
22.1	117, 135
22.7	132
22.9	131
22.11-13	123
22.13	132
23–27	130
23.3	130
23.4	137
23.11	131
23.24	131

24.3	131, 136	5.9	292	7.22	295
24.6	136	5.10	122	8.1–9.24	290
24.19	131	5.11-13	295	8.1	290
24.31	136	5.11	295	8.11	294
25.1	240	5.13	295	9.25-28	290
26	138	5.14	295	10–36	124
26.29-32	137	6	123, 289,	12–36	92
26.29	138, 140		295	12.2-12	117
26.30	131	6.1-42	290	12.2	96, 97, 116,
26.32	131, 138	6.1	295		117, 150
27	130, 132,	6.2	295	12.6-7	119
	140	6.3	295	12.7	120
27.1-15	136	6.4	295	12.10	131
27.1	130	6.6	292, 295	13.15	130
27.3	137	6.12-13	289	13.22	95, 118
27.5	137	6.12	289, 290	14.8	130
27.22	130	6.13	289, 290	14.10 MT	130
27.23-24	130	6.14-15	291	17.10	130
27.23	117, 136,	6.16	292, 293	17.14	131
	137	6.17	292	17.17	130
27.24	130, 136	6.18	127, 294	18–23	123
27.27	137, 138	6.19	294	19.10	131
28.2	131, 132	6.22-37	291	20.7	121
28.5	139	6.22	292, 294	20.11	121
28.7	123	6.24	292	20.15	130
28.9	277	6.26	292	20.17	130
28.29	102	6.27	294	20.29	130
29.15	126	6.28	292	22.7	118
29.18	270	6.29	294	23.14	131
29.22	136	6.32	292	23.16–24.14	132, 133,
29.30	127	6.34	292		140
		6.36-39	123	23.18	131, 132
2 Chronicles		6.36	292	24.4	132
1–9	17, 289	6.40-42	291	24.5	132
1–7	293	6.40	292	24.6	132, 138
1.1-13	290	6.41	292	24.9	138
1.5	26	6.42	292	24.11	131, 133
1.14-17	290	7	294, 295	24.18	131
1.18	291	7.1-10	290	24.27	95, 118, 137
2.1-17	290	7.1-3	290	25.4	293
3.1–5.1	290	7.1	103, 290	25.5-10	134, 140
3.1	104	7.3	103	25.5	131
3.19-24	62	7.6	290	25.8	130
4.6-8	293	7.7	295	26.11	131
5	294	7.11	291	26.16-21	97
5.2-14	290	7.12-22	290	26.16-18	98
5.2	295	7.14	119, 293,	26.16	96, 97, 116
5.6	295		294	26.18	96, 97, 116

2 Chronicles (cont.)

26.19	98	34.10	131	9.1	162
28.3	131	34.12	131	11–13	91
28.10	131	34.17	131	11	94, 150
28.13	131, 293	34.33	131	11.3-19	93, 94
28.16-20	97	35.1–36.1	125	11.3-17	94
28.19	96, 97, 116	35.1-9	202	11.3	93, 94
28.22	96-98, 116	35.3	138	11.18-22	94
28.24	98	35.24	124	13.27	96, 110
29–31	101	35.25–36.23	125		
29	98	35.25	125	*Job*	
29.5	99	36.1-23	121	21.34	96
29.6-7	98	36.6	125	42.16	174
29.6	96, 97, 116,	36.8	131		
	123	36.9-10	122	*Psalms*	
29.8	99	36.11-14	97	27.12	177
29.9	98	36.12	125	39.13	126
29.10	99, 132	36.13	122	48	239
29.16	99	36.14	96-98, 101,	56.9	269
29.19	96, 97, 116		116, 117,	69.29	269
29.21	99, 293		131, 150	74.12-15	236
29.23	99, 293	36.15-16	104, 122	78	251
29.24	99, 293	36.20	122	78.24	251
29.25	99	36.21	120, 125	78.27	251
30.6	98, 270	36.22-23	90, 92, 93	78.43-51	230
30.7	96, 97, 116,	36.22	125, 126	81.8	245
	123	36.23	126, 131	95.8	245
30.9	98			101.1	239
30.27	102	*Ezra*		105.40	252
31	119	1–4.5	91	106.32	245
31.1	126	1.1-4	92, 93	110.4	239
31.10	102	4.6-23	91	118.14	239
31.11	138	4.24–6.22	91	132	291
31.12-13	138, 140	6.19-22	201	139.16	269
31.13	131	7–10	91	145.1-2	239
32.7-8	130, 135	7.9	162		
32.8	130	8–10	91	*Proverbs*	
32.21-23	92	9.2	96, 110	1.7	72
32.27-29	137	9.4	96, 110	6.19	177
33.2	131	10.2	96, 110	16.10	96
33.9	121	10.6	96, 110		
33.10	118	10.9	162	*Isaiah*	
33.18-20	97	10.10	96, 110	1–39	101
33.18	118	10.16-17	162	1–35	66
33.19	96-98, 116,			2.10	239
	293	*Nehemiah*		2.19	239
33.23	131	1–7	91	2.21	239
34.9	134	1.8	96	5.1	239
		8.2	162	7.14	130

12.2	239	33.26	270	*Daniel*	
13.1–23.1	137	34.9	223	9.2	68
36–39	200	45.4	183	9.7	96
40–66	101	52	31, 37, 200	12.1	269
44.15	174				
44.17	174	*Lamentations*		*Hosea*	
46.6	174	3.39	253	1.9	23
51.9-10	83			2.7	35
		Ezekiel		2.16	35
Jeremiah		1.26	190	4.2	195
2.4	183	1.27-28	190	8.11-14	103
5.9	157	3.17-21	259	9.5	166
5.20	183	10.1	190	9.10	35
7.9	195	11.16	151	10.4	176
7.20	253	14.13	96	11	299
14.12	228	15.8	96	11.1	35
21.2	192	17.20	96	12.10	23
21.9	228	18.24	96	12.12	176
23.37	183	20	105, 151	12.14	35, 44
27.8	228	20.5	23, 183	13.4	23, 35
27.13	228	20.27	96	13.5	35
31.31-34	106, 298, 299	25.4	109		
		33.27	183	*Amos*	
31.31	191, 192	39.23	96	3.7	43
31.32	224	45.21	201	9.7	35
32.21	221, 224, 238	47.19	245		
		48	109	*Malachi*	
				3.16	269

NEW TESTAMENT

Luke		8.18-25	306	*Philippians*	
16.31	86	11.32	304	2.13	299
		13.9-10	306	3.8-9	303
Romans					
1.2	299	*Galatians*		*2 Timothy*	
2.29	299	3.2	306	2.13	303
3.3-4	303	3.7-9	304		
4	304	3.16	305	*Hebrews*	
4.1	304	3.29	305	11.28	208
4.11	304	4.9	303		
5.8	303	5.11	305	*Revelation*	
7.7-25	304	5.14	306	7.5-8	111
8.1	305				
8.11	306	*Ephesians*			
		2.14	303		

OTHER ANCIENT REFERENCES

Mishnah			*Yom.*			Midrash	
Sanh.			1.6	114		*Exod. R.*	
1.6	165					15.26	124
			Talmud				
			b. Pes.				
			6b	295			

INDEX OF AUTHORS

Abraham, W.J. 288
Achenbach, R. 256
Anderson, B.W. 11
Andrew, M.E. 172
Auld, A.G. 13, 217

Bartoloni, P. 284
Barton, J. 143, 285, 288
Beardsley, M.C. 282-84, 287
Becker, J. 68
Begg, C.T. 153, 154
Bertheau, E. 111
Bimson, J.J. 76
Black, J.S. 57
Blenkinsopp, J. 9
Blum, E. 18-28, 31-38, 42-46, 226
Bodkin, M. 287
Boer, P.A.H. de 263
Bokser, B.M. 100
Boorer, S. 263
Bowden, J.S. 12
Braulik, G. 211
Brekelmans, C.H.W 263, 279
Brenner, M.L. 238
Brett, M.G. 283, 286
Bright, J. 10, 11, 55
Brooks, C. 287
Buber, M. 24
Buis, P. 90

Caloz, M. 203
Calvin, J. 299
Cameron, G.G. 56
Carmichael, C. 211
Carpenter, J.E. 63, 142, 151
Carroll, R.P. 198
Childs, B.S. 64, 158, 221, 267, 282, 297

Chrystal, G. 57
Clements, R.E. 164
Clines, D.J.A. 286
Coggan, F.D. 106
Cohen, R. 161
Coleridge, S.T. 72, 73
Crüsemann, F. 194, 195

Dahood, M. 287
Danby, H. 61, 114
Daube, D. 212
Davies, G.I. 18, 35-48, 209, 232
Davies, P.R. 89
De Wette, W.M.L. 63
Dohmen, C. 174, 178, 194, 200, 201
Dozeman, T.B. 9
Dunn, J.D.G. 15
Durham, J.I. 200, 201

Eichhorn, J.G. 73
Eissfeldt, O. 152, 203
Eliot, G. 72, 73
Evans, C.F. 54, 72
Ewald, H. 68

Fell, B. 51
Fohrer, G. 152
Fox, M.V. 18
Freedman, H. 124
Friebe, R. 226
Frost, H. 51, 284
Fuller, R.C. 59

Galling, K. 78
Geddes, A. 59, 60, 62, 71-73
George, J.F.L. 207
Gershevitch, I. 50

Gerstenberger, E. 194
Gibson, J.C.L. 239
Giveon, R. 80, 83
Goedicke, H. 233
Goren, A. 160
Graf, K.H. 63
Graupner, A. 173, 176, 177
Gray, J. 58
Greenberg, M. 233
Gunkel, H. 60
Gunn, D.M. 66
Gunneweg, A.H.J. 75, 142
Gutschmid, A. von 151

Hanson, P.D. 69
Har-El, M. 160
Harford-Battersby, G. 63, 142, 151
Harrison, R.K. 145
Hartmann, B. 221
Helck, W. 79, 84
Henniger, J. 81, 202
Herder, J.G. 73
Herrmann, S. 54, 76, 79
Hirsch, E.D. 283, 286
Holzinger, H. 176
Hossfeld, F.-L. 173-97, 200
Houtman, C. 9
Hyatt, J.P. 152, 158, 218

Japhet, S. 16, 21, 116, 118-27, 130
Jenkins, A.K. 55
Johnstone, W. 15, 52, 239, 284

Kallai, Z. 264
Kegler, J. 226
Kelly, B.E. 128, 136
Kennedy, A.C. 56
Kennedy, A.R.S. 56
Koch, K. 175
Kohata, F. 202
Kraus, H.-J. 82
Kremers, H. 176
Kuenen, A. 57

Lang, B. 172, 194, 196
Levin, C. 172, 176-78, 195
Liverani, M. 76
Lohfink, N. 153, 211

Lust, J. 18, 34, 154, 262

Magnusson, M. 54
Martin, J.D. 89
Martínez, F.G. 263
Mathias, D. 63, 67, 68, 70
Mayes, A.D.H. 221
McCarthy, D.J. 163
McHardy, W.D. 56
McKenzie, J.L. 54
Meinhold, J. 175
Milgrom, J. 100, 105
Moberley, R.W.L. 217
Moriarty, F.L. 68
Mowinckel, S. 172

Neusner, J. 95, 114
Newton-De Molina, D. 297
Nicholson, E.W. 9, 18, 27, 28, 30, 31,
    35
Nicoll, A. 56
Nielsen, E. 172
Nöldeke, T. 151
Noth, M. 11, 60, 208

Oren, E. 161

Patrick, D. 65
Paul, S.M. 164
Paulus, H.E.G. 73
Pelon, O. 242
Perlitt, L. 12, 32, 155, 183
Phillips, A. 170
Pyper, H. 284

Rad, G. von 11
Rashdall, H. 72
Renaud, B. 13, 154, 219
Ricoeur, P. 282
Robinson, B.P. 213
Rogerson, J.W. 15, 207
Rost, L. 81
Rothenberg, B. 165
Rowley, H.H. 55, 172
Rowton, M.B. 76

Sanders, E.P. 304, 306
Sarna, N.M. 64

Sawyer, J.F.A. 115
Schaeffer, C.F.A. 52, 242
Schenker, A. 134
Schmidt, L. 234
Schmidt, W.H. 24, 79, 198
Schmitt, H.-C. 18
Segal, J.B. 202
Selman, M.J. 128
Shaffer, E.S. 73
Simon, M. 124
Ska, J.L. 18
Smend, R. 18, 63
Smith, G.A. 56
Smith, M. 62, 67
Smith, W.R. 56-62, 65, 72
Snaith, N.H. 111
Stalker, D.M.G. 11
Stamm, J.J. 172

Thiel, W. 106
Thompson, T.L. 11, 142
Tillotson, G. 287

Van der Woude, A.S. 66
Van Seters, J. 18, 25, 47, 154, 202, 207,
    222, 242
Vaux, R. de 16, 53, 76, 79, 80
Vermeylen, J. 66, 153, 263, 279
Vervenne, M. 9, 18, 19, 34, 154, 238,
    242, 262

Wallace, M.I. 282, 283, 297
Watson, N. 288
Weimar, P. 77, 80, 86
Wellhausen, J. 18, 57, 63, 70, 155, 172,
    175
Wevers, J.W. 288
Williamson, H.G.M. 66, 92
Wilson, A.N. 300
Wimsatt, W.K. 282-84, 287
Wolff, H.W. 11, 144

Zenger, E. 77, 80, 86
Ziesler, J.A. 302
Zimmerli, W. 174
Zunz, L. 70

JOURNAL FOR THE STUDY OF THE OLD TESTAMENT
SUPPLEMENT SERIES

149 Eugene Ulrich, John W. Wright, Robert P. Carroll & Philip R. Davies (eds.), *Priests, Prophets and Scribes: Essays on the Formation and Heritage of Second Temple Judaism in Honour of Joseph Blenkinsopp*

150 Janet E. Tollington, *Tradition and Innovation in Haggai and Zechariah 1–8*

151 Joel Weinberg, *The Citizen–Temple Community* (trans. Daniel L. Smith Christopher)

152 A. Graeme Auld (ed.), *Understanding Poets and Prophets: Essays in Honour of George Wishart Anderson*

153 Donald K. Berry, *The Psalms and their Readers: Interpretive Strategies for Psalm 18*

154 Marc Brettler and Michael Fishbane (eds.), *Min`ah le-Na`um: Biblical and Other Studies Presented to Nahum M. Sarna in Honour of his 70th Birthday*

155 Jeffrey A. Fager, *Land Tenure and the Biblical Jubilee: Uncovering Hebrew Ethics through the Sociology of Knowledge*

156 John W. Kleinig, *The Lord's Song: The Basis, Function and Significance of Choral Music in Chronicles*

157 Gordon R. Clark, *The Word Ḥesed in the Hebrew Bible*

158 Mary Douglas, *In the Wilderness: The Doctrine of Defilement in the Book of Numbers*

159 J. Clinton McCann (ed.), *The Shape and Shaping of the Psalter*

160 William Riley, *King and Cultus in Chronicles: Worship and the Reinterpretation of History*

161 George W. Coats, *The Moses Tradition*

162 Heather A. McKay and David J.A. Clines (eds.), *Of Prophets' Visions and the Wisdom of Sages: Essays in Honour of R. Norman Whybray on his Seventieth Birthday*

163 J. Cheryl Exum, *Fragmented Women: Feminist (Sub)versions of Biblical Narratives*

164 Lyle Eslinger, *House of God or House of David: The Rhetoric of 2 Samuel 7*

166 D.R.G. Beattie and M.J. McNamara (eds.), *The Aramaic Bible: Targums in their Historical Context*

167 Raymond F. Person, *Second Zechariah and the Deuteronomic School*

168 R.N. Whybray, *The Composition of the Book of Proverbs*

169 Bert Dicou, *Edom, Israel's Brother and Antagonist: The Role of Edom in Biblical Prophecy and Story*

170 Wilfred G.E. Watson, *Traditional Techniques in Classical Hebrew Verse*

171 Henning Graf Reventlow, Yair Hoffman and Benjamin Uffenheimer (eds.), *Politics and Theopolitics in the Bible and Postbiblical Literature*

172 Volkmar Fritz, *An Introduction to Biblical Archaeology*

173 M. Patrick Graham, William P. Brown and Jeffrey K. Kuan (eds.), *History and Interpretation: Essays in Honour of John H. Hayes*

174 Joe M. Sprinkle, *'The Book of the Covenant': A Literary Approach*

175 Tamara C. Eskenazi and Kent H. Richards (eds.), *Second Temple Studies. II. Temple and Community in the Persian Period*

176 Gershon Brin, *Studies in Biblical Law: From the Hebrew Bible to the Dead Sea Scrolls*

177 David Allan Dawson, *Text-Linguistics and Biblical Hebrew*

178 Martin Ravndal Hauge, *Between Sheol and Temple: Motif Structure and Function in the I-Psalms*

179 J.G. McConville and J.G. Millar, *Time and Place in Deuteronomy*

180 Richard L. Schultz, *The Search for Quotation: Verbal Parallels in the Prophets*

181 Bernard M. Levinson (ed.), *Theory and Method in Biblical and Cuneiform Law: Revision, Interpolation and Development*

182 Steven L. McKenzie and M. Patrick Graham (eds.), *The History of Israel's Traditions: The Heritage of Martin Noth*

183 John Day (ed.), *Lectures on the Religion of the Semites (Second and Third Series) by William Robertson Smith*

184 John C. Reeves and John Kampen (eds.), *Pursuing the Text: Studies in Honor of Ben Zion Wacholder on the Occasion of his Seventieth Birthday*

185 Seth Daniel Kunin, *The Logic of Incest: A Structuralist Analysis of Hebrew Mythology*

186 Linda Day, *Three Faces of a Queen: Characterization in the Books of Esther*

187 Charles V. Dorothy, *The Books of Esther: Structure, Genre and Textual Integrity*

188 Robert H. O'Connell, *Concentricity and Continuity: The Literary Structure of Isaiah*

189 William Johnstone (ed.), *William Robertson Smith: Essays in Reassessment*

190 Steven W. Holloway and Lowell K. Handy (eds.), *The Pitcher is Broken: Memorial Essays for Gösta W. Ahlström*

191 Magne Sæbø, *On the Way to Canon: Creative Tradition History in the Old Testament*

192 Henning Graf Reventlow and William Farmer (eds.), *Biblical Studies and the Shifting of Paradigms, 1850–1914*

193 Brooks Schramm, *The Opponents of Third Isaiah: Reconstructing the Cultic History of the Restoration*

194 Else Kragelund Holt, *Prophesying the Past: The Use of Israel's History in the Book of Hosea*

195 Jon Davies, Graham Harvey and Wilfred G.E. Watson (eds.), *Words Remembered, Texts Renewed: Essays in Honour of John F.A. Sawyer*

196 Joel S. Kaminsky, *Corporate Responsibility in the Hebrew Bible*

197 William M. Schniedewind, *The Word of God in Transition: From Prophet to Exegete in the Second Temple Period*

198   T.J. Meadowcroft, *Aramaic Daniel and Greek Daniel: A Literary Comparison*

199   J.H. Eaton, *Psalms of the Way and the Kingdom: A Conference with the Commentators*

200   Mark Daniel Carroll R., David J.A. Clines and Philip R. Davies (eds.), *The Bible in Human Society: Essays in Honour of John Rogerson*

201   John W. Rogerson, *The Bible and Criticism in Victorian Britain: Profiles of F.D. Maurice and William Robertson Smith*

202   Nanette Stahl, *Law and Liminality in the Bible*

203   Jill M. Munro, *Spikenard and Saffron: The Imagery of the Song of Songs*

204   Philip R. Davies, *Whose Bible Is It Anyway?*

205   David J.A. Clines, *Interested Parties: The Ideology of Writers and Readers of the Hebrew Bible*

206   Møgens Müller, *The First Bible of the Church: A Plea for the Septuagint*

207   John W. Rogerson, Margaret Davies and Mark Daniel Carroll R. (eds.), *The Bible in Ethics: The Second Sheffield Colloquium*

208   Beverly J. Stratton, *Out of Eden: Reading, Rhetoric, and Ideology in Genesis 2–3*

209   Patricia Dutcher-Walls, *Narrative Art, Political Rhetoric: The Case of Athaliah and Joash*

210   Jacques Berlinerblau, *The Vow and the 'Popular Religious Groups' of Ancient Israel: A Philological and Sociological Inquiry*

211   Brian E. Kelly, *Retribution and Eschatology in Chronicles*

212   Yvonne Sherwood, *The Prostitute and the Prophet: Hosea's Marriage in Literary-Theoretical Perspective*

213   Yair Hoffman, *A Blemished Perfection: The Book of Job in Context*

214   Roy F. Melugin and Marvin A. Sweeney (eds.), *New Visions of Isaiah*

215   J. Cheryl Exum, *Plotted, Shot and Painted: Cultural Representations of Biblical Women*

216   Judith E. McKinlay, *Gendering Wisdom the Host: Biblical Invitations to Eat and Drink*

217   Jerome F.D. Creach, *Yahweh as Refuge and the Editing of the Hebrew Psalter*

218   Gregory Glazov, *The Bridling of the Tongue and the Opening of the Mouth in Biblical Prophecy*

219   Gerald Morris, *Prophecy, Poetry and Hosea*

220   Raymond F. Person, Jr, *In Conversation with Jonah: Conversation Analysis, Literary Criticism, and the Book of Jonah*

221   Gillian Keys, *The Wages of Sin: A Reappraisal of the 'Succession Narrative'*

222   R.N. Whybray, *Reading the Psalms as a Book*

223   Scott B. Noegel, *Janus Parallelism in the Book of Job*

224   Paul J. Kissling, *Reliable Characters in the Primary History: Profiles of Moses, Joshua, Elijah and Elisha*

225   Richard D. Weis and David M. Carr (eds.), *A Gift of God in Due Season: Essays on Scripture and Community in Honor of James A. Sanders*

226 Lori L. Rowlett, *Joshua and the Rhetoric of Violence: A New Historicist Analysis*

227 John F.A. Sawyer (ed.), *Reading Leviticus: Responses to Mary Douglas*

228 Volkmar Fritz and Philip R. Davies (eds.), *The Origins of the Ancient Israelite States*

229 Stephen Breck Reid (ed.), *Prophets and Paradigms: Essays in Honor of Gene M. Tucker*

230 Kevin J. Cathcart and Michael Maher (eds.), *Targumic and Cognate Studies: Essays in Honour of Martin McNamara*

231 Weston W. Fields, *Sodom and Gomorrah: History and Motif in Biblical Narrative*

232 Tilde Binger, *Asherah: Goddesses in Ugarit, Israel and the Old Testament*

233 Michael D. Goulder, *The Psalms of Asaph and the Pentateuch: Studies in the Psalter, III*

234 Ken Stone, *Sex, Honor, and Power in the Deuteronomistic History*

235 James W. Watts and Paul House (eds.), *Forming Prophetic Literature: Essays on Isaiah and the Twelve in Honor of John D.W. Watts*

236 Thomas M. Bolin, *Freedom beyond Forgiveness: The Book of Jonah Re-Examined*

237 Neil Asher Silberman and David B. Small (eds.), *The Archaeology of Israel: Constructing the Past, Interpreting the Present*

238 M. Patrick Graham, Kenneth G. Hoglund and Steven L. McKenzie (eds.), *The Chronicler as Historian*

239 Mark S. Smith, *The Pilgrimage Pattern in Exodus* (with contributions by Elizabeth M. Bloch-Smith)

240 Eugene E. Carpenter (ed.), *A Biblical Itinerary: In Search of Method, Form and Content. Essays in Honor of George W. Coats*

241 Robert Karl Gnuse, *No Other Gods: Emergent Monotheism in Israel*

242 K.L. Noll, *The Faces of David*

243 Henning Graf Reventlow, *Eschatology in the Bible and in Jewish and Christian Tradition*

244 Walter E. Aufrecht, Neil A. Mirau and Steven W. Gauley (eds.), *Aspects of Urbanism in Antiquity: From Mesopotamia to Crete*

245 Lester L. Grabbe, *Can a 'History of Israel' Be Written?*

246 Gillian M. Bediako, *Primal Religion and the Bible: William Robertson Smith and his Heritage*

248 Etienne Nodet, *A Search for the Origins of Judaism: From Joshua to the Mishnah*

249 William Paul Griffin, *The God of the Prophets: An Analysis of Divine Action*

250 Josette Elayi and Jean Sapin (eds.), *Beyond the River: New Perspectives on Transeuphratene*

251 Flemming A.J. Nielsen, *The Tragedy in History: Herodotus and the Deuteronomistic History*

252 David C. Mitchell, *The Message of the Psalter: An Eschatological Programme in the Book of Psalms*

253 William Johnstone, *1 and 2 Chronicles, Vol. 1: 1 Chronicles 1–2 Chronicles 9: Israel's Place among the Nations*

254 William Johnstone, *1 and 2 Chronicles, Vol. 2: 2 Chronicles 10–36: Guilt and Atonement*

255 Larry L. Lyke, *King David with the Wise Woman of Tekoa: The Resonance of Tradition in Parabolic Narrative*

256 Roland Meynet, *Rhetorical Analysis: An Introduction to Biblical Rhetoric* translated by Luc Racaut

257 Philip R. Davies and David J.A. Clines (eds.), *The World of Genesis: Persons, Places, Perspectives*

258 Michael D. Goulder, *The Psalms of the Return (Book V, Psalms 107–150): Studies in the Psalter, IV*

259 Allen Rosengren Petersen, *The Royal God: Enthronement Festivals in Ancient Israel and Ugarit?*

260 A.R. Pete Diamond, Kathleen M. O'Connor and Louis Stulman (eds.), *Trouble with Jeremiah: Prophecy in Conflict*

261 Othmar Keel, *Goddesses and Trees, New Moon and Yahweh*

262 Victor H. Matthews, Bernard M. Levinson and Tikva Frymer-Kensky (eds.), *Gender and Law in the Hebrew Bible and the Ancient Near East*

264 Donald F. Murray, *Divine Prerogative and Royal Pretension: Pragmatics, Poetics and Polemics in a Narrative Sequence about David (2 Samuel 5.17–7.29)*

266 J. Cheryl Exum and Stephen D. Moore (eds.), *Biblical Studies/Cultural Studies: The Third Sheffield Colloquium*

269 David J.A. Clines and Stephen D. Moore (eds.), *Auguries: The Jubilee Volume of the Sheffield Department of Biblical Studies*

270 John Day (ed.), *King and Messiah in Israel and the Ancient Near East: Proceedings of the Oxford Old Testament Seminar*

272 James Richard Linville, *Israel in the Book of Kings: The Past as a Project of Social Identity*

273 Meir Lubetski, Claire Gottlieb and Sharon Keller (eds.), *Boundaries of the Ancient Near Eastern World: A Tribute to Cyrus H. Gordon*

275 William Johnstone, *Chronicles and Exodus: An Analogy and its Application*

276 Raz Kletter, *Economic Keystones: The Weight System of the Kingdom of Judah*

277 Augustine Pagolu, *The Religion of the Patriarchs*

278 Lester L. Grabbe (ed), *Leading Captivity Captive: 'The Exile' as History and Ideology*

279 Kari Latvus, *God, Anger and Ideology: The Anger of God in Joshua and Judges in Relation to Deuteronomy and the Priestly Writings*

291 Christine Schams, *Jewish Scribes in the Second-Temple Period*

292 David J.A. Clines, *On the Way to the Postmodern: Old Testament Essays, 1967–1998 Volume 1*

293 David J.A. Clines, *On the Way to the Postmodern: Old Testament Essays, 1967–1998 Volume 2*

DATE DUE

NOV 2 0			
			Printed in USA